Data Modeler's Workbench

Advance Praise for
Data Modeler's Workbench

"This book is chock-full of useful techniques and tips for improving data models and designs. And it's easy and an entertaining read as well—a terrific combination!"

Wayne Eckerson
Director of Education and Research,
The Data Warehousing Institute

"Any data modeler should own a copy of Steve Hoberman's book on data modeling tools and techniques. Steve does an outstanding job of walking the reader through real-world data modeling situations and shows how to successfully apply the tools and techniques contained in this book."

David Marco
President, Enterprise Warehousing Solutions, Inc.

"Steve Hoberman has written a truly valuable book that is sure to advance the discipline of data modeling. His concepts, definitions, and classification schema help advance data modeling as a learnable and repeatable process. Many aspects of this book added to my knowledge of data modeling—and I'm a modeling practitioner with nearly twenty years of experience. I believe the single greatest impact this book will make is in its attention to data modeling as a human process as well as a technical one."

David Wells
Founder and Principal Consultant, Infocentric

Data Modeler's Workbench

Tools and Techniques for Analysis and Design

Steve Hoberman

Wiley Computer Publishing

John Wiley & Sons, Inc.

NEW YORK • CHICHESTER • WEINHEIM • BRISBANE • SINGAPORE • TORONTO

Publisher: Robert Ipsen
Editor: Robert Elliott
Developmental Editor: Emilie Herman
Managing Editor: John Atkins
Associate New Media Editor: Brian Snapp
Text Design & Composition: ATLIS Graphics & Design

Published by John Wiley & Sons, Inc., New York

Published simultaneously in Canada.

This publication is designed to provide accurate and authoritative information in regard to the subject matter covered. It is sold with the understanding that the publisher is not engaged in professional services. If professional advice or other expert assistance is required, the services of a competent professional person should be sought.

Library of Congress Cataloging-in-Publication Data:

Hoberman, Steve 1968-
  Data modeler's workbench: tools and techniques for analysis and design/Steven Hoberman.
    p.cm.
"Wiley Computer Publishing."
Includes bibliographical references and index.
ISBN 0-471-11176-9 (pbk.: alk. paper)
  1. Database design. 2. Data structures (Computer science) 3. Information technology.
I. Title.

QA76.9.D26 H62 2001
005.74—dc21   2001046562

Printed in the United States of America.

10 9 8 7 6 5 4 3 2 1

To Jenn

CONTENTS

It would be interesting to draw a map of all the challenges faced by professional modelers in their day-to-day work and then to assess how well each one is addressed by the literature. It would be a very uneven picture.

Normalization would probably win the prize for the most-addressed topic. Indeed, an outsider could easily conclude that data modeling was primarily about the resolution of complex normalization problems and that the prime tools of the data modeler were relational algebra and calculus.

Languages and diagramming conventions would be more than adequately covered. There has been a steady stream of alternatives proposed over the years, and a great deal of debate—sometimes passionate debate—as to their relative suitability.

Thanks to more recent publications, largely by practitioners, we would see some useful contributions in the previously barren areas of data model patterns and business rules.

These are important topics, but they address only a fraction of what data modelers actually do. The choice of conventions is usually a one-time decision, often made by someone else. If normalization is done at all, it is usually as a final check on what has been done intuitively. Thirty years of research since the original articulation of the first three normal forms has made little difference to the models that are produced in practice.

What is missing in this lopsided map is material on the *process* of data modeling: the practicalities of project planning, communicating with end users, verifying rules and assumptions, presenting models to diverse audiences, even convincing stakeholders that data modeling needs to be done at all. This is the messy, inexact stuff that consumes the time of real data modelers—and very often determines whether a project will succeed or fail.

The glib response is that we learn these things from experience, rather than from books. This should not be an acceptable answer. True, many of these topics may be unattractive to researchers: they are not easily compartmentalized, they require a detailed knowledge of practice and organizational settings, and there is seldom a single solution. But there is a real need to codify experience if we are to avoid reinventing the wheel or paying for data modelers' education with failed projects.

Steve Hoberman has tackled a large uncharted area with this book. He identifies a range of challenges facing data modelers, and this is an achievement in its own right. Many of them are common problems that we all face, but have not always stopped to think about or discuss.

He then offers his own solutions: tools, ideas, ways of communicating. They have the ring of truth about them; one senses that they have been born of necessity and evolved through repeated use. For the novice, these should provide an excellent starting point; for the experts, they should stimulate re-examination, and updating, of their own toolkits.

Steve has resisted any temptation to offer a methodology or recipe. Data modelers have had their share of "one approach fits all" solutions. The profession has, I hoped, matured to the stage where we realize that what we require is an extensive common body of knowledge and the ability to adapt it.

In this book, we have not only a substantial contribution to the data modeling profession's body of knowledge, but a mapping out of new territory for debate and discussion. I hope that both practitioners and researchers will take up the challenge to explore further these important areas of data modeling practice.

Graeme Simsion
September 2001

Do you find yourself always packing the same items before you go away on vacation? I usually find myself packing a toothbrush, travel alarm, razor, shaving cream, and so on. These items are important for the comfort of my vacation. When I forget any of them, I usually have to purchase them at a local store. Bringing these items with me saves the time and expense of shopping for replacements.

Similarly, when we are about to embark on a data modeling adventure, there is a set of items, or tools, we need to bring with us and use on our designs. These tools take the form of spreadsheets, guidelines, questions, tips, and so on, designed to make the data modeling effort run more efficiently and result in a high-quality design. Using existing data modeling tools will save you the time and expense of creating your own tools or not using tools at all. This book contains a collection of tools to make the data modeling process run more efficiently and produce high-quality data model deliverables.

Overview of the Book and Technology

A data model is the heart and soul of our applications. A good data model provides a foundation for efficient data entry and retrieval. It also needs to be consistent with other models, at least in your organization, and needs to accurately capture the appropriate business requirements. A good data model must enable an application to expand and evolve gracefully to support changing business requirements. Despite the high value attributed to the data model, I am still amazed at how often we give little thought to the process of creating a data model and how little we rely on tools and techniques to continuously improve the data modeling process.

When I teach data modeling, I usually start off with a short exercise in which I ask the students to create a data model based on a particular form or report. As I walk around the room, I am always impressed by how many different ways I see people creating the models. Sometimes people jump right into a data model, others start with spreadsheets, and still others list all of the data elements. Some of the people in the room might complete this small classroom model correctly in the allotted 10 minutes. Others might spend 10 minutes and hardly scratch the surface. One thing is certain: Those that complete the model correctly have data modeling processes or tools that work for them.

I have been data modeling since 1990 and have developed a set of processes and tools that work for me. This book contains a collection of finely tuned data modeling tools organized according to when they should occur in the life cycle. These tools will assist us in capturing, modeling, and validating data requirements to improve the speed, accuracy, flexibility, and consistency of data warehouse and operational applications.

This book has two main purposes:

1. **To provide you with a set of data modeling tools that you can start using today on your data model designs.** This book will take you through a number of data modeling tools, starting with several tools that need to be applied before any analysis or modeling work takes place and ending by properly arranging the data elements on the model.

2. **To stimulate your imagination to create your own tools or variations of those in this text.** Because I could not possibly discuss all data modeling tools, you should be able to think up your own that are most appropriate for your assignments, organizations, and industries after reading about the tools in this book.

I wrote this book because I believe using data modeling tools that already have been proven to improve designs can save data modelers lots of time, effort, and trial and error in creating their own data modeling tools. This book fills a very important niche in our industry, because many data modeling books exist that deal with formal data modeling "how to" or are specific to a type of application, such as data warehousing. What is lacking is a book on practical tools to help with the data modeling process and data modeling deliverables. These practical tools are ones that can be applied to any type of application, regardless of whether they are reporting or operational in nature and regardless of your industry or application methodology.

I know that at certain points during the reading of this book you might ask yourself, "Are these data modeling techniques for data warehouse designs or for operational designs?" The answer is that most of the techniques presented in this text are for all types of applications. The answers or results of some of these tools might vary, depending on whether it is a reporting or operational application; however, the tools can be used for both. There are a few exceptions to this general rule, which I will mention when I discuss the specific tools in the text.

How This Book Is Organized

This book is organized into three parts, according to when these tools should be applied in the data modeling process. For example, the Subject Area Family Tree in Chapter 5 should always precede the Data Element Family Tree in Chapter 7. Although I recommend reading the text in the order in which it appears, once you have read Chapters 2 and 4, you will have a very good understanding of the sequence for the rest of the text. Then you can jump to the sections that most interest you. I refer back to previous tools in each chapter, however, making it more logical to read the text from beginning to end.

Here is an overview of each of the three parts:

■ **Part 1, Building the Foundation.** Chapters 1 through 4 offer several tools to help you as the data modeler utilize the data modeling education and communication process.

- **Part 2, Analyzing the Requirements.** Chapters 5 through 7 focus on capturing and validating the subject area requirements for an application, as well as on the detailed data elements that will provide the inputs to our logical data modeling phase.

- **Part 3, Modeling the Requirements and Some Advice.** Chapters 8 through 10 focus on creating the optimal logical and physical data models for our application. A series of tools is presented for modeling the data requirements in a flexible way, while considering the database performance and storage ramifications. As a bonus, Chapter 11 is included in this part. Chapter 11 concludes this book with some advice that I have learned over the years and continuously follow as a data modeler.

Here is a summary of each chapter:

Chapter 1, "Using Anecdotes, Analogies, and Presentations to Illustrate Data Modeling Concepts," focuses on the most effective ways to clearly communicate facets of data modeling. Anecdotes are short stories that can work very well to explain a concept or term. Analogies compare data modeling concepts with something the audience is very familiar with, to highlight some of the data modeling traits. Presentation steps are the sequence of steps to go through when creating a data modeling presentation.

Chapter 2, "Meta Data Bingo," helps define the standard types of meta data for your project and organization. Meta Data Bingo is a game where the people on your project team complete Bingo cards identifying which types of meta data are most important to capture. These Bingo cards capture meta data at a number of different levels, including project, data model, subject area, entity, and data element levels of detail.

Chapter 3, "Ensuring High-Quality Definitions," focuses on a tool called the Definition Checklist. Examples of applying the Definition Checklist at the subject area, entity, and data element levels are provided.

Chapter 4, "Project Planning for the Data Modeler," includes four project planning templates that contain the complete and sequential set of tasks required to successfully finish data modeling deliverables in a realistic timeframe.

Chapter 5, "Subject Area Analysis," offers tools to complete the deliverables for identifying and capturing the subject areas for an application. The Subject Area Checklist is a complete list of subject areas within the new application, along with their definitions. The Application Subject Area CRUD (Create, Read, Update, and Delete) Matrix contains the subject area gaps and overlap that can exist between your new application and existing applications. This is a powerful tool for scoping your application. The In-the-Know Template identifies the people and documentation you will need as resources to complete your data modeling deliverables of this new application. The Subject Area Family Tree contains the source applications for each subject area and several other critical pieces of information. The Subject Area Grain Matrix captures the reporting levels for each measurement or fact subject area using a spreadsheet format.

Chapter 6, "Subject Area Modeling," focuses on three types of subject area models, each being a very powerful validation and scoping tool. The Business Clean Slate model helps us understand a business area independent of any applications. The Application Clean Slate builds on the Business Clean Slate and focuses only on what is important for the application. The Early Reality Check compares the new application with an existing application architecture to assess overlap and impact.

Chapter 7, "Logical Data Analysis," presents four powerful data element capture and validation tools. The Data Element Family Tree captures data element name, alias, definition, business purpose, default value, transformations, format, and nullability. The Data Element Grain Matrix captures the relationships between the facts and their reporting levels. The Data Quality Capture Template contains the criteria and comparison information between data and meta data, and the Data Quality Validation Template provides proof that the data quality of each data element has been properly reviewed.

Chapter 8, "The Normalization Hike and Denormalization Survival Guide," presents the tools for normalizing and denormalizing your data requirements. The Normalization Hike is a set of rules and guidelines that can lead you to the summit of complete understanding for your application. The Denormalization Survival Guide is a question-and-answer approach to determining where to denormalize your data model. When you are done asking these questions for each relationship, you will have a physical data model at the appropriate level of denormalization.

Chapter 9, "The Abstraction Safety Guide and Components," helps minimize the impact future data requirements will have on our model and the resulting database design. The Abstraction Safety Guide is a set of three questions that will help you determine where, if at all, you need to abstract on your data models. The Abstraction Components tool is a collection of the most useful of these abstraction building blocks. The components I discuss in this chapter are those you can use in your own application models to replace sections of your models that need more flexibility. These components can exist at the entity, relationship, or data element levels.

Chapter 10, "Data Model Beauty Tips," takes your design beyond the immediate application requirements, by focusing on tips for improving the visual appearance of the logical and physical data models. These tips are offered at the entity, relationship and data element levels of detail.

Chapter 11, "Planning a Long and Prosperous Career in Data Modeling", focuses on my advice, which I follow as a data modeler. This advice consists of what I have learned over the years, either from my own experiences and from the successes and failures of those around me. Following this advice can help you become a more successful data modeler. This advice is phrased in the format of a Top Ten list.

Notation and Structure in This Book

I have used several consistent formats to show information throughout the chapters.

NOTE

■■■■ **I show Notes, Warnings, and Tips throughout this text in this format. In this way you can easily spot these as you read each chapter. Notes provide additional information on the topic being discussed, Warnings contain pitfalls and problems you want to avoid, and Tips are short yet important words of advice.**

I use italics to discuss real-life situations you might one day find yourself in. For example, in Chapter 7 you will see this story:

> *You have completed all of the subject area analysis tools for your application, including the Subject Area Family Tree. Now what? You need to identify the data elements within each subject area, along with their sources and any transformations. You need to take the Subject Area Family Tree down to the next level. What you identify at this detailed level will be the data elements that will be used in the remainder of the development. This means that data elements we do not identify in this stage will probably not exist in the final application. Therefore, it is extremely important to organize these data elements in as simple and clear a way as possible to maximize capturing the most complete and accurate information. We need the Data Element Family Tree.*

In addition, at the beginning of this Introduction and at the beginning of each of the chapters is a short story that relates a personal vacation experience to the tools in each chapter. There are two areas I find very near and dear to my heart: data modeling and vacation. So why not bring them both into each chapter?

You will also note that each chapter has similar headings:

About This Chapter. Describes in a few paragraphs what is contained in the chapter, along with the sequence of topics to be discussed and a very short overview of each of the tools contained in the chapter. Also in this section there usually are a few sentences about how this chapter relates to the previous chapters in the text.

What Is This Tool? An explanation of the tool, including its goals and usually a few simple examples. Note that this section and the next two sections are repeated for each tool in the chapter.

Using the Tool. Includes the steps you would take to apply this tool.

The Tool In Practice. Contains a detailed example of applying the tool, using the steps described under the section Using The Tool.

Summary. Briefly summarizes the key points from the chapter and relates the chapter to subsequent chapters.

Who Should Read this Book

This book is for you if you have some familiarity with data modeling and data modeling concepts. Included are data modelers and administrators, analysts, designers, and system and data architects. You should not read this book if you are brand new to data modeling, because there are many very good introductory texts on data modeling, some of which are listed in the suggested reading list at the end of this book. You should read this book if you have had some practical data modeling experience. I strongly believe that even those of us with a dozen or more years of data modeling experience might find a few useful tools and techniques between the covers of this book.

If you have less than 3 years' experience in data modeling, I would highly recommend reading this book from cover to cover. If you have more than 3 years' experience, I would start with Chapter 4, "Project Planning for the Data Modeler," which provides a good overview for Chapters 5 through 10 and will help you navigate directly to the sections of the text that most interest you. If you have a lot of experience, I would recommend skipping the section Normalization Hike in Chapter 8 and reading only the second half of Chapter 8, What Is the Denormalization Survival Guide. For all, I recommend reading Chapter 11 at some point. Although it is short, it contains valuable advice for the data modeler.

I would also recommend marking those sections that you find most interesting in this text and referring back to them as you are doing your data modeling activities. Many times when we read a text, we nod our heads with understanding as we complete each chapter but forget to apply the information as we are actually doing the work. I recommend using this book as an active reference as you are modeling. For example, you might ask yourself, "How do I structure my Data Element Family Tree again?" and then quickly find the answer in Chapter 7.

What's on the Web Site?

If you visit my Web site, www.wiley.com/compbooks/hoberman, you will find additional tools and templates and updates for existing tools from this text. If you do not want to recreate some of the spreadsheets in this book, you can go to this Web site and download an empty spreadsheet as your starting point. I also will continue to update this Web site with new tools and advice for the data modeler. This Web site also contains pointers to some of my favorite data modeling sites on the World Wide Web.

You can contact me through the companion Web site or at me@stevehoberman.com.

From Here

I have written this book with the intention of making it very practical and having it contain information that easily can be applied to any type of application. I would like you to use your imagination in dreaming up new tools as you are reading about the tools in these pages. Think up new tools or customizations to the tools included herein that can directly impact your current assignments.

As the field of data modeling increases in importance, there will be more demands placed on the data modeler. To look at it in a more positive light, there will be more challenges and exciting opportunities for the data modeler. These opportunities translate into quicker turnaround for data models and more flexible and efficient resulting designs. In other words, tools such as those in this text will become critical to successful designs, not only in our current environment but also in the near future.

ACKNOWLEDGMENTS

I can summarize my acknowledgements for this book with the following equation:

Wife + Reviewers + Managers + Coworkers + Family + Me = Book

Input and support from all of these people helped me complete this book.

Wife. Being my partner through everything, and this book was no exception, Jenn was very supportive in my need to work what seemed like endless nights and weekends. Jenn not only reviewed each chapter but also took on additional household responsibilities for 8 months, letting me type away without diversion. While writing this text, I was excused from shopping, cooking, laundry, cleaning, mowing grass, paying bills, and the list goes on. (I am hoping that I will continue to be excused now that the book is done.)

Reviewers. This content of this book was enhanced significantly with the help of professional reviewers. I thank Bruce Horowitz, Emilie Herman, and Irving Nichols for their help in reviewing and proofing this text. Bruce has an incredible amount of experience in the field, and he provided both advice on broad subject matters and detailed comments on each chapter. Emilie from John Wiley & Sons coached me through each step along the way, offering timely and valuable comments on each chapter. Irving (a.k.a. Mr. N) provided many excellent comments on the tone of the text and opened my eyes to the difference between "complement" and "compliment."

Managers. Over the years in my career, I was very lucky to have great data administration and data modeling managers. I thank Cynthia Silber, Artie Mahal, and Phil Maxson for their insight and mentorship, and for giving me the opportunity to work on challenging projects. Cynthia taught me to "feel the data." I admire Artie's passion for data and his ability to tell a great story. Phil helped me understand the communication and education sides to data modeling necessary for its success.

Coworkers. I have worked with talented groups of people over the years and am grateful for the interactions and challenges they have provided, which have broadened my understanding of this field.

Family. I thank my family for their support, advice, and sense of humor during this project, including our little dog Francis, who stood guard at my office door while I worked into the night.

Building the Foundation

Have you ever been in a situation where a lack of effective communication with the project manager led to unreasonable expectations from you as the data modeler? An example is a situation where unrealistic timeframes to complete the models were dictated; another is where the project team felt that many of the data modeling activities were unnecessary and a waste of time. The project manager, the data modeler, and the rest of the project team need to have realistic and mutually acceptable expectations of the data modeling activities. Expectations must be realistic in terms of which modeling tasks are required and how long it should take to complete them. Expectations must be mutually acceptable in that all members of the project team, including the data modeler, agree to and understand the modeler's task and time commitments.

Realistic and mutually acceptable expectations do not happen automatically, nor are they solely arrived at through the power of positive thinking. In your role as data modeler, you have the capability and obligation to educate and influence. These communication prerequisites form the foundation of the application analysis and design activities. Having this foundation in place before the design work begins will increase the project manager's satisfaction with and appreciation of the overall modeling activities. Therefore, this foundation is critical for a successful modeling experience.

Part 1 of this book, "Building the Foundation," offers several tools to help you as the data modeler utilize the data modeling education and communication process. Chapters 1 through 4 contain tools that focus on aspects of data modeling education and communication. Here is the purpose of each of these four chapters:

Clearly explain data modeling concepts. Chapter 1, "Using Anecdotes, Analogies, and Presentations to Illustrate Data Modeling Concepts," focuses on the most effective ways I have found to clearly communicate facets of data modeling. *Anecdotes* are short stories that can work very well to explain a concept or term. *Analogies* compare data modeling concepts with something the audience is very familiar with to highlight some of the data modeling traits. *Presentation steps* are the sequence of steps to go through when creating a data modeling presentation.

Gain agreement on the required types of meta data. Chapter 2, "Meta Data Bingo," will help define the standard types of meta data for your project and organization. Meta Data Bingo is a game where the people on your project team complete Bingo cards identifying which types of meta data are most important to capture. These Bingo cards capture meta data at a number of different levels of detail, including project, data model, subject area, entity, and data element levels.

Improve the quality and consistency of definitions. Chapter 3, "Ensuring High-Quality Definitions," focuses on a tool called the Definition Checklist. Examples of applying the Definition Checklist at the subject area, entity, and data element levels are provided.

Offer a set of data modeling tasks and how they fit into the larger development life cycle. Chapter 4, "Project Planning for the Data Modeler," includes four project planning templates that contain the complete and sequential set of tasks required to successfully finish data modeling deliverables in a realistic timeframe.

Using Anecdotes, Analogies, and Presentations to Illustrate Data Modeling Concepts

While vacationing in Europe, we decided to spend a few days at a very small village in Northern Italy. It was an extremely picturesque town surrounded by snow-capped mountains full of great hiking trails. There were only four restaurants in the town, and the first one we decided to try was located in a building several hundred years old. On entering, we were immediately impressed with the restaurant's atmosphere and character—lots of antiques and paintings, with the warm smell of a fireplace and food. After we were seated, we realized that the restaurant did not use menus. Apparently any food that is seasonable or available is served for dinner. This would not have been a problem except that no one in the restaurant spoke English and the only Italian I knew was the word *ciao*, which means *bye*.

We needed a way to clearly communicate our dinner preferences. It took several minutes of unsuccessful and frustrating attempts at communication with the waiter before an idea came to us. We started to make animal sounds. Apparently animal sounds are universal. By mooing, we were able to inquire whether beef was available that evening. We were also able to oink and shake our heads, meaning we did not want pork. We successfully acted out all of our animals and were served exactly what we expected. I was amazed at how well this technique worked. We were able to clearly communicate using this animal sound approach. I think this dinner is a great example that no matter how different your backgrounds or interests may be, there are always ways for people to communicate clearly.

For many people with limited application development experience, the field of data modeling can sometimes be just as foreign as a foreign language. This can lead to a lack of understanding of data modeling concepts and terminology, causing confusion and unrealistic expectations in completing the modeling deliverables. We can avoid this confusion by clearly explaining the different aspects of data modeling. To successfully explain data modeling concepts at times requires being as creative as imitating a cow in a restaurant. We need to think of innovative and creative approaches to get our message across. Sometimes a short story or anecdote can clearly explain a data modeling concept. Sometimes analogies can be a very powerful technique. Sometimes a short and focused presentation will suffice. I find that one or a combination of anecdotes, analogies, and presentations can be used to effectively communicate with and in some cases influence those who are having difficulty grasping data modeling concepts and terms.

About This Chapter

This chapter focuses on the most effective tools for clearly communicating data modeling concepts. Some people with whom we work on projects, such as managers and business users, may not easily grasp concepts such as a data model or a data warehouse. How effective do you think it would be to rattle off the textbook definition of a data model to these individuals? Their eyes probably would glaze over, and although they may occasionally nod their heads in the hope of understanding, most likely they will be bored out of their minds and even more confused than before. What is needed is a simple and captivating approach to explain modeling concepts.

I sometimes am asked what I do for a living. As a data modeler, how would you respond? Because the people asking usually have very little technical background, when I proudly say, "I am a data modeler," I often receive blank expressions. I could reply with something such as, "I create representations of the data requirements for a system that can be then transformed into a relational database where the actual data can be entered and retrieved, blah, blah, blah." How many people would really understand or appreciate that explanation? Or, I could think of a simple and interesting way to explain what I do and say, "I create blueprints for applications" or "I make sure applications contain the correct and complete information that the business needs."

There are tools that improve the communication process. We will discuss three data modeling communication tools within this chapter:

Anecdotes. Short stories can work very well to explain a concept or term. Most of us love to hear a story. We look forward to knowing what is going to happen next. You can use a combination of humor, facts, and relevant situations as input to clearly explain a complex topic. We will review the steps to create a data modeling anecdote and go through a detailed example of an actual anecdote that I have used many times.

Analogies. *Analogies* are comparisons between two or more concepts. Analogies can compare something the audience is familiar with to a data modeling concept we would like them to understand. We will discuss a work sheet to help with creating an effective analogy and go through a number of my most favorite data modeling analogies. Six of these data modeling analogies will be described. Because I often have used these analogies and they are effective, I will dedicate a fairly large portion of this chapter to this topic.

Presentation steps. How often have you listened to a presentation and lost interest in it because you could not understand how it related to you? When we explain data modeling concepts through formal presentations, we need to make sure our material has been tailored or customized so that it hits home with the audience and demonstrates how this information directly impacts them. We will review the steps to create a presentation that gets this customized message across to your audience. Well-structured presentations can clearly communicate the required concepts at the appropriate level of detail with content that the audience can relate to and appreciate. We will discuss the steps for creating these customized presentations and go through a detailed example.

If you visit the companion Web site, www.wiley.com/compbooks/hoberman, you will find templates for each of the tools in this chapter, additional tools and more information about tools within this book, including empty templates that you can download.

What Are Data Modeling Anecdotes?

In our normal daily communication, we probably tell and hear many stories, or anecdotes, on a wide range of topics. Some examples are stories of what happened to us over the weekend, stories of things that have happened to people we know, and stories related to our work projects. These anecdotes help strengthen relationships with those around us and entertain and educate us. We can visualize what the speaker is saying. Sometimes, when the story is complete, we leave with a message or additional understanding we did not have before. Anecdotes are extremely effective in explaining data modeling concepts for a number of reasons:

They create lasting visual. Our minds are much more easily able to absorb and retain a story than a fact, a statement, or an explanation. For example, on a job interview simply telling the interviewer that you are a hard worker would not have the same lasting impact as would describing a situation or story where you had to work nights and weekends to complete a task. The interviewer picturing you working nights and weekends creates a much more lasting impression than does just hearing you say you are a hard worker. There are many courses that teach how to improve your memory. Most of these memory improvement techniques involve creating a story or visual image for the concept you need to remember. For example, if you would like to memorize the name Mary Doe, you might visualize a deer wearing a name tag that says Mary. This visual image might sound rather strange, but I bet that even a few paragraphs from now you will still remember the name Mary Doe. A manager with whom I once worked is an excellent storyteller. I still remember many of his stories. Once he used a story to convince a senior level manager of the benefits of data modeling. This manager was so inspired that he told his entire staff, "No application gets developed without a data model." Whenever I think of this story, I have a visual image of him passionately communicating why data modeling is so important.

They captivate and entertain. A story can grab your attention and keep you at the edge of your seat. As children, we were always eager to hear a story: "Read me about those three little pigs one more time!" When we get older, we still have this interest in hearing stories. Telling a story is so much more captivating and entertaining than explaining a concept in dry technical terms. Have you ever been to a presentation where the speaker used a story to lure you into her topic? It is a good way to catch your interest. You are eager to know what is going to happen next. When I teach data modeling, I usually start off with a story on sports. This story is a great attention-getting device for the rest of the presentation and communicates the theme for the entire talk. I get everyone's attention because they all are very much interested in the story.

They strengthen relationships. When you tell a story, you are sharing an experience with your audience. They learn more about you through the story. This brings you closer together with other people and thus strengthens relationships. While in college, I did a number of student orientations to get freshman feeling more comfortable on campus. One of the get-to-know-you activities I did quite often was to sit with about a dozen freshman in a circle and pass around a roll of toilet paper, asking each freshman to take as many pieces as he or she would like. When each freshman had one or more pieces of toilet paper, I would ask them to tell something about themselves for every piece of toilet paper they are holding. This sharing helps make people feel comfortable and closer with each other. Many students chose to tell a story from their past. Several years ago I worked with a senior manager who was very much against data modeling and would constantly blame the data modeling team for any delays in her projects. Telling this story to fellow data modelers strengthens my relationships with them and also encourages them to share their war stories with me.

They alleviate tension. I have been in a number of meetings where accusations and emotions run high. Sometimes a story told during these tense situations can reduce the stress level and put the situation into perspective. Recently, I was in a very intense design session where somebody was bold enough to tell a joke. This brief interruption from our stressful situation made us all laugh. We then were able to attack our problem once again, with a less rigid and less serious attitude.

WARNING

Sometimes too many stories or a story that is too long can distract and annoy your audience. Use stories only for a specific purpose, and keep them as short as possible.

Data Modeling Anecdotes In Use

There are three simple steps to creating and telling a successful data modeling anecdote:

1. **Define a topic.** Make sure the anecdote you tell has a specific objective or topic in mind, in this case to explain a data modeling concept or term. I like to phrase a topic in the form of a question that I plan on answering with the story. Topics can be either just an explanation or also include the need to influence the audience. Here are some examples of good topics or objectives that explain something to the audience:

   - What is a data model?

   - What does normalization mean?

- What is a dimension? A fact table?
- What is meta data?
- What does data quality mean?
- When does data modeling take place in the software life cycle?

Here are some examples of good topics or objectives that are designed to influence the audience:

- Why do I need a data warehouse?
- Why is data modeling so important?
- Why do I need definitions?
- Why does data modeling take so long?
- Why do I need naming standards?
- Why do we need a meta data repository?

2. **Choose your story.** There are many different types of stories from which to choose. Think of an entertaining yet informative and brief story that clearly communicates your topic. We can select true stories that happened to us, war stories that we have heard about, stories about the future, jokes, and so on. For example, for the topic "Why do I need a data warehouse?" I might describe a situation in which the business had a great deal of valuable data but lacked a convenient and efficient way to report on and understand these data.

3. **Practice your story.** Once you have your story, practice telling it until you feel confident that it conveys your topic in less than two minutes. Avoid telling a story that drags on. Unfortunately, almost everyone at one time or another has had to listen to a long, boring story. We need to keep our data modeling anecdotes short and sweet and to the point. For example, I would practice telling the "Why do I need a data warehouse?" story until I can tell it smoothly in less than two minutes.

TIP

Keep your anecdotes short and sweet. The purpose of the data modeling anecdote is to support your topic as quickly and clearly as possible. Avoid long, boring stories. Try to have entertaining, short stories. For example, one very-well-known person in our industry almost always starts his presentation with a parrot joke, which he uses to explain the topics he will discuss. The joke is always short and entertaining. The parrot joke is a great attention-getting device and helps us visualize his points clearly.

Data Modeling Anecdotes In Practice

To illustrate the steps to come up with a useful anecdote, I will go through an example of one that I use quite often. Let's go through each of these three steps.

Define Your Topic

I wanted to explain why definitions were so important for the entities on a particular data model. This data model had many entities that had very encompassing and broad names, such as Business Party and Transaction. It had these broad names because we were applying abstraction, which we will learn more about in Chapter 9, "The Abstraction Safety Guide and Components." For now, picture several entities that are not intuitive to know what they mean by reading their names. We would need to read their definitions to really understand what they are. For this particular project, the functional analyst was creating some resistance in providing these entity definitions. Therefore, my topic will be "Why do I need definitions?" My goal is to convince the functional analyst that we need to take the time to fully define abstract and generic entities, such as Business Party and Transaction.

Choose Your Story

I prefer to choose true stories that have happened to me. After data modeling for many years, I have a large collection of stories that illustrate different aspects of our data modeling industry. I also can tailor the same story for many particular topics. In this way, I can reuse my well-practiced story instead of preparing and practicing a new story. I prefer stories that make the audience laugh. In general, people like to be entertained.

For this particular case, I will choose to tell a story of what happened to me a little over a year ago. I can tailor this story slightly to convey a different purpose or explain a slightly different concept. I am listing it here in text, and this is similar to how I would verbally tell it to the functional analyst:

> I was on a plane preparing for a very important data model walk-through presentation I was to give to a group of managers in Latin America. I sat in a window seat studying the data model in front me, holding it several inches from my face. The model was on two large pieces of paper taped together, providing a sound and visual barrier between me and everyone else on the airplane. I was intently studying each of the entities and relationships on this model. I was planning the sequence and techniques I would use to walk through each of the concepts the following day.
>
> "What are you working on?" This question that penetrated the relatively quiet airplane silence came from the little girl sitting next to me, who was probably about eight years old. I was speechless for a moment, recovering from being interrupted from my work and being surprised by this little girl's interest in what I was working on. Was she bored, or was she really interested in this sheet of paper filled with rectangles and lines? I thought, "Here lies a great opportunity to educate someone about data modeling." We data modelers know we could never pass up this kind of opportunity. This was especially true because I had a meeting the next day where I would need to explain this model to a group of managers. I thought that explaining the data model now to this captive audience might be good practice for my presentation.
>
> I proceeded to explain what a data model is and what this particular model was showing. I was very careful to use terms and examples that I thought an eight year old would understand. I described the data model as a set of instructions, just like instructions for building a dollhouse or model plane. Then she asked a question that I will never forget: "What is a Business Party?"
>
> Business Party was one of the entities on this model. I thought to myself, "This girl is a genius. She is going to make a great data modeler when she grows up." The name "Busi-

ness Party" is vague and does not convey any business concepts or anything that we can really relate to. Therefore, we need to have documented a solid definition for Business Party. If we did not have a solid definition, we would be asking the same question in the near future that this eight year old asked on first seeing this model.

I was very excited that she asked this question, and so I proceeded to explain in detail what a Business Party is. "It is a customer, and an employee, and a flight attendant. . . ." I went through many examples until the little girl interrupted me with another question: "Can I watch the movie now?"

You see, a movie was about to start on the airplane, and I guess she had had enough data modeling for one day. Although my ego was slightly hurt by her comment, I did use some of the explanations the next day with the group of managers, which helped me a lot. I also made sure my Business Party definition was comprehensive enough to make Business Party better understood for a long time to come.

Practice Your Story

Once you have identified your story, practice it over and over again until you can tell it smoothly and clearly. Once you have the story sounding smooth and taking a minimal amount of time to tell, you can keep it in mind for other topics that might be relevant. For example, the airplane story just told can be used for more than just explaining the importance of definitions for entities. I can also use it for keeping explanations simple. If I can explain a data model to an eight-year-old girl, I should be able to explain a data model to people with whom I work. I can just focus on different aspects of the story and use the same story to support multiple topics.

What Are Data Modeling Analogies?

An analogy is a comparison between two or more concepts to highlight their similarities and/or differences. Something is like something else for certain reasons. It is a very good technique for introducing something foreign or new. By comparing something foreign to something familiar, the foreign concept is no longer as foreign and an initial level of understanding has been created.

A good example of an analogy within the development arena is the waterfall approach to software development. This technique of developing applications is based on the outputs of a high-level phase flowing into the inputs of a more detailed phase. For example, the business requirements phase flows into the functional requirements phase, which flows into the technical requirements phase, and so on, just like a waterfall. A waterfall gives us the picture in our minds of water flowing from a high to a low level. By picturing a waterfall, we can imagine the different software development phases flowing from one to the other. This is a very effective way of picturing one method for developing an application.

I have found that using an analogy is sometimes the most effective method for educating and influencing someone on what data modeling is or why it is important. An analogy has several benefits:

It creates a lasting visual image. Just as does a good story, an analogy creates a picture in our minds that we do not soon forget. I learned the waterfall methodology over 15 years ago, yet I clearly remember it because of the analogy to an actual waterfall. For many people who are less technically oriented, it is hard to visualize a data model or model-related concepts. By using analogies, you can compare these intangible data modeling concepts to things with which people are more familiar.

It offers easy customization. You can easily tailor an analogy to your audience. In the examples that follow you will see that you can change the familiar concepts, depending on your audience's needs and interests. For example, the blueprint analogy, which we will discuss shortly, can be tailored to your audience to be as flexible as a blueprint for a house, a building, an amusement park ride, and so on, and still provide the same effect.

It provides quick comparisons. Most analogies are short and to the point. Name each concept and explain why they are similar. We do not have the same risk as we do with anecdotes, where stories have the potential to drag on.

WARNING

■■■■ **Try not to appear condescending when using analogies. Many times when we try to simplify, we find ourselves sounding like a first-grade teacher talking to a group of children. Keep your analogies simple but professional.**

Data Modeling Analogies In Use

To use an analogy, I simply fill in a template, such as the one in Table 1.1.

This Analogy Work Sheet lists the concepts you are comparing and a few phrases of what the concepts have in common. This is a valuable tool to clearly capture and document your analogies. Also, add to this table over time as you develop new analogies. Any concept in data management that has been misunderstood is a prime candidate for an analogy.

Table 1.1 Analogy Work Sheet

THIS EASILY UNDERSTOOD CONCEPT ...	... IS LIKE THIS CONCEPT I'M TRYING TO EXPLAIN ...	... FOR THESE REASONS

TIP

▬▬▬▬ Remember the high-level components of an analogy from the Analogy Work Sheet. If you just remember the easily understood concept, the data modeling concept you are trying to explain, and the reasons they are similar, you will have the basic building blocks for any analogy.

Data Modeling Analogies in Practice

Let's go through a number of analogies that I use most often in data modeling. I will fill in the Analogy Work Sheet for each one of these analogies and then go through an example using a dialog format to explain how these might be used in normal conversation. These analogies are not listed in any particular order:

The subject area model is a high-level view. A view from the top of a skyscraper provides a high-level understanding of the surrounding city in much the same way as the subject area model provides a high-level understanding of our business.

The data model is a blueprint. A blueprint provides the same types of clarity, consistency, and formal representation of a structure, such as to a house or building, as the data model provides to a database design.

The enterprise model is a world map. A world map provides a single view of all the land and water on earth, just as the enterprise data model provides a single view of all the information within an organization. Both the world map and enterprise data model can be used for issue resolution and for building common ground and agreement among parties.

Standards are city planning. City planning provides consistency and conformity for the greater good of the towns in which we live. In much the same way, standards provide consistency and conformity for the greater good of our departments and organizations.

A meta data repository is a library. A library contains books organized in a way that allows for easy location and retrieval. A meta data repository contains information about our applications and business also organized in a way that allows for easy location and retrieval.

A data warehouse is a heart. A heart is the central hub to our bodies. Blood is carried through veins to our heart, and carried through arteries from our heart. Similarly, the data warehouse is the central hub to our reporting environment. Lots of applications pass information through interfaces to the data warehouse, and lots of data marts need information passed through interfaces from the data warehouse.

NOTE

▬▬▬▬ There are many great analogies that I have used over the years, and many more are still waiting to be discovered. Think of some new analogies as you read this section. Use the blank form on the Web site www.wiley.com/compbooks/hoberman to record the components of your analogy.

The Subject Area Model Is a High-Level View

This analogy explains the benefits of a subject area model by comparing the high-level view of the business from this model with the high-level view of the city from the top of a skyscraper. You can use any skyscraper and city. I prefer using New York City and the Empire State Building, because I grew up in Queens and never fully understood the layout of New York City until I visited the top of the Empire State Building one summer night several years ago. The similarities between the skyscraper and the subject area model are outlined in the Analogy Work Sheet in Table 1.2.

NOTE

If you are unfamiliar with the meaning and concept of a subject area model, we discuss them in depth in Chapter 6, "Subject Area Modeling." We discuss several different types of subject area models; we can apply a variation of this analogy to all of them.

Let's go through each of the similarities between the skyscraper and subject area model:

Easily understood view. As mentioned previously, I prefer to use the Empire State Building as my skyscraper. The view from the Empire State Building is breathtaking on a clear day. The Empire State Building is over 1,400 feet tall, with more than 100 stories. It casts its shadow over neighboring buildings, many of which are also very tall. The minor details of the city disappear from this height, and the main sections of the city are visible. Without being caught up in the details of the city, the important points can be more easily understood and digested. Important points of interest seen from this height in New York City would be the different bridges, the Statue of Liberty, Yankee Stadium, Uptown, Downtown, and so on. You can learn a lot by seeing these larger points of interest from this high level. For example, I had no idea how close the Throgs Neck and Whitestone Bridges were to each other until I went to the top of the Empire State Building one summer night several years ago. Everything is clear and easily understood at this level.

High-level view. The subject area model is a high-level view of the business. This model contains the subject areas and how they relate to each other. Subject areas are the critical and basic concepts to the department or company. These subject

Table 1.2 Skyscraper Analogy Work Sheet

THIS EASILY UNDERSTOOD CONCEPT ...	... IS LIKE THIS CONCEPT I'M TRYING TO EXPLAIN ...	... FOR THESE REASONS
View from a skyscraper	Subject area model	• Easily understood view • High-level view

areas are at a very high level. The details of entities, their business rules, and data elements are all hidden and not relevant at this level. Thus, for example, subject areas that are at the same level of detail as the Statue of Liberty and Yankee Stadium include the following:

- Customer
- Associate
- Account
- Product
- Order

We would see Customer on the subject area model and not Customer Last Name, Customer Demographics, and Customer Type. An example of a subject area model is shown in Figure 1.1.

NOTE

Both a skyscraper and the subject area model provide a high-level view to make understanding a concept easier. By understanding at this level, a high-level view becomes an efficient tool to use in gaining agreement on differences between business concepts.

A Short Dialog to Show How This Analogy Is Applied

Let's say you are given the following situation and want to put this analogy to the test:

Management is trying to decide whether to purchase a very expensive piece of packaged software and is very concerned about how it will fit into the existing applications. Some existing applications will be replaced, and others will become source and destination applications for information from this packaged software. Management is worried that there might be substantial integration issues in introducing this software. You would like to suggest that a subject area model be created to show how this new software fits into the existing applications. John and Janet are two managers who have the authority to approve

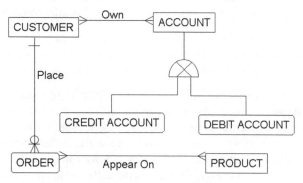

Figure 1.1 Sample subject area model.

the purchase of the software. They are meeting with you, the star data modeler for your company, in a conference room.

John: Another question I have is on the area of logistics. I wonder if this packaged software is going to meet our need for logistics, and if it does, will we throw away our current logistics system from the 1980s?

Janet: Good question. Also, how about Customer Location information. We can today only handle one location per customer, which I hear is starting to cause some data quality issues. I would love this new software to be able to support multiple locations per customer. Do you think that it will do that?

John: I'm not sure. What do you think?

They are asking for your opinion. Now these are two high-level managers sitting in a room with you, the data modeler, asking what you think. You know this can never happen in the real world. You also know that the packaged software would have probably been purchased and half implemented before these kinds of questions are usually asked. Sad, but true! But this is a data modeling book, and we are telling a story for data modelers. So, let's pretend. Imagine you are in the same room with these high-level managers and they want to know what you think. Enjoy it!

You: I think you are both asking exactly the right kinds of questions. The problem we are facing is that we don't have a high-level understanding of the existing systems and how they will relate to this new packaged software. You need a view as if you are on top of a skyscraper looking out over an entire city. Everything makes sense from that height. You need the same high-level view that encompasses both our existing systems and this new piece of software.

Note how short we kept this analogy. Because these are busy folks, we keep the comparison very short and sweet.

John: You're right. We are missing that high-level view. How do you get it?

You: You need a subject area model. This model contains our understanding of our subject areas, such as logistics and customer, and also can show which subject areas this new software can provide. We can represent the overlap between what we have today and what this packaged software application can support. We can use different colors to differentiate our applications from this new one. For example, I did the data modeling in our logistics area and this is how logistics looks in our business.

You draw several subject areas on the white board and draw lines as you relate the subject areas to each other. Then you use a different color for the packaged software.

You: So we need to ask this software vendor to define which types of logistics information it stores, or to provide me with its data model or some type of meta data dictionary. If the vendor carries the same concept of logistics that we have here, then we can color the entity green, meaning it overlaps with our functionality. If the vendor has some of our functionality in its software, we can color the entity yellow. If the vendor does not have any of the functionality we need, we better color the entity red. Red is a very large warning signal and could be the make-or-break decision as to whether we purchase this package. A large number of yellow items can also be a problem.

Janet: This sounds like a great idea. What next?

You: I need a few business experts from each subject area. I can work with them over this week to create a subject area model of our business. Then I will need several hours of time from this software vendor. Hopefully the vendor can provide us with a technical person who knows the internal data structures. I can color in the entities with the appropriate colors based on this technical person's answers. If there is a lot of green, not a lot of yellow, and no red, I think we would be in good shape and could more easily justify purchasing this piece of software.

John: You're brilliant! After this modeling effort, we will be doubling your salary!

Why not? If you are lucky enough to be meeting with senior management on this issue, anything is possible—even doubling of your salary!

TIP

Know your audience. Tailor the analogy comparisons to your audience. If you are using an analogy with someone who is currently building a house, try to work it into the analogy. This can make the difference between a successful analogy and a disaster. Be very aware of your audience's verbal and nonverbal cues when using the analogy. If you feel you have already made your point, there is no need to go any further. If you feel your audience still does not understand the concepts, try a different analogy or solicit questions from them.

The Data Model Is a Blueprint

This analogy explains the benefits of data modeling and why it requires time and effort. A comparison is made between the data model and a blueprint of something the audience is familiar with, such as a house, a building, an airplane, or even a roller coaster. See Table 1.3 for the Analogy Work Sheet.

Table 1.3 Blueprint Analogy Work Sheet

THIS EASILY UNDERSTOOD CONCEPT ...	... IS LIKE THIS CONCEPT I'M TRYING TO EXPLAIN ...	... FOR THESE REASONS
Blueprint	Data model	• Unambiguous representation • Standard industry syntax • Connections and relationships • Optimized design • Different levels of granularity

In much the same way an architect creates a blueprint for a future metal, stone, glass, or wood structure, the data modeler creates a data model for a future set of database tables.

A blueprint is the final working drawing created by the architect that shows exactly where everything will go inside and outside of the finished building. Builders use blueprints as guidelines so that the design created by the architect is reflected in the finished structure. Blueprints are covered with special standard industry symbols used by architects to tell the builder exactly where everything should go, including windows and doors, light fixtures, electrical outlets, water and gas lines, and so on.

A data model is an accurate representation used to assist business users, data modelers, developers, and database administrators in understanding and validating data requirements. A data model can be at subject area, logical, or physical level of detail.

Let's go through each of the similarities between the blueprint and data model:

Unambiguous representation. An unambiguous representation means that there is only a single interpretation in the design. In a blueprint for a house, for example, a ceiling might be nine feet high. The method used to note this fact on the blueprint is not up for interpretation. The height is nine feet. It is not eight or ten feet high, or even nine feet, one inch high. A data model provides the same level of rigor. A Customer must have at least one Account. This also is not up for interpretation. If a person does not have an Account, then the person is not a Customer. There is no room for multiple interpretations, as opposed to conversational language where there can be numerous interpretations. A business requirements document, for example, might contain the sentence "A Customer can have Accounts." But what does this sentence really mean? Can a Customer have no Accounts? Can a Customer have more than one? Once the rule is defined on the data model, there is only one interpretation.

Standard industry syntax. Standard industry syntax means that the icons and representations used in the design are widely understood around the country and sometimes worldwide. The notation for an electrical outlet on a blueprint is the same whether the blueprint is for a house in California or an office building in New York. In this way, electricians can be trained to recognize the meaning of a certain icon and get right to work instead of spending time first understanding the meaning of the icons and then the electrical requirements. A data model also has standard syntax. Entities are represented with labels inside rectangles, relationships through lines, and so on.

Connections and relationships. Connections and relationships mean that all portions of the design relate to each other and serve a purpose. In a blueprint for a roller coaster, for example, you would never have a drop that goes nowhere. Imagine the safety issues with a drop that just goes down, and not back up again! Similarly, on a data model, you would never have an entity or relationship that does not contribute in some way to the whole. Customer has relationships to Account, Salesperson, Order, and so on. Customer has value only when it relates to the other concepts within the business.

Optimized design. Optimized design means that certain laws of nature or industry rules are applied to the final design. A blueprint for a roller coaster, for example, takes into account the laws of physics and centrifugal force in designing the drops, loops, and corkscrews. The blueprint would have to take into account that the roller coaster car would need to have enough energy after the first drop to carry it through to the next drop, and so on, until the ride is completed. The data model enforces the laws of normalization and relational database design. By the completion of the logical data model, each data element is assigned to its appropriate entity based on the dependencies to the primary key. This provides for maximum flexibility and minimum redundancy within the resulting set of database tables.

Different levels of granularity. Different levels of granularity means that there can be different views of the same structure, depending on audience and purpose. For example, the owners of a house looking to expand their dining room do not need to know the same levels of detail as the contractors doing the work. The owners of the house know they need to have two electrical outlets in their expanded dining room. The electrical contractors need to know many more details to help with the new wiring and connections to the existing wiring. This allows the architect to explain the requirements at different levels of detail, depending on the audience, just as the data model can be at subject area, logical, or physical level of detail. Senior management might just need to understand the subject area level of detail, whereas the functional team needs to understand the logical level and the technical team the physical level. The Vice President sees CUSTOMER in the subject area model, for example. The functional analyst sees and validates the detailed business rules between CUSTOMER and CUSTOMER DEMOGRAPHICS. The database administrator needs the *volumetrics*, which is the number of initial rows and daily updates required to the CUSTOMER structure.

TIP

For the blueprint analogy, we use a new design comparison for a new application and a design for an addition on something to compare to an enhancement for an application. For example, for a new application you might want to compare the data model to a blueprint of a new home, building, or roller coaster. For an enhancement, you might want to compare the data model to a blueprint of an addition on a home or a new elevator in an office building.

It is very important to be as flexible as possible with your choice of blueprint yet still cover the most important similarities mentioned previously. Two dialogue examples using this analogy follow. The first is an example of applying this analogy to a new application; the second is an example of applying this analogy to an application enhancement.

A Short Dialog to Show How This Analogy Is Applied to a New Development Effort

Let's say you are given the following situation and want to put this analogy to the test:

Congratulations! You've been chosen as the data modeler for a very visible project! It is a brand new order processing application. You are feeling great, that is until you review the project plan and note that the only data modeling task listed is database design (that is, physical data modeling). Subject area and logical data modeling have been completely left off the project plan. Has this ever happened to you? You explain to the project manager that she is missing some critical tasks. She adds them reluctantly to the project plan and assigns each one a single day for completion. You have had a chance to review the updated project plan and business requirements documents over the weekend (you are very dedicated!) and are planning to meet with the project manager on Monday. You will need to educate her on why we do data modeling and why it requires time and effort. You will use the blueprint analogy.

For this example, you are the data modeler and Mary is the project manager. You walk into Mary's office.

Mary: Hi. How are you doing?

You: Pretty good. How was your weekend?

Mary: Great! I took the family to that new amusement park. The rides are amazing, especially the roller coaster. A drop of over 100 feet! Have you ever been there?

Your mind: Hmmm. A roller coaster. The blueprint for a roller coaster is similar to the data model for a database. This might make a good analogy.

You: I haven't been there yet, but I do love to ride roller coasters. Maybe I'll pay the amusement park a visit as a reward for completing the data models for your project. Say, Mary, I've had a chance to review the updated project plan this weekend and frankly was a little surprised by how little time was allocated to the data modeling phase of this project.

Mary: Wow, you worked on the weekend! That's dedication! In terms of the project plan, as long as the database is ready to go, that's what is important. If you need an extra day or two to theorize what the database design might look like, I suppose I can give it to you.

Your mind: Theorize is a euphemism for useless task. Calm down, calm down. Mary needs a good explanation of the data model and its benefits. Let's try out this Blueprint Analogy using the roller coaster as the example.

You: Thanks for being flexible, Mary. There is a lot more to data modeling than just the theory. Imagine if only a day or two were allocated to design that roller coaster you rode this weekend. If so, then in two days the architect had to meet all of the requirements for safety and enjoyment on that roller coaster. How do you think it would have turned out? Would you go for a ride on it?

Mary: Probably not. But I like where you're going with this. Please continue.

Your mind: Now I got her attention. I might want to sketch some of this on the white board.

You: If given appropriate attention, the benefits of that roller coaster blueprint are very similar to the benefits your project will derive from the data model. I can think of five characteristics these two have in common. They both have unambiguous representation, standard industry syntax, connections, optimized design, and different levels of granularity. (You might want to list these on the whiteboard. You explain each of these in sufficient detail, similar to how we described them in the previous section.)

Mary: I understand a bit better what you're trying to do for my project. How much time do you need to complete the subject area and logical data models?

You: Well, assuming the business requirements document I read this weekend is accurate, I estimated it would take. . . .

A Short Dialog to Show How This Analogy Is Applied to an Application Enhancement Effort

The same situation exists as described under the new application effort, except this is for a system enhancement. For this example, you are the data modeler and Mary is the project manager. You walk into Mary's office.

Mary: Hi. How are you doing?

You: Pretty good. How was your weekend?

Mary: Really hectic. We're building an addition onto our house.

Your mind: Hmmm. An addition to a house. That's just like a system enhancement to an existing application. The blueprint for a house addition is similar to the data model for a database. This might make a good analogy.

You: That's something you really need to plan for. Did you spend a lot of time with an architect?

Mary: You bet! I'm so glad we did, too. If we didn't have that blueprint, this new addition would be like a shot in the dark. Who knows how it would turn out.

You: Speaking of blueprints, I've had a chance to review the updated project plan this weekend and frankly was a little surprised by how little time was allocated to the data modeling phase of this project.

Mary: Wow, you worked on the weekend! That's dedication! In terms of the project plan, as long as the database is ready to go, that's what is important. If you need an extra day or two to theorize what the database design might look like, I suppose I can give it to you.

You: Thanks for being flexible, Mary. There is a lot more to data modeling than just the theory. Imagine if only a day or two were allocated to planning your house addition. If so, then in two days the architect had to meet all of your requirements. How do you think it would have turned out? Would you be satisfied? If given appropriate attention, the benefits of your addition blueprint are very similar to the benefits your project will derive from the data model. I can think of five characteristics these two have in common. They both have unambiguous representation, standard industry syntax, connections, optimized design, and different levels of granularity. (You might want to list these on the whiteboard. You explain each of these to her in sufficient detail.)

Mary: I understand a bit better what you're trying to do for my project. How much time do you need to complete the subject area and logical data models?

You: Well, assuming the business requirements document I read this weekend is accurate, I estimated it would take. . . .

The Enterprise Model Is a World Map

This analogy explains the benefits of an enterprise data model and the efficiency of limiting it to a subject area level of detail. A comparison is made between the enterprise data model and a world map. By comparing the enterprise data model to a world map, the audience can get a feel for the value of a complete big picture. See Table 1.4.

In much the same way as a world map is used to show the countries, nations, bodies of water, and their relationships, the enterprise data model is used to show all of the concepts or subject areas of a corporation and their relationships.

A world map is a graphical representation of the entire globe. It helps us understand how we fit into the rest of our environment. It needs to be complete, consistent, and accurate. By complete we mean that the world map needs to contain all of the land and water and country boundaries that exist. By consistent we mean that there is agreement as to the depiction of the land, water, and boundaries. It needs to be agreed to by all participants who might have more detailed maps that need to fit into the higher-level world map. By accurate we mean that it is correct and up-to-date. It also is a representation, meaning Earth is depicted in a two-dimensional form for mobility and practicality. The world map can fit on a single page or be several hundred pages of details. The more detailed, however, the greater the cost to create and maintain. The level of detail depends on the audience and purpose of the map.

An enterprise data model is a graphical representation of the entire business or corporation. It helps us understand how we fit into the rest of our environment. It needs to be complete, consistent, and accurate. By complete we mean that the model needs to contain all of the subject areas and concepts that exist in the company. By consistent we mean that there is agreement across departments as to the meaning and relationships of these subject areas. By accurate we mean that it is correct and up-to-date. It also is a representation, meaning that the internal, and sometimes external, environment of a company is represented in a two-dimensional model for mobility and practicality. The model can fit on a single page or be several hundred pages of details. The more detailed, however, the greater the cost to create and maintain. The level of detail depends on the audience and purpose of the enterprise data model.

I always recommend an enterprise data model be created only at the subject area level. Any more detailed than this level and the model loses its effect. An enterprise model that is too detailed is a like a world map where the mileage scale is actual size. This means there is no scale of one inch equals 100 miles. Instead, one inch equals one inch

Table 1.4 World Map Analogy Work Sheet

THIS EASILY UNDERSTOOD CONCEPT ...	... IS LIKE THIS CONCEPT I'M TRYING TO EXPLAIN ...	... FOR THESE REASONS
World map	Enterprise data model	• Agreement • Planning • Issue resolution

on the map. This is not only extremely complicated to imagine but cost prohibitive to create and maintain. If the enterprise data model was created at a logical or physical level, as soon as it is published it will probably be out-of-date because something has changed in the enterprise's data structures. The point here is to keep the enterprise data model at as high a level as possible.

Let's go through each of the similarities between the world map and enterprise data model:

Agreement. Agreement means that people with very different backgrounds, cultures, and beliefs understand and concur that this is the way the world is. Americans and Australians agree as to their countries' boundaries and locations on the globe. On the enterprise data model, both the accounting and sales departments agree as to the meaning of a Customer and the customer's relationship to an Account.

Planning. Planning means that the complete picture can be used as a tool to decide which future projects will have the most positive impact. Looking on a world map can help individuals choose exotic vacation destinations, or help corporations decide where to build factories or distribution centers. On the enterprise data model, companies can decide which data marts will give the biggest bang for the buck; where a certain packaged software fits in; and where data integration problems, data redundancy, opportunities for reuse, and so on, exist.

Issue resolution. Issue resolution means that the complete picture can be used as a tool to scope problems and prioritize them. Border disputes in the Middle East can be scoped, and parties from each country can use this scoped section as a common point for discussion. On the enterprise data model, companies can resolve name and definitions clashes across areas (for example, you call it Customer, I call it Consumer), as well as relationship conflicts.

When you use this analogy, think of current issues or projects that would benefit from the enterprise data model. For example, in describing the value of issue resolution, think of an issue your audience had recently that would have been solved more efficiently if the enterprise data model existed.

A Short Dialog to Show How This Analogy Is Applied

Let's use the following situation and see the dialog that develops.

> *Budgets are becoming increasingly tighter in your department. You are one approval signature away from receiving the initial funding for your enterprise data model project. Unfortunately, that one signature needs to come from your own department manager, Bob, who is not fully convinced of the value of an enterprise data model. You have scheduled a meeting with Bob, who has only offered to give you 15 minutes of his time to explain your case. You will need to explain the benefits of the enterprise data model. One of the points you need to make to Bob is that the initial funding for the enterprise data model is only for the subject area level of detail. It is a relatively small amount of money, a fraction of what it would cost to create an enterprise logical data model. You will make your pitch using the world map analogy.*

You walk into Bob's office.

Bob: I'm very busy today. You have 15 minutes to tell me more about your enterprise data model project. Your time starts now. Go!

Your mind: Bob currently thinks this is a total waste of time. Aha! He's got a world map on his office wall. Perfect for this analogy.

You: Thanks for making time for me, Bob. I know you're very busy. That world map on your wall is just like this enterprise data model project that we are eager to start working on.

Bob: You are wasting my time. Twelve minutes left!

You: You see, both that map on your wall and our enterprise data model provide three very important benefits: agreement, planning, and issue resolution. (You proceed to explain each of these three, customizing them for Bob's particular needs.)

Agreement means that people with very different backgrounds, cultures, and beliefs understand and concur that this is the way the world is. On the enterprise data model, your data warehouse department and the accounting department can finally agree on which financial data are in the data warehouse. That's probably one of the thorns in your side right now.

Bob: You got that right. Go on. Ten minutes left.

You: Planning means that the enterprise model can be used as a tool to decide which future projects will have the most positive impact. Looking on a world map can help our company decide which markets to penetrate next. Similarly, you can use the enterprise data model to meet with the business on how that new packaged software application will fit into the current systems architecture. It can be used to determine which subject areas will overlap. This new packaged software application is a big project on your plate now.

Bob: You are again right about that. Tell me more.

Your mind: Now I've got his interest!

You: Third, but not last, is issue resolution. Issue resolution means that the enterprise model can be used as a tool to scope problems and prioritize them. You can use the enterprise data model to resolve that Consumer versus Client debate that's been going on for some time.

And the best part is this first phase is only for the subject area level of detail. There is not a lot of funding involved, and in several weeks you will have your completed model. With all of the budget issues going on now, you more than anyone else are going to need a complete subject area view of our company to discuss the status of the projects with your management. If you are not yet convinced, I can create the Consumer/Client portion of the model for you in two days and we can see the benefits in action. What do you say Bob? Is it worthwhile?

Bob: You've convinced me. And wow! You did it in less than 10 minutes.

Standards Are City Planning

This analogy explains the reasons behind following standards by comparing data standards to zoning and city planning standards. See Table 1.5 for the Analogy Work Sheet.

Many of us have been in situations where we have encountered zoning or city planning rules and regulations. One of us may have said that "My neighbor's fence is too high!" or "There's no way they're building that townhouse complex in our town!" Whether you are influenced positively or negatively by these rules and regulations, their purpose is generally for the greater good of the entire community. Naming standards for entities and data elements are for the good of the entire company.

Let's go through each of the similarities between city planning and standards:

Good for the whole. There are books of standards that each town uses to shape its environment. These standards help ensure one building does not stick out or look exceptionally odd compared with the rest of the town storefronts or residences. Some towns are much stricter than other towns. Cape May, New Jersey, for example, which prides itself on being a Victorian town, has such strict ordinances that owners of Victorian homes cannot even replace their outside doorknobs without first seeking approval from the township. The purpose of these standards is to maintain the aesthetic appearance of the town. There are also safety and health reasons for standards. Standard electrical current is a safety issue. Standards for city sewer and water are health issues. Standard naming conventions are also good for the whole. For example, all of my data elements that are financial amounts end their data element name with the suffix AMT. This helps me identify financial data elements across projects and, therefore, increases the overall consistency, look, and feel of the data element names.

Conformity. Data standards also help ensure conformity. Data elements with the same name or naming structure can more easily be understood and reused. For example, using a standard that says all financial data elements end in the suffix AMT would help enormously when reviewing data elements.

GROSS_SALES_AMT tells us this is in dollars, and all other data elements that end in AMT are also in dollars. In addition, using the same naming abbreviations for the entire data element name can help in identifying common data elements across applications. For example, CUST_LAST_NAM appearing in two different applications appears to be the same data elements. Are CUST_LAST_NAM and

Table 1.5 Standards Analogy Work Sheet

THIS EASILY UNDERSTOOD CONCEPT ...	... IS LIKE THIS CONCEPT I'M TRYING TO EXPLAIN ...	... FOR THESE REASONS
City planning	Standards	• Good for the whole • Conformity

CONSUMER_LAST_NAM the same data elements? We really cannot tell by the name.

NOTE

▬▬▬▬ **In order to facilitate their understanding and reuse, standards help make concepts conform and be consistent with each other. In the case of naming standards, they are for the good of the company and not just for a specific project.**

A Short Dialog to Show How This Analogy Is Applied

Let's use this situation and see the dialog that develops.

In almost every project, you are constantly being asked variations of the question "Why do we follow naming standards?" Sometimes colleagues question the strange abbreviations, but almost all question the effort that goes into standardizing the data elements. You have been explaining that it is for the good of the company, not just your specific project. That usually does not work too well, because project managers pay the development costs and do not feel they should pay for effort that does not offer some amount of value to them. You have just been asked the question again, and this time you will try an analogy. Bill has asked the question. You plan on using the city planning analogy.

Bill: Why do we need to follow these archaic naming standards?

You: You just built a new house, right?

Bill: Yes, but what does that have to do with it?

You: Well, what if there were no standards on the type of sewer pipes that were needed? Or, what if any wattage would be allowed for your electrical outlets? How about the height of your neighbor's house? Imagine if your neighbors could build their houses as tall as they would like, without any regulations on maximum height?

Bill: I would probably move to a new town!

You: If we didn't follow standards for this project, you would probably want to move to a new company. Data standards help ensure conformity.

You proceed to explain the conformity and good for the whole similarities described previously. You relate each of these similarities to Bill's house example.

Bill: I'm convinced. I'll never ask about naming standards again!

A Meta Data Repository Is a Library

This analogy explains the need for a meta data repository by comparing it to a library. See Table 1.6 for the Analogy Work Sheet.

Both a library and meta data repository share a number of important characteristics for this analogy:

Table 1.6 Library Analogy Work Sheet

THIS EASILY UNDERSTOOD CONCEPT ...	... IS LIKE THIS CONCEPT I'M TRYING TO EXPLAIN ...	... FOR THESE REASONS
Library	Meta data repository	• Storage place for valuable information • Central location • Easy location and retrieval

Storage place for valuable information. A library can contain hundreds of thousands of books, all safely kept on shelves within aisles. A meta data repository can contain hundreds of thousands of pieces of important business information, all neatly kept within the realm of a single application. I can go to the library to take out books on gardening, travel, and web development. I can equally access topics that are just as broad from the meta data repository when I request the customer last name, associate stewardship information, and the latest version of a particular data model.

Central location. It is a single place to go for all your needs. For any book I need, I can go to the library. For any piece of meta data I need, I should go to the meta data repository. Whether I am looking for stored procedures or data element definitions, I can look in the same meta data repository application.

Easy location and retrieval. It is very easy to find a book on the shelf in the library. For example, if I am looking for a book on traveling to California, I could easily find out where the travel books are located and start looking for travel books on California. Likewise, I will have easy access to the information within the repository. For example, I will be able to easily find all of my customer location meta data.

A Short Dialog to Show How This Analogy Is Applied

Let's use this situation and see the dialog that develops:

A new person named Al on your data modeling team is questioning why so much effort has been put into designing and developing your company's meta data repository. Al believes that all of the required meta data can exist within the data modeling tool and does not need to be stored within a repository. You will try to explain the benefits of the repository to Al using the library analogy.

Al: I still don't see why we need a meta data repository. Everything I care about is right here in my model: definitions, names, format information. I can store and retrieve everything I need.

You: It's true that all of the meta data you need right now is in the model, but can other people who need to see it get to it? Mary on the reporting team would probably love to have many of our definitions that today exist only within our data models. Think of a library. We all have shelves of books in our homes, but these books cannot be as shared as easily and are not as accessible as those same books in a library. In a library, books are centrally located and provide easy location and retrieval. Just like with the meta data repository, all of the meta data is easily accessible and centrally located.

You continue to go into the details, explaining the similarities between the library and meta data repository mentioned in the previous section.

You: What if you need some meta data that cannot be captured within our current data modeling tool?

Al: Actually, I was looking for a place to store stewardship information. I was thinking of putting in the definition spot for each entity. . . .

You: Ouch! Imagine how inaccessible that would make stewardship. By storing all of the meta data within the repository, every type of meta data you can think of can be easily captured and represented. You do not need to fit a square peg into a round hole, so to speak. So, would you rather go to a friend's house for a book or tap the huge and easily accessible resources of your local library?

Al: Sounds like the library's a better choice. Will the meta data repository charge a late fee if I don't return the meta data in time? Just joking.

A Data Warehouse Is a Heart

This analogy explains why a data warehouse is so useful by comparing it to a heart. See Table 1.7 for the Analogy Work Sheet.

Both a heart and data warehouse share a number of important characteristics in this analogy:

Many veins or interfaces in, many arteries or interfaces out. Both a heart and data warehouse have many conduits going in and out. A heart has many veins and arteries carrying blood from one part of the body to another. Blood goes into the heart from many veins and out from the heart to other locations from many arteries. Likewise, many source system interfaces send data to the data warehouse from which much data are sent to other applications, such as data marts.

Centrally located. The heart is the hub within our body. Lots of blood and nutrients travel through this central location, just as in a data warehouse lots of data travel through the central reporting location.

Table 1.7 Heart Analogy Work Sheet

THIS EASILY UNDERSTOOD CONCEPT ...	... IS LIKE THIS CONCEPT I'M TRYING TO EXPLAIN ...	... FOR THESE REASONS
Heart	Data warehouse	• Many veins or interfaces in, many arteries or interfaces out • Centrally located

TIP

You can use this heart analogy on any application effort that is an integration hub; it is not limited to a data warehouse. Thus, this heart analogy is applicable whenever an application has lots of data elements coming in and going out.

A Short Dialog to Show How This Analogy Is Applied

Let's use this situation and see the dialog that develops.

> You are trying to convince the project manager, Betty, that it makes more sense to design her data mart through the data warehouse architecture instead of by building direct interfaces between the source applications and her mart. She believes it will be less expensive and more efficient to go directly against the source applications instead of pulling all her data from the data warehouse.

Betty: I know exactly what source applications to get my data from. Why do I need to go through the data warehouse?

You: Well, let's say you get your data directly from the source applications. Do you know the syntax for looking up the customer identifiers on the order information against the customer reference data? You see, there are many cases where you will need to do the integration and data checking that today is already done within the warehouse. It is true that you might know exactly what you need from each source application, but do you know how to integrate everything?

Betty: Not quite. But how complicated can it be?

You: Imagine all of the veins and arteries in the human body. There are incredible numbers of veins passing blood and nutrients to the heart; in turn, many arteries from the heart pass blood and nutrients to the rest of the body. Imagine if instead of having the central heart, we had all the veins and arteries directly connected to where they needed to pass their information. Imagine how complicated and wasteful that would be. Well, the same would be true if we built all of the interfaces directly to the source applications.

You proceed to explain the similarities between the heart and the data warehouse. Betty looks convinced.

Betty: Ok, ok. Let's give it a shot your way—through the data warehouse—and see what happens.

What Are the Presentations Steps?

The average data modeler probably gives hundreds of presentations throughout his or her career. These presentations can span many topics, including data model reviews, explanations of modeling concepts, accomplishments for the year, and so on. These presentations need to succinctly present your topic in an interesting way. The surest way to lose your audience is to fall into one of the following presentation traps:

No direction. This is when a presentation appears to go from slide to slide without a goal or objective. The slides touch on many topics without clearly explaining any one of them. You leave these types of presentations with many unanswered questions and a feeling that you wasted your time. Data modeling presentations with little or no direction can be very frustrating for the audience, because the smallest data modeling subject can take hours to debate and explain. Have you ever presented a data model or sat in on a data model review where the discussions seemed to spend hours on a very small section of the model or on a single issue? I have been in meetings where the entire meeting focused on a very small topic and never went anywhere else. Afterward, I was left wondering what the original purpose of the meeting was.

Audience cannot relate. This is when there is nothing included in the presentation to make the members of the audience feel that listening is an important use of their time. There are no examples or scenarios that show how the material directly impacts them. The question "What's in it for me?" needs to be incorporated into your presentation, because this is the question the members of the audience are going to be asking themselves. Thus, a presentation showing the benefits of data modeling needs to clearly articulate how data modeling will benefit the specific audience and should not include generalities to which the audience cannot relate.

Too much. This is when there are too many slides for a particular topic. There might be extraneous slides that are not needed for the explanation, or too many facts or statistics that do not directly add value to the topic. A presentation that is unnecessarily long is a very good way to lose the audience and make them want to be in the dentist's chair rather than in your audience.

Too dry. This is when we have a presentation that is in presentation slide format but reads more like a textbook. There are no graphics, and the wording is very dry and boring. A data modeling presentation on the benefits of data modeling, which lists the mathematical and relational database benefits in technical terms, might be too dry for the audience.

Over the years, I have noticed that my technical presentations have similarities in the way the material is created and in regard to the general discussion topics. I have developed a process for creating presentations that is quick and results in a high-quality presentation. That is the tool I discuss in this section. I consider it a tool because this process helps me create presentations, which I use in my projects to communicate with the business, functional, and technical teams. Just as with anecdotes and analogies, the process of creating a presentation is a tool for clearly getting the word out.

WARNING

▬▬▬ **This tool does not discuss how to present your information but only how to organization it in the presentation format. There are many great books on presenting in front of people, but usually the best way to sharpen this skill is through practice.**

This section walks you through the high-level steps for creating an effective presentation to communicate a data modeling concept. The benefits of following these steps include the following:

Faster creation of presentations. The process I will present separates the subject headings within your presentation from their content. The process is made more efficient by focusing on the headings first and then the content. You will save time creating your presentations by using this divide-and-conquer strategy because you will not be jumping from headings to content, back to headings, back to content, and so on. You first focus on the headings; when they are completed, you focus on the content. By identifying the headings for my presentation, I can use them as placeholders and fill in the text as I am preparing for my presentation.

Greater consistency between presentations. The same format means greater consistency across presentations. Your presentation should have a look and feel similar to other presentations within your organization. A common process also makes it easier to reuse existing presentations. When I do a model walk-through, I try to reuse as much material as possible from previous model walk-through presentations.

More complete presentations. Because I use a divide-and-conquer strategy, I will be less likely to miss a concept or subject within my presentation. By focusing only on headings and then only on content, I am more likely to cover all of my topics.

NOTE

You might have your own techniques for creating presentations that work for you. You might, therefore, choose not to use these presentation steps or incorporate only certain parts of this process into your own set of steps.

Presentations Steps in Use

Let's go through the steps to create a data modeling presentation. In the next section we will apply this to a detailed example:

1. **Define your topic.** What are you trying to communicate in this presentation? This should be phrased in a question format. I try to use a question starting with what or how when my presentation is explaining something. I try to use a question starting with why when I am trying to convince the audience or influence them in some way. Note the similarities between defining the topic for the presentation in this section and defining the topic for the anecdotes mentioned toward the beginning of this chapter.

   Examples of explanatory topics include the following:

   - What is data modeling?
   - What is a meta data repository?
   - How do you normalize?
   - What is a data warehouse?
   - What does our customer subject area model look like?

   Examples of influencing topics include the following:

   - Why do we do data modeling?
   - Why is a data warehouse a necessity?

- Why do we need definitions?
- Why do we normalize? Why do we denormalize?
- Why do we have naming standards?

2. **Define your headings.** What are all of the possible subjects you can discuss within your topic? A very good technique for defining all of the possible subjects is to ask yourself the following basic high-level questions:

- Why?
- What?
- Where?
- When?
- Who?
- How?

By asking yourself these questions, you will increase the chances that you will completely cover your topic. It is an effective brainstorming technique that generates a list of possible headings within your presentation. After you have this initial list, put the headings in the order in which you plan to discuss them. Most presentation tools offer an outline view of the headings within the presentation. I prefer to use the outline view for this step. In this way, I am only viewing headings and am not tempted to start adding the details.

Note that after you have your initial list of headings, you might need to update your topic. There have been a number of cases where my topic changed slightly because I identified something very relevant to the audience in one or more of the headings. Make sure that your updated topic is still the one that is going to meet the purpose of your presentation and that you did not modify it just to accommodate a cool new heading.

3. **Add the details under each heading.** Now I focus on each heading and add the initial bullet points or statements that I would like to discuss. If the heading is "What is an entity?" my bullet list might include the following:

- Representation of a person, place, thing, or concept
- A noun
- Always singular

Remember that sometimes after adding the details your headings might change. Therefore, revisit Step 2 and make sure your headings are still correct. In checking your headings, there is a chance that your topic also might need to be adjusted slightly.

TIP

Iteration is extremely important when creating a presentation. You will note throughout these presentation steps that we are always going back to previous steps and reviewing and possibly updating the information. For example, after we finish our initial list of headings, we revisit our presentation topic and see if it is still relevant.

4. **Customize to your audience.** Put yourself in the shoes of the audience. What are they looking for out of your presentation? I might add lots of examples that they would understand, or include benefits to which they can relate. If the audience is from the logistics department within my company, I will use logistics examples that they will easily be able to comprehend. In adding examples you might find yourself updating some of the content on the slides. If this happens, you might update the headings and, in turn, update the topic. Note the iteration here.

5. **Add an agenda and a summary slide.** There is a famous saying that you can use when creating presentations: "Tell them what you are going to tell them, tell them, and then tell them what you told them." The first and last parts of this saying are extremely important to remind your audience what the presentation is about. The agenda and summary slides help with this overview. These are very easy to create. Just take your headings and put each on its own slide. If you have a fairly short presentation (that is, 10 or fewer slides), you can just list the heading names on two slides. If you have a longer presentation, you might need to summarize into topics and then list these topics on the agenda and summary slides. My agenda and summary slides usually are the same.

6. **Add an attention-getting device as the first slide.** I always like to start my presentations with something entertaining and captivating. Try not to spend a lot of time on the attention-getter, because it should not take away from the rest of the presentation. Rather, it should pull the audience in and keep them interested. This is my favorite slide to create because it really taps my creativity to think of something funny and relevant to say in a minute or two. I consider it a challenge.

7. **Add graphics where appropriate.** I usually do not add graphics until the end. Sometimes if I add them too early I find myself trying to change my text to accommodate a cute graphic, or spending too much time making the graphics look a certain way. It is better to add the graphics when you are done with all of your text. This is because you will not waste time and your graphics will be much more relevant. That is, there will be a greater chance you will know what types of graphics you are looking for.

Presentations Steps In Practice

Let's go through an example of creating a data modeling presentation.

1. **Define your topic.** Let's say we are giving a 30-minute presentation on convincing people that normalization is a good thing. Therefore, our topic could be "Why do we normalize?" Note that we will be trying to convince the audience that normalization is important for this topic.

2. **Define your headings.** Before we define the headings, we might want to get more of an idea of who the audience is. That is, will they need to be given background information on normalization before we explain why it is important? If I am not sure of their expertise or know that some of the members of the audience will not understand normalization, I will usually put in a slide or two as background information. Using the who, what, where, and so on, questions, we come up with the following initial set of headings:

- What is normalization?
- What are the business benefits of normalization?
- What are the application benefits of normalization?

I may add a few more, but this is good for an initial list. Is there any heading here that would change my topic? Let's assume the answer is no at this point.

3. **Add the details under each heading.** Now let's do some brainstorming as to what should be included under each heading:

- What Is Normalization?
  - Process to assign data elements to entities
  - Putting data elements where they most likely belong
- What Are the Business Benefits of Normalization?
  - Increases understanding of data elements and business rules
- What Are the Application Benefits of Normalization?
  - Maximizes flexibility
  - Minimizes redundancy
  - Maximizes reuse
- What Are the Costs of Normalization?
  - Requires more time and, therefore, more money

We could have added a few more, but this is enough to explain the process. Note that a new slide came out of this step. In listing the details, we realized that we missed a subject, that is, the cost of normalization. We, therefore, added a new heading and the relevant details. Be aware of this iteration when you are applying these steps.

4. **Customize to your audience.** This is where I would add a few examples for my particular audience. Let's say my audience is mainly from the finance area. I would add a few examples relevant to finance:

- What Is Normalization?
  - Process to assign data elements to entities
  - Putting data elements where they most likely belong
- What Are Some Examples?
  - Show customer/account example.
- What Are the Business Benefits of Normalization?
  - Increases understanding of data elements and business rules
- What Are Some Examples?
  - Use same customer/account example and go through a few values for customer and account to highlight these benefits for the business.
- What Are the Application Benefits of Normalization?
  - Maximizes flexibility

- ■ Minimizes redundancy
- ■ Maximizes reuse
- ■ What Are Some Examples?
  - ■ Use same customer/account example and go through a few values for customer and account to highlight these benefits for the application.
- ■ What Are the Costs of Normalization?
  - ■ Requires more time and, therefore, more money
- ■ What Are Some Examples?
  - ■ Use same customer/account example and go through on average how long it might take to normalize.

5. **Add an agenda and a summary slide.** This is a very easy step. Just take the steps we just listed and copy them to their own two slides.

6. **Add an attention-getting device as the first slide.** As I mentioned previously, this is my most enjoyable step. I usually like to use an anecdote as the attention-getter. Following the rules earlier in the chapter under anecdotes, I have decided to use a baseball card analogy that clearly explains normalization and its benefits.

7. **Add graphics where appropriate.** I might add a few graphics throughout the presentation. Remember not to overdo it with graphics. They can take away from your text and take too long to create and incorporate.

Summary

This chapter focused on the most effective ways I have found to clearly communicate data modeling concepts. We discussed three data modeling communication tools:

Anecdotes. Short stories can work very well to explain a concept or term. Through this use of personal stories, work-related war stories, various scenarios, and the like, we can clearly get our points across to a captivated audience.

Analogies. Analogies are comparisons between two things. Analogies can compare something the audience is familiar with to something in data modeling to highlight some of the data modeling traits.

Presentation steps. We listed the sequence of steps to go through when creating a data modeling presentation. Even though data modelers give a variety of different types of presentations, they all will benefit from this sequence of steps.

This chapter built the data modeling education foundation with techniques that help create stronger communication channels so that you can more easily and efficiently complete the rest of the analysis and modeling tools in this text. The next chapter will build the data modeling meta data foundation, identifying the types of meta data that will be captured and validated throughout the rest of the text.

CHAPTER 2

Meta Data Bingo

A recent vacation was a Caribbean cruise. I really enjoyed relaxing on the deck, eating *lots* of food, and participating in the daily activities, one of which was Bingo. A large group of passengers gathered in a ballroom and purchased one or more Bingo cards. The goal was to match a specific pattern first, such a straight line or an X, and win the money prize. Playing was very exciting and entertaining. I thought it be great if I could take a topic that some of us outside the data modeling field might find rather boring, such as meta data, and make it equally as exciting and entertaining. This idea led to the creation of the Meta Data Bingo game.

About This Chapter

This chapter focuses on the Meta Data Bingo tool. Meta Data Bingo is a game where the people on your project team complete Bingo cards identifying which types of meta data are most important to capture. This chapter includes an explanation and the benefits of Meta Data Bingo, a philosophical discussion on the levels of meta data, a listing of tools from the rest of this text that can help with meta data capture, and a detailed example of Meta Data Bingo.

The full explanation of the game is included here as well as goals and when it should be played. The project team roles that you would want to identify as players in this game also are explained. This will ensure that you will not miss some important people, whose input you need to sign off on the data model and validate the meta data. In addition, we will review each of the actual Meta Data Bingo cards and describe the types of meta data on each. Shortly after we present the concept of Meta Data Bingo, we will need to create the appropriate context for meta-meta data. We do this by explaining some of the different levels around data, meta data, meta-meta data, meta-meta-meta data, and so on. Put your thinking hat on for this discussion!

This chapter also provides a handy reference to a large percentage of the tools in the rest of this book. Thus, once you know you need a certain type of meta data, you will know where to look for the best tool or tools to help capture it. This can help you decide on the best order to read the rest of this book. Note that this chapter relates the tools in this book in terms of the types of meta data they capture; whereas Chapter 4, "Project Planning for the Data Modeler" ties together the tools in terms of sequence, or when they are performed in the software development life cycle. Therefore, view this chapter (and Chapter 4) as providing an overview or compass for the rest of the tools in this book.

This chapter ends with a section on applying Meta Data Bingo. We will use one of the Bingo cards as an example and average the individual player scores to come up with the types of meta data we will capture for this project.

As you are reading this chapter, you might be thinking, "OK, so I need this particular type of meta data. But what is the level of quality I am required to maintain when capturing this information?" For example, if it is very important to capture the definition of a data element, is a five-word, terse, and vague definition just as acceptable as a two-paragraph one? I need to know the level of quality I am responsible for with each type of meta data. Chapter 3, "Ensuring High-Quality Definitions," focuses on gauging the quality of a definition. Therefore, view this chapter as an identification phase to the types of meta data, and view Chapter 3 as the acceptability or standards associated with one particular type of meta data: the definition.

What Is Meta Data Bingo?

Not too long ago I was chosen as the data modeler for a large and very visible data warehouse project. This project had team members that were distributed across many states, and even the users and functional analysts were spread out across time zones. Each analyst had already started capturing meta data for this project in preparation for the design work. Good idea, but the types of meta data they were capturing were not consistent with each other. One analyst was capturing the business purpose for each data element, whereas the others captured only the definition. One analyst was capturing stewardship information, whereas the others were not. You can see the problems that will develop in the near future with this scenario. The single deliverable produced at the end of this project potentially could have huge amounts of information missing, where one group captured meta data the other groups did not. Aware that this was a possibility, I quickly drafted and sent out the following email (specific phrases were deleted and names were changed to maintain confidentiality):

> *Subject:*   *Meta Data Bingo!*
> *Before we start the design work for this project, we need to agree on what meta data we need to capture. Everyone sent this email, please play this game:*
> *On the list below, please put an "H" next to those rows that are critical to capture, an "M" next to those that might be nice to capture, and a "L" next to those that are not important to capture. We will use everyone's answers to structure our meta data deliverable.*

Please respond before tomorrow 2 P.M. EST. Call me if you have any questions.
Thanks,
Steve
For each data element:
_____ *NAME (e.g., Total Sales Value)*
_____ *DEFINITION (e.g., Total Sales Value is the. . . .)*
_____ *CALCULATION (e.g., Total Sales Value = X + Y − Z. . . .)*
_____ *BUSINESS PURPOSE (e.g., Total Sales Value is useful for. . . .)*
_____ *OWNER (e.g., John Doe/XYZ Department/555-1212)*
_____ *USER ALTERNATE NAME (e.g., Users call Total Sales Value "XYZ")*
_____ *SAMPLE VALUES*
_____ *Others?*

I titled the subject line in this email "Meta Data Bingo!" for two reasons:

1. **My questionnaire was similar in format to a Bingo card.** When we play Bingo, we have a card with letters and numbers in front of us and eagerly wait for the caller to yell out just the right combination of letters and numbers to form a particular pattern on our card. The goal is to be the first to obtain a straight line or another particular pattern. When you do, you win and get to scream Bingo! at the top of your lungs. Meta Data Bingo also contains letters or words. But in this game you fill out the card yourself, instead of being driven by a caller who does not understand your wants or needs and creates a competitive environment with those other players around you. You fill in the Meta Data Bingo card based on what you think is important; at the end of the game, what you think is important is compared and graded with what everyone else thinks is important. Individual scores are averaged, and as a team, the most important types of meta data are selected. Hopefully, at the end of this game everyone wins and gets to yell Bingo!

2. **I needed an attention-getting subject line.** Meta Data Bingo is an interactive process to encourage the entire project team to agree on what types of meta data are most important to capture. Having an entertaining subject line to your email will get a lot more interest than your typical data administration email. Imagine if the subject line was "Meta data type identification" or "Meta-meta data synchronization." These boring subject lines subconsciously tell the reader to "Delete me!" or "Don't read me!" The Meta Data Bingo subject line subconsciously says, "Open me quick. I am a fun email!"

TIP

Always try to use attention-getting subject lines that are relevant to the content of your email. During our data modeling work, not everyone is excited and always eager to read data administration—and data modeling—related emails. Think in terms of catchy and visual when choosing your words, and you will make your team look forward to your emails and read and respond quickly.

Within a day I heard back from almost everyone to whom I sent this email. I assumed that those who did not respond would go along with the majority on the importance of each of these meta data types. I then sent out the following email to summarize the results of Meta Data Bingo:

Subject: *Meta Data Bingo—And the winner is. . .*

The moment you've all been waiting for! Below is a list of the types of meta data we will capture for our project (I used "majority rules" on these—if you feel something is not listed below that should be, let me know ASAP):

For each data element:

H_____ *NAME (e.g., Total Sales Value)*

H_____ *DEFINITION (e.g., Total Sales Value is the. . . .)*

H_____ *CALCULATION (e.g., Total Sales Value = X + Y − Z. . . .)*

ExtraH_____*OWNER (e.g., John Doe/XYZ Department/555-1212)*

These are the ones we will not be capturing (If we come across these, we'll take them but they're not part of the deliverable):

L_____ *BUSINESS PURPOSE (e.g., Total Sales Value is useful for. . . .)*

M_____*USER ALTERNATE NAME (e.g., Users call Total Sales Value "XYZ")*

M_____*SAMPLE VALUES*

L_____*REPORT NAME*

M_____*BUSINESS UNIT*

Thanks for everyone's input,

Steve

Utilizing this game, we were very quickly able to identify everyone's desires and set the expectations of the team. Before I distributed this email, it was agreed that only the H or high-priority types of meta data will be required and all other types would be extra credit and nice to have but not required. Note that there is even an ExtraH above, for extra important. You can see that capturing owner information was extremely important to the team. This game of Meta Data Bingo was very successful and helped correctly identify the types of meta data we needed for this project.

Meta Data Bingo is a game where the people on your project team complete Bingo cards identifying which types of meta data are most important to capture at different levels of detail. We then consolidate these cards and tally the scores to see which types of meta data win and thus will be captured. By knowing up front as a team which types of meta data we will capture, we will meet expectations in this area during our data modeling. There should be no surprises with the types of information we capture, and nothing should fall through the cracks. For example, if the entity name is important to your project, then this is a type of meta data that will be identified while using this tool.

Meta Data Bingo contains most of the possible types of meta data we will encounter during the data analysis and modeling phases. It does not include meta data for the rest of the software life cycle. For example, during development and testing there is a substantial amount of meta data captured and possibly needed later on. This is outside the scope of this tool. So you will not see types of meta data, such as report average run times, security settings, stored procedure and technical documentation locations, job dependencies, and so on, as part of this tool. If you need to capture types of meta data outside the data analysis phase, you might consider creating your own Meta Data Bingo game using the cards in this chapter as guidelines.

There is also the possibility that the Meta Data Bingo cards in this chapter do not contain all of the meta data you need for the data analysis and modeling phases. Departments and companies might have their own types of meta data or variations of meta data in these cards. A popular example would be different types of notes, such as notes on data elements or entities. I encourage you to modify these cards to the needs of your own project or organization, including renaming, adding, or deleting types of meta data. One of the types of meta data I listed in the Meta Data Bingo email in my previous example was Other. This opened the door for other types of meta data that I may not have considered when I sent the email.

TIP

Use the types of meta data and their names that appear within this chapter as a guide. You might need to modify these Bingo cards to accommodate your own particular needs. For example, if your organization uses the term Description or Comment instead of Definition, you would need to make this change to the appropriate Bingo cards.

There are several different project team roles that need to play this game. These roles span the business, functional, and technical levels of the project. Picking the right players will ensure that this game gets played once per project, or hopefully less, depending on the scope of the players. If you do not pick the right participants, you might find yourself in the unfortunate position of playing this game again in some form during the data modeling phase, where there is a very high risk that you might have to go back and capture different types of information. You do not want to be in this situation. It will not be a game at that point. Just pick the right players, and you will do fine.

It is important to note that Meta Data Bingo can also be played just once for the entire department or company, instead of for each individual project. If you have the right players and the right management support, the results of your one game of Meta Data Bingo could last a very long time and be useful for many projects. Just be prepared, because user needs can change over time and you might need to make changes to your list of meta data over time. Determining the requirements for a meta data repository is a great example when you want to play Meta Data Bingo just once. This is because once you identify the types of meta data you need, you can then research the meta data repository market or build your own.

TIP

The more Meta Data Bingo is played at the department and enterprise levels, instead of at the project level, the more integration, consistency, and meta data reuse is possible within a company and between projects.

Please be aware that Meta Data Bingo does not concern itself with the things current development tools can or cannot support. The meta data list is tool-independent. For example, if your data modeling tool does not currently capture the expert for a subject area, it does not mean that this information is unimportant. Please make sure in identifying the relevant meta data that you do not limit yourself by your current toolset. Tools change. Every month improved versions of existing tools and new tools go on the market. Meta Data Bingo should focus on requirements and not on current software functionality.

Timing is critical in doing this exercise. Try to make sure you play this game as early as possible in a project's history. Meta Data Bingo should be played before any type of data analysis or modeling is done for a project. Remember that if you play this game at the department or enterprise level, you will have the advantage of just reusing the results instead of playing the game over and over again for each project.

The goals of Meta Data Bingo are to correctly identify the types of meta data that are important to capture for your project or organization, increase consistency, create common expectations, and improve project integration.

Meta Data Bingo accomplishes the goal of meta data type identification through the following benefits:

Providing an easy-to-use set of Bingo cards for capturing individual or department requests for meta data needed for a project. Meta Data Bingo contains all of the possible types of meta data that you might want to consider capturing for your project. There are several different types of cards that help ensure that during your work you will not miss recording any types of information. Cards are easy to fill out, as easy as regular Bingo cards. Each person checks off whether each type of meta data is of high, medium, or low priority. There is also a Questions and Issues column in case follow-up is required.

Including a scoring system and guidelines for selecting the most important meta data to capture for a project. The scoring system and guidelines help in analytically determining the most important meta data to capture for a project. You need to consolidate player requests into one list and average the results. Many of the types of meta data will be no-brainers in terms of whether or not they are captured. For example, of course, you will keep track of the physical data element name. You cannot have a database without this. But there will be a set of meta data types that will require making a decision as to whether they are important enough to keep. This grading system will standardize and make consistent these decisions. In this way, the group decides what to capture and emotion and organizational position are not the primary drivers of the decision-making process.

Note that on several of the Bingo cards you will see in this chapter, there is meta-meta data already checked off as a high priority; that is, it is prefilled. This is because these types of meta data are mandatory and it is not worth the time or effort to have participants question their value. An example on the Data Model Bingo Card is the file name for the data model. You cannot have a data model saved without a file name. Therefore, it is already checked off on the card because this information needs to be captured for the project. Thus, there is no need to include it in the scoring. This is similar to the blank center square on a regular Bingo card.

Offering a communication format to publish the total scores and document which types of meta data will be captured. Once you have graded the cards and know which meta data types appear to be the most desirable, it is time to let all of the participants know the results. If anyone objects to the results, an informal meeting or quick Meta Data Bingo rematch might be required. After agreement is reached, you will have a set of meta data that can be used as a sign-off document between the business and project team. In this way, down the road when you are nearing your completion of the data model, a user will not innocently ask, "So where can I find the steward for this data?" when capturing stewardship was not agreed on.

Adding entertainment to this otherwise tedious and potentially boring task. The last of these guiding principles, and one that you will see reiterated throughout this chapter, is the entertainment value. This is a game and has rules. We hope everyone will be a winner. Keep this activity light, but ensure that the participants know the value and long-term effects of the results of this game, which is to correctly capture the meta-meta data.

Understanding the Meta-Meta Data

Before we begin playing this game, we need to have a very strong understanding of a key concept: meta-meta data. *Meta-meta data* is descriptive information about the meta data. This sentence may not help a lot; the best way to explain varying levels of meta data is through examples. Let's put meta-meta data in the context with the rest of the meta data levels. Here are a few of the various degrees of data and meta data:

- Data
- Meta data
- Meta-meta data
- Meta-meta-meta data

Each level requires the level below it for its description and context. Thus, for example, the data level requires the meta data level for its description, the meta data level requires the meta-meta data level for its description, and so on. Let's use this level structure and apply values from each of these four levels for a more detailed explanation.

Data

Data are something we capture as part of the normal process of doing business. We use data for purposes of reporting, taxes, billing, and so on. Data drives our business processes; it would be very difficult if not impossible to get along without it. See Table 2.1 for some examples of data.

Table 2.1 Examples of Data

DATA	5	MAX	YES	WEDNESDAY	08701
Meta Data					
Meta-Meta Data					
Meta-Meta-Meta Data					

Meta Data

What do you think about the data examples above? Do they make sense to you? Take the number 5. It is a nice number and is probably stored in many different places throughout our applications. However, it has no value or meaning without a description. Is 5 the total sales for this month, the number of complaints received in January, or the customer's shoe size?

Meta data is the descriptive information that makes the data meaningful. This includes each of the value's name, definition, format, nullability, and many other descriptors. See Table 2.2 for examples of meta data listed below the respective data.

You can see how the meta data has framed each data value according to its descriptive information. When you first noticed Wednesday, you might have made the assumption that this represents a certain day of the week. The meta data, however, provided the descriptive information that clarified that this is the character Wednesday from the TV series *The Addams Family*.

Meta-Meta Data

Now this is where it starts getting interesting. If the meta data is descriptive information about the data, then meta-meta data is descriptive information about the meta

Table 2.2 Examples of Meta Data

DATA	5	MAX	YES	WEDNESDAY	08701
Meta Data	Customer shoe size, decimal (3), can be null, it is defined as the length of a person's foot, from the ...	Contact pet name varchar (30), can be null, it is defined as the full name of each contact's pet, including cats, dogs, but not birds, which are ...	Chocolate indicator, character (1), not null, it is defined as whether this particular dessert contains chocolate ...	Favorite TV character name, varchar (30), null, it is defined as the most popular TV character of all comedy series during the 1960s ...	Zip code, character (10), not null, it is defined as the post office location ....
Meta-Meta Data					
Meta-Meta-Meta Data					

data. The meta data might say, "Shoe size," but what information do we know about this? Is this a data element name or a definition? What is the maximum length of this name? Let's jump right to the examples. See Table 2.3 for examples of meta-meta data listed below the respective meta data and data.

You can see how the meta-meta data has framed each piece of meta data into a category, such as name or format. When you use data modeling tools or spreadsheets, you are storing the meta data within meta-meta data forms, spreadsheet cells, or lists. For example, in a data modeling tool you might enter a definition for shoe size. There is a meta-meta data type called Definition in which the shoe size definition will be stored.

Meta-Meta-Meta Data

We are getting pretty abstract at this level. If the meta-meta data is descriptive information about the meta data, then meta-meta-meta data is descriptive information about the meta-meta data. The meta-meta data might say Definition; whereas the meta-meta-meta data might contain the information about the definition, including what makes a good definition (see Chapter 3, "Ensuring High-Quality Definitions"), the maximum length of a definition, the language it is in, and so on. See Table 2.4 for examples of meta-meta-meta data listed below the respective meta-meta data, meta data, and data.

Wow! You can see where we are going with this. Much of the meta-meta-meta data has to do with the quality or structure of the meta-meta data, which for definitions will be covered in Chapter 3, "Ensuring High-Quality Definitions." Realize at this point that we can keep on going up, probably for at least a whole line of meta-meta-metas. As you go higher than meta-meta-meta data, you start getting way into the clouds. Usually the only interested parties at these levels are the tool vendors and developers. They need to build meta data repositories or data dictionaries and need to treat the meta-meta data as data. Therefore, this data has its own meta data. You can see how we get into very abstract meta levels quickly here.

Now that you know the context of the meta-meta data, which is the main driver for playing the game Meta Data Bingo, let's talk about the players.

Who Plays Meta Data Bingo?

All of the major players during data analysis and design need to participate in this game. If there are multiple people playing the same role, such as three business users, try to have all three participate. It is very important that you have representation from each area. Within each area those individuals with the most knowledge and influence should be prime candidates to participate. The same person might also play multiple roles. For example, the same person from the business could be a business user for the new application, the subject area expert, and the source system business expert. There are three main categories to which these roles belong: business, functional, and technical. The roles listed here also include the manager for that area, so that the business user role also includes the business user manager.

Table 2.3 Examples of Meta-Meta Data

DATA	5	MAX	YES	WEDNESDAY	08701
Meta Data	Customer shoe size, decimal (3), can be null, it is defined as the length of a person's foot, from the ...	Contact pet name varchar (30), can be null, it is defined as the full name of each contact's pet, including cats, dogs, but not birds, which are ...	Chocolate indicator, character (1), not null, it is defined as whether this particular dessert contains chocolate ...	Favorite TV character name, varchar (30), null, it is defined as the most popular TV character of all comedy series during the 1960s ...	Zip code, character (10), not null, it is defined as the post office location ....
Meta-Meta Data	*Customer shoe size* = data element logical business name *decimal (3)* = format *can be null* = nullability indicator *it is defined as the length of a person's foot, from the ...* = definition	*Contact pet name* = data element logical business name *varchar (30)* = format *can be null* = nullability indicator *it is defined as the full name of each contact's pet, including cats, dogs, but not birds, which are ...* = definition	*Chocolate indicator* = data element logical business name *character (1)* = format *not null* = nullability indicator *it is defined as whether this particular dessert contains chocolate ...* = definition	*Favorite TV character name* = data element logical business name *varchar (30)* = format *null* = nullability indicator *it is defined as the most popular TV character of all comedy series during the 1960s ...* = definition	*Zip code* = data element logical business name *character (10)* = format *not null* = nullability indicator *it is defined as the post office location ...* = definition
Meta-Meta-Meta Data Meta Data					

Here are the specific roles for the business category:

- Business users
- Subject area experts
- Architects
- Data modelers

Here are the specific roles for the functional category:

- Functional analysts
- Data modelers
- Project manager
- Architects

Here are the specific roles for the technical category:

- Data modelers
- Database administrators
- Architects
- Developers

Thus, a person, such as Stu, can play the roles of source system business user and subject area expert. Both roles belong to the functional category. The data modeler plays a role in subject area, logical, and physical data modeling; thus, this role belongs to all three categories. Stu plays the role of subject area expert, but so do Polly and Sam. Thus, there is a many-to-many business rule between person and role, and between role and category.

Each of these roles can provide very valuable insight into the types of meta data that we need for the project. Much of this meta-meta data might already have been defined in terms of what is required for a project by the data administration department or data warehouse team. If so, then you might want to tailor Meta Data Bingo to those types of meta data that were not mentioned by the data administration team, or just use what they have.

With all of these roles, and there could be many more in your company or department, it is important to realize that we have only the three categories: business, functional, and technical. Not all categories need to fill out every Meta Data Bingo Card. Here are my recommendations for which role needs to complete which Bingo cards. The X in the intersection cell indicates that this role should complete this Bingo card. These role/Bingo card relationships are discussed for each Bingo card section in Table 2.5.

Using Meta Data Bingo

There are several different Meta Data Bingo cards, corresponding to the different areas for which we capture meta data. There are Project, Data Model, Subject Area, Entity (or Table), and Data Element Bingo cards. The Project Bingo card contains types of

Table 2.4 Examples of Meta-Meta-Meta Data

DATA	5	MAX	YES	WEDNESDAY	08701
Meta Data	Customer shoe size, decimal (3), can be null, it is defined as the length of a person's foot, from the ...	Contact pet name, varchar (30), can be null, it is defined as the full name of each contact's pet, including cats, dogs, but not birds, which are ...	Chocolate indicator, character (1), not null, it is defined as whether this particular dessert contains chocolate ...	Favorite TV character name, varchar (30), null, it is defined as the most popular TV character of all comedy series during the 1960s ...	Zip code, character (10), not null, it is defined as the post office location ....
Meta-Meta Data	*Customer shoe size* = data element logical business name *decimal (3)* = format *can be null* = nullability indicator *it is defined as the length of a person's foot, from the ...* = definition	*Contact pet name* = data element logical business name *varchar (30)* = format *can be null* = nullability indicator *it is defined as the full name of each contact's pet, including cats, dogs, but not birds, which are ...* = definition	*Chocolate indicator* = data element logical business name *character (1)* = format *not null* = nullability indicator *it is defined as whether this particular dessert contains chocolate ...* = definition	*Favorite TV character name* = data element logical business name *varchar (30)* = format *null* = nullability indicator *it is defined as the most popular TV character of all comedy series during the 1960s ...* = definition	*Zip code* = data element logical business name *character (10)* = format *not null* = nullability indicator *it is defined as the post office location ...* = definition

Table 2.4 *(Continued)*

DATA	5	MAX	YES	WEDNESDAY	08701
Meta- Meta- Meta Data	*data element logical business name* = must be very descriptive, cannot contain the name of any application or department, must be at least six characters, and less than fifty ... *format* = must be one of the values Decimal, Integer, String, ... *nullability indicator* = must be a one-character data element containing Yes or No ... *definition* = must be very descriptive, at least two sentences long, in English cannot use the name of the data element in the definition, ...				

meta data around project planning and deliverables. The Subject Area Bingo card contains types of meta data around each subject area, including definition, sourcing, and history requirements. The Entity Bingo card contains types of meta data around each entity, including definition and volumetrics. The Data Element Bingo card contains types of meta data around each data element, including definition, calculations and transformations, and data quality. This section describes in detail each of these Bingo cards. If you visit the Web site www.wiley.com/compbooks/hoberman, you will find additional tools and more information about tools within this book, including empty templates that you can download.

Project Meta Data Bingo Card

The Project Meta Data Bingo Card is the highest level. See Table 2.6. Not all players need to complete this card. I would recommend managers and team leaders complete it, including business user managers, project managers, data administration and modeler managers, and developer managers (for example, the data warehouse development manager if it is a reporting application). This card is completed by putting a check in the appropriate column, depending on whether the type of meta data is of

Table 2.5 Role/Bingo Card Relationships

ROLE	PROJECT	DATA MODEL	SUBJECT AREA	ENTITY	DATA ELEMENT
Business user	X	X	X		
Subject area expert		X	X		
Data modeler	X	X	X	X	X
Functional analyst		X	X	X	X
Project manager	X	X			
Architect		X	X	X	
Developer	X	X		X	X
Database administrator		X		X	X

Table 2.6 Project Meta Data Bingo Card

CODE	DESCRIPTIVE INFORMATION	HIGH	MEDIUM	LOW	QUESTIONS AND ISSUES
A	Current project plan, including tasks, dates, and resources				
B	History of all project plans, including task, date, and resources				
C	Current project teams and roles and individuals				
D	History of all project teams and roles and individuals				
E	Where to find all project deliverables				
F	Who created each deliverable and when				
G	Who last changed each deliverable and when				
H	Who signed off on each deliverable and when				

high, medium, or of low priority. All Bingo cards should have a Questions and Issues column to let the players record thoughts or follow-up questions while they are filling in the card. Below the card is a description of each type of meta data followed by my recommendations and what other tools in this text can help you capture this information. Note that the far left-hand column contains a code that makes it easy to refer to each meta data type by letter instead of by full description.

A. Current Project Plan, Including Tasks, Dates, and Resources

The current project plan includes the most current version of where you are in the project. It usually takes the form of a project planning tool and includes all of the tasks, when they need to be done, and who is responsible for them. The usefulness of the plan is based on how current and accurate it is. It needs to be updated on a task or periodic (daily or weekly) basis and needs to be the context for all project status meetings.

B. History of All Project Plans, Including Task, Date, and Resources

The history of all project plans is something that is rarely captured yet could prove interesting for the project. This type of meta data includes all of the changes, or history, that have been applied against the plan over the duration of the project. For example, the current project plan would show the logical data model being completed some time next week. The history, however, might show that it was supposed to be completed some time last month. By tracking the changes of each of the project plans, you can play detective and find out when the delay occurred. Note that there are two ways to keep track of this history of the project plans. You can either save the project plan under a new name whenever a change is made or save under a new name on a periodic basis. Thus, using the first approach, if the data modeling due date changes from last month to next week, you would save a copy of the project as soon as this change is applied. Or, you can save the project plan every Friday (or at any other periodic interval) and keep changes at a point in time.

C. Current Project Teams and Roles and Individuals

The project plan contains the resource working on each task but usually does not provide an overview to the organizations working on the project. That is what this type of meta data is for. Here we keep track of the organizational structure, including job positions and people. This is only the most current view however. For example, if Stu moved from data modeler to developer, you would only see Stu as developer here. This is very useful to understand the project in the context of the project team organization.

D. History of All Project Teams and Roles and Individuals

Instead of keeping track of just the most current view of what the project organizational team looks like, this type of meta data keeps a record of all changes. This can help in targeting weak or ailing areas of the development. If the data modeling dates slipped a month, keeping a record of all project plans will tell you when it slipped; however, having a history of the people and teams might shed more light on why the date slipped. Because Stu moved to a developer position, Polly, who already has several data modeling projects going on, also needs to complete the data model for this project. This is the reason the date slipped.

E. Where to Find All Project Deliverables

Usually during project development there are so many interim, not yet complete documents that no one really seems to care where they are located. Most of them probably exist on people's local machines instead of network drives. We capture this type of meta data to keep a record of the location of all documents so that even after completion of the project there is a reliable place to refer to the most current documentation. This usually becomes a folder on a shared drive or Web site. Here are examples of documentation you need to keep track of:

- Project plan
- Business, functional, and technical requirements documents
- Subject area, logical, and physical data models
- Issues and their resolutions
- Data element source and transformation documentation

F. Who Created Each Deliverable and When

Most of the time shortly after the project is completed—it could be several months or even over a year—people start to forget who created each deliverable. It is important to keep track of this information, especially for existing applications that are used to design or source new applications, such as data warehouse and reference database applications. By doing so, you will be able to find who did the work when questions arise. We also might want to keep track of date information.

Note that because we are mentioning this descriptive information at the project level, we do not need to mention it at the next level of detail, the data model level. This is because the subject area, logical, and physical data models are considered project deliverables and, therefore, are included under this description. For example, if it is deemed important to keep track of who created each deliverable and when, we would know who created each data model and when.

G. Who Last Changed Each Deliverable and When

Just as we might want to keep track of who created each deliverable, we might want to keep track of who made the last changes to each deliverable. Usually for small projects, last-changed and created-by activities are done by the same people. For large projects, there can be many players involved; therefore, it might be important to know who made the last change. This person probably has the most recent knowledge of the project. If a problem with the application arises suddenly, it might have something to do with these changes. By keeping track of who created each deliverable and when, you can quickly find the person and fix the problem. The same note in the preceding paragraph applies here. This descriptive information also includes data models, and thus we do not need to redundantly mention who last changed each deliverable under the Data Model Meta Data Bingo Card.

H. Who Signed Off on Each Deliverable and When

Who signed off on each deliverable and when is a record of the person who said the deliverable met expectations and it was acceptable to move on in the development. This information is important to capture, and therefore, you define checks and balances when progressing through each of the phases. Also, if there is ever a problem, you have a record of who approved the deliverable. The same note in the preceding paragraph applies here. This descriptive information also includes data models, and thus we do not need to redundantly mention who last signed off on each deliverable under the Data Model Meta Data Bingo Card.

My Recommendation

At a minimum I would capture A, E, and H. A must be captured so that there is an up-to-date view of where the project is and where it must be going to meet deadlines within budget. Luckily, this type of meta data is captured quite frequently by the project manager, who usually needs to keep it up-to-date. E probably takes the least amount of time to complete and yet is useful for the longest amount of time. People will always need to refer back to documentation, and knowing where to look is a great asset and time saver. H is the most important resource to capture on a deliverable. You might argue that the name of the person who created the deliverable should be captured, and this of course also is useful to capture. However, the approver is the person held responsible for the deliverable being declared complete and therefore the most accountable.

Tools That Can Help

Chapter 4, "Project Planning for the Data Modeler," contains several project planning tools, including the Phase-to-Task-to-Tools Template, which contains the data analysis and modeling tasks for any development effort. In addition, for capturing and publishing the individual resources (people and documentation) for a project, you will find the In-the-Know Template in Chapter 5, "Subject Area Analysis," very useful.

Data Model Meta Data Bingo Card

The Bingo card in Table 2.7 captures the meta data for the subject area, logical, and physical data models. Each type of descriptive information can exist at any of these three levels. Note that this is the first Bingo card where there are certain rows already filled in as being high priority. You cannot complete this deliverable without this information. For example, you cannot have a data model without a name. Therefore, the name row is already populated with Hs, which stands for high priority. It is not a discussion point and not worth spending each participant's time deciding how important it is. It is a given that you will have a data model name.

All players should complete this Bingo card: business user, subject area expert, functional analyst, project manager, architect, developer, and database administrator. This is because the data model spans each level of analysis and, therefore, the data model can impact all the categories: business, functional, and technical. The subject area

Table 2.7 Data Model Meta Data Bingo Card

CODE	DESCRIPTIVE INFORMATION	SUBJECT AREA (SA)			LOGICAL DATA MODEL (LDM)			PHYSICAL DATA MODEL (PDM)			QUESTIONS AND ISSUES
		L	M	H	L	M	H	L	M	H	
A	File name	X			X			X			
B	Business name										
C	Definition										
D	Mappings to next level of model										
E	Most recent data models	X			X			X			
F	History of all data models										

L, low priority; M, medium priority; H, high priority.

model impacts the business category, the logical data model impacts the functional category, and the physical data model impacts the technical category.

You might need to explain some of the abbreviations on this card. SA is subject area model, LDM is logical data model, PDM is physical data model, L is low priority, M is medium priority, and H is high priority. It is a good idea to abbreviate column headings when your spreadsheet has many columns. Note that the far left-hand column contains a code that makes it easy to reference these rows.

NOTE

You can customize all of these Bingo cards to your own needs. On this Data Model Bingo Card, you may not always have distinct logical and physical models; therefore, you would not need to include LDM and PDM. You might just show the PDM columns and possibly capture some of the logical information, such as Business Name on the PDM.

A. File Name

The file name is the name under which the data model is saved on your computer or network server. It usually is a short name, such as the project acronym, along with a file extension. For example, sales.er1 is the file name for the Sales data mart data model, using the Erwin data modeling tool. But can you tell by sales.er1 whether this is a subject area, logical, or physical level of detail? You might also want to embed this as part of the name. Thus, the subject area model for the Sales data mart might be called salessa.er1; the logical model, salesldm.er1; and the physical model, salespdm.er1. You can also embed version information into the file name, such as salesv1sa.er1, the Sales Subject Area Model, version 1.

In the Bingo card in Table 2.7, under file name, high priority is checked off for all three levels because you cannot have a data model without saving it somewhere.

TIP

In naming your data model, choose a descriptive yet flexible name. Think about what your model might be tomorrow in addition to what it is today. For example, suppose I recently saved a model with the application name as part of the model's file name. Then, after adding several other applications to this same data model file, I realized that the name was no longer relevant and accurate. I should have originally renamed this model's file to make it more encompassing.

B. Business Name

The business name is the full, unabbreviated name of the data model. This usually includes at a minimum the full name of the project or application. It might also include a phase or stage for the project and possibly even a version for the data model. If salesv1sa.er1 is the file name, "The Sales Data Mart Version 1 Subject Area Model" might be the full business name. For a data model where the file name is sales.er1, it is easy to decipher the business name. However, most of our file names might look like abc.er1, making it difficult to know that abc.er1 stands for the All Big Customers data mart. The business name is very useful when it is hard to understand the meaning of the file name.

C. Definition

Definitions are critical for data elements and entities, yet they also can be very useful for data models. The definition for a data model might include a number of important pieces of information:

- Overview to the subject areas included in the model
- Model scope and fit with existing applications
- The type of design, whether reporting, operational, and so on
- The purpose and function of the application being modeled
- The role of the model within the systems architecture; for example, for a data warehouse the role of this application might be a data mart, integration area, or staging area
- The status of the data model, including whether it is signed off on, under review, or pending resolution of several issues
- Reasons for some of the noteworthy or unusual design structures on the model; for example, certain structures that are overdenormalized, overnormalized, over-abstracted, or heavily recursive

The items above, which you might want to include in the definition of the model, are also types of meta data. I did not list them separately in the Bingo card because they might be included on other cards (for example, the status of the model might be included under the Project Bingo card) or they might be much less important than the types mentioned on the Bingo card. You do not want to clutter the card with very detailed and potentially less useful information. If you feel that some of these data might be very useful to capture, however, you might want to list them as separate types of meta data on this Bingo card.

TIP

 Some of these types of meta data require not just capturing the information once but also maintaining it. For example, the status of the model is a type of meta data that needs to be kept up-to-date.

D. Mappings to Next Level of Model

When you go from a subject area model to a logical model, you need to keep a mapping, or translation, of how each subject area and relationship on the subject area model translates into entities, relationships, and data elements on the logical data model. If there is a Customer entity on your subject area model, you would keep track that this Customer entity maps into Customer, Customer Location, Customer Association, Customer Classification, and so on, on the logical data model. The same is true when you go from the logical data model to the physical data model. You would keep track of how the entities translate into tables. This is very useful to make sure nothing fell through the cracks, or suddenly appeared on the logical but not the subject area or on the physical but not the logical. If a Customer entity is on the subject area, you will be able to trace it through to the physical tables. Likewise, if there is a Customer Demographics table in the database, it should be represented somewhere on the subject area model. Although this is useful information, it is very difficult to maintain manually and will quickly become out-of-date. Once it does, it is useless.

E. Most Recent Data Models

The most recent data models are the actual data models that are the most current for an application. If you are still doing your data modeling, these will be the models on which you will be working. If you have completed your data modeling, these will be the models that you will review with the rest of the project team. If these models have already been reviewed, these are the final models for the project. Note that these are already checked off on the card as a high priority, because these are the actual data models and you have to have them. Having the most recent data model does not mean having an up-to-date data model. For example, I might have the most recent subject area model but if the logical and physical models have been expanded with functionality that was never updated back in the subject area, I now have a recent yet out-of-date subject area model.

F. History of All Data Models

Is it important to keep track of all changes made to the data models over time? Do you need a record of when a new entity is added or any other change is made to the model? Keeping track of each of these changes might involve an incredible number of copies of data models, which can take lots of space and potentially cause confusion when deciding which one is the most current. Imagine saving your model under a different name every day when the slightest changes are made.

This history includes not just changes to each model but transitions between models. As part of the normal data modeling process, we will be creating a number of interim models. These models might be considered interim because they have not yet been standardized with the corporate naming standards, or maybe all parties have not formally reviewed these models. In either case, this type of meta data keeps track of each of these models in case there is a need to refer back to them over time. Without a formal way to keep track of these interim models, they usually only find themselves in paper format in someone's folder in their desk drawer, usually with lots of notes scribbled on them.

Note that under the Project Meta Data Bingo card in Table 2.6, one of the options was to keep track of who created each deliverable, last changed each deliverable, and approved each deliverable. The difference here is that the history on all data models includes the actual models as they change over the life of the project, not just the people and dates.

My Recommendation

At a minimum, go with the two rows that are already checked off, A and E. The next most valuable type would be D. This is extremely valuable, especially from logical to physical data models where heavy denormalization can make finding the logical entities very difficult. I would suggest not capturing D, however, unless there is a plan to maintain this information. It is useless as soon as it becomes out-of-date.

Tools That Can Help

The Data Element Family Tree in Chapter 7 , "Logical Data Analysis," is a great tool for capturing the relationships from each subject area to each of the data elements and entities within that subject area. For example, this tool will capture that the Customer Last Name, Social Security Number, Address, and so on, all belong to the Customer subject area. This can help with the row D in Table 2.7.

Subject Area Meta Data Bingo Card

The Subject Area Meta Data Bingo Card (see Table 2.8) is the first level of detail where we are starting to look at the content within the application. Subject areas, which we will learn more about in Chapter 5, "Subject Area Analysis," are the concepts that are both basic and critical to the business. By basic we mean that they are probably mentioned a dozen times a day in normal business conversation. By critical we mean that the business will be very different or nonexistent without these concepts. Examples of subject areas are Customer, Account, Associate, Vendor, Competitor, and Order. All players in the business and functional categories should fill in this card. Note that the subject area definition is already checked off as high priority, and therefore, this is a type of meta data that must be captured.

This card is completed by putting a check in the appropriate column, depending on whether the type of meta data is of high, medium, or low priority in capturing. Note again the questions and issues column. Below this Bingo card is a description of each type of meta data followed by my recommendations and what other tools in this text can help you capture this information. Note that the column at the far left-hand side is a code that makes it easy to reference these rows.

A.   Standard Enterprise Name

The standard enterprise name is the name given to a subject area that is consistent with the rest of the organization. Subject areas might start off with a name that is only meaningful to the business users from the department whose application for which

Table 2.8   Subject Area Meta Data Bingo Card

CODE	DESCRIPTIVE INFORMATION	HIGH	MEDIUM	LOW	QUESTIONS AND ISSUES
A	Standard enterprise name				
B	Alias				
C	Definition	X			
D	Steward name and department				
E	History requirements				
F	Source				

you are creating the subject area model. Eventually, before the subject area modeling is complete, you will need to standardize the name, which means that people from outside the department will easily be able to recognize and understand this concept. For example, during a subject area modeling session the users identify Client as one of their subject areas. You will need to make sure that Client is also the standard name for this concept in the rest of the company. You might learn that the standard name is Customer, in which case you need to reconcile this with the users and change the name of this subject area to Customer. This is important information to capture because it is the link to the rest of the company at the subject area level. Any development effort that has anything to do with other applications or other departments needs a standard subject area name.

B.   Alias

With so many different names for the same concepts, there is a strong need for aliases. An *alias* is another name or reference for something. For example, pop might be an alias for soda. Pop is used in certain areas of the country and is recognized as meaning the same thing as soda. We have many aliases in our businesses. *Internal aliases* are different names for the same thing assigned within a company, and *external aliases* are different names for the same thing assigned by parties outside the company. Aliases are especially important when reconciling department views with company views. A department has its own terminology. In many cases in order to fit its information in with the business the department needs to give up its terminology and use the standard names. An alias provides a place to keep the original department name so that those familiar with the department concept can recognize the enterprise concept.

In many cases, aliases for subject areas are the unstandardized names given by the business users. Using the same example mentioned under Standard Enterprise Name, Client would be an alias for the standard name Customer. Aliases are important to capture because they provide the translation for the business users back to their own terminology. If a user does not understand the concept of the standard enterprise name Customer, it makes sense to provide an alias to Client, which they do understand.

C.   Definition

The definition provides more meaning to the subject area than just the name. Definitions at a subject level are nonnegotiable, which means you must have definitions at this level. If you do not, chaos will ensue when you get into more detail. Imagine trying to define Customer Location and Customer Demographics, without having a good definition for Customer. Thus, this high-priority column is already checked off on the Bingo card.

D.   Steward Name and Department

The steward name is the name of the person or department responsible for the actual data within a subject area. This is a person from the business who are the recognized experts and who have the authority to impact the subject area or data element meta data.

In many situations, your users or their managers will be your stewards for the data. Exceptions tend to be for Item and Customer, where there is usually a separate reference database to manage the information and, therefore, also a separate department or person.

Steward information is one of the most underrated types of meta-meta data. It is very rarely captured yet very useful, especially when there are questions, changes, or approvals required around this data. I think one of the biggest reasons this information is not captured has to do with maintenance. People come and go all the time and departments reorganize; therefore, it is likely that these data will become out-of-date. Bob Jones might be the steward for an item today, and Mary Smith tomorrow. Without a maintenance process, capturing stewardship information will not prove useful for very long.

E. History Requirements

The subject area level is the optimal level to capture how much history the users request. Capturing this information at this level, and as early as possible in the analysis process, can prevent a major problem. You do not want to find yourself in a situation such as this: the user wants 3 years of history and you can only provide 2 years, and the user does not know about this until the project plan and budgeted dollars already have been allocated. A subject area level is sufficient because I have rarely seen a case where within a subject area there were differences in the level of history required. Usually the request is something such as, "I need 3 years of customer data" and not "I need 2 years of customer address information and 3 years of customer classification information."

F. Source

Capture basic source information at the subject area level for each subject area to make sure you can meet the expectations of the user based on the source. For example, if the source application has 1 year of customer history but your user has requested 2 years, you can raise this issue immediately. Capturing source at this high level also makes more detailed analysis easier because you already know where to look for each subject area. For example, if I am determining the source data element names for customers, I already know where to start looking because I know the application defined as the source for the Customer subject area.

My Recommendation

At this subject area level, I would recommend capturing all of this information. Information captured at this level also is generally extremely useful for the more detailed entity and data element levels. Therefore, I can save a lot of time and address issues very early by knowing the sourcing and definition information for each subject area. If I could not have all of these types, my picks would be C, E, and F. C is a given, and I have mentioned previously why it is so important. E and F are important because they set the stage for things to come. It is extremely proactive to capture history and source at the subject area level to make the detailed analysis go more smoothly and identify important issues very early.

Tools That Can Help

A number of tools are given in Chapter 5, "Subject Area Analysis," that can help capture subject area information. The Subject Area Checklist provides a list of subject areas with generic definitions and business rules to help you start your analysis. The In-the-Know Template captures the people, documentation, and reports that can provide and validate the data requirements, including stewardship information. The Subject Area Family Tree provides the source and definition for each subject area. The Subject Area Grain Matrix captures the different levels within each subject area at which each measurement needs to be reported. It is for data warehouse applications only and can rapidly identify the levels of reporting for each subject area and help in estimating and scoping a data mart effort.

Entity Meta Data Bingo Card

The Entity Meta Data Bingo Card (see Table 2.9) is relatively small, because most of the meta-meta data, such as source and history information, have already been captured at the subject area level. You might want to call this card a Table Meta Data Bingo Card if most of your players are technically oriented. All roles in the functional and technical categories should complete this Bingo card, including the data modeler, functional analyst, architect, developer, and database administrator.

This card is completed by putting a check in the appropriate column, depending on whether the type of meta data is of high, medium, or low priority in capturing. Note again the questions and issues column. Below this card is a description of each type of meta data followed by my recommendations and what other tools in this text can help you capture this information. Note that the column at the far left-hand side is a code that makes it easy to reference these rows.

A. Standard Enterprise Name

The standard enterprise name is the name given to an entity or table that is consistent with the rest of the organization. For an entity this is the standard logical name, and for the table this is the standard physical name. The standard logical name is the full business name for the entity, whereas the standard physical name is the abbreviated name for the table. For example, CUSTOMER DEMOGRAPHICS might be the standard entity name and CUST_DEM might be the standard table name. Again, standard means that it is not specific to a group of users or a department but, rather, is consistent with the entire business or enterprise.

Table 2.9 Entity Meta Data Bingo Card

CODE	DESCRIPTIVE INFORMATION	HIGH	MEDIUM	LOW	QUESTIONS AND ISSUES
A	Standard enterprise name				
B	Alias				
C	Definition				
D	Volumetrics				

B. Alias

Just as we saw with the subject area, an alias is another name for something. In most cases, it is used by such entities as the user or department-specific name. This allows for mapping back from standard name mentioned previously to the name with which the users are more familiar. If the standard name is CUSTOMER DEMOGRAPHICS, aliases might be CUSTOMER PATTERNS or CLIENT DEMOGRAPHICS. The alias provides a link back to the term that is most comfortable for the users.

C. Definition

This definition is more detailed than the subject area definition, and at this level the definition helps provide a context for all the data elements contained within. I do not consider definitions at the entity level as important as definitions at the subject area or data element level, because if I know what the high level and details mean, I do not necessarily need to know what the entities in the middle mean. I think definitions are extremely valuable at the entity level but not as important as the subject area and data element levels. If I know what CUSTOMER means and I know what CUSTOMER DEMOGRAPHICS TYPE CODE means, I could easily infer the definition of CUSTOMER DEMOGRAPHICS.

D. Volumetrics

Volumetrics is a fancy word for table sizing information. It is important to capture during the analysis phase because it can impact the design of the physical data model and can make the database creation phase run more efficiently. This information is needed to accurately allocate space for each table in the database. Sizing information includes the following:

- Initial number of rows in the table
- Maximum number of rows in the table
- Expected updates to rows each year
- Expected new rows each year

My Recommendation

My number one pick here would be just to have a standard entity name, A. The others may be just as important; however, if you capture this information at the subject area and data element levels, the entities in this middle level of detail usually can be inferred.

Tools That Can Help

The Data Element Family Tree mentioned in Chapter 7, "Logical Data Analysis," captures much of this meta-meta data, including names and definitions.

Data Element Meta Data Bingo Card

The Data Element Meta Data Bingo Card is the most detailed of the cards (see Table 2.10). You will see a lot of the same information that you have seen in previous cards,

Table 2.10 Data Element Meta Data Bingo Card

CODE	DESCRIPTIVE INFORMATION	NUMERIC			CODE			DATE			ID			TEXT			QUESTIONS AND ISSUES
		H	M	L	H	M	L	H	M	L	H	M	L	H	M	L	
A	Standard enterprise name	X			X			X			X			X			
B	Alias																
C	Definition	X			X			X			X			X			
D	Business purpose	X															
E	Sample values				X												
F	Default value																
G	Transformation or derivation logic and rules																
H	Format	X			X			X			X			X			
I	Nullability	X			X			X			X			X			
J	Keys and indexes										X						
K	Data quality factors or criteria																
L	Data quality results of factors or criteria																

such as name and definition. However, there are many types of meta data that only pertain to data elements, such as format and nullability information. This Bingo card is also unique in that the types of meta data captured can vary based on the different types of data elements that exist. To keep this card simple, each data element is assigned to one of five buckets:

Numeric. Numerics include all of the measurements in our application, for example, quantities, weights, volumes, and amounts. This also includes those nonadditive numbers, such as telephone number and customer age.

Code. Codes include any shortened phrase for something else. Examples of codes include state (NJ is short for New Jersey), gender (M is Male), and reason (C is Complaint).

Date. Dates include time and date information in any format.

Identifier. Identifiers (IDs) include all identifiers for our large tables, such as Customer and Item. IDs are used everywhere except for code tables, which are identified by codes.

Text. Text includes name, definition, decode (the longer text version of what the code represents), and other types of text-based fields.

You may feel that it might be too complicated for your players to have separate columns on this card for the different types of data elements. If so, you might want to have just the three columns of high, medium, and low priority and not separate this Bingo card by the categories of data elements.

This card is completed by putting a check in the appropriate column, depending on whether the type of meta data is of high, medium, or of low priority in capturing. Note again the questions and issues column. Below this card is a description of each type of meta data followed by my recommendations and what other tools in this text can help you capture this information. Note that the column at the far left-hand side is a code that makes it easy to reference these rows. This card is completed by most of the functional and technical categories, including the roles of data modeler, functional analyst, developer, and database administrator.

A.   Standard Enterprise Name

Just as we have seen for the entity and subject area Bingo cards, we have a type of meta data called Standard Enterprise Name. This includes both the logical and physical corporatewide standard name. Logical is the full business name, whereas physical is the abbreviated database name. Both these names should end in a valid class word, such as amount, code, number, name, and identifier. We will discuss class words in more detail in Chapter 9, "The Abstraction Safety Guide and Components." An example of a logical standard enterprise name would be Customer Last Name. Its physical counterpart might be CUST_LAST_NAM. Most organizations have standard abbreviation codes for each portion of the data element name. For example, Customer's standard abbreviation might be CUST or CUS. The standard enterprise name is critical to have for all data elements and, therefore, is already checked off.

B. Alias

Aliases have several different uses when it comes to data elements. They can provide mappings back to the following:

Business user understanding terminology. This is the same purpose we provided for the entity and subject area aliases, so that users can still hang onto their names while using standard corporatewide terminology in the actual design. Thus, users want to see Client Last Name, which would be an alias for the actual standard business name of Customer Last Name.

Legacy applications. Aliases are very useful to map legacy information. Perhaps there is a very old application that allows a maximum of eight-character names, and this application is a source for our data warehouse, which follows our 32-character standard naming length format. Obviously, we cannot rename the source system names; however, using aliases provides the mapping mechanism from the legacy name to the new name.

Report labels. Report labels are another use of aliases. Users might be intimidated by seeing CUST_MIDL_INITL_NAM on the report screen. This also takes up a lot of space and can be very difficult to translate to anything meaningful for users. Instead, they might prefer to see Middle Initial. Middle Initial becomes the report label alias for the CUST_MIDL_INITL_NAM standard physical name.

C. Definition

Most definitions I have seen seem to fall into one of three categories: nonexistent, poor, or average. In the next chapter we will discuss what makes a good definition. For now, we will concern ourselves with determining whether we want to capture a definition. A *definition* is textual information that describes something. Definitions during the analysis and modeling phase help determine the context of data elements and entities. What does a data element mean, and how is it to be used? Which entity should it be stored in? Does the data match its meanings?

A definition is the most important type of meta data to capture. You can always derive a name from a definition, but how often can you derive a definition from a name? My recommendation is to make sure definition is included in this list. You will note that the high-priority columns already have been checked in the data element Bingo card.

It is ironic that the definition, the most important type of meta data, is also the most corrupted. It is for this reason that in addition to requiring a definition you also define criteria to make sure only precise definitions are accepted. See Chapter 3, "Ensuring High-Quality Definitions," for these criteria.

WARNING

▬▬▬ **I have found that when enterprise definitions exist in a company, project definitions sometimes are not checked under the guise that you can just plug in the enterprise definitions. This is a very big mistake. This means that the project team fully trusts definitions that might have been created a long time ago by different departments for different purposes. A serious checkpoint is missed when these definitions are** not validated, and not validating them also shows a general lack of caring about them. Try not to fall into the trap of relying too heavily on existing definitions. Challenge the users to come up with their own, and use the existing definitions as a validation step to make sure you have the right data element.

D. Business Purpose

Many times I have seen the business purpose combined with the definition. This is a serious mistake because by combining them you might omit one and thus miss important information. A business purpose is the reason we have this concept. For example, Gross Sales Amount might be defined as the total amount received in a particular time period by multiplying list price by quantity purchased. This is the definition. The business purpose for Gross Sales Amount might be to routinely gauge company performance over time using a standard metric. I have seen business purpose substituted for definition many times, and you can see how this can cause trouble because you still do not fully understand what this concept means.

The business purpose helps ensure that what you are identifying as information to have in the application will be useful to someone. I usually recommend having a business purpose for transaction types of data, not for reference data. Transaction data can contain many variations of the same information, such as Gross Sales Amount, Gross Sales Volume, and Gross Sales Quantity. By identifying the purpose of each data element, you can ensure that only useful data elements are brought in. Because we are afraid to delete them, we may retain many useless data elements, a high percentage of which are transaction data elements. These elements may sound valuable but in reality they are no longer being used or they contain erroneous or useless information. I remember seeing a data element called Gross Amount in a table that I initially thought would be valuable but then found out it was always null, meaning completely empty. It was just never deleted from the model. A business purpose reduces the chance that this situation will arise. Also, with the amount of transaction data in our business, the business purpose might be the deciding factor as to whether we keep certain measurements or facts. Reference data is usually much less in question. After all, what is the business purpose of the Customer Last Name data element? Much of the time the business purpose of reference data is redundant with the definition. Therefore, you should focus on business purpose but only for transaction data. Note that this is prefilled as being high priority on the card for the numeric or transaction data in your project.

E. Sample Values

Sample values provide additional explanation to the definition. Showing some actual values is extremely useful for codes, where a definition might only go so far. For example, a business unit code might have a definition such as "the code that helps us identify one of our six business units." But sample values would add a lot more. You can list all the possible values of a business unit:

1 = Northeast Automotive

2 = Bob's Best Birdseed

3 = Mary's Magnificent Marionettes

Showing actual values adds much more meaning to the definition. Obviously, for unique identifiers and description data elements there is limited value, except for showing certain types of format information. For example, showing several values of a primary key would help us understand the format of the key.

It is very important to always show samples for codes. In fact, you will note that H is prefilled for codes on the Bingo card. If there are less than 20 distinct codes, show all values. Make sure you do not just list the codes but that you also include the descriptions. For example, instead of documenting A, B, C, document A = Apples, B = Bananas, C = Carrots. Sample values for other types of data elements also help, but they are most useful for codes.

F. Default Value

Having a default value means if the data element is left blank another value will be stored in it. For example, the default can be Yes, No, Blue, or some other value. Be very careful with default values. Many times, especially with reporting applications, they can skew results. The person entering the data must understand what will happen if this data element is left blank. For example, whenever a certain code is left blank, it will default to the code value corresponding to Unknown. Whenever the Previous Customer Flag is left blank, it will default to No.

G. Transformation or Derivation Logic and Rules

Transformation or derivation logic and rules are the formulas or equations that are applied to a target data element. For example, the list price and total quantity data elements are multiplied to arrive at a gross sales amount. The transformation rules capture this multiplication equation. Most of the time, transformations apply to amount data elements; however, they can also apply to other types of data elements, such as those defined as character when performing changes such as character substitution or concatenation. These rules need to be documented in a business language and technical language. The business language provides a record of how the data elements change in plain English terms that a business user can understand. The technical language provides how to manipulate the source data elements to arrive at the target data element. This technical transformation is only useful until the development is complete. Afterward, this information should be easily accessible through the development tool, such as an Extract, Transform, and Load utility.

This information is useful to capture as soon as you capture other source information, such as the source data element name. This way you will know what the source data elements are as well as how they change when they arrive at the target data element.

H. Format

Format information is a requirement to capture at the technical level. You cannot have a database data element without specifying some sort of length and type. Examples include Character(16), Integer, Decimal(15,2), Varchar(256). Note that this meta-meta data is checked off on the Bingo card as being high priority.

I. Nullability

Nullability is an indicator that determines whether the data element can be left blank, or empty. If it can be left blank, then it can be null. If it must always be filled in with something, even if it is a blank space, then it is not null. The business user needs to identify from a business process perspective if this data element always must be filled in. The functional analyst then needs to identify from an application perspective if this data element always must be filled in. In this way, the correct null option can be selected in the database. Sometimes a default value is used to make a data element contain a value that would otherwise be null.

As early as possible for each data element, identify whether or not it can be null. Spend time with the business users to educate them about what this means to make sure you are capturing accurate information. Note that this information must be populated for the database to be created; hence it is already checked off on the Bingo card as being high priority.

J. Keys and Indexes

Keys (primary, foreign, and alternate) and indexes are extremely important to capture for each data element. *Primary keys* are one or more data elements that uniquely define a value within this entity. All of the data elements within the entity depend on the primary key. *Foreign keys* are primary keys from other entities that are used to connect entities and to navigate from information in one entity to information in another entity. *Alternate keys* are one or more data elements that, as do primary keys, also uniquely identify all of the values in the entity but are not defined as the primary key. *Indexes* are any data elements that are accessed for retrieval purposes often enough to warrant a quick reference to speed up retrieval.

Identify key information as early as possible because it will help you with the data modeling effort. The correct defining of primary and alternate keys is critical for a successful data model. Indexes are important to capture during the physical data modeling phase and are less important than identifying the keys. The ID column is prefilled with an H for this type of meta data.

K. Data Quality Factors Or Criteria

Data quality has many factors, which are described in Chapter 7, "Logical Data Analysis," when we discuss the data quality capture and validation templates. Examples include checking whether or not a data element is null, whether the data matches the definition, any reference constraints that are being violated, and so on. This information is useful to capture because it ensures consistent and mutually defined data quality checks.

L. Data Quality Results of Factors or Criteria

This is the actual analysis and results of the criteria and factors mentioned previously. So, who performed the data quality check, when, what percentage of the rows met the quality criteria, what percentage are problem records, and are there any additional comments? Examples of meta data we care about include the following:

Results of factors or criteria. The results of the data quality check include examples such as 50% null, all rows numeric except one that is all character, only the first four of the 30 characters are being populated, and so on.

Validated by whom. Validated by whom provides the necessary audit tracking to provide responsibility and credit for those doing the checking. For example, Tom approved the results of the quality checking within the customer area.

Validated when. Validated when provides the date this validation took place.

My Recommendation

At a minimum, I would capture all of the types of meta data that are prefilled with X s in the high-priority columns. For all data elements these include A, C, H, and I. A, H, and I, are required to create the physical database tables; therefore, these are non-negotiable and must be captured. The definition is probably the most important of the logical types of meta data we capture, because it clarifies the data element name and values and is needed by data modeler, functional analyst, and user alike. The definition is also where you can resolve disputes between department and enterprise. I would also capture all of the possible values for codes under sample values. There are many different types of meta data where we do not need to show sample values, such as total order amount, which we know will be just a number. However, for codes it is imperative you list all possible values (I would list them up to the first 20 distinct code values) to enhance understanding. I would capture business purpose for transaction or numeric data elements and primary key information for all ID data elements.

Tools That Can Help

The Data Element Family Tree mentioned in Chapter 7, "Logical Data Analysis," captures much of this meta-meta data. Other useful tools include the Data Element Grain Matrix, which captures the reporting levels for the data elements, also mentioned in Chapter 7. Chapter 7 also provides some very useful tools on data quality checking, the Data Quality Capture Template and Data Quality Validation Template.

Meta Data Bingo Grading Process

Now that you have all of the filled-in cards returned to you, what next? You need to go through each card and assign each type of meta data a final grade. High means that you will capture the meta data and low you will not. Medium means you might need management to make the call. A follow-up email only to the project manager and data administration manager, and possibly the data warehouse manager, is needed to determine thumbs up or down.

My grading system is very simple. I assign H five points, M three points, and L one point. I then add up all of the cards and average the values. When the averages are greater than 3, I grade as high; we must capture these meta data. When the averages are less than 3 but greater than 2, I grade as medium; these go to management for the final decision. When the average is 2 or less, I grade as low; we do not capture these.

For example, let's say you got back five cards at the subject area level. The scores for stewardship were 3 Hs, 1 M, and 2 L. Translating these into numerics, we get a total of

20. We divide this total by 5, which gives us 4, meaning we capture this meta data. If the scores were 1 H, 2 Ms, and 2 Ls, we would get an average of 2.6, which means management would need to decide.

An alternate to having management decide, depending on how much authority you have (or how much courage!), is to round up to high or round down to low. Take a chance, and then when you publish the results see what kind of feedback you get. Usually this technique of rounding works fairly well and means that management does not need to have lengthy and heated discussions to determine whether we must capture the types of meta data that are borderline.

Once you have completed your grading, send out an email with the final grades. Write this email with the same tone as the opening email, meaning entertaining and to the point. Make sure you put in this email that if anyone does not agree with these results to please contact you as soon as possible. This is an extra precaution that will help get support from everyone. Also, by saying people should contact you, you avoid those Reply to All emails that could make the whole game of Meta Data Bingo a waste of time because of lengthy email messages going back and forth. Thus, make sure you handle these disagreements one on one.

Meta Data Bingo In Practice

Let's say you are in the following situation:

You and several colleagues in your organization have been data modeling many operational and data warehouse applications over the years. You have become very aware of the differences in the types of meta data captured in each modeling effort. These differences appear to be a result of different styles of data modeling, operational versus data warehouse designs, user requests, project resources, and so on. However, there appears to be a core set of meta data, which everyone captures, that mostly encompasses the physical

Table 2.11 Jean's Card

CODE	DESCRIPTIVE INFORMATION	HIGH	MEDIUM	LOW	QUESTIONS AND ISSUES
A	Standard enterprise name	X			
B	Alias			X	
C	Definition	X			
D	Steward name and department		X		
E	History requirements			X	
F	Source			X	How far back sourcing are we talking about?

Table 2.12 Irving's Card

CODE	DESCRIPTIVE INFORMATION	HIGH	MEDIUM	LOW	QUESTIONS AND ISSUES
A	Standard enterprise name	X			
B	Alias			X	Don't understand what an alias is, so I guess it's not important!
C	Definition	X			
D	Steward name and department	X			
E	History requirements		X		
F	Source		X		

database area, such as column name or data element format. Despite this small amount of common meta data, there are too many differences within your organization, which have led to differences in project expectations and difficulty integrating across applications. You would like to bring a level of consistency to your organization in terms of types of meta data captured and are looking for a good tool to assist.

Let's say you decide to play Meta Data Bingo and send out cards to the relevant players on the project team. Your Subject Area Meta Data Bingo Card went out to 10 people, and you have only received four responses by your deadline. You are a little discouraged by the poor response but have convinced yourself that the other six people will go along with whatever these four people have said. Tables 2. 11 through 2.14 show the four responses on the subject area card.

Adding up these numbers and assigning averages based on the grading criteria mentioned in the previous section, your final scores look like those in Table 2.15.

Therefore, in your email announcing the results, you will keep A and, of course, C. You will not keep B, E, or F. You should respond to Irving's comment on an alias before do-

Table 2.13 Jenn's Card

CODE	DESCRIPTIVE INFORMATION	HIGH	MEDIUM	LOW	QUESTIONS AND ISSUES
A	Standard enterprise name	X			
B	Alias		X		
C	Definition	X			
D	Steward name and department			X	
E	History requirements		X		
F	Source			X	

Table 2.14 Eric's Card

CODE	DESCRIPTIVE INFORMATION	HIGH	MEDIUM	LOW	QUESTIONS AND ISSUES
A	Standard enterprise name		X		
B	Alias			X	
C	Definition	X			
D	Steward name and department		X		
E	History requirements			X	
F	Source			X	

ing your final grading because after you explain what an alias is, Irving might determine that it is very important. You should also respond to Jean's question on sourcing before doing the final grading. Stewardship information has a very solid medium score so you might send an email to management asking for an opinion, or the round the results and make the decision yourself.

TIP

 Make sure you answer all the outstanding questions and address all the issues on these Bingo cards before summarizing and making decisions as to which types of meta data to capture. Sometimes answers to questions can change people's initial scores and, therefore, may impact the final results.

Summary

This chapter focused on the game of Meta Data Bingo. This tool involves people on your project team completing Bingo cards, with the goal of identifying which types of meta data are most important to capture. We went into the details of playing the game

Table 2.15 Subject Area Bingo Results

CODE	DESCRIPTIVE INFORMATION	HIGH	MEDIUM	LOW	QUESTIONS AND ISSUES
A	Standard enterprise name	4.5			
B	Alias			1.5	
C	Definition	5			
D	Steward name and department		2.5		
E	History requirements			2	
F	Source			1.5	

and describing each of the Meta Data Bingo cards of Project, Data Model, Subject Area, Entity, and Data Element. We also discussed meta-meta-meta data, the various meta data levels, and how these levels relate to each other. The chapter finished up with an application of the game, including sample grading using the Subject Area Bingo card. After playing Meta Data Bingo, you know the types of meta data you would like to capture. Next, in Chapter 3, "Ensuring High-Quality Definition," we will discuss some of quality criteria for one of the most important types of meta data, the definition.

Ensuring High-Quality Definitions

The weather in Los Angeles was beautiful. The temperature was around 70 degrees, and the clear blue skies were much preferred over the 50-degree rainy day I left behind in New Jersey. It would be a perfect day to lie on the beach and relax, listening to the sounds of the ocean waves. However, I was not in Los Angeles on vacation, but for business. My company sent me on a very important short-term assignment. I only had two 2 to complete this assignment and publish my findings. Two days of my time and travel expenses was a fairly large investment. Was this to create a quick data model, gather requirements for an estimate to an existing application, or review the logical data model of a packaged piece of software to see if it would meet our business requirements? It was none of these. It was to capture an agreed-on definition for a single data element! There were several different definitions for gross sales amount, including different definitions from two systems that were in the process of being integrated and a different definition at the enterprise level. After an intensive couple of days with no time to spare outside enjoying the beautiful weather, I reported back with the agreed-on definition. With this extra effort, this complete and consistent definition has withstood the test of time and is still being used to this day.

About This Chapter

In Chapter 2, "Meta Data Bingo," we identified the different types of meta data and came up with Bingo cards to make selecting the types of meta data to capture as straightforward and interactive as possible. If a type of meta data were identified as being important for a project, we would require capturing this information. Very few types of meta data that are captured have values that can vary in quality. For example, format does not vary in quality. The format for a data element might be identified as character (15), for example. It is not up for discussion or interpretation; it is 15 characters long. That is all. Can we judge the quality of this format information? We can analyze this data element to see if it really is 15 characters; however, once we identify it as 15 characters long, we cannot judge its quality.

In contrast, the definition of a data element is a type of meta data that can be of high or poor quality. I am always surprised to see how much of the time the definition is of poor quality. A checklist or set of guidelines is needed to measure the level of quality of definitions. This chapter focuses on a tool called the Definition Checklist, which contains criteria for ensuring definitions are of the highest quality.

This chapter begins by defining what we mean by a definition and then explains the Definition Checklist in detail, including this tool's goals, categories, and criteria within these categories. We then conclude with examples of applying the Definition Checklist at the subject area, entity, and data element levels. If you visit this Web site, www.wiley.com/compbooks/hoberman, you will find the Definition Checklist Template; additional tools; and more information about tools within this book, including empty templates that you can download.

What Is a Definition?

Before we describe the Definition Checklist, it is important to make sure we have a solid understanding of the meaning of a definition. I define a definition of a subject area, entity, or data element as a text description that provides valuable insight into the meaning of a term. The definition supplements other key pieces of meta data, such as the term name. The definition will not only describe the term but may also clarify the actual data values the term contains. For example, if I read a definition on total sales amount, I would expect this data element to have the data values and derivations that match this text description. The text description acts as a prologue or introduction to the actual data values.

To give more of an explanation of a definition, I pulled out the trusty dictionary, or in my case the trusty Web site, and looked up the word definition. According to Webster's dictionary, *definition* can have several meanings, including:

- A statement conveying fundamental character
- A statement of the meaning of a word, phrase, or term, as in a dictionary entry
- The act of making clear and distinct

The first meaning focuses on character. Each subject area, entity, and data element definition should capture the essence or character of each term it describes. Character is a very strong term that emphasizes the importance of a definition. Think about the character of an individual. If I have strong character, it means I am more than just what appears on the surface; I have depth and meaning. Likewise, the definition of a term captures its character. A poor definition leads to shallow character, whereas a very good definition leads to strong character and depth. When a term has a good definition, I can see beyond the name or surface and understand and appreciate more about the term. The second meaning is what we think of when we define a term in the data modeling world, that is, the text that accommodates the subject area, entity, or data element. Although not very exciting, this definition makes sense.

The third meaning is very interesting and is my preferred definition. It contains two of my favorite words: clear and distinct. Our definition needs to be clear and understandable to those within and outside of the area that creates and is responsible for the definition. It also needs to be distinct and unique from other definitions in our world. If two definitions are too similar, perhaps they are the same term under two separate names. Make sure your definitions are unique enough to warrant separate terms.

Definitions are important because they provide the clarity and character for common understanding and a basis for discussion for any object or concept. They help us resolve debates on terms with the same names but different definitions *(homonyms),* as well as with different names that appear to mean the same *(synonyms).* Definitions help us integrate discrete structures by identifying where the overlap or common definitions are. Integrating or relating order information into customer reference data requires ensuring that the definition of the customer identifier from the order structure is identical in meaning to the definition of the customer identifier from the customer area. Definitions help us resolve and integrate new structures within the enterprise, regional, or data warehouse existing structures. Definitions help shed light on areas we do not understand. For example, when we come across a word that we do not recognize, we simply look it up in the dictionary. It is very ironic that as important as a definition is, it is usually the most abused type of meta data in existence. I am always shocked to see that such a high percentage of terms continue to lack definitions. Of those terms with definitions, I have observed that between 70 and 80 percent are lacking in quality in at least one area. This is alarming considering how much we need to rely on definitions, especially in the data warehousing arena where running reports and performing analyses rely heavily on understanding the measurements.

What Is the Definition Checklist?

Have you ever read a really poor definition for an entity or a data element? How about a really good one? You have probably found that the more definitions you review, the more you can develop a gut feel for what is good and what is bad. For example, some definitions might appear to be a rephrasing of the actual term name, such as "Customer Last Name means the last name of the customer." Other definitions might be very vague or contain spelling or grammatical errors. These are quickly ruled out as bad definitions. A small minority are considered fairly good. When reviewing a large number of definitions, you need to suppress your gut feeling and rely on unbiased and factual criteria to measure the quality of a definition. This will increase the overall consistency and quality of definitions and highlight the specific weaknesses that needs correcting. These unbiased and factual criteria are contained in the Definition Checklist, which will validate the quality of existing definitions and provide the guidance to ensure new definitions are also of high quality.

The Definition Checklist, which we will discuss in this section, will help detect the areas of improvement in the 70 to 80 percent of terms that need some reworking. It will also provide assistance in completing definitions for those terms missing definitions and for any new terms that come up during our data modeling activities.

The single goal of the Definition Checklist is to increase the quality of each definition in your organization. This includes improving existing definitions as well as preventing poor quality in new definitions. Quality includes clarity, completeness, accuracy, punctuation, and length. Each of these five categories represent different sections of the Definition Checklist, and each category is described in detail in the following section. Each category contains several specific criteria that will help determine whether a definition meets the requirements of this category.

The Definition Checklist in Use

We use the Definition Checklist to determine the quality of subject area, entity, and data element definitions. It is broken down into five categories: clarity, completeness, accuracy, punctuation, and length. Within each category are a number of detailed criteria. In this section we will describe each category and its criteria. For each criterion we will review at least one poor example that violates it and discuss how we can fix the example so that it meets the criteria. In the next section, we will show you how to apply this checklist in a spreadsheet format using three examples: subject area, entity, and data element. This checklist can be applied to review a definition and provide guidance to make sure new definitions are of high quality. Here is the Definition Checklist:

- Clarity
    - Not a restatement of the obvious
    - No obscure technical terminology
    - Only widely understood abbreviations
    - No ego-building words
- Completeness
    - Not too generic
    - Not too specific
    - Stands alone
    - Has derivation if applicable
    - Has examples
- Accuracy
    - Approval by data quality steward
    - Consistent with the enterprise
- Punctuation
    - Spellcheck
    - Good grammar
- Length
    - Not too long
    - Not too short

In what order should you apply these to your definition? Clarity and completeness should be the first and second categories to apply. It does not matter which is first. The next three categories should be applied in the order in which they appear in this checklist. Within each category, you can apply each criterion in the order in which it appears. You may need to apply some of these more than once. For example, if you make a change to a definition to improve the grammar, you will need to run a spellcheck again. Thus, there is iteration here. Be alert to changing your definition to satisfy one of these criterion and potentially causing a violation of another criterion or other criteria as a result of your changes.

Clarity

This category focuses on how clear and understandable the definition is. Usually the first few words that appear as the definition are redundant with the name of the term, or the first few words are difficult to comprehend. It is sad to say that in many cases these first few words, which might otherwise be more of a start on a good definition, usually wind up being the finished definition. Either through oversight or lack of care, this poor definition goes unnoticed until someone needs it, which is almost guaranteed to happen. This category will help you prevent this sad situation from occurring.

Not a Restatement of the Obvious

Just to restate the obvious, "restating the obvious" means that we are not providing any new information. We are just describing something, which already has been mentioned or is easy to find elsewhere. A definition left in this state is not only annoying but also dangerous. It is annoying because it gives the appearance of being a definition when in reality it is not. If I write a query to bring back all of the missing definitions, definitions that restate the obvious are not returned because there is some text in the definition field. However, this text provides no value. It is dangerous because it adds a layer of dependency such that if the name of the term were to change, the definition would make no sense.

NOTE

Restating the obvious is fine as long as it supplements the actual definition. For example, defining an Associate Identifier as "The Associate Identifier is the unique number assigned to associates on their hire date" is an acceptable use of restating the obvious. Just make sure all of your definitions are consistent, meaning either all or none start with repeating the term name.

How to Detect It

There are several indicators that the definition is a restatement of the obvious:

The definition has the same text as the name. For example, the definition for Associate Identifier is "Associate Identifier." Someone obviously copied and pasted the name into the definition field. This is the most easily detected offense.

The definition contains the same words as the name, with one or two additional

words. For example, the definition for Associate Identifier is "The identifier for the associate." This phrase by itself is offensive and embarrassing, yet I believe we have all seen (or written) definitions such as this.

The definition contains synonyms of the name. For example, the definition for Associate Identifier is "The primary key for an employee." This is tricky. At first glance it looks like a fairly good definition. On close inspection we note that primary key is a synonym for identifier and employee is a synonym for an associate. This type of definition usually goes undetected. Be alert for definitions like this one that only contain synonyms of the term being defined, with no additional words to shed light on what the term actually means.

The definition defines the parent instead of the actual term. This is most prevalent when defining a child of something else. For example, when we define an entity we might also redefine the subject area, when we define a data element we might also redefine the entity, and so on. Thus, for Associate Identifier, a redefined definition might be "An associate is someone who works for our company. This is their unique identifier." Here we defined associate. But associate was also defined for the entity Associate. We do not want to repeat or denormalize the definition. The one case where it is acceptable to repeat the definition is when you are using the same term for both parent and child, for example, if you used the same definition for the Associate entity and the Associate subject area. Associate in this case should have the same definition. Repeating a definition is the most difficult of these offenses to detect. This is a problem because by redefining a term, you build in redundancy and create a synchronization issue where if the definition of the parent term is updated, the definition of the component will also need to be updated.

The definition defines the child or children instead of the actual term. This is the opposite of the previous offense and occurs when we list what children the parent contains instead of actually defining the parent. For the definition of a subject area, all of the entities are mentioned; for an entity, all of the data elements are mentioned; and so on. Doing this not only restates the obvious but also introduces redundancy that will need to be kept up-to-date or the definition can become out of synch with the actual values. Here are two examples of this offense:

A customer contains the CUSTOMER LOCATION, CUSTOMER ASSOCIATION, CUSTOMER DEMOGRAHICS, and CUSTOMER CLASSIFICATION entities.

A customer contains the concept of a customer location, its relationships to other customers, where the customer lives, and different ways of classifying customers.

The first example is fairly obvious as a restatement of what we will find when we look at the data model. It provides no additional information. Note also that if the customer subject area data model is updated with a new entity, say CUSTOMER ACCOUNT, this definition would also have to be updated. The second example is a little trickier. It appears to make a nice sounding sentence, but there is that word "contains" again. It is a "contains" sentence that just lists the entities on the customer subject area data model. However, it also is a rephrasing of each of the entities on the model. For example "relationships to other customers" is really a restatement of the CUSTOMER

ASSOCIATION entity! Because both of these restatement scenarios are combined in a single definition, it can be even more difficult to detect.

How to Fix It

If the repetition refers to a parent or child of the term, remove this part of the definition. If it is a data element and the entity to which it belongs is defined within the data element definition, or if a subject area definition lists all of the entities, this type of repetition creates a synchronization problem and is a repetition of a definition found elsewhere. Before you remove this part just make sure that if it is a definition for the parent of the term, it is not better than the actual definition for the parent. For example, if the definition of associate in Associate Alternate Identifier is better than the definition for associate within the Associate entity, you might want to use this definition instead.

If the repetition is between a term and its definition, the repetition might be acceptable as long as the actual definition is also included. For example, this is acceptable:

> *The associate identifier is the unique number assigned to associates on their hire date. It is a counter, which increments by one for each new associate. This number stays with the associates for their career with the company. Even if associates move to other departments within the company, they will keep this identifier.*

You can see that this definition contains the phrase "unique number assigned to associates," which has some redundancy with the name of the data element, Associate Identifier. It works as a nice supplement in this case, however, because of the additional text that clarifies this data element. I find the use of examples to be another way to supplement the redundancy and yet still provide additional meaningful information.

No Obscure Technical Terminology

Every department, company, and industry has at least a few words that have meaning only within that department, company, or industry. For example, a Lot Number has meaning within the manufacturing area as a time and location timestamp for a particular product and has several purposes, including for product recall. The Lot Number is well understood within the manufacturing industry. There are equally specific words on the scope of company and department that we come across quite often during our data modeling activities. We need to make sure that if these words are used in a definition, everyone who needs to know this definition will understand its meaning. We can probably use the term Lot Number freely in all our definitions within the manufacturing area, because it is an standard industry term. However, if we have a term, let's say *mudrins,* which makes sense only to a particular department within the company, we may want to reconsider using it or briefly defining it, if it is not defined elsewhere.

Industries with a rich history, such as the telecommunications and manufacturing industries, are more likely to use obscure terminology than other industries. A phone company I once worked for had entire manuals on just the telecommunications terminology!

How to Detect It

This criterion is fairly straightforward to evaluate against our definitions. We need to first understand the scope of the term being defined. Is this term only going to be referred to within a department? Is it an enterprise term? We also need to think whether the scope will be broader in the future. Always err on the side of caution and take the broader scope. In today's applications, where integration and consistency is the trend, it is usually the enterprise scope.

Once the scope is defined for this term, we need to ask ourselves if there are any words in the definition of this term that would be difficult to understand. Think about the individuals in different departments who might need to look at this enterprise definition one day. Would they understand this word or words? If the answer is Yes, then it is not obscure terminology and your definition passes this criterion. If the answer is No or Maybe, then you need to clear up the potential confusion.

For example, let's look at the following definition for the term smitrins (I made up this term. Can you tell?):

> *A smitrin is the general location of where our consumer parks his or her car in our department store parking lots. A consumer tends to park in the same general area. It takes up the same square footage as our mudrins.*

In order to understand how large a smitrin actually is, we also need to understand what a mudrin is. (I made up the word mudrin, too!) Let's say we identify the term smitrin to be an enterprise term, and therefore, its definition needs to be understood by people outside of this department. Do they understand what a mudrin is? Let's say you bump into someone in the hall who you know works in another department. In casual conversation after discussing your plans for the weekend, you strategically use the word mudrin in a sentence. This person, who you know has years of experience with the company and within the industry, looks at you with a confused expression and admits he does not know what this word means. You've found a word in the category of obscure terminology. Now we have to fix this.

How to Fix It

Now that we have identified this obscure word, we need to fix this definition. There are four ways to do so. The first involves doing nothing. This assumes that the obscure word eventually will become clear in everyone's minds and that people outside the department will one day know what this word means. If you have identified an obscure word, you are more than half way there in fixing the problem; therefore, this first solution usually is not adequate. The second solution is to replace this obscure word with a word that makes more sense within the scope of the enterprise. Is there a synonym for mudrins within your company? Does this synonym make more sense to people? If the answer is Yes, you might want to replace mudrins with this synonym. If the answer is No, there are still two more ways left to fix this problem. The third way is to replace this obscure word with its definition. For example, using the same definition we had for smitrins previously, we need to replace mudrins with the definition of mudrins:

> *A smitrin is the general location of where our consumer parks his or her car in our de-*

partment store parking lots. A consumer tends to park in same general area. It takes up the same square footage as a 200-square-foot piece of land.

So we have replaced the word mudrin with its definition of 200 square feet. This definition now makes a lot more sense. Everyone in the company probably would understand it now. The fourth way of fixing this problem is to add the definition of the obscure word instead of replacing it. For example, back to smitrin:

A smitrin is the general location of where our consumer parks his or her car in our department store parking lots. A consumer tends to park in same general area. It takes up the same square footage as a mudrin, which is a 200-square-foot piece of land.

This solution is also viable. However, as we have seen with repeating any definitions, if mudrins are defined elsewhere, we now have built in redundancy in our definition, although relating the terms smitrin and mudrin would probably add value. I can see people asking, for example, "How does a smitrin relate to a mudrin?" Having the term mudrin in the definition would answer this question. Thus, both the third and forth solutions are my preferred methods of solving this problem. There is a tradeoff with the fourth method. Is the redundancy we create by repeating the definition of mudrin worth the added value of understanding the relationship between a smitrin and mudrin? This is an important question that you need to answer on a case-by-case basis based on what you think the chances are that the definition of mudrin will change and your definitions will get out of synch.

Only Widely Understood Abbreviations

For the same reasons we have obscure terminology in our definitions, we might also have abbreviations that are understood only within certain circles of the company. Many departments might use abbreviations freely within their department and may one day realize no one outside the department understands them. Types of abbreviations include the following:

System acronyms. These are the abbreviations for an internal application, for example, System XYZ and the ABC Interface.

Slang. These are the words we might use in written or verbal communication that are not really part of our agreed-on language. That is, you would not find these words in the dictionary. For example, in popular email slang, btw stands for By the Way and imho stands for In My Humble Opinion.

Company- and industry-specific abbreviations. These abbreviations are well understood within certain circles but not widely understood, for example, the PING process or the DUNs (Dun and Bradstreet) number.

Only some of these abbreviations might be acceptable to keep in our definitions.

How to Detect It

We need to be alert to understanding the scope of the term being defined, just as when looking for obscure terminology. When doing so, we identified whether the term was department-specific, companywide, or industrywide. Most of the time, in these days of application integration, terms need to be at least at the company or enterprise level. Thus, to detect little understood abbreviations, ask someone outside of the department in which the definition was created. For example, here is the definition for bleeps (another word I made up):

A bleep is the major product produced from the PING process. Although it has a pungent odor, it is the main ingredient in many candles and household air fresheners. The PING process produces this very distinctive odor.

Do you know what PING stands for? You and the department that created the definition might understand the full name, but ask Bruce who has lots of experience and works in another department. "Hey Bruce, got a minute? Are you aware of the PING process? Do you know what it stands for?" Very quickly you can determine if there is a general understanding of this abbreviation. Let's assume Bruce is not aware of this abbreviation.

How to Fix It

Once you understand the scope and have determined that the abbreviation will cause confusion in the definition, you need to update this definition. There is really only one approach to fixing the definition with this offense, and it is very easy. Add the fully spelled out name along with the abbreviation in parenthesis the first time the abbreviation appears. After spelling out what it stands for, any future reference to this abbreviation can be made just using the abbreviation. Applying these changes to the previous definition might give us something such as this:

A bleep is the major product produced from the Porous Ingenious Napkin Gene (PING) process. Although it has a pungent odor, it is the main ingredient to many candles and household air fresheners. The PING process produces this very distinctive odor.

Note that even with the fully spelled out name, if Bruce or someone outside the department still does not understand what this means, you might have an example of obscure terminology in your definition. You then need to choose one of the four solutions discussed previously under obscure terminology.

TIP

Sometimes fixing one problem in the definition might uncover other problems. In the example just discussed, listing the full name for an abbreviation still might not clarify understanding in the definition. Therefore, we need to revisit the obscure terminology criterion. Maybe Porous Ingenious Napkin Gene fits under the category of obscure terminology. Therefore, be alert to revisiting some of these criteria based on updates to the definition.

No Ego-Building Words

I can honestly say that vocabulary is not a strong point of mine. I have been in situations where while reading or listening to someone, the meaning of a word escapes me. Does this ever happen to you? I know in a corporate setting, through written prose such as memos, emails, and even definitions, that every once in a while one of these ego-building words finds its way into the text and confuses not only me but many of my colleagues. I call these ego-building words because either the author expects everyone to understand them as they do, or they are showing off their vocabulary skills and feeding their ego. If the author expects everyone to understand the word, it shows a lack of understanding of the audience. I would rather err on the side of caution and assume the author is just feeding his or her ego. Memos and emails usually have a limited lifetime; we read and then recycle them. In contrast, it is hoped that definitions live a much longer time. Thus, you really want to avoid having these ego-building words in the definition of a subject area, entity, or data element. A definition needs to be clear to the masses, and just as we have seen with obscure terminology and unknown abbreviations, ego-building words can cause confusion and misunderstandings.

I have used very archaic and difficult words to exaggerate the point. Do you know what these mean?

- Iswonk
- Latrant
- Hanaper
- Thingus

The reader of a definition might also have an ego. They may quickly make an assumption as to what the word means. If this assumption is incorrect, we have a misunderstanding. A minority of the readers might look up the definition; however, this takes time and will have to be done continuously as new readers encounter the same definition. We need to detect these ego-building words and fix the definition.

How to Detect It

Detecting ego-building words is very easy. Just ask yourself if you are not very clear on the meanings of any of the words in the definition. If you consider yourself to have a fairly large vocabulary, ask a colleague or several colleagues (with small egos!) if any words give them trouble. For example, "Hey Eric, for a free cup of coffee, define the term. . ." You can make a game out of it to make it more entertaining.

How to Fix It

Solving this problem is just as easy as detecting it. Replace the confusing word with its meaning or a simple synonym. For example, referring back to the words mentioned previously, here are their meanings:

- Iswonk (to work hard)
- Latrant (constantly complaining)
- Hanaper (a place to keep documents)
- Thingus (a nobleman or knight)

It is relatively easy to get these meanings and synonyms because most word processors support a thesaurus—or you can always refer to that reliable old 20-pound paperweight, called a dictionary, sitting on your shelf.

Completeness

This category focuses on making sure the definition is at the appropriate level of detail and that it includes all of the necessary components, such as derivation information and examples. Having a definition at the appropriate level of detail means that it is not so generic as to provide very little additional value, and not too specific as to provide value only to an application or department or provide only a business purpose or a point in time definition. A complete definition leaves no gaps that need to be filled in at a later time and ensures consistency across definitions, because definitions will contain the same types of information.

Not Too Generic

To meet the needs of the entire company, or even the entire industry, we sometimes will create a very generic definition so that all parties can agree on the meaning. It is usually a very short definition, one that does not offend anyone. A definition that leaves little up for debate because it meets everyone's needs at a high level. Generic definitions can include these traits:

Dictionary quotations. Generic definitions can quote the dictionary and because there is little argument as to what a word means in a dictionary, it is generally accepted by all parties. If the term being defined is multiple words, sometimes the dictionary definition is supplied for each part of the word.

Ambiguous terminology. To avoid conflict, we can purposely use words that can mean many things to different people, such as associate, relate, and interact.

Abstraction. When we abstract our designs, as we will see later in the book, we create more generic and flexible design structures. In our definitions we sometimes apply this same level of abstraction. Thus, to be flexible and meet conflicting needs, we might use terms such as person and party to mean customer, employee, supplier, and so on.

Unit of measure omissions. A *unit of measure* is a term that categorizes an amount or quantity. For example, if we come across the number 5, we have limited understanding of what it means unless we know its unit of measure. For example, the 5 can be the following:

- 5 pounds
- 5 ounces
- 5 pallets
- 5 cups
- 5 feet

Many of the data elements we define have a unit of measure that characterizes them. For example, Order Total Weight might be measured in pounds. Generic definitions can sometimes omit this unit of measure, leaving us guessing as to what the amount really means unless the unit of measure is embedded within the data element name, such as Order Total Pounds Weight.

How to Detect It

This is one of the more difficult criterion to detect. It is not difficult to identify a generic phase within a definition; however, it is difficult to detect when it is too generic. Thus, the first step is to identify a generic definition or phrase within a definition. Let's say you have identified the following very generic definition:

A person, persons, or organization of importance to the business.

Wow! This is extremely generic. After identifying a generic structure, we need to do the fairly difficult step of determining whether it is too generic. We need to ask ourselves the question "Is the definition generic because the term we are defining needs to be generic?" This means that for reasons such as flexibility, integration, and future needs, we needed to create a generic term; therefore, we need a generic definition to accompany it. For example, if the term we were defining with the previous definition was Party, perhaps this is an appropriate level of detail for the definition and, therefore, not too generic. However, even if this definition were at an acceptable level of detail, examples would be required to add more relevance, as we will see in the subsequent examples. Let's say the term we were defining was Customer. Would this definition still be appropriate? Probably not. If I want to represent a competitor, who is by no means a customer, this definition does not exclude it. Therefore, the definition allows more leniency than the term, and we have identified a definition that is too generic. Now let's try and fix it.

TIP

■■■■■ **The scope of the definition needs to match the scope of the term. If the definition does not exclude concepts that the name appears to exclude, we have a mismatch in level of detail between term and its definition. In many cases, this mismatch is caused by a definition that is too generic. A test to determine this is to come up with concepts you know are not included by this term and make sure the definition excludes them.**

How to Fix It

Consider a definition that is too generic as a starting point toward a better definition. It just needs more information to increase its usefulness. The definition will need more information either as a clarification, in the case of examples, or as a way of making sure what is excluded by the term is also excluded by its definition. Let's revisit our example:

A person, persons, or organization of importance to the business.

If this is the definition for a Party, then we mentioned that this definition might be acceptable, with the addition of examples to add relevance. Thus, this definition might become:

A person, persons, or organization of importance to the business.
    Examples include:
    Customer
    Supplier

> *Competitor*
> *Employee*

If this definition is for a Customer, then we need to add the text that excludes everything but a customer. For example:

> *A person, persons, or organization of importance to the business that purchases our products and services.*

If this definition is for an internal party concept, the definition might look like this:

> *A person, persons, or organization of importance to the business that is internal to the organization.*
>   *Examples include:*
>   *Employee*
>   *Department*
>   *Examples that are not included:*
>   *Competitor*
>   *Government agency*

Not Too Specific

The opposite of making a definition too generic is making it too specific. Too specific means that the definition is correct within a certain scope, yet does not address the complete scope implied by the term being defined. Specific definitions can exhibit the following traits:

References to specific departments. The definition incorrectly refers to a smaller subset of the organization than the term implies. For example, "The Sales Department enters the commission information based on the accepted formula."

References to specific applications. The definition incorrectly refers to an application that is not implied by this term. For example, "The Account Identifier is uniquely generated by the XYZ application."

Just includes a business purpose. The definition only includes the "Why" and not the "What". For example, "Total Sales Amount is needed to correctly measure our company's gross revenues." Note there is no mention as to what Total Sales Amount means, only its business purpose.

Just includes a point in time definition. The definition only includes what the term means today and excludes what the term means in general. We see these definitions quite often during application transitions. For example, the definition for Company Name might be "Today this represents the company's email address." This is a point-in-time definition that does not include what the term will mean in the future. When will it include the Company Name, and what does Company Name mean?

Just includes examples. Examples are very important to a definition, but sometimes they can be all we find in the definition. For example, when we defined Party previously, just including the examples would only list the following for the complete definition:

Examples:
- *Customer*
- *Supplier*
- *Competitor*
- *Employee*

As you can see, this does not give us much information.

Just includes derivations. Derivations are very important for certain terms. If all that exists is a derivation, however, we have a definition that is too specific. For example, if the only text accompanying Total Sales Amount is "Quantity times Adjusted Base Price," this provides some value but still requires a business explanation of what Total Sales means.

How to Detect It

The first step in detecting whether a definition is too specific is to identify any potential definitions that fall into one of the previous categories. Once we have, we need to ask ourselves whether we have a problem. If we only have a business purpose, derivation, or example as a definition, we automatically have a problem: This definition needs more information. It needs a true definition, instead of just one of these supplements to a definition. If we have a point-in-time definition, we need to ask ourselves can this term mean something else, other than this point-in-time definition, at any time in the future. If the answer is yes, we need to fix this definition. If there are references to specific departments or systems, we need to ask ourselves whether this term can ever mean something outside this scope. There could be many valid concepts that will only ever be specific to a system or application, such as internal date or audit information. Here is how we know if we have a problem for each of the previous solutions:

References to specific departments. What is the scope of this term? If it will only be used by this department, then the definition is not too specific. I have very rarely seen examples where references to specific departments are not too specific. Most of the time, the scope is broader than a specific department.

References to specific applications. What is the scope of this term? I have seen many date and audit data elements that are application-specific and, therefore, their definition is not too specific.

Just includes a business purpose. This always means we have a definition that is too specific and will require fixing.

Just includes a point-in-time definition. Can this term mean something else in the future? If the answer is yes, we have a problem here.

Just includes examples. This always means we have a definition that is too specific and will require fixing.

Just includes derivations. This always means we have a definition that is too specific and will require fixing.

How to Fix It

As are generic definitions, these usually are not bad definitions but just a starting point for the complete definition. We need to add more information to each of these:

References to specific departments. The original example was "The Sales Department enters the commission information based on the accepted formula." This is a phrase within a larger definition. Is the Sales Department the only one that can enter this information? If the answer is yes, this is acceptable to keep in the definition. Let's assume that several departments can enter this information. Then we can either list all of the departments that can enter the commission information, or remove this information from the definition so that we might be left with the phrase "The commission information is entered based on the accepted formula."

References to specific applications. The original example was "The Account Identifier is uniquely generated by the XYZ application." Is the XYZ information the only place or source where this identifier is generated, now and in the future? If the answer is yes, then we do not have a problem here. However, do we see this application being around for a very long time? If the application changes, we need to update this definition. If the answer is no, then we need to remove the application reference from this definition. Thus, we might be left with "The Account Identifier is uniquely generated by the Account Entry Application, which today is handled by the XYZ application," or something similar. Note that I also added an element of time into this definition when I added that the XYZ application is handling this today. You need to be very cautious when you add the element of time, as we will see under this separate category.

Just includes a business purpose. The original example was "Total Sales Amount is needed to correctly measure our company's gross revenues." We need to fix this definition by adding the actual meaning of this term. For example, the definition might become "Total Sales Amount is the gross revenues our company makes, which is calculated based on multiplying the adjusted price by the total quantity sold. It is a key indicator in measuring our company's gross revenues."

Just includes a point-in-time definition. The original example was "Today this represents the company's email address." If this is the definition for all time, then we can remove the word Today, and hopefully rename this term from Company Name to Company Email Address. If this is just the definition for this month or the next few months, we need to understand what this terms means independent of time and optionally add what it represents today, or store this information in a separate place such as a Notes field.

Just includes examples. The original example was:

Examples:
- *Customer*
- *Supplier*
- *Competitor*
- *Employee*

This is an easy one to fix. Just add the definition to Party before these examples occur, and we now have a fairly robust definition.

Just includes derivations. The original example was Total Sales Amount is "Quantity times Adjusted Base Price," This is a good start. We need to add meaning, and therefore, we arrive at a definition similar to the definition under business purpose that we have seen previously: "Total Sales Amount is the gross revenues our company makes, which is calculated based on multiplying the adjusted price by the total quantity sold. It is a key indicator in measuring our company's gross revenues."

You can see that the techniques used to fix a definition that is too specific are heavily dependent on which of the situations seen earlier makes it too specific.

Stands Alone

It is very important that the definition for each term be explainable independent of other terms. This means that when we are reading a definition, we do not have to have knowledge of the structure of related data elements, entities, and subject areas. Note the word structure. When we read a definition, and find ourselves looking at the data model to clarify something in it, this definition does not stand alone and requires knowledge of the structure. It requires knowing how this term relates to other data elements, entities, and subject areas. There are two situations where we might find definitions that are not standalone ones: containment dependency and peer-to-peer dependency.

Containment dependency. This means that the definition for a term requires understanding the structure and the category to which that term belongs. For example, each data element should have a definition that does not require researching to which entity this data element belongs. Likewise, each entity should have a definition that does not require researching to which subject area this entity belongs. Let's examine the data element ID. ID is defined as follows:

The unique identifier for this entity, which guarantees uniqueness and is just a counter so there is no meaning implied in any of the values.

Note that we cannot tell what this data element identifies unless we know to which entity it belongs. Is it a Customer ID, an Employee ID, a Product ID, and so on? We could tell if it had a more specific name, such as Customer Identifier. In this situation we would know the term to which it refers.

Peer-to-peer dependency. This means that a data element requires understanding its relationship to another data element to fully understand its definition. The most prevalent example of this is a fact or measurement requiring a dimensional data element for its meaning. Let's say Total Sales Amount is defined as follows:

Total Sales Amount is the gross revenues our company makes, which is calculated based on multiplying the adjusted price by the total quantity sold. It is a key indicator in measuring our company's gross revenues. It is calculated on a monthly basis, by customer, by product.

Note the last sentence adds the requirement that we need to understand the structure of how Total Sales Amount relates to time, customer, and product. We have built the grain levels into the dimension.

How to Detect It

The best way to detect this definition violation is to read the definition and see if you find yourself referring to the data model to completely understand the definition. If you find yourself examining the entities to which data elements belong, or the relationships between fact and dimension tables, this would be a definition that does not stand alone. Both examples mentioned previously, ID and Total Sales Amount, would require that the average reader of the definition refer back to the data model for complete understanding.

How to Fix It

If we have a containment standalone, simply add the parent term to the definition. For example, let's say for the ID data element, we refer to the data model and learn that this is the identifier for a Customer Location:

> *The unique identifier for each Customer Location, which guarantees uniqueness and is just a counter so there is no intelligence implied in any of the values.*

Note that you want to make sure you do not start defining what a Customer Location is, because this will be in the Customer Location entity and you do not want to repeat it here. If you do, you will be restating the obvious and, therefore, cause another definition offense on the Definition Checklist.

Has Derivation If Applicable

There can be a large number of derived data elements in our applications, especially in the fact and summary tables of our data marts. A business derivation is very valuable supplemental information to the definition, for a derived data element. A business derivation is the business meaning of how a data element is derived, as opposed to the physical derivation, which is at a physical data element level and is usually captured in the Extract, Transform, and Load tool. The physical derivation provides little business insight into the derivation but does associate the derived data element with its specific components. Let's revisit the definition of Total Sales Amount:

> *Total Sales Amount is the gross revenues our company makes, which is calculated based on multiplying the adjusted price by the total quantity sold. It is a key indicator in measuring our company's gross revenues.*

Note that this data element has the derivation. But is this derivation good enough? Derivation offenses fall into two categories:

No derivation. This is when we have a derived data element whose definition does not include the derivation. For example, for Order Weight:

> *Order weight is the total tonnage of the order.*

This is a fairly light definition to begin with; however, you can see that one of its traits is that the derivation is missing.

Not enough derivation. This is when there is a derivation, but it may not be adequate. Look at the Total Sales Amount definition again:

> *Total Sales Amount is the gross revenues for our company, which is calculated based on multiplying the adjusted price by the total quantity sold. It is a key indicator in measuring our company's gross revenues.*

We learn from this definition that total sales amount is derived by multiplying adjusted price and quantity. But let's say there are several different adjusted prices. We might have one after promotions, one after freight discounts, one after returns, and so on. Which price should we use? Thus, this derivation needs more information.

How to Detect It

There are three steps to detecting definitions lacking derivation information. The first step is to identify the derived data elements. Usually these are easy to find by looking for words in their name such as total, net, and gross. Once you have identified these data elements, highlight those that have no derivations. These you will need to fix. Out of those that have derivations, which ones are good enough? This is not always an easy question to answer. Ask yourself whether this derivation leaves room for multiple interpretations. Is it ambiguous? Can more than one data element fit the description for part of the derivation, as we saw in trying to determine which price to use in the previous example? If the answer is yes, then we need to improve this derivation.

How to Fix It

For both of the derivation scenarios, the solution is the same. Clearly identify the single terms that are used in the derivation and add them to the definition. By single terms, I mean leave no room for ambiguity. Also, there is no need to specify the physical data element names, just include business names and terms. Thus, to add the derivation information to Order Weight:

> Order weight is the total tonnage of the order. It is the standard weight for a product multiplied by the number of products ordered, divided by 2,000 to convert pounds to tonnage.

For the Total Sales Amount data element, we need to make the existing derivation information more detailed:

> Total Sales Amount is the gross revenues for our company, which is calculated based on multiplying the adjusted price after applying promotions to the gross price, by the total quantity sold. It is a key indicator in measuring our company's gross revenues.

Note the more specific information on the price component of the derivation.

Has Examples

Examples always provide additional insight into the meanings of terms and are required in two situations:

Codes. Many times codes just have a few values. Although an explanation of the code is useful, a significant amount of additional value can be provided by listing all or a subset of the actual values of the code. For example, the data element State Code might have the following definition:

> An abbreviated version of the name of a state within the United States, maintained and used by the United States Postal Service.

Are you certain you know what the possible values are for this code? There is more than one set of abbreviations for a state code; therefore, examples or sample values would be very useful.

Abstraction. Whenever we abstract a concept, which we will learn more about in Chapter 9, "The Abstraction Safety Guide and Components," we lose business representation on the model yet gain flexibility. This loss sometimes needs to be made up in the definition. Recall that the examples for Party were:

- Customer
- Supplier
- Competitor
- Employee

This adds a significant amount of information to the definition. Note that you do not have to list all the possible values, because such a restriction on an abstraction concept forces inflexibility in your definition where you wanted flexibility. By introducing just a few examples, however, you add a lot more clarity to your definition.

TIP

■■■■■■ Use sample values or examples as much as possible. Examples are nice to have in all definitions but are a requirement for codes, their decodes or descriptions, and abstract structures.

How to Detect It

First, identify all of your data elements that are codes or *decodes* (descriptions) that currently do not have sample values. Next, identify all of the abstract terminology that was not covered under codes. These are the two categories that need sample values. This includes subject areas, entities, and data elements. Add a few examples under each. Again, we do not need a complete list here but just enough to add understanding.

How to Fix It

For codes, I usually recommend listing all values for a code when there are 20 or less distinct values, or just the first 20 if there are more than 20 values. Using classwords, which we will discuss in Chapter 9, will make more apparent which of the data elements are codes. For example, these might be the examples for the state code definition:

01 = Alabama

02 = Arkansas

03 = New York

04 = New Jersey

05 = California

06 = . . . and so on for the first 20 states

Note that the sample values are actually different than we might expect. We expected Alabama to be AL, for example. This highlights the value of having these example values.

Accuracy

This category focuses on having a definition that totally matches what the term means and is consistent with the rest of the business. An expert in the field would agree that this term matches this definition. Note that we are not validating the term and definition against the actual data at this point. This data validation happens later in this process, and there are tools in this book for assistance when you have access to the actual data. As ironic as it may sound, accuracy can sometimes be up for interpretation. It can be interpreted possibly multiple ways, depending on scope and on the business experts that validate the definition. The scope issue is addressed when viewing each definition in terms of its place in the enterprise. When business experts disagree, there needs to be a single steward for the subject area. A steward is someone who is responsible for a particular term or subject area. Note that some of the validation we address in this category might have already been done when requesting feedback from people outside the department.

Approved by Data Quality Steward

Has the agreed-on expert in this area signed off on this definition? The expert is someone who is independent of a particular application. The expert is the business expert and owns the official stewardship title because the expert alone has the final say for data and meta data associated with this subject area. Note that I say subject area, not entity or data element. This is an important point. The steward should be defined at a subject area level so that there is consistency with other stewards. This will prevent stewardship scope from overlapping. This will also minimize the number of stewards and the maintenance process associated with who is the steward for which data. Imagine how many stewards there would be if we assigned stewardship at the entity or data element level?

How to Detect It

This is easy to do. Has a data steward reviewed the definition? If the answer is yes, then you are done with this criterion. If the answer is no, then you need to have the definition reviewed and approved.

How to Fix It

There are two steps to having a definition approved by a steward. The first is to identify who the steward is. This can be fairly challenging, especially in a large company or department where multiple people might be authorities on this term. Usually what happens is the manager of the department who is responsible for creating or changing the data becomes the steward. Next the steward must approve this definition. Make sure that it is not a rubber stamp approval, meaning the steward barely looks at the definition and then signs off on it. It is important to make the steward aware that there is a lot of responsibility associated with being the steward and the role should not be taken lightly. Always obtain a commitment that the steward will provide feedback and agree on a date of review, because there is probably a lot of work on the steward's plate.

Consistent with the Enterprise

Once a definition is written and approved, you need to ensure that it is consistent with the larger scope, such as the enterprise. You need to make sure it does not conflict with any existing enterprise terms and definitions.

How to Detect It

Validating your term and definition against the enterprise list will produce one of four results:

No match. In the enterprise list you did not find anything similar to your term and definition, in which case the definition approved by your steward will become the enterprise definition. The Customer term and definition were not in the enterprise list.

Exact match. You have found the term with the same name and almost exact definition as your own. Your definition of Customer matches that of the enterprise.

Synonym. You have found a term with a similar but not exact name, with the same definition. For example, the term Client on the enterprise list has the same definition as your term Customer.

Homonym. You have found a term with the same name, but the definition appears to be different. For example, your definition of Customer means something quite different from that of the enterprise.

How to Fix It

There are different ways to meet this criterion, depending on which situation has occurred:

No match. If the definition is not found in the enterprise, you are done with this criterion, because there is nothing to which to compare your definition. Your final definition will probably become the enterprise definition. Therefore, your definition for Customer will become the enterprise definition for Customer.

Exact match. You also have very little work to do to fix this situation. Just make sure the definitions match exactly. If they are even slightly different, make them the same. Update your definition of Customer to match exactly that of the enterprise.

Synonym. If you found a similar term name with the same definition, you might need to meet with your team and suggest they change the name. Therefore, you would suggest to your team that they use the term Client instead of Customer.

Homonym. If you found a homonym, you probably need to change the name of your term and start the enterprise search over again. Ask your business users for another term name, such as Client, instead of using the term Customer. See if Client exists in the enterprise list and matches your definition.

Punctuation

This category focuses on the appearance of the definition instead of the content, including spelling and grammar. Although they take a back seat to the other criteria already reviewed, violating spelling and grammar could take away from the good traits of the definition. For example, when I see a lot of spelling errors in a definition, I tend to look more for spelling errors and less at the content. When I find these types of errors, I question the credibility of and often discount much of the information.

Spellcheck

It is very interesting to note that although spelling is the easiest and quickest definition criterion to get right, it is usually the one least done. I believe this is due to a lack of a spellchecker in many of the modeling and analysis tools we use. I get annoyed whenever I see spelling errors in the definitions because they can be corrected easily and quickly.

How to Detect It

You can detect misspellings by either going through the definition by hand looking for errors or using the preferred method of using a spellchecker.

How to Fix It

If your modeling tool does not support a spellchecker, then I recommend that you copy and paste the definitions into a tool that supports one, such as Microsoft Word or Excel, and then copy and paste back into your modeling tool if you have made any changes.

Good Grammar

This is much more difficult to detect and, in some cases, might not be necessary to correct. Many times we want our definitions to be easy to read and sound more like verbal communication than written prose. Therefore, we make many allowances for grammar. This is ok to do.

How to Detect It

If you did want to correct the grammar, you probably will not be able to do so in the modeling tool. You can either check for it by hand or copy and paste into one of the many tools that can check for grammar.

How to Fix It

My recommendation would be not to worry so much about this criterion. What you might want to do is copy and paste the definition, as we did for spelling, into a software package that can also check for some types of grammar and then copy and paste back into your modeling tool if you have made any changes.

Length

This category focuses on the word length of the definition instead of the content. A very long definition can include so much irrelevant information that it hides its really important meaning. Likewise, a really short definition can contain too little information to explain the term clearly.

Not Too Long

Although very rare, sometimes our definitions can be too long. As a general rule of thumb, if you find yourself with a definition spanning two paragraphs, you might need to reevaluate it. Many times looking through such a long definition leads to discovering definitions of other terms or relationships between terms.

How to Detect It

Each sentence in the definition should focus only on the term being defined. If you find the following phrases in your definition, perhaps your definition is too long; you should remove them:

Under the Customer entity definition: A Customer can have one or more accounts associated with him or her.

Under the Customer Last Name data element definition: In addition to this last-name data element, there is also a first-name data element in the same entity.

Under the Product subject area definition: A Product can have many promotions applied against it.

You can see from these examples that they reference information outside the scope of the term. The first definition phrase is redundant with what the relationship will say, for the business rule between Customer and Account. The second definition phrase is not related at all to the last name data element, and we will find both data elements in the same entity if we briefly examine the model. The important point, however, is that references to the first-name data element are not relevant in defining the last-name data element. The last of these definition phrases again describes a relationship that is quick to find on the model and not relevant to the definition of a Product.

How to Fix It

Remove the extraneous information. Only keep verbiage directly related to this term, and leave out the information that appears to relate to similar but different terms. Thus, all the phrases mentioned previously would be removed from the definition, making it shorter.

Not Too Short

Likewise, we can have a definition that is too short. For example, a five-word phrase might be too short. You do not want to sacrifice meaning or understanding by being too succinct.

How to Detect It

Can the definition be just a short phrase and not even a short sentence? For example:

Customer Credit Rating. Assigned by industry for general rating

Product. Item or service

These definitions provides some value but still lack clarity and appear very light. The first example is missing a large part of the definition, and the second example appears to be more of an alias list than a definition. Note that by applying all of the criteria mentioned previously, you will never have a short, meaningless definition. Corrections would have already been applied earlier on in the definition review process.

How to Fix It

Ask yourself if the definition is clear and complete. Willingly add verbiage if need be. The extra words do not cost anything. Just remember to expand only the actual term you are defining. If you use the criteria in this chapter, you will not develop a definition that is too short and will ensure that the correct types of information are included.

The Definition Checklist In Practice

This section contains three examples of using the Definition Checklist, one each for subject areas, entities, and data elements. Note the format. I find a spreadsheet mechanism works best to easily see which definitions are acceptable and which are lacking certain criteria. Also, many times data modeling tools or other data analysis tools can easily export subject areas, entities, and data elements into a spreadsheet format.

Note throughout these examples that the criteria are rows in the spreadsheet, and the terms whose definitions we are evaluating are the columns. I chose this layout because I am showing only about four different terms for each example. Thus, it is easy to keep the spreadsheet in a portrait format. When you use the Definition Checklist, you might prefer to create your spreadsheet in the landscape mode and put the criteria in the columns and the terms in the rows. This works especially well when you are defining many terms. You might even want to use a single spreadsheet for all subject areas, entities, and data elements and choose to divide the spreadsheet into three sections.

Subject Area Example

Here are four subject areas and their definitions followed by a filled-in Definition Checklist (see Table 3.1):

Customer. An individual, group of individuals, or company that purchases our products and services.

Product. An item. According to Webster's dictionary, "Something produced by human or mechanical effort or by a natural process."

Employee. A person who works in the Accounting Department.

Account. According to Webster's dictionary: "1. A formal banking, brokerage, or business relationship established to provide for regular services, dealings, and other financial transactions. 2. A precise list or enumeration of financial transactions. 3. Money deposited for checking, savings, or brokerage use."

Validation of Customer Definition

This definition appears to meet most of the criteria. For clarity, it meets all of the criteria, because there are no obscure terms or restating the obvious. For completeness,

Table 3.1 Filled-In Subject Area Definition Checklist

CRITERIA	CUSTOMER	PRODUCT	EMPLOYEE	ACCOUNT
Clarity				
Not a restatement of the obvious	X		X	X
No obscure technical terminology	X	X	X	X
Only widely understood abbreviations	X	X	X	X
No ego-building words	X	X	X	
Completeness				
Not too generic	X			
Not too specific	X	X		X
Stands alone	X	X	X	
Has derivation if applicable				
Has examples				
Accuracy				
Approval by data quality steward	X	X		X
Consistent with the enterprise	X		X	X
Punctuation				
Spellcheck	X	X	X	X
Good grammar	X	X	X	X
Length				
Not too long	X	X	X	X
Not too short	X		X	X

the one criterion I would question would be "Not too generic." It appears that this definition will work in any industry. Is there additional information we can add to make it more specific and more informative to our company? For example, should we specify the types of customers we have? If we do this, we might find ourselves describing another term, namely Customer Type, that we would define somewhere else. Describing Customer Type twice would lead to a violation of the restating the obvious criterion, because we are redundantly defining Customer Type.

In several industries in which I have worked there has been a point of discussion about how a customer differs from a consumer. If this was an issue for a particular company, I might say in their customer definition how a customer differs from a consumer. Again, be careful not to completely define the consumer in this definition. I think there is only so much more we can say with this definition without describing something else. You will find that at a subject area level, most of our definitions will tend to be more on the generic side. As long as the definition completely describes the term, we will check off the "Not too generic" criterion. Under accuracy and punctuation, let's assume we did the necessary checks to make sure it meets these criteria.

To give this definition more substance, the only text we might consider adding more of are examples. Examples provide a direct link between this somewhat generic definition and actual values described by the term Customer. Examples would be especially useful if we did decide to compare a Customer and Consumer, because we can show through values what is a Customer and not a Consumer and vice versa.

Validation of Product Definition

The first sentence restates the obvious and, therefore, violates this Clarity category. Specifically, it violates restating the obvious because the definition contains synonyms of the name. An item might be a synonym for a product. This sentence provides no additional value. Is a Product something we sell, is it something we buy as a raw material, does it include the packaging of the product, and so on? This definition leaves much room for questions and must be expanded. For example, we might replace the "Item" sentence with the following:

> *Something we manufacturer or purchase from a reseller and sell to customers for profit. A product can be a raw material, the packaging for a product, and the finished product ready for resale. According to Webster's dictionary, "Something produced by human or mechanical effort or by a natural process."*

Note that although this is still generic, it is now at the same level of detail as the term, and therefore, we can now check off this spreadsheet cell under "Not too generic." It is interesting that sometimes violating one of these criterion can cascade into violations in other criteria. For example, because the definition contained synonyms of the name, we did not check off "Not a restatement of the obvious," and we also did not check off "Not too generic" and "Not too short." Once we fix "Not too generic," these other criteria are also met and get checked.

This definition did not get a check mark under accuracy for "Consistent with the enterprise." This could mean that there is another definition for Product out there that we have not resolved against yet. It could also mean there is a similar concept, such as Item, and we do not know how Product and Item compare to each other. Either way, not having this option checked should raise eyebrows to quickly address this.

Note also the dictionary quote in this definition. It becomes fairly useful as a supplement to this enhanced definition.

TIP

 It always adds validity and strength to a definition to include a quote from a reliable source, such as the dictionary or industry reference document, that supports your definition.

Validation of Employee Definition

Employee is a clear definition, with no obscure terminology or restating the obvious. Under completeness, however, it is very interesting to see that it is too generic and too specific. It is too generic because there are more terms that can be covered under this definition that are outside the scope of an employee. For example, a contractor or consultant would be a person who meets this definition and yet is not an employee. Finding such an example means that we need more information in this definition to match the term Employee. I might choose to expand this definition:

> *A person who works in the Accounting Department. Someone we financially compensate and withhold taxes from. We also provide the person with additional benefits, such as a 401K, retirement pension, health benefits, and vacation and sick days.*

This adds enough information to rule out contractors and consultants and now appears to be at the same level as Employee, with one exception: "Accounting Department." We see that specifying "Accounting Department" for a generic term such as Employee again causes a mismatch in scope between definition and term. It appears in this case that the definition is more restrictive than the term. We need to either remove "Accounting Department" from the definition or change the name of the term to just Accounting Department Employee.

Note that a data steward has not yet approved this definition. This is a red flag. You need to make sure a steward approves this definition before it is considered complete. It is especially important at the subject area level, where not having steward approval means that all of the entities and data elements contained within the subject area also do not have steward approval. To reiterate, all changes a steward makes to the definition require reexamination of all the criteria to make sure the definition still satisfies each one.

Validation of Account Definition

I would not consider the definition of Account to be very clear. For one thing, it only contains a dictionary quotation. Note, however, that there are multiple definitions from the dictionary and variations in their meanings. For an account, are we talking about the relationship, the list of transactions, or the deposits? Three separate meanings are all in the same definition. We need to choose one. Or, if it means more than one, we need to elaborate on each. Let's say this particular definition of account means the second definition, the list of transactions. I would consider the word enumeration to be an ego-building word; however, because we cannot change the dictionary quotation, we need to leave this the way it is. This is what the definition looks like so far:

> *According to Webster's Dictionary, "A precise list or enumeration of financial transactions."*

This still violates several other criteria. Under completeness, it does not appear that this word stands on its own. Without a clear understanding of what a transaction is, we do not know what a list of transactions means. We need to remove the dependency on transaction or explain what a transaction is. If we explain what a transaction is, we now have the term transaction redundantly defined, because transaction will probably be defined elsewhere. Doing this would violate the "Restating the obvious" criterion. Instead of a detailed definition of a transaction, I would recommend using some examples of transaction, such as the following:

> *According to Webster's Dictionary, "A precise list or enumeration of financial transactions." For our company, this includes debits, credits, and settlements.*

This change also now satisfies the "Not too generic" validation. We have information specific to our company. We now also can check off the "Has examples" validation.

Entity Example

Below are four entities and their definitions followed by a filled-in Definition Checklist (see Table 3.2).

Customer Location. The address for a customer.

Product Classification. A grouping of products, such as by brand, size, or price.

Table 3.2 Filled-In Entity Definition Checklist

CRITERIA	CUSTOMER LOCATION	PRODUCT CLASSIFICATION	EMPLOYEE ASSOCIATION	ACCOUNT TYPE
Clarity				
Not a restatement of the obvious			X	
No obscure technical terminology	X	X	X	X
Only widely understood abbreviations	X	X	X	
No ego-building words	X	X		X
Completeness				
Not too generic		X		X
Not too specific	X	X	X	
Stands alone	X	X	X	X
Has derivation if applicable				X
Has examples		X		X
Accuracy				
Approval by data quality steward	X	X	X	X
Consistent with the enterprise	X	X	X	X
Punctuation				
Spellcheck	X	X	X	X
Good grammar	X	X	X	X
Length				
Not too long	X	X	X	X
Not too short	X	X	X	X

Employee Association. Juxtaposition between two employees with the same company.

Account Type. The type of account a customer can have, which currently only contains GL.

Validation of Customer Location Definition

Under the criterion Clarity, we immediately note that this definition is a restatement of the obvious. Address is a synonym for location. Customer is used redundantly in the name and definition. How often have we seen entity definitions list this one? One way to solve this problem is add some examples. Examples will shed light on whether this is the full street address, longitude and latitude, some point within a Geographical Information System, and so on. After adding examples, the updated definition for Customer Location might look like this:

> *The address for a customer.*
> *Examples:*
> *14 Main St*
> *PO Box 10*

Be cautious when using examples for entities. You need to make sure that you do not find yourself explaining an entity as if it were one of the data elements it contains. Examples need to elaborate on the entity as a whole. These examples we've listed appear more as data element values than an entity value. The example "14 Main St." might be a good one for a data element, such as Street Address Line 1 Text, but not for the entity Customer Location. Let's update the definition with examples that refer to the entire entity:

> *The address for a customer.*
> *Examples:*
> *14 Main St., Apt 5B, New York, NY 11111*
> *PO Box 10, Somecity, NJ 12222*

Note that examples did help a lot in this case. The Customer Location entity still might require additional text, however, because it might contain more than just the address. It may contain the preferred days of the week that we would like to deliver product to this customer, for example. Thus, we might need to clarify this definition a bit more.

Validation of Product Classification Definition

Although I like the second part of this definition, the first part is a restatement of the obvious, similar to Customer Location. "Grouping" is a synonym for classification, and the term products is used redundantly. Often when we do not want to spend time on definitions—yet we still want something that sounds good—we find ourselves using these redundant definitions with synonyms. They are more difficult to detect than just repeating the term name in the definition. Note that I did not have to define product again, because this term was defined under the subject area and should not be repeated here.

I think even more examples would be useful in this definition. Specifically, I would like to know if one classification can contain other classifications, which I can explain either through the description or examples. Examples are needed for this definition, because classification is such an abstract concept. The revised definition might look like this:

The assignment of a product to one or more categories. A category can contain one or more other categories, creating a hierarchy. There are over 20 different hierarchies in our business.
 Examples:
 Automobile
  Luxury Car
   Luxury Car Convertible
    BigBucks400 Convertible

This example shows actual classifications as well as the hierarchy depicted by indenting classifications contained within other classifications.

Validation of Employee Association Definition

The definition for Employee Association violates the "No ego-building words" criterion under the Clarity category. This is because of the use of the word juxtaposition. This is one of those words that might impress someone at a cocktail party or on a standardized vocabulary examination but has no place in a definition. You can replace this word with an easily understood synonym for "Association," and then add examples so that you are not simply restating the obvious. Whenever I have a generic term such as association or classification, examples become a very valuable part of the definition. Updating this Employee Association definition gives us:

—A corporate relationship between two employees with the same company. Examples include management, team members, and counterparts. If Bob works for Mary, their Employee Association would be "management." If both Bob and Mary were on the same team as colleagues, their Employee Association would be "team members." If Bob performs the same role in the United States as Mary does in Europe, their Employee Association would be "counterparts."

Validation of Account Type Definition

As we have seen with some of the other definitions, Account Type suffers from a restatement of the obvious. The first part of this sentence needs to change to provide more meaning, or we can add some examples, or both. In addition, everyone might not understand the abbreviation GL; therefore, there is no check mark under "Only widely understood abbreviations." Those in the accounting department might know that GL stands for general ledger account, but someone outside that department might not. Err on the side of caution and include what GL stands for in this definition.

Note also that this definition might appear to be too specific. It potentially violates the "Just includes a point in time definition" situation within the "Not too specific" criterion. It only makes reference to general ledger accounts. If this entity means something more than general ledger, this definition is too restrictive. In your definitions, try not to use terms such as "currently" and "for the moment." I would recommend using a separate field, or type of meta data, for this information, such as Notes. The new definition might look something like this:

—The kind of account we use to handle customer interactions, including general ledger, accounts receivable, and accounts payable.

Data Element Example

Below are four data elements and their definitions followed by a filled-in Definition Checklist (see Table 3.3).

Customer Location City Name. The full name of the city in which the customer has his or her primary residence. Note this is just in the United States and not global.

Product Classification Description. The full description of the assignment of a product to one or more categories. Categories can belong to a hierarchy. For example, a product belongs to the luxury car category, which in turn belongs to the car category, which in turn belongs to the automotive category, and so on. There are over 20 different hierarchies in our business.

Employee Association. The unique identifier for the manager of the employee.

Account Type Code. The code for the kind of account we use to handle customer interactions, including general ledger, accounts receivable, and accounts payable.

Validation of Customer Location City Name Definition

Customer Location City Name has a fairly good definition. The only addition I might make is to list some example values, because I am using synonyms in the first sentence and I want to make sure I am not restating the obvious. What I also like about this definition is that it provides the added piece of knowledge that this represents the primary residence of the customer. I would also be slightly concerned as to the scope of this definition. It appears it is just a United States and not a global term, and when we validate against the enterprise definition hopefully it will provide insight as to whether we need a more generic name for a city that can be used globally instead.

Validation of Product Classification Description Definition

Product Classification Description appears to have the same definition as its entity. Because the first sentence appears as a restatement of the obvious, we need good and easily understood examples to shed more light on this term. Let's follow the outline for the Production Classification entity from the previous example: Here is an updated definition:

The full description of the assignment of a product to one or more categories. Categories can belong to other hierarchies. There are over 20 different hierarchies in our business.
    Examples:
    Automobile
        Luxury Car
            Luxury Car Convertible
                BigBucks400 Convertible

Table 3.3 Filled-In Data Element Definition Checklist

CRITERIA	CUSTOMER LOCATION CITY NAME	PRODUCT CLASSIFICATION DESCRIPTION	EMPLOYEE ASSOCIATION WORKS FOR IDENTIFIER	ACCOUNT TYPE CODE
Clarity				
Not a restatement of the obvious	X			X
No obscure technical terminology	X	X	X	X
Only widely understood abbreviations	X	X	X	X
No ego-building words	X	X	X	X
Completeness				
Not too generic	X	X	X	X
Not too specific	X	X	X	X
Stands alone	X	X	X	X
Has derivation if applicable				
Has examples		X		
Accuracy				
Approval by data quality steward	X	X	X	X
Consistent with the enterprise	X	X	X	X
Punctuation				
Spellcheck	X	X	X	X
Good grammar	X	X	X	X
Length				
Not too long	X	X	X	X
Not too short	X	X	X	X

Note that we are repeating the examples and some of the phrases from the entity this data element belongs to but are not redefining any terms. This is an important distinction. Using the same examples and phrases increases consistency across definitions. However, repeating term definitions causes redundancy and a restatement of the obvious.

Validation of Employee Association Works for Identifier Definition

I do consider the Employee Association Works for Identifier definition to be a restatement of the obvious. After all, "works for" and "manager" appear to be very close, and "identifier" is used both in the term and definition. If I cannot think of another way to phrase the definition so that it is not a restatement of the obvious, I will need to do as we have seen before and add examples to clarify the term. Here is how I would update the definition:

> *Employee Association Works for Identifier—The unique identifier for the employee's manager. For example, Bob works for John and therefore this value would contain John's unique identifier.*

Validation of Account Type Code Definition

I like the definition for Account Type Code. My only recommendation would be to list all of the values up to the first 20. This is a code, and previously we discussed the importance of listing many if not all of the values for each code. Updating this definition we have:

> *The code for the kind of account we use to handle customer interactions.*
> *Examples:*
>   - *GL = general ledger*
>   - *AR = accounts receivable*
>   - *AP = accounts payable*

Summary

This chapter discussed a tool called the Definition Checklist, which contains criteria to ensure each definition is of the highest quality and consistency within your company. These criteria fit into five categories: Clarity, Completeness, Accuracy, Punctuation, and Length. This tool built on the Meta Data Bingo game in the previous chapter. Meta Data Bingo identified the types of meta data that are important to capture. This chapter identified the measurements of quality required for one of the most important types of meta data, the definition. Now that we have built a foundation on identifying the types of meta data and the criteria that categorize a high-quality definition, we can discuss the actual project deliverables in Chapter 4, "Project Planning for the Data Modeler."

CHAPTER 4

Project Planning for the Data Modeler

W eekends are so important. After working hard for 5 days, we have 2 days off to recover, run errands, relax, celebrate, and prepare for the upcoming week. Therefore, we need to make the most of this valuable time. I usually list my planned weekend activities in a spreadsheet, an example being shown in Table 4.1.

Planning my weekend with this spreadsheet allows me to allocate time on Saturday during the day to cut the grass and pick up mulch, and to spend some time on Sunday evening surfing the Internet. This helps me make the most of my time during the weekend, and helps prevent me from getting diverted onto unplanned and less important activities. This weekend planning approach is very similar to our project planning approach. We need spreadsheets and other planning tools to make the most of the data modeling effort dedicated to a project.

About This Chapter

One of my first big data modeling assignments was a complete disaster. The project took twice as long as originally intended; cost more than double the original estimate; and with all this extra effort and money, still did not meet the users' needs. What caused this to occur? After much thought, I attribute it to the lack of planning. There was no real project plan. As the data modeler for this project, I constantly found myself in one of two modes: either working intensely to complete a task in an unrealistic timeframe, or not working at all for huge gaps of time. I became increasingly aware of very interesting working patterns among the team. For example, developers were happily coding while I was working on the data model. When I updated the data model, they had to change their code. They were not happy for very long. I was working on the logical data model, while the functional analyst was updating the functional requirements document. When the functional requirements document changed, I had to update my data model. I was not happy either.

Table 4.1 Steve's Weekend Plan

	FRIDAY	SATURDAY	SUNDAY
Day	• Work • Unwind—go for a jog	• Go to a few tag sales • Cut grass • Pick up mulch	• Sleep late • Go for a short hike, maybe Delaware Water Gap
Evening	• Dinner at local restaurant • See movie or rent video	• Take dog for nice long walk • Alicia and Jon coming over for barbeque	• Eat at home • Prepare for upcoming week • Surf net

You can see the problems here. There was no project plan and no defined deliverables, with dependencies and timelines. Even with a technically skilled group of individuals, we still failed because of inadequate planning. I get frustrated even to this day when I think of this project. This failure could have been avoided had more time been put into planning and estimating tasks. A project plan would have taken a relatively small amount of time to create and led to a much more efficient use of time and money. If I had a time machine, I would read this chapter thoroughly and then go back to the beginning of this project. I would make sure my data modeling deliverables were defined in the context of project deliverables, with an agreed-on timeline and sequence of tasks. I would work closely with the project manager to make sure dates and dependencies within the entire project plan were followed and enforced. The tools discussed in this chapter can help us avoid these poorly planned situations.

This chapter includes four project planning tools that contain the complete and sequential set of tasks required to successfully finish data modeling deliverables in a realistic timeframe. These tools are designed so that you can provide the project manager with a detailed and proven set of data modeling tasks with well-defined dependencies. Detailed, proven, and well-defined dependencies are the key words. By detailed we mean that you can capture each and every modeling task that needs to be performed for the specific project. If the project manager prefers to see only a high-level set of tasks, he or she can view just the high-level data modeling phases. By proven we mean that these tasks have been used successfully over and over again on many different types of projects. By well-defined dependencies we mean that certain tasks cannot be started until others are finished. For example, you would not want to start the logical data modeling phase without completing the logical data analysis phase.

This chapter has two main goals:

To describe the four tools that define the data modeling phases, tasks, tools, and timelines. Phases contain tasks, which can be completed with a number of useful tools. Phases and tasks have dependencies and an order in which they must occur. Tasks take varying amounts of effort to complete, and it is important to accurately gauge the amount of time required. An understanding of the phases, tasks, tools, and timelines will help ensure that you do not find yourself in the same unfortunate situation as I was in the previous story. The four tools presented in this chapter will help with the planning, dependencies, and durations for the data modeling deliverables.

To provide a context for the rest of the book. This chapter presents the order and a brief description for the phases, tasks, and tools you will read about in the remaining chapters. You can view this chapter almost as a detailed table of contents or compass for the rest of the book. Every data modeling tool will fit within a task in the tools in this chapter. The remaining chapters appear sequentially according to when they should occur as mentioned in these tools.

These tools are designed to meet the needs of every project. Each project has some variations based on the types of project and department or company sponsoring it. Be flexible and know when to customize these tools for your specific purposes.

Two categories contain most of the projects we work on: new applications and enhancements to existing applications:

Examples of new applications follow:

- Custom-built operational application
- Brand new data mart
- New packaged software application

Examples of enhancements to existing applications follow:

- New functionality to an existing operational application
- New functionality to an existing data mart
- Enhancement to an existing data warehouse architecture

Each of these types of projects might contain all of the high-level data modeling phases mentioned in this chapter and, perhaps, all of the detailed tasks as well. More than likely, however, some of the detailed tasks will vary. For example, data mart and data warehouse applications require a report analysis step that is not required for other types of applications. These variations are mentioned when discussing the tasks in this chapter. We will also go through several detailed examples, showing how the tools can be applied to the two previously mentioned categories.

Variations within companies or departments cannot all be accounted for in this chapter. For example, some of us have enterprise data models and some do not. Having an enterprise data model will no doubt lead to an additional task in the project plan of conforming the project data models into the enterprise. Some of us might perform this integration to the enterprise data model at the subject area or logical levels of detail, depending on the level of detail that exists in the enterprise data model. Another variation is the use of standards. Some of us have very rigorous naming standards, and some do not. If you do, you might need to add tasks or expand existing steps accordingly. Sometimes, for example, I will create an unstandardized model followed by a standardized model, depending on data administration practices. You can see that there are too many variations to mention them all in this chapter.

TIP

Customize these project planning tools for your own needs. There are variations in data modeling standards and practices within industries, organizations, and departments.

There are four project planning tools reviewed in this chapter that will be discussed, in the following order:

Data Modeling Phase Tool. The data modeler starts with the Data Modeling Phase Tool. This tool fits the data modeling phases in the context of the rest of the detailed project plan. For example, subject area modeling occurs during the business requirements section of the project. This tool also helps ensure that all data modeling phases are accounted for, not just the logical or physical ones. In addition, this tool provides a reference from which each of the tools within the chapters can be discussed in the order in which they occur. For example, it lists Chapter 5, "Subject Area Analysis," as the chapter where you can learn more about subject area modeling.

Phase-to-Task-to-Tools. After completing the Data Modeling Phase Tool, each of these phases is then broken down into the relevant tasks described in the Phase-to-Task-to-Tools. For each task, the relevant tools within this book are listed along with their chapters. In this way you can create a detailed project plan and know where to look to make each of the tasks go more quickly and with greater efficiency and consistency. In some cases, the task level of detail will not be required from the project manager; that is, the project manager might only want to see your plan at the phase level. Regardless, always keep track of your progress at the task level.

Priorities Triangle. The Priorities Triangle demonstrates, through a diagram, that you cannot have it all. You can pick a maximum of two out of three:

- Very high quality
- Minimum amount of time
- Minimum cost

You can never have all three. This tool makes it easy to picture the three options and helps describe the tradeoffs among these three. This realization can be applied to your data modeling tasks and the project as a whole. Make sure that the two being followed for the data modeling tasks are the same being followed for the project as a whole.

Good Guess Estimating Tool. The Good Guess Estimating Tool has two sections. The Subject Area Effort Range identifies which percentage of the entire project the data modeling phase should consume based on the type of application. The Task Effort Tool takes each of the tasks identified in Phase-to-Task-to-Tools and lists which percentage they should be of the entire set of data model deliverables. The combination of these two sections will allow you some degree of contingency, with it providing a reasonable estimate to the project manager.

There are times when even if the correct tasks are identified, incorrect timelines and estimates are given. This leads to the potential for missed deliverables or a lot of overtime. This tool can calculate how much time the tasks should take. If there is a relevant discrepancy between what the tool recommends and what the project manager expects, a meeting fairly quickly is in order. In this way expectations will be realistic from the inception of the project.

This chapter goes into two detailed examples on applying the Good Guess Estimating Tool. The first is a new data mart, which also involves making changes to the data warehouse architecture to support this data mart. This example demonstrates both a new application, which is the data mart, and an enhancement, which are the updates required to the architecture to support this data mart. The second example is an enhancement that needs to be made to a custom-built operational application. This example demonstrates when only a system enhancement is required.

If you visit the companion Web site, www.wiley.com/compbooks/hoberman, you will find blank templates for the tools in this chapter; additional tools; and more information about tools within this book, including empty templates that you can download.

What Is the Data Modeling Phase Tool?

You have been assigned to be the data modeler for a project, which has just been approved by senior management and is now ready to be allocated funds. The project manager would like to know what your involvement is going to be during each phase of the project. She is not as much interested in your deliverables at this point. That will come in the next iteration. She first wants to understand the high-level data modeling phases. You need to provide her with a comparison of where your work fits into the context of each software development life cycle phase.

The Data Modeling Phase Tool presents at a high level each of the data modeling steps and where they fit into the software development life cycle. It provides a number of benefits:

Assigns data modeling deliverables to sections of the project plan. Too often, we focus on looking for sections in the project plan where we can put or hide the logical and physical data model deliverables. In reality, there are many other steps in which the data modeler is involved. Each is part of a phase, and each phase has its role in the life cycle. For example, subject area analysis and subject area modeling are the data modeling phases that fit within the business requirements section of the project.

Offers a communication medium with the project manager. This tool can be reviewed with the project manager during the development of the project plan. In the opening story to this section, you can use this tool to meet with the project manager and help her understand where the data modeling phases fit within her project.

Provides context for many of the tools within this book. Each phase in this tool corresponds with one or more chapters of this book. It is a very good way to understand how the different sections of the book relate to each other. For example, this tool documents that subject area analysis is discussed in Chapter 5, "Subject Area Analysis," and subject area modeling is discussed in Chapter 6, "Subject Area Modeling."

Becomes the starting point for the Phase-to-Task-to-Tools. The Phase-to-Task-to-Tools takes each of the phases in the Data Modeling Phase Tool and breaks them down into more detailed tasks. For example, subject area modeling is broken down into creating the Business Clean Slate, Application Clean Slate, and Early Reality Check data models.

Using the Data Modeling Phase Tool

The Data Modeling Phase Tool is divided into project sections with the corresponding data modeling phase. Table 4.2 is this tool with a description of each phase and the chapter(s) where the topic is covered.

Project Definition

The project definition includes everything in terms of project justification and scope. Why are we doing this project? What benefits do we expect from this application? Justification usually takes the form of a Request for Funding, or similar document, designed for management to agree on the value of this project. The *scope* is how this project fits in with other development efforts and existing applications. Much of this information usually is a guess at this point because complete subject area analysis has not been done yet, and therefore, the subject areas of the project have not been validated. There are times when this phase is not considered to be complete until part of the Subject Area Analysis phase is completed so that we know the subject areas and how they will be impacted by this project.

Table 4.2 Data Modeling Phase Tool

PHASE	PROJECT	DATA MODELING	CHAPTER(S)
I	Project Definition		
II	Project Planning	Project Planning for Data Modeling Deliverables	4
III	Business Requirements	Subject Area Analysis	5
		Subject Area Modeling	6
IV	Functional Requirements	Logical Data Analysis	7
		Logical Data Modeling	8,9,10
V	Technical Requirements	Physical Data Modeling	8,10
VI	Development	Data Model Maintenance	
VII	Testing	Data Model Maintenance	
VIII	Rollout and Training		
IX	Maintenance		

Project Planning

Project planning includes identifying the resources, tasks, and timeline to complete the project. Resources include the people and departments assigned to this project, along with the necessary funding. Steps include the tasks required to complete the project, including identifying task dependencies. The timeline includes the effort and duration to complete the tasks in a timely and high-quality manner. Project planning is not something that happens once and is finalized and never changed. Rather, it is defined at the beginning of the project and is constantly being monitored and revisited throughout the life cycle. By the end of this chapter, you should have a good idea of the data modeling tasks required in the plan, their dependencies, and how much effort they require, depending on the type of project.

Business Requirements

Business requirements include identifying how the business operates and the problems currently facing the business or department that this new application will hopefully solve. For example, a business requirements document might describe the current logistics or inventory subject area and identify the areas prioritized for improvement. An example of such an area might be a very manually intensive process for monitoring inventory. Here is an example of what a paragraph from a business requirements document might look like:

> The consumer contacts our department either by phone or email. If the consumer contacts us by phone, one of our representatives will answer the call. The representative quickly needs to determine whether this call is a complaint or a compliment. If the caller is complaining about something, the representative must get the caller's complete address and phone number. This information is vital for following up with or sending the caller something in the mail to satisfy the caller. Next, the representative should identify what he or she believes will satisfy the customer, whether free coupons, a letter back from a manager, or something else.

For data model deliverables, business requirements correspond with the subject area analysis (Chapter 5, "Subject Area Analysis") and modeling phases (Chapter 6, "Subject Area Modeling").

Subject Area Analysis

The subject area analysis phase includes all of the analysis in identifying the subject area data requirements. Subject areas are concepts that are both basic and critical to your business. Examples include Customer, Account, Supplier, Employee, and so on. The data modeler needs to capture relevant subject area information during this phase, including:

- The complete list of subject areas for the application, including subject area definitions

- The source systems that contain each subject area

- The resources, including the people and documentation, that have information on each subject area

■ The reporting levels required for each subject area (if this is a reporting application, such as a data mart)

Subject Area Modeling

The subject area modeling phase includes the actual modeling of subject areas and the relationships that exist between them. This phase helps with a high-level understanding of the application and sets the stage for more detailed design during the functional and technical phases. Subject area modeling is heavily dependent on the findings from the Subject Area Analysis phase. Several different types of subject area models required will be discussed:

■ Business Clean Slate

■ Application Clean Slate

■ Early Reality Check

Functional Requirements

This phase includes all of the tasks that transform the business requirements into application-specific requirements. Functional requirements include the data requirements and process functionality for the application. For example, data flow diagrams and, yes, logical data models!

> *The consumer contacts our department either by phone or email. If the consumer contacts us by phone, one of our representatives will answer the call. The first option presented to the representative on the application screen will be to select whether the incoming call is a complaint or compliment. If the representative clicks on complaint, the next screen that pops up will have a place to enter the caller's complete address along with up to two phone numbers. Under the contact information is a free form text field that the representative should use to capture what he or she thinks will satisfy the irate consumer, whether free coupons, a letter back from a manager, or something else.*

For data model deliverables, functional requirements correspond with the logical data analysis (Chapter 7, "Logical Data Analysis,") and modeling phases (Chapter 8, "The Normalization Hike and Denormalization Survival Guide," Chapter 9, "The Abstraction Safety Guide and Components," and Chapter 10, "Data Model Beauty Tips").

Logical Data Analysis

The logical data analysis phase includes all of the work in identifying the detailed data requirements:

■ The complete list of data elements for the application and their definitions

■ The source and transformations for each data element

■ The reporting levels for each measurement (if this is a reporting application, such as a data mart)

■ The data quality of each data element

If a data element is identified during this phase, it will be in the resulting application.

Likewise, if a data element is not included, it will not be in the resulting application. Many user interviews happen during this phase.

Logical Data Modeling

The logical data modeling phase is creating the actual normalized data model based on the data elements identified during the analysis phase. This includes not just the normalization process (Chapter 8), but also abstraction (Chapter 9) and the correct organization and arrangement of the data model (Chapter 10).

Technical Requirements

The technical requirements phase includes all of the tasks that transform the functional requirements into physical database and development requirements. Technical requirements are the "How." How will this application be implemented? For example, the functional requirements would describe a report and the technical requirements would describe how the report will be generated.

> *After the representative logs in through the password screen, create a new record in the CONTACT database table and show the complaint/compliment indicator field from this table to the user. Use the functionality in the reporting tool to display this field in the clickbox style, where a 1 will be stored in this field in the representative clicks Complaint, and a 0 will be stored in this field in the representative clicks Compliment. If the user selects Complaint, create a new record in the CONSUMER table and display the consumer address and phone number fields on the next screen. Also display the free form text field from the CONTACT table that the representative should use to capture what he or she thinks will satisfy the irate consumer, whether free coupons, a letter back from a manager, or something else.*

Physical Data Modeling

The physical data modeling phase is creating the actual denormalized physical data model based on the data elements identified during the logical phase. This includes not just the denormalization process (Chapter 8) but also abstraction (Chapter 9) and the correct organization and arrangement of the data model (Chapter 10).

Development

The development phase is the actual implementation of the database and code. Tables are generated from the physical data model and reports, and screens are developed. For data warehouse projects, Extract, Transform, and Load tools are used to develop source-to-target mappings. Source system interfaces and transformations are implemented.

Data Model Maintenance

In data model maintenance the data modeler plays a reactive mode, responding to questions from the developers or making design changes to the physical (and, therefore, possibly the logical and subject area) models based on performance issues. This can include additional indexing, denormalization, summarization, and so on.

Testing

Testing includes several different types of testing, including unit, system, and user acceptance testing. *Unit testing* is when each individual development component is tested separately for technical accuracy. Technical accuracy translates into making sure the values that appear are consistent with what should appear. That is, the code appears to work for a subset of the development, such as a particular dimension or fact table. *System testing* includes putting together the development components to see if the entire application, or a large portion of the application, functions according to the technical specifications. *User acceptance testing* is when the business and functional people view the data in the resulting application to determine if it is consistent with the data they were expecting.

Data Model Maintenance

The data modeler also plays a reactive mode in data model maintenance. If something unusual in the data comes up during this phase, the data modeler might be required to change the models. Users also might need an overview of their design at this point. This overview usually is done when the users are fairly technically oriented or not afraid to learn the technical details of the model.

Rollout and Training

Rollout and training include everything to get the new application on the machines of the users and to have them productively using the application. There is both a technical and people component to this task. The technical component includes the most efficient architecture for getting the application on the machines of the users. Examples of media include Web, CD, and mass transmission. The people component involves showing the users how to utilize the application and usually consists of several day-long training sessions on the new application.

Maintenance

Maintenance includes the ongoing support and enhancements to the application. Resources usually are budgeted to bring up the application if it crashes and for routine maintenance, such as backup and index rebuilding. The data modeler usually will get involved if another phase of the project is considered. There usually are no major model changes here, unless driven by new requirements. A minor modeling change could be the addition of new indexes based on monitoring the actions of the user with the application.

What Is the Phase-to-Task-to-Tools?

Now that you have provided the high-level data modeling phases to the project manager, the next step is to plan the more detailed tasks within each phase. These tasks are either analysis or modeling tasks. Some tasks produce data models, whereas other tasks produce documents to aid the data modeling tasks. An example would be identifying your subject areas (analysis) to complete the task of subject area model design (data modeling). Some of these tasks will never be seen by anyone outside of data administration or the data modeling group.

The Phase-to-Task-to-Tools presents the detailed tasks required within each data modeling phase, along with the tools that can help assist with each of these tasks. It provides a number of benefits:

Documenting the detailed modeling tasks. All of the tasks required to complete the data modeling deliverables are presented and described. Each task is part of a tightly designed sequence that needs to be followed. You need to completely identify the data elements and their definitions before creating the logical data model. The tasks within this tool can be inserted directly into a project plan or just used to manage your own modeling progress.

Referencing the tools to assist with each modeling task. To make each task go more smoothly, tools are referenced at a high level in this tool and described in more detail in other parts of this book. The chapters containing each tool are provided for easy reference. For example, the Data Element Family Tree in Chapter 7, can assist with the task of identifying the data element sources, transformations, and definitions.

Using the Phase-to-Task-to-Tools

An example of the Phase-to-Task-to-Tools template is shown in Table 4.3.

Each of these tasks is described in the following sections, along with the tools to make the tasks go more smoothly and more quickly. Please refer to the specific chapters mentioned previously for each task for more detailed information. I will briefly describe each tool in a few sentences and show an example in this chapter; however, I will give detailed explanation in the appropriate chapter of the book.

Project Planning

The project planning phase contains the tasks for developing the data model project plan and arriving at a good estimate of how long the tasks will take.

Create Data Modeling Project Task List

The data modeling project task list is one of the main purposes of this chapter. There are two levels of detail to this effort. The first purpose is to create the high-level list of data modeling phases required during the project. The second purpose is to take each phase down to the detail of the individual tasks that need to be completed. For example, the Subject Area Analysis phase consists of several smaller tasks, including identifying the subject areas affected by the application. By the end of this task you should have a complete list of steps for your project and know the order in which these steps need to take place. Remember to be flexible and customize the steps shown previously according to your specific company or project needs.

Table 4.3 Phase-to-Task-to-Tools

TASK NO.	DATA MODEL PHASE	TASKS	TOOLS	CHAPTER
1.	Project Planning	Create data modeling project task list	Data Modeling Phase Tool Phase-to-Task-to-Tools	4
2.		Create data modeling estimates for project plan	Priorities Triangle Good Guess Estimating Tool, including Subject Area Effort Range and Task Effort Tool	4
3.	Subject Area Analysis	Identify subject areas affected by application	Subject Area Checklist	5
4.		Identify fit with existing applications	Application Subject Area CRUD Matrix	5
5.		Identify resources for each subject area	In-the-Know Template	5
6.		Identify subject area sources and definitions	Subject Area Family Tree	5
7.		Identify levels of reporting by subject area (for reporting applications only)	Subject Area Grain Matrix	5
8.	Subject Area Modeling	Create Business Clean Slate	Business Clean Slate	6
9.		Create Application Clean Slate	Application Clean Slate	6
10.		Create Early Reality Check	Early Reality Check	6
11.	Logical Data Analysis	Identify data element sources, transformations, and definitions	Data Element Family Tree	7
12.		Identify the fact levels of reporting (for reporting applications only)	Data Element Grain Matrix	7
13.		Check the data	Data Quality Capture Template Data Quality Validation Template	7
14.	Logical Data Modeling	Create a normalized logical data model	Normalization Hike	8
15.		Apply abstraction	Abstraction Safety Guide Abstraction Components	9

Table 4.3 *(Continued)*

TASK NO.	DATA MODEL PHASE	TASKS	TOOLS	CHAPTER
16.		Appropriately arrange logical data model	Logical Data Element Sequence Tips Entity Layout Tips Relationship Layout Tips Attention-Getting Tips	10
17.	Physical Data Modeling	Denormalize the logical into a physical design	Denormalization Survival Guide	8
18.		Appropriately arrange physical data model	Physical Data Element Sequence Tips	10

Tools to Help with This Task

The two tools to help with this task are the Data Modeling Phase Tool and the Phase-to-Task-to-Tools, which represent a large portion of this chapter. The Data Modeling Phase Tool is a handy list of the data modeling phases and how they correspond with the life cycle phases during project development. The Phase-to-Task-to-Tools describes the tasks and tools associated with each phase.

Create Data Modeling Estimates for Project Plan

The chapter on creating data modeling estimates is also about the estimating approach. How long will each task take? This can be a very tricky task because there is a high probability that the project manager, and other individuals with a stake in the cost and overall timeline of the project, might try to influence you. Focus on the facts, and come up with a reasonable effort based on your experience and the tools provided in this chapter. Keep in mind that in many cases your estimate will have to be changed, most likely to fewer days. Thus, in coming up with this estimate, also keep in the back of your mind where you might be able to cut corners without much sacrifice to save time. Very rarely is the first estimate the only one. Be flexible without compromising your deliverables.

Tools to Help with This Task

This section on tools to help with this task has two tools to help with estimating: the Priorities Triangle and Good Guess Estimating Tool. Each depends heavily on the Data Modeling Phase Tool and the Phase-to-Task-to-Tools. The Priorities Triangle basically says that you can never have all three: very high quality, minimum amount of time, and minimum cost. At least one will need to be sacrificed. For example, if you want your project done in very little time and costing very little money, the end result usually will be very little quality.

The Good Guess Estimating Tool contains two smaller tools: the Subject Area Effort Range and Task Effort Tool. The Subject Area Effort Range provides the short, long, and average length of time it would take to complete a subject area in days. What is meant by short, long, and average is determined mainly by how much high-quality information is provided to the data modeler and how experienced the entire project team is, including the data modeler. If you are new to estimating or are not sure of the quality of information available for the project, always err on the side of caution. This translates into selecting an average-to-high amount of time for the subject area. Examples of subject areas are Customer, Account, Product, and so on. The Task Effort Tool takes the tasks we have come up with and assigns each a percentage. Multiplying the number of days per subject area by task percentage gives us the amount of time in days to complete the task by subject area. If we are requested to provide effort at the project level instead of the subject area level, then simply get a total number of days for all subject areas (sum up all subject areas) and multiply by the percentage for each task. We will go through an example of applying these formulas shortly.

Subject Area Analysis

The subject area analysis phase contains all of the tasks at the subject area level of detail.

Identify Subject Areas Affected by Application

The first step in starting the subject area analysis is to generate a list of the subject areas that are required for your project, including names and definitions. You need to get agreement and commitment on what each subject area means before data requirements work can get to any level of detail. Also, make sure you are using the appropriate names for each subject area. For example, if the business refers to a Customer as a Client, use Client as the name for this subject area. For this reason, you might break down this task into two smaller tasks: first identify the subject areas based on the terminology of the user and then translate the project-specific subject area names and definitions into corporatewide standards.

Tools to Help with This Task

The Subject Area Checklist provides a starting point to generate the list of subject areas you need for your subject area model. If you do not have much information to start with, or need to encourage project and business teams to get out from the weeds (meaning they are talking at too detailed a level for this point in the project), this tool provides a list of subject areas with generic definitions as your starting point. Work with the team to choose from this list those subject areas relevant to the project. If the resources you are working with disagree with a name or a definition, that is good. This list of subject areas and definitions is provided as a starting point for discussion. Disagreements are good. Document any differences between what the resources say it should be and the standard definition, and work with experts in the subject area to agree on the correct definition or name. There could even be more than one definition for the same name, which means choosing the right definition or selecting pieces from each could be a daunting task.

Compare the names captured on this checklist with your preferred or standardized company names. Make sure you use the right names on this checklist. Doing so means that you are consistent with your department or company and that you will be consistent with the business in future, more detailed phases.

Table 4.4 contains a sample Subject Area Checklist. To learn more about this tool refer to Chapter 5, "Subject Area Analysis."

Identify Fit with Existing Applications

How do the subject areas identified up to this point fit in with the rest of the applications in your company? Or, on an even smaller scale, how do the subject areas identified for this project compare with other data mart developments (if this is a data mart development effort), or with packaged or customized operational applications? You need to identify at a subject area level the gaps that this application will fill. For example, if there are currently no data marts that report on logistics and your data mart will report on logistics, then this is a gap that can be filled. In contrast, this task could identify a strong redundancy with other applications, causing the scope of the application to change or accept the redundancy. It also could mean the end to this project. This is a critical task. It can be accomplished just as effectively by referring to a company's enterprise data model, which we may need to first create if we do not already have one that is up-to-date.

Tools to Help with This Task

The Application Subject Area CRUD Matrix shows the applications as rows and the subject areas as columns. A filled-in cell tells us that this particular application either creates, reads, updates, or deletes information in this subject area. Table 4.5 is one example of what a simple implementation of this tool looks like. Chapter 5, "Subject Area Analysis," goes into detail about this tool.

Identify Resources for Each Subject Area

Once the subject areas are completely identified, and each has an agreed-on definition or well-documented definitions that have not been agreed on, you need to know where to look or with whom to speak to get more detailed information on a subject area. For example, if customer will be within your application scope, who from the business side in your organization is the expert on customer? Is there any valuable documentation on customer reference data? You also will need to be able to show management where gaps exist, that is, where there are no resources or documentation. It is exceptionally good to identify gaps at this early stage, because there is still time to find somebody or locate that folder of useful documentation. If there is no person or documentation available for a subject area, this is the time to raise a red flag. Use the Subject Area Checklist as your list of subject areas in which to identify the experts.

Table 4.4 Subject Area Checklist

NAME	SYNONYMS OR INDUSTRY-SPECIFIC TERMS	DEFINITION	QUESTIONS
Account	General ledger account, accounts receivable, expense account	Structure to facilitate the financial transactions carried out by the company. A formal banking, brokerage, or business relationship established to provide for regular services and financial transactions.	Can an account exist without an owner? What uniquely identifies an account? Can an account have more than one owner? These questions will be answered during the subject area modeling phase when we are trying to understand the business rules between the subject areas. However, I have found that account and owner are usually so intertwined that, in many cases, they might be considered the same concept. Understanding their relationship at this point can help you come up with a solid definition.
Asset	Machine, part, capital, stock, wealth, supply	Something our company owns that is considered valuable.	Does this also include purchases we plan on making for the upcoming year? A question such as this adds the element of a life cycle into these definitions. It is really asking how broad we want to go with this definition. Does it include past, present, and future assets, or only present assets? You can ask questions such as this for each of these subject areas. It will help you refine the definition and possibly introduce new subject areas that were originally overlooked. Is rented and leased equipment considered assets? This question tests the scope of the definition.
Associate	Employee, worker	A person employed in a full- or part-time capacity by our company to perform a service or function for our company.	Clearly distinguish the rules that differentiate an associate and contractor. There is usually a fine line between the concepts of employee and contractor. Make sure you have documented this fine line.

Table 4.5 Application Subject Area CRUD Matrix

SUBJECT AREAS	YOUR NEW DATA MART	CUSTOMER REFERENCE DATABASE	XYZ APPLICATION	DATA WAREHOUSE
CUSTOMER	R	C	C	R
ITEM	R		C	
ORDER	R		C	
ASSOCIATE	R			R

Tools to Help with This Task

The In-the-Know Template captures the people, documentation, and reports that can provide and validate the data requirements. This tool is great for finding gaps or redundancies in your resources. It also can be used as a document that is signed off on by management. Therefore, if a person is identified as a resource for a particular subject area, his or her management can be aware and allocate the person's time accordingly. In this way you will minimize the chances that your customer expert is pulled in another direction when you need that person to help you. Chapter 5, "Subject Area Analysis," goes into detail about this tool. Table 4.6 is a sample of the In-the-Know Template.

Identify Subject Area Sources and Definitions

If the application you are modeling is going to require information from other systems, you will need to identify those sources, even if you are designing a data mart that is part of a data warehouse architecture and supposedly getting all of its information

Table 4.6 In-the-Know Template

SUBJECT AREA	RESOURCE	TYPE	ROLE/HOW USED	LOCATION/ CONTACT
Customer	Tom Jones	Subject Matter Expert	Customer Reference Data Administrator	212-555-1212
Customer	Customer classification list	Documentation	To validate and create new customer classifications	S:/customer/custcl sfn.xls
Item	Current Item Report	Report	To identify all current item information	www.item.com

from the data warehouse. At the subject area level of detail, this means you will need to identify the source system for each subject area. This will be very helpful later when you need to identify the sources for each data element. It is rare but possible that the source system at a subject area level will not be the same source as that for one of its data elements. Not all of our applications are scoped by subject areas, and therefore, it is possible for data elements from the same subject area to span applications. Most of the time, however, the subject area source will be equal to the data element source.

Use the Subject Area Checklist as your list to gather sources and definitions. You might already have the appropriate definitions based on how well the Identify Fit with Existing Applications task went. Also, in many cases, the resources identified on the In-the-Know Template would be your contacts to identify the sources. In other words, you can put your resource list to the test starting with this task.

Tools to Help with This Task

The Subject Area Family Tree is a tool that provides the columns to enter the source and definition for each subject area. It helps to rapidly identify the agreed-on source system for each subject area and to set the stage for more detailed data requirements gathering at the data element level. It also includes the agreed-on subject area definitions. It will also help in determining work effort. This task is one of those that, if possible, should be done before finalizing the work estimate, because it can help in determining the complexity of each subject area. Chapter 5, "Subject Area Analysis," goes into detail about this tool. Table 4.7 shows a sample.

Note that you can use this tool to show more than just the immediate source system. If resources permit, you can go all the way back to the strategic source, which is usually somebody typing something in or a transaction generated electronically somewhere. Make sure you do not duplicate the work already done in capturing information for the Application Subject Area CRUD Matrix described earlier. Reuse as much information as possible from the CRUD matrix. Note also the importance of the Questions and Impact column. Even at the subject area level, there can be many questions. They must be answered as soon as possible, because this can affect project scope and avoid rework and more questions later.

Identify Levels of Reporting by Subject Area

Once the subject areas have been identified, sourced, and defined, you will need to determine at a high level how to report on them. This is only for reporting applications, such as data marts. You can examine both the transaction and reference information at the subject area level and note how each transaction subject area needs to be viewed. For example, you might have Customer Sales viewed by Time, Customer, and Company. Note the limited value unless you break down the reference subject areas into levels. For example, you might have Customer Sales viewed by Year, Customer Type, and Sales Organization Level. This provides much more value. If you keep it only at the reference subject area level, probably all of the transaction reference data will need to be reported against at all of the reference subject area levels. Keep in mind that an important factor here is to know not just the lowest level the user would like to see the data but all the levels the user needs. For example, an ad hoc reporting environment would probably require all of the levels of detail in a reference or dimension area. A predefined or canned report may not go down to the lowest level, however, but instead stop at a fairly summarized level.

Tools to Help with This Task

The Subject Area Grain Matrix is a tool for easily capturing and viewing the different levels at which each transaction subject area needs to be reported. It can rapidly identify the levels of reporting for each subject area and help in estimating and scoping a data mart effort. It is flexible enough to handle both ad hoc and canned reporting. There are many situations where you might create more than one Subject Area Grain Matrix for a single project, depending on reporting needs. Chapter 5, "Subject Area Analysis," goes into detail about this tool. Table 4.8 shows a sample.

Subject Area Modeling

The subject area modeling phase contains the tasks for capturing the subject areas for the application in a subject area model, including the relationships that exist between the subject areas.

Create Business Clean Slate

In the Business Clean Slate model, the area you are modeling can be designed in isolation from other applications or business areas. It is a brand new area. You do not need to be concerned with how the major business entities in this model relate to the rest of the company. This is the easier of the two types of models to create and is also the most common subject area model. Most of the time when people use the term subject area model, the Business Clean Slate model is what they are talking about. It can usually be designed using a minimal number of subject experts. Most of the time the actual users of the application being designed will suffice. The Business Clean Slate model can be used for understanding a new business area. It becomes the starting point for the Application Clean Slate.

Tools to Help with This Task

Chapter 6, "Subject Area Modeling," goes into detail about the Business Clean Slate model. A sample is shown in Figure 4.1.

Create Application Clean Slate

In the Application Clean Slate model, the area you are modeling can be designed in isolation from other applications or business areas. It is a brand new area. You do not need to be concerned with how the major business entities in this model relate to the rest of the company. It usually can be scoped from the Business Clean Slate. In some cases, it is as easy as taking a marker and outlining those subject areas on the Business Clean Slate that will be in your application.

Table 4.7 Subject Area Family Tree

FROM HERE				TO HERE				TO ARRIVE HERE		
NAME	SOURCE	DEFINITION	HISTORY	NAME	SOURCE	DEFINITION	HISTORY	NAME	DEFINITION	HISTORY
				Customer	Customer Reference Database	The recipient and purchaser of our products.	10	Customer	The recipient and purchaser of our products.	3
	Order Entry	A contract to buy a quantity of product at a specified price.	4	Transaction	Transaction Integration Application	An individual change or action within our environment.	2	Order	A contract to buy a quantity of product at a specified price.	3
				Item	Item Reference Database	Anything we buy, sell, stock, move, or make. Any manufactured or purchased part, material, component, assembly, or product.	10	Product	Anything we buy, sell, stock, move, or make. Any manufactured or purchased part, material, component, assembly, or product.	3

Term	Source	Definition	
Party	Data Warehouse	A person or company that is important to our business in some way.	5
Time	Data Warehouse	A measurable length of seconds, minutes, hours, days, weeks, months, or years. Can include both fiscal and Julian time measurements.	10
Associate		A person who is employed in a full- or part-time capacity by our company, to perform a service or function to our company.	3
Time		A measurable length of seconds, minutes, hours, days, weeks, months, or years. Can include both fiscal and Julian time measurements.	3

Table 4.8 Subject Area Grain Matrix

SUBJECT AREA	TIME				CUSTOMER		PRODUCT		SALES ORGANIZATION	
	YEAR	QUARTER	MONTH	DAY	CATEGORY	CUSTOMER	BRAND	ITEM	DIVISION	REGION
Shipments	AB	AB	AB	A	AB	A	AB	A		
Debits	A	A	A	A	A	A				
Credits	A	A	A	A	A	A				
Balances	A	A	A	A			A	A		
Production	AC	AC	A	A			AC	AC		
Contact	A	A	A	A	A	A	A	A		

A, ad hoc reporting; B, shipments summary report; C, production summary report

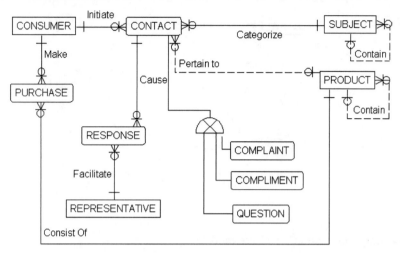

Figure 4.1 Business Clean Slate model.

Tools to Help with This Task

Chapter 6, "Subject Area Modeling," goes into detail about the Application Clean Slate model. Figure 4.2 shows a sample that is a scoped down model of our previous Business Clean Slate.

Create Early Reality Check

This is called the Early Reality Check because it provides an overview on how something new fits in with something existing very early in the development process. This model is concerned with not only modeling the required area but also with how the resulting model fits in with something that already exists, usually something with a much larger scope. I have found this type of subject area model to be the most powerful. I have some great success stories using this type of model. I usually use a color key to differentiate what is new from what already exists. The Early Reality Check model can be used for the following types of applications:

New data mart within current data warehouse architecture. The Early Reality Check will show how the new data mart requirements fit into what currently exists within the data warehouse. I have used this type of model where I color in the major business entities that exist as green, those that exist in some form as yellow, and those that do not exist in the current environment as red. The red ones require the most effort to provide to the new data mart. This provides a great high-level estimate to the project team. The more yellows and reds, the more expensive the project is to develop.

New functionality to an existing operational or data mart application. The Early Reality Check will highlight the new functionality and show how it fits in with current functionality. It is a very good technique for identifying issues and integration challenges very early in the project.

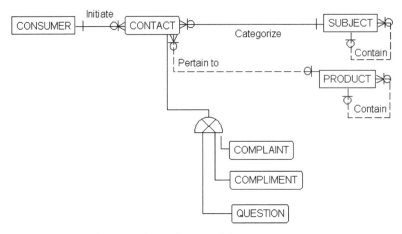

Figure 4.2 Application Clean Slate model.

Customization to a packaged piece of software. More and more we will be implementing packaged software, the most popular being Enterprise Resource Planning (ERP) applications. These expensive and very encompassing pieces of software need to be analyzed (it is hoped before they are purchased!) to see how they fit into the current environment. The Early Reality Check will allow management to see the impact and overlap caused by introducing packaged software.

Tools to Help with This Task

Chapter 6, "Subject Area Modeling," goes into detail about the Early Reality Check model. Figure 4.3 shows an example in which different-sized entities are used. In Chapter 6 you will learn that there are different techniques in addition to color for highlighting overlap between new and existing development.

Logical Data Analysis

The logical data analysis phase is where all of the data elements are fully analyzed in preparation for the logical data model. We have enough knowledge about our application at this point to start identifying and capturing the data elements. Examples of questions we need to answer follow:

- Which data elements do we need?

- What do they mean?

- Where do they come from?

- What reporting levels do they require?

- Do they contain values that are consistent with their meta data?

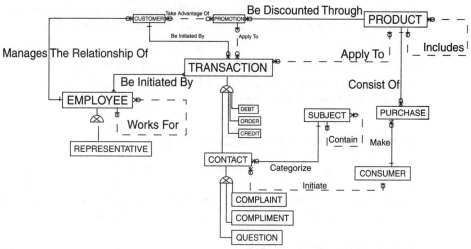

Figure 4.3 Early Reality Check model.

Identify Data Element Sources, Transformations, and Definitions

Just as you did at the subject area level where you identified the source application for each subject area, you need to identify the sources for each data element. This can build on the work you did earlier. Keep in mind that at the data element level there are several more details you need to capture. These include derivations and calculations, if appropriate, especially on data mart fact tables where many facts can be summarized. You need to identify all of your data elements at this point. If you leave a data element out, even a derived data element, there is a good chance that it may not be in your finished application. There are many other types of meta data you should consider when identifying source information, including format, nullability, and definitions. Note that nullability captures whether the data element can be empty (meaning null) or must always be filled in with some value (meaning not null). The Meta Data Bingo tool you used in Chapter 2 will give you a good indicator of what types of meta data you need. The data elements in this task are also good input for your logical data model. You can look at them as the components or building blocks of the data model. You just need to correctly assign each data element to the most appropriate entity based on normalization rules.

Tools to Help with This Task

Just as we had the Subject Area Family Tree, we also have the Data Element Family Tree. It has the same basic structure and purpose but several more columns. Its purpose is to clearly identify and define each data element (including derived data) that will be needed for the project, along with enterprise definitions and source system. It can be built using the Subject Area Family Tree as a starting point. These spreadsheets can get very detailed and complicated, especially if you consider all the types of meta data you might need, such as format, nullability, and so on. Therefore, be selective when choosing the types of meta data you need. Each column you add decreases the font size.

Chapter 7, "Logical Data Analysis," goes into detail about the Data Element Family Tree. Table 4.9 is a simple example of a Data Element Family Tree (more complicated examples are shown in Chapter 7).

Identify the Fact Levels of Reporting

Just as we have identified the subject area levels of reporting for each transaction subject area, we also need to identify the levels of reporting for each fact. For data marts, it is essential that we understand the different levels that exist within each dimension and which ones are required as reporting levels for each fact.

Tools to Help with This Task

The Data Element Grain Matrix captures the levels of reporting for each fact, which will seamlessly translate into an initial data mart design. All of the facts with the same levels of reporting can be grouped together, which gives a very good indicator that these facts will be in the same initial fact table. This will help us validate the decisions made during the Denormalization Survival Guide discussed in Chapter 8 as well as help us determine where we should introduce summary level entities. This tool also provides a common language between business users and the technical project team. Many business users are afraid of or have a lack understanding of data modeling, but everyone can understand a spreadsheet. The Data Element Grain Matrix is built on the Subject Area Grain Matrix.

Chapter 7, "Logical Data Analysis," goes into detail about this tool. Table 4.10 shows a sample.

Check the Data

Many people do not perform this task at this early point during the logical data analysis phase. They wait until they are into development, and when the data found in the tables does not match the meta data on the model, large issues develop. Something has to change when this occurs. The smallest change would be an update to a definition on the model to be consistent with the data. Rarely is this the case. More often, changes are required to data element format, nullability, name, and so on. Not only are updates to the model required because of these change but also changes to database tables and possibly code. The better approach is to examine the data much earlier in the life cycle. An appropriate time to do so is right after identifying the data elements required in the application. Thus, as soon as a data element is identified, look at the data to make sure it is what you think they are. The challenge is that because it is still very early in the development life cycle, it might be difficult to actually get access to the data. It might require being pretty creative to find ways to get to the data so early, such as getting access to the source application or requesting any types of existing source system extract files. However, it will be worth it!

Table 4.9 Data Element Family Tree

	FROM HERE (SOURCE)					TO ARRIVE HERE (TARGET)				
NAME	SOURCE	DEFINITION	FORMAT	NULL ?	TRANSFORMA-TION LOGIC	NAME	DEFINITION	FORMAT	NULL ?	QUESTIONS
		CUSTOMER					**CUSTOMER**			
ID	Customer Reference Database	The unique way to refer to each customer. A customer's ID will never change or be reused.	Number(8)	N	Straight Map	CUST_REF_DB_ID	The unique way to refer to each customer, assigned by the Customer Reference Database application. A customer's ID will never change or be reused.	Number(8)	N	
F-NAME	Customer Reference Database	The first name of the customer. Can be a nickname.	Char(15)	Y	Straight Map	CUST_FRST_NAM	The first name of the customer. Can be a nickname.	Char(20)	Y	
L-NAME	Customer Reference Database	The last name of the customer.	Char(30)	N	Straight Map	CUST_LST_NAM	The last name of the customer.	Char(20)	N	

Table 4.10 Data Element Grain Matrix

DATA	TIME	CUSTOMER			PRODUCT				ASSOCIATE		
ELEMENT		YEAR	MONTH	DAY	CUSTOMER	CATEGORY	BRAND	PRODUCT	DEPARTMENT	ASSOCIATE
Order										
ORD_QUANTITY		AB	AB	A	A	AB	AB	A	A	A
ORD_AMOUNT		AB	AB	A	A	AB	AB	A	A	A
ORD_WEIGHT_POUNDS		AB	AB	A	A	AB	AB	A	A	A
ORD_WEIGHT_TONS		AB	AB	A	A	AB	AB	A	A	A
ORD_WEIGHT_TONNES		AB	AB	A	A	AB	AB	A	A	A

A, ad hoc reporting; B, shipments summary report

Tools to Help with This Task

There are two tools to help in validating the data: the Data Quality Capture Template and Data Quality Validation Template. The first compares the data against the meta data for each data element. It includes documenting nullability, format oversizes, name and actual data consistency, and so on. Someone who does not need to fully understand the data can make comparisons involving nullability and format. For example, if data element A is defined as not null but any of the rows examined is null, we have a problem. Even without a deep understanding of A, we know there is a discrepancy. However, the data element Gross Amount with a value of $5.00 may or may not be correct.

Chapter 7 goes into detail about this tool. Table 4.11 shows a sample.

Many of the comparisons contained on the Data Quality Capture Template need to be validated by an expert in the particular subject area in the Data Quality Validation Template. To find the appropriate expert, refer to the In-the-Know Template. The Data Quality Validation Template is designed for someone to go through and grade the comparison of the data versus the meta data. It allows the subject matter expert to approve those data elements where the data matches the meta data, and, therefore are of high quality, and to resolve data quality issues on the problem data elements. It includes definition, nullability, and format questions that have been identified in the previous spreadsheet. In this way there is documentation from a subject area expert indicating the quality of the data. This will be an extremely useful piece of documentation as the team develops the data mart and will help put minds at ease because seeing surprises in the data will be much less likely. In addition, any problem identified can be addressed quickly and usually without holding up development tasks because the problem has been caught at this early stage in the life cycle. It is a very proactive approach.

Chapter 7 goes into detail about this tool. Table 4.12 shows a sample.

Logical Data Modeling

The logical data modeling phase identifies and represents the relationships between the data elements identified during the logical data analysis phase. The end result is an accurate and flexible logical data model.

Create a Normalized Logical Data Model

Before a set of database tables can be created, there must be a complete understanding of the data elements and their relationships to each other. This translates into maximizing the amount of normalization on the logical data model. The logical data model cannot be considered complete until it is in Fifth Normal Form (5NF). Even star schema data mart designs need to have a 5NF logical data model. We need to follow a process to go from the initial unnormalized collection of data elements to a fully normalized and fully understood structure. Too often we do not normalize to the extent that we should, sometimes stopping this process at Third Normal Form (3NF) or even

Table 4.11 Data Quality Capture Template

	META DATA			RESULTS			
NAME	DEFINITION	FORMAT	NULL	FIRST 10 TO 25 DISTINCT VALUES	PERCENT NULL	MAXIMUM LENGTH	PERCENT FAILED LOOKUPS
CUST_REF_DB_ID	The unique way to refer to each customer, assigned by the Customer Reference Database application. A customer's ID will never change or be reused.	Number(8)	N	12345 39385 38595 37584 38494 38393 30349 94847 18238	0	8	0
CUST_FRST_NAM	The first name of the customer. Can be a nickname.	Char(20)	Y	Jane Emily Lori Gary Serena Stu Sandy Jenn Mitch John	9	10	N/A
CUST_LST_NAM	The last name of the customer.	Char(20)	N	Smith Doe Klein Carter Nixon Reagan Bush Clinton Lincoln Washington	0	20	N/A

Table 4.12 Data Quality Validation Template

META DATA				RESULTS				VALIDATION (Y / N / ?)				
NAME	DEFINITION	FORMAT	NULL	FIRST 10 TO 25 DISTINCT VALUES	PERCENT NULL	MAXIMUM LENGTH	PERCENT FAILED LOOKUPS	MEANING	NULL	LENGTH	LOOKUP	COMMENT
PRO_ITEM_REF_DB_ID	The unique identifier generated for a product.	Char(5)	N	12452 33855 85958 37580 38447 38936 33490 48476 38111	0	5	95	Y	Y	Y	?	Are you sure you are doing the lookup properly? Make sure you ignore the last character on each value in this data element when you do the lookup. This last character means something else. Call me if you need more of an explanation.
PRO_BRAND_CD	The label by which our customers recognize our products.	Char(5)	N	DKDKD EIDMD EIFKF DLFPO DD DKFK DLFKD EIEIE PEOE DKDL	0	5	N/A	Y	Y	Y	Y	
PRO_CTGY_CD	The internal grouping of our brands.	Char(5)	N	A W D Q S U T E S B	0	1	N/A	Y	Y	N	Y	I would like to see this data element defined as a single character. Why waste five characters? This data element will never have values that are longer than a single character.

sooner. However, we need to understand and strive to reach the higher levels of normalization, including Fourth Normal Form (4NF), Boyce/Codd Normal Form (BCNF), and 5NF.

Tools to Help with This Task

The process of normalizing is a quest, a challenging hike that culminates with the completed normalized model. The Normalization Hike is a set of questions and guidelines to help you reach the summit of your hiking adventure. There is a lot of sweat and effort to get to the top; however, once you are there, the view is amazing. It is important to have a consistent and straightforward approach to fully normalize your design. This tool is not the standard set of normalization rules that we see in numerous data modeling texts. We do not include dependency algorithms, mathematical proofs, and the like. Instead, I tried to take the topic of normalization in a slightly different direction. I explain each of the levels of normalization in simple terminology and practical situations instead of mathematical equations and complicated syntax. Also, I have included special tips and guidelines that have assisted me in completing each level. Consider the Normalization Hike the practical approach to normalization. The Normalization Hike is discussed in detail in Chapter 8, "The Normalization Hike and Denormalization Survival Guide." Here are its goals:

To practically explain the levels of normalization. The Normalization Hike provides a less mathematical and theoretical explanation of normalization than your standard book. For example, this tool avoids words such as determinate and join-dependency.

To offer normalization guidelines, tips, and warnings. The hike provides useful pointers for each stage of normalization. For example, looking for data elements that are codes with fairly long lengths can help detect situations where multiple pieces of business information are being stored within the same data element.

To provide the visual. The hike is a progression we go through whenever we do a design. Just as in any long hike with a challenging destination, the more we progress along the trail the greater our understanding and the more sweat and effort go into arriving at the normalized logical design. This visual image is very effective for explaining the value of normalization and the effort that normalization requires. It also is a good visual image to show how sometimes we take shortcuts along the mountain. These shortcuts involve only going up a few levels of normalization before trekking across the mountain and denormalizing. This shortcut on the Normalization Hike shows how much understanding we miss by not normalizing completely up to 5NF.

To be the starting point for the Denormalization Survival Guide. Once we have hiked up to the lookout point and have a fully normalized data model, we need to start working our way down and denormalizing. The Normalization Hike makes sure we have gone up as high as we can go before descending using the Denormalization Survival Guide.

Apply Abstraction

Abstraction is one of the most powerful tools we have as data modelers. A major goal of the finished data model is to have structures that can withstand the changes of time.

We are designing not just for the immediate data requirements but also with an eye on future requirements. We are trying to avoid the situation where the users come back to the project manager shortly after the application goes live and ask for something slightly different that would require a data model, database, and coding changes. Abstraction is very powerful because it adds a layer of flexibility to our models. For example, the concepts of employee, customer, and vendor might all be abstracted into a concept called person. Person could then handle new types of individuals, such as consumer or competitor, with minimal or no design changes. Figure 4.4 shows an example of abstraction that can be used to capture the data requirements for the typical meta data repository. This and many other abstraction examples are discussed in detail in Chapter 9, "The Abstraction Safety Guide and Components."

Tools to Help with This Task

The Abstraction Safety Guide will make sure we apply the appropriate level of abstraction in our design. This safety guide contains three questions that will help us determine where, if at all, we need to abstract on our data models. It helps introduce consistency in deciding where to abstract, makes sure we do not miss any opportunities for abstraction, and helps us avoid overabstraction. Here are the three Abstraction Safety Guide questions that will be discussed in detail in Chapter 9:

1. Does this data element, entity, or relationship have something in common with one or more other data elements, entities, or relationships?

2. If yes, are there concrete situations that would warrant an abstract structure?

3. If yes, is the extra development effort now substantially less than the development effort down the road?

The Abstraction Components Tool is a collection of the most useful abstraction building blocks, which can exist at the entity, relationship, or data element level. For entities, we discuss the six most prevalent abstract entities. For relationships, we discuss the three most powerful abstract relationships. For data elements we discuss the basic building block of any data element: the class word. An example of a relationship abstraction component, called classification, is shown in Figure 4.5.

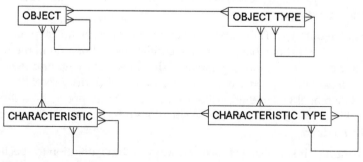

Figure 4.4 Meta data repository abstract data model.

Figure 4.5 Classification abstraction component.

Appropriately Arrange the Logical Data Model

As your logical data modeling phase draws to an end and you are preparing to review and validate the model with the users and project team, you need to make sure the visual appearance of the logical data model is most appropriate for business understanding. For example, in the Customer entity you might want your address data elements immediately below the customer name data elements. You might want the city data element immediately above the state data element and immediately below the address line data element. In this step, you need to apply a set of rules to make sure all the entities, relationships, and data elements are in the best arrangement and layout for user understanding.

Tools to Help with This Task

In Chapter 10, "Data Model Beauty Tips," I discuss in detail four categories of data modeling beauty tips that can improve the appearance and, therefore, the readability of your logical data model. Here is an overview of each of these categories:

Logical Data Element Sequence Tips. These tips propose ordering or sequencing of the data elements within each entity on your logical data model. This sequencing is done to improve the readability and understanding of the data elements within each entity.

Entity Layout Tips. These tips focus on the optimal layout of each of the entities on both the logical and physical data models. This is purely for readability and understanding purposes. It is amazing how much of a difference the positions of the entities on a data model can impact a data model review. When the entities are correctly positioned, a data model review is much easier and more intuitive than if there is no thought given to the placement of the entities. Without focusing on placement, there will be more time spent trying to find entities than trying to understand entities during model reviews. A proper entity layout saves time spent locating entities on the model and can uncover design issues that otherwise would remain hidden.

Relationship Layout Tips. These tips focus on rearranging relationship lines that overlap and relationships that go through entities instead of around them to the entities they connect. Just moving a relationship line slightly up or down on the model can make the difference between confusion and clarity. I recently completed a data model where there were several instances of poorly placed relationships. Luckily, I was able to catch these situations on my model and correct them before the model review.

Attention-Getting Tips. These tips focus on ways to draw attention to specific parts of the logical and physical data models. There are times when we need to highlight data elements, entities, or relationships on our design. Reasons for highlighting might include that we may only want to show a portion of the model that might have outstanding issues or certain reporting needs.

Physical Data Modeling

The physical data modeling phase contains all of the tasks to convert the logical data model into an efficient database design.

Denormalize the Logical into a Physical Design

Once you have the 5NF logical data model, it is now time to brace yourself for the real world. Performance of the relational databases of today is such that the more tables we are joining against, the slower the retrieval speeds. This leads us to denormalization, where we combine the data elements from different normalized entities based on their common retrieval patterns. In this step, we need to make some very difficult yet calculated decisions on what we should denormalize.

Tools to Help with This Task

The Denormalization Survival Guide discussed in detail in Chapter 8, "The Normalization Hike and Denormalization Survival Guide," is a question-and-answer approach to determining where to denormalize your logical data model. The survival guide contains a series of questions in several different categories. These questions need to be asked for each relationship on our model. There are point values associated with answers to each question. By adding up these points, we can determine whether to denormalize each specific relationship. If our score is 10 or higher after summing the individual scores, we will denormalize the relationship. If our score is less than 20, we will keep the relationship normalized and intact. When you are done asking these questions for each relationship, you will have a physical data model at the appropriate level of denormalization.

The questions within the Denormalization Survival Guide belong to several areas that we will review in detail in Chapter 8, including the following:

- Type of relationship
- Participation ratio
- Parent entity size
- Commonality or usage
- Placeholder factor
- Change factor

Appropriately Arrange the Physical Data Model

Your physical data modeling phase is drawing to an end and you are preparing to review the model with the users and project team. You want to make sure that the order of the data elements in each entity is most appropriate for performance and storage. For example, long character strings that are usually null should not be the first data element in your table.

Tools to Help with This Task

Just as we focused on the proper sequence of data elements on the logical data model, we need to have guidelines for the proper sequence of data elements on the physical data model. In Chapter 10, "Data Model Beauty Tips," we have these, including the Physical Data Element Sequence Tips. These tips are less of visual tips and more of memory storage and performance tips. From a physical perspective, ordering the data elements a certain way can potentially save space in the database and reduce data retrieval times. Therefore, we think less about the layout that increases readability and understanding on the physical data model. Instead, we focus more on data element length, nullability, and composite alternate and primary keys. Larger, emptier data elements listed toward the end of each entity can save valuable storage space. Following is the Physical Data Element Sequence discussed in detail in Chapter 10:

1. Primary key

2. Alternate keys

3. Not nulls from shortest to longest

What Is the Priorities Triangle?

> *The project manager has extremely high expectations from you, the data modeler for a highly visible project. She expects the highest quality. You also expect to deliver the highest quality design. However, she also would like your deliverables in a very unrealistic and tight timeframe. As if that were not enough, she also wants the deliverables completed at a minimal cost. Thus, you are required to complete your data modeling work with the highest quality, yet for a minimal amount of time and money. Is this even possible?*

The purpose of the Priorities Triangle is to demonstrate pictorially that you cannot have everything. See Figure 4.6. You can pick a maximum of two out of three:

- Very high quality
- Minimum amount of time
- Minimum cost

This tool makes it easy to picture the three options and helps describe the tradeoffs among them. This realization can be applied to your data modeling tasks as well as the project as a whole. Make sure that the two being followed for the data modeling tasks are the same two being followed for the project as a whole.

Using the Priorities Triangle

Table 4.13 includes descriptions of the different combinations of the triangle and an example of each.

Figure 4.6   Priorities triangle.

Table 4.13 shows each of the possible options in the triangle, along with examples of the types of projects that usually choose the particular option. When deciding which of the three priorities to select, think more about what you lose than what you gain. For example, if you are contemplating high quality for minimal time for your project, think about running over budget or the larger expense of the data modeling effort. Can you afford to spend the extra money? Let's look at each of these options:

High quality and minimal time. This is the most expensive option. The data modeling work must be done correctly and in the least amount of time. This option is very popular for projects that are on the critical path. This means that if several other projects cannot be started until a particular project is completed, it will usually be driven by high quality and minimal time, especially if the content in this project will be used by many other projects. This option also is very effective when you create a high-impact data mart, where the users have the money and just need to access their reporting data as soon as possible. Keep in mind that this is not sacrificing quality. If you just choose minimal time, for example, you will

Table 4.13   Priorities Triangle Uses

OPTION	EXAMPLES OF PROJECTS THAT MAINLY USE THIS OPTION
High quality and minimal time	• Critical path projects • High visibility data marts • Small operational applications • Y2K projects
High quality and minimal cost	• Meta data repository • Standards development
Minimal time and minimal cost	• Prototypes • Proof of concepts

lose quality. Thus, in the long term, the expense will be much greater regarding support costs and loss of credibility than if you had chosen both high quality and minimal time. I worked on a project where time was a prime motivating factor. The quality of the worked suffered and ultimately minimized the usefulness of the project.

TIP

Make sure you select two of three and not just one of three. Selecting just one will cause the other two to be significantly worse than originally planned. For example, just selecting minimal time will mean quality will substantially suffer and the expense will be much higher through support costs and lost credibility.

High quality and minimal cost. This solution will work when you do not have to rush and the attitude is just take your time and get the work done, and make sure you are not wasting money. Long-term projects such as a meta data repository or standards development make the best candidates for this option. Never use this option when time is a major factor, such as in the Y2K effort, where all work needed to be complete by a certain date.

Minimal time and minimal cost. This is also known as the quick and dirty solution. Although you might be thinking that we never, ever want to select this option, it might be most appropriate in certain situations. Prototyping or proof of concept comes to mind. You need to show something quickly to the project team or the users, and therefore, time is of the utmost importance. It can be mentioned that after showing the prototype, substantial work is necessary to improve the quality within the prototype. For example, maybe the prototype is just demonstrating a few of the possible scenarios in the application. The end result must correctly handle all possible scenarios, however, costing more money and time to do the analysis and development.

In selecting one of these options, be very careful to choose the same option you feel the project as a whole has already chosen. Being inconsistent at this point can lead to raising flags about your performance and speed. For example, if in your opinion the project appears to be moving ahead with the theme of minimal time and minimal cost, then your focus on delivering a high-quality data model will be futile. You will be blamed for slowing down the project or increasing the cost. On the plus side, however, being aware that the project implicitly selects one of these three options should increase the chances that you will choose and comply with the preferred option.

TIP

Be aware of the option the project, as a whole, has selected. Even without formally stating an option, be attuned to the culture and atmosphere within the project team and what appears to be driving the team forward. No matter how strong you feel about one of these three options, choose the same option for your data modeling that the project team has chosen for the overall project. Usually the data modeler selects quality over all else, which is not consistent with the project as a whole. This can lead to the data modeling tasks taking up more time and money than the other project phases.

What Is the Good Guess Estimating Tool?

How much effort will the data modeling tasks take? You have identified the tasks and have selected the Priorities Triangle option you believe to be most effective. Now the project manager has asked you this question. You do not know a whole lot about the project at this point. You need to get a more information and apply two tools to give a fairly realistic estimate.

The goal of this tool is provide a good guess-timate of the amount of effort for the data modeling tasks. There is no amount that is accurate all of the time. For example, "The data modeling will take three weeks" should never be a standard response to the request for an estimate. It depends on a number of tasks, including the type of project, how much information is available, and how good it is. These tools should take some of the guesswork out of the process by applying a formal procedure to arriving at an accurate estimate.

TIP

Be aware of the difference between effort and duration. *Effort* is the amount of time it takes to complete the tasks, measured in days or hours. It is usually based on one person performing the work on a full-time basis, that is, one person working 8 hours a day, 5 days a week. *Duration* is how long the project will take, which takes into account factors such as dependencies between tasks, the number of people working on the tasks, other projects going on that will take time away from your tasks, and so on. Effort provides the actual time to complete the tasks, whereas duration provides how long it will actually take to complete the tasks. The Good Guess Estimating Tool focuses on effort; whereas duration varies, depending on the particular project, team, and situation.

Using the Good Guess Estimating Tool

Thus, the first step after identifying the tasks is to get a rough idea of how long the activities will take per person. You can come up with this number, let's say in days, by going through each task and determining a conservative estimate. Then add these estimates together to come up with the total. The more of these estimates you do, the more you can look at the type of project and develop an accurate estimate. To this end I have developed the Good Guess Estimating Tool.

There are two parts to this tool. The first part is the Subject Area Effort Range spreadsheet, which has by project the short, long, and average length it would take to complete the data modeling deliverables. The second part is the Task Effort Tool, which takes each of the tasks we have come up with and assigns them a percentage. After you have chosen the type of project from this table, you multiply that number by the percentage to get how much time for each of the tasks.

If the project manager dictates a time length to you, then skip the spreadsheet and just multiply the time length by each percentage to get the amount of time for each task. Note that you might want to use the first spreadsheet anyway, so that you can tell the project manager how long the data modeling tasks should take as opposed to how long the project manager would like them to take. This can also help in obtaining additional resources to shorten the duration of the tasks.

Both spreadsheets appear in the following sections. We will present each one and then go through a number of examples to show how to use these two tools.

Subject Area Effort Range

The Subject Area Effort Range has by project the short, long, and average length of days in effort it would take to complete. Short, long, and average are determined mainly by how much high-quality information is provided to the data modeler and how experienced the entire project team is, including the data modeler. Generally, to play it safe, choose the average or high-range amount. The time amounts are given by subject area. Subject areas correspond with the early tasks in the project plan. Unfortunately, it can be a Catch-22 situation where you need the complete list of subject areas to give a valid estimate, yet to get the subject areas you have to start the project and complete the subject area analysis portion of the tasks. I usually recommend some startup funds to at least do the subject area tasks in the plan, which can help with the accuracy of the estimate and shave off some time from the resulting project plan. See Table 4.14.

All of the applications we work on should fit into one of these project types: a new operational application, new packaged software, new data mart, operational enhancement, or data mart enhancement. A new operational application is one being built from scratch. Examples include a new order processing or contact management application. New operational applications usually take the least time of all new applications, because from a design point of view, your physical model will be very similar to your logical highly normalized model. After getting your design to 5NF, there will be only minor changes to create the physical data model and subsequent database tables.

The trend in companies lately has been to buy the big operational applications from other companies and build only small-scale (maybe department level) applications.

Table 4.14 Subject Area Effort Range

TYPE OF PROJECT	LOW RANGE*	HIGH RANGE*	AVERAGE RANGE*
New operational application	2	10	4
New packaged software	3	12	6
New data mart	3	11	5
Operational enhancement	1	5	2
Data mart enhancement	1	6	3

*Per subject area in days.

From the point of view of complete development and implementation, these packages might take less time per subject area than would a customized effort. From the data modeling point of view, however, analyzing the packaged software can take much more time. This is because you need to understand the generic structures within the packaged software and have the added task of mapping your company's data requirements to this generic structure. Thus, although you do not have to create data models from scratch, you still have the huge mapping task, which must be consistent and correct. That is why packaged software usually takes slightly longer when estimating the data modeling tasks.

Designing a new data mart requires slightly more effort than designing a new operational application, because the data modeler has the extra tasks of analyzing reporting requirements. For each fact or measurement in the design, the data modeler needs to capture the levels of reference data or dimensionality reporting. These extra requirements add time to the plan.

Operational and data mart enhancements have a fairly wide time range, depending on the scope of the enhancements. For example, adding a new data element to an existing table will take less data modeling effort than adding several new entities to a model. Data mart enhancements could take slightly longer than operational ones owing to the additional reporting tasks required of the data modeler.

Task Effort Tool

The Task Effort Tool (see Table 4.15) takes each of the tasks we have come up with and assigns them a percentage. If you have chosen your project from Table 4.14, you multiply that number by the percentage to get how much time is required for each of the tasks.

There are separate columns in this tool for reporting and operational activities. You will note that the reporting columns assign percentages to the two analysis tasks, which involve determining levels of reporting: Identify levels of reporting by subject area, and identify the fact levels of reporting. Doing this analysis up front leads to less time being spent during the physical data modeling phase because you already have a very good idea of what the report design might look like. It will be a star schema or a variation of a star schema. That is why the physical data modeling phase takes less time for reporting applications.

The operational column obviously requires no time for the two reporting tasks mentioned previously. More time will be required during physical data modeling to denormalize where appropriate, because we do not yet have a good handle what the final design might look like. It might be very close to the logical design; however, there probably will be sections of the model that need to be carefully analyzed for folding tables together. If the physical will almost match the logical, then use the extra time to check your work and look for areas of the model that might become hot spots later in development. In other words, the extra time can be used to be proactive and look to prevent design rework in the future. This is why there is extra effort to creating a normalized data model for the operational application.

Table 4.15 Task Effort Tool

DATA MODEL PHASE	TASKS	PERCENT OF TOTAL DA ACTIVITIES (REPORTING)	PERCENT OF TOTAL DA ACTIVITIES (OPERATIONAL)
Project Planning		5	5
	Create data modeling project task list	2	2
	Create data modeling estimates for project plan	3	3
Subject Area Analysis		8	7
	Identify subject areas affected by application	2	2
	Identify fit with existing applications	3	3
	Identify resources for each subject area	1	1
	Identify subject area sources and definitions	1	1
	Identify levels of reporting by subject area (for reporting applications only)	1	0
Subject Area Modeling		7	7
	Create Business Clean Slate	2	2
	Create Application Clean Slate	2	2
	Create Early Reality Check	2	3
Logical Data Analysis		40	30
	Identify data element sources, transformations, and definitions	15	15
	Identify fact levels of reporting (for reporting applications only)	10	0
	Check data	15	15
Logical Data Modeling		25	35
	Create a normalized logical data model	19	29
	Apply abstraction	5	5
	Appropriately arrange logical data model	1	1

Table 4.15 *(Continued)*

DATA MODEL PHASE	TASKS	PERCENT OF TOTAL DA ACTIVITIES (REPORTING)	PERCENT OF TOTAL DA ACTIVITIES (OPERATIONAL)
Physical Data Modeling		15	16
	Denormalize the logical into a physical design	10	11
	Appropriately arrange physical data model	5	5

Remember if your project includes a combination of a new application and an enhancement, you need to break down the effort into these two pieces, apply the estimating approach to each, and then add them together for the total effort. This situation is prevalent in our data warehouse area when we create a new data mart and introduce a new source system into the data warehouse architecture.

Good Guess Estimating Tool In Practice

To put these pieces together, let's go through an example of estimating a new application and an enhancement. For new applications, we have new custom-built operational applications or data marts, or new packaged operational applications or data warehouses. For enhancements to existing applications, we have new functionality to an existing operational application or data mart, including a customization to a new packaged piece of software. We also have enhancements to the existing data warehouse architecture. To demonstrate this estimating approach, for a new application we will choose building a new data mart within an existing architecture. This will give us a taste of both the new application and enhancement estimate approach. We will choose an enhancement to an existing operational application. We could go through an example of each type of project; however, by going through these two examples you should be comfortable using these tools for any type of project.

New Data Mart within an Existing Data Warehouse Architecture

You have been assigned to be the data modeler on a new data mart effort. You already know by using the task spreadsheet which activities and in what order they should be performed in your role as data modeler. Now you need to give an estimate for each task to the project manager. He has already told you that the project must be completed by the end of April, which is a full 6 months for analysis through implementation.

Table 4.16 Effort Break Down for Each Task for the New Data Mart

DATA MODEL PHASE	TASKS	PERCENT OF TOTAL DA ACTIVITIES	DAYS FOR TOTAL DA ACTIVITIES	TOTAL DAYS PER ACTIVITY
Project Planning		5	20	1
	Create data modeling project task list	2	20	0.4
	Create data modeling estimates for project plan	3	20	0.6
Subject Area Analysis		8	20	1.6
	Identify subject areas affected by application	2	20	0.4
	Identify fit with existing applications	3	20	0.6
	Identify resources for each subject area	1	20	0.2
	Identify subject area sources and definitions	1	20	0.2
	Identify levels of reporting by subject area (for reporting applications only)	1	20	0.2
Subject Area Modeling		7	20	1.4
	Create Business Clean Slate	2	20	0.4
	Create Application Clean Slate	2	20	0.4
	Create Early Reality Check	3	20	0.6
Logical Data Analysis		40	20	8
	Identify data element sources, transformations, and definitions	15	20	3

Table 4.16 (Continued)

DATA MODEL PHASE	TASKS	PERCENT OF TOTAL DA ACTIVITIES	DAYS FOR TOTAL DA ACTIVITIES	TOTAL DAYS PER ACTIVITY
	Identify fact levels of reporting (for reporting applications only)	10	20	2
	Check data	15	20	3
Logical Data Modeling		25	20	5
	Create a normalized logical data model	19	20	3.8
	Apply abstraction	5	20	1
	Appropriately arrange logical data model	1	20	0.2
Physical Data Modeling		15	20	3
	Denormalize the logical into a physical design	10	20	2
	Appropriately arrange physical data model	5	20	1

Based on your understanding of the project so far, highly experienced individuals from the business and the technical team are assigned to this project. In addition, you have had experience in modeling data marts in the past. Based on this information, you referred to the Subject Area Effort Range, and because of the high level of expertise assigned to this project, you have decided that this data mart should be in the low range of effort for a new data mart. Therefore, you estimate that 4 days per subject area is sufficient.

You ask the project manager for 2 days to do some quick analysis on the number of subject areas and return with two figures, one for the data mart and one for the data warehouse architecture. You believe there will be five subject areas within the data mart. Therefore, the data mart data modeling effort should take roughly 20 days. You also believe adding this new data mart will mean creating one new subject area within the data warehouse and substantially updating two more subject areas. This gives us three subject areas within the data warehouse architecture. You believe it will take roughly 5 days per subject area in the data warehouse. Therefore, the data warehouse architecture data modeling effort should take roughly 15 days. Table 4.16 shows how tasks are broken down.

This shows the total time for each of these tasks for the data mart. Now let's do the enhancement to the data warehouse architecture. Table 4.17 is the same tool, except with 15 days' duration instead of 20.

Table 4.17 Effort Break Down for Each Task for Data Warehouse Enhancement

DATA MODEL PHASE	TASKS	PERCENT OF TOTAL DA ACTIVITIES	DAYS FOR TOTAL DA ACTIVITIES	TOTAL DAYS PER ACTIVITY
Project Planning		5	15	0.75
	Create data modeling project task list	2	15	0.3
	Create data modeling estimates for project plan	3	15	0.45
Subject Area Analysis		8	15	1.2
	Identify subject areas affected by application	2	15	0.3
	Identify fit with existing applications	3	15	0.45
	Identify resources for each subject area	1	15	0.15
	Identify subject area sources and definitions	1	15	0.15
	Identify levels of reporting by subject area (for reporting applications only)	1	15	0.15
Subject Area Modeling		7	15	1.05
	Create Business Clean Slate	2	15	0.3
	Create Application Clean Slate	2	15	0.3
	Create Early Reality Check	3	15	0.45
Logical Data Analysis		40	15	6
	Identify data element sources, transformations, and definitions	15	15	2.25
	Identify fact levels of reporting (for reporting applications only)	10	15	1.5
	Check data	15	15	2.25

Table 4.17   (Continued)

DATA MODEL PHASE	TASKS	PERCENT OF TOTAL DA ACTIVITIES	DAYS FOR TOTAL DA ACTIVITIES	TOTAL DAYS PER ACTIVITY
Logical Data Modeling		25	15	3.75
	Create a normalized logical data model	19	15	2.85
	Apply abstraction	5	15	0.75
	Appropriately arrange logical data model	1	15	0.15
Physical Data Modeling		15	15	2.25
	Denormalize the logical into a physical design	10	15	1.5
	Appropriately arrange physical data model	5	15	0.75

If you add these two amounts together, you get a total of 35 days of effort. Duration can be longer or shorter, depending on your own experience of how long these tasks take and how many people can work on them to reduce the overall length of time. Remember this is a guide, or tool, that can help you. Projects vary based on many different factors.

Enhancements to an Existing Operational Application

You have been assigned to be the data modeler to make a quick enhancement to an operational application. The project manager assures you that it is a very minor change. You do a quick analysis to see which subject areas are affected, however, and find there are three. You believe that this project will not be a slam dunk. Rather, it will be the exact opposite and take a substantial amount of time to complete. For this reason, you go to the high end of the scale for effort and choose 5 days per subject area for a total effort of 15 days. Table 4.18 shows how the effort breaks down into tasks.

You can see that even though this is a system enhancement, it can still take a substantial amount of time. Make sure this total amount is quickly communicated to the project manager who is under the impression that this is a very quick change.

Table 4.18 Effort Break Down for Each Task for Operational Application Enhancement

DATA MODEL PHASE	TASKS	PERCENT TOTAL DA ACTIVITIES	DAYS FOR TOTAL DA ACTIVITIES	TOTAL DAYS PER ACTIVITY
Project Planning		5	15	.75
	Create data modeling project task list	2	15	.3
	Create data modeling estimates for project plan	3	15	.45
Subject Area Analysis		7	15	1.05
	Identify subject areas affected by application	2	15	3
	Identify fit with existing applications	3	15	.45
	Identify resources for each subject area	1	15	.15
	Identify subject area sources and definitions	1	15	.15
	Identify levels of reporting by subject area (for reporting applications only)	0	15	0
Subject Area Modeling		7	15	1.05
	Create Business Clean Slate	2	15	.3
	Create Application Clean Slate	2	15	.3
	Create Early Reality Check	3	15	.45
Logical Data Analysis		30	15	4.5
	Identify data element sources, transformations, and definitions	15	15	2.25
	Identify the fact levels of reporting (for reporting applications only)	0	15	0
	Check the data	15	15	2.25

Table 4.18 *(Continued)*

DATA MODEL PHASE	TASKS	PERCENT TOTAL DA ACTIVITIES	DAYS FOR TOTAL DA ACTIVITIES	TOTAL DAYS PER ACTIVITY
Logical Data Modeling		25	15	3.75
	Create a normalized logical data model	29	15	4.35
	Apply abstraction	5	15	.75
	Appropriately arrange logical data model	1	15	.15
Physical Data Modeling		27	15	4.05
	Denormalize the logical into a physical design	12	15	1.8
	Appropriately arrange physical data model	5	15	.75

Summary

This chapter focused on the four tools that define the data modeling phases, tasks, tools, and timelines:

- Data Modeling Phase Tool
- Phase-to-Task-to-Tools
- Priorities Triangle Tool
- Good Guess Estimating Tool

Each tool is designed to make the data modeling project planning process as painless, quick, and accurate as possible. The Data Modeling Phase identifies the data modeling steps at the highest level. It is a very good starting point in fitting data modeling deliverables into the detailed project plan. Then the Phase-to-Task-to-Tools takes all of the phases from the Data Modeling Phase and breaks them down into data modeling tasks. For each task, the relevant tools within this book are listed. In this way you can create a detailed project plan and know where to look in this book to make each of the tasks go more quickly and with greater efficiency and consistency. Then the Priorities Triangle demonstrates through a diagram that you cannot have it all. You can pick a maximum of two out of three: very high quality, minimum amount of time, and minimum cost. You can never have all three. This tool makes it easy to picture the three options and helps describe the tradeoffs among them.

The chapter concludes with the Good Guess Estimating Tool. There are two sections to this tool. The Subject Area Effort Range identifies which percentage of the entire project each data modeling phase should consume based on the type of application. The Task Effort Tool takes all the tasks identified in Phase-to-Task-to-Tools and lists which percentage they should be of the entire set of data model deliverables. The combination of these two sections will allow you to provide, with some degree of accuracy, a reasonable estimate to the project manager. In subsequent chapters we will go into detail about each of the data modeling tasks and tools mentioned in this chapter, starting with Chapter 5, "Subject Area Analysis."

PART TWO

Analyzing the Requirements

Have you ever completed your data modeling tasks and realized afterward that you still lacked understanding of the big picture? By that I mean the high level and encompassing view that shows the scope of the application in the context of the rest of the organization. To obtain such a big picture, you should follow a set of tasks that are discussed in this part of book that will greatly help with the understanding and capturing of the data requirements for an application. After establishing the foundation reviewed in the first part of this text, we are now ready to start analyzing the application. The proper approach to thoroughly understanding the requirements is to first represent them at a high level, the subject area level, at which we can understand the scope and content we will need to analyze in detail in future steps. Once we understand each of the subject areas within an application, we can capture the data elements that belong to each subject area.

This section of the book focuses on capturing and validating the subject area requirements for an application as well as the detailed data elements that will provide the inputs to our logical data modeling phase. Chapter 5, "Subject Area Analysis," Chapter 6, "Subject Area Modeling," and Chapter 7, "Logical Data Analysis," present a series of tools for analyzing the requirements of an application. Here is the purpose of each:

Identify and define the subject areas. Chapter 5 offers tools to complete the deliverables for identifying and capturing the subject areas for an application. The Subject Area Checklist is a complete list of subject areas within the new application, along with their definitions. The Application Subject Area Create, Read, Update, Delete (CRUD) Matrix contains the subject area gaps and overlap that can exist between your new application and existing applications. This is a powerful tool for scoping your application. The In-the-Know Template identifies the people and documentation you will need as resources to complete your data modeling deliverables for this new application. This is a straightforward method to gain agreement on the resources you can tap for your data modeling activities. The Subject Area Family Tree contains the source applications for each subject area and several other critical pieces of information. This clarifies where the subject area data will come from. The Subject Area Grain Matrix captures the reporting levels for each measurement or fact subject area, using a spreadsheet format. This offers a very easy-to-read document for validating reporting requirements.

Create the subject area models. Chapter 6 focuses on three types of subject area models, each being a very powerful validation and scoping tool. The Business Clean Slate model helps us understand a business area independent of any applications. The Application Clean Slate builds on the Business Clean Slate and focuses only on what is important for the application. The Early Reality Check compares the new application with an existing application architecture to understand overlap and impact.

Identify and define the data elements. Chapter 7 presents four powerful data element capture and validation tools. The Data Element Family Tree captures data element name, alias, definition, business purpose, default value, transformations, format, and nullability. The Data Element Grain Matrix captures the relationships between the facts and their reporting levels. The Data Quality Capture Template contains the criteria and comparison information between data and meta data, whereas the Data Quality Validation Template provides proof that the data quality of each data element has been properly reviewed.

Subject Area Analysis

O ne of my favorite types of vacations is a road adventure. We pick a place that we have never been to before, rent a car, and then explore. We do a limited amount of research about this place, such as which towns are a must-see, where is the best hiking, and where are the most scenic drives. We also expect a certain amount of chaos and un-planned adventures during our trip, with the goals of arriving at these must-see places. To plan such a trip requires a certain amount of preparation. We do not want to study and memorize a detailed map of this state or country, because that sounds more like work than vacation. Rather, the level of preparation or analysis done is at a very high level. We create a high-level map, where our must-see places are just dots; by connecting these dots, we know we can reach each place. These dots represent our vacation requirements at a high level. Similarly, we use subject area analysis to repre-sent our data requirements at a high level. The five tools that can help during this sub-ject area level analysis are the subject of this chapter.

About This Chapter

Subject area analysis lays the foundation for the subject area modeling and logical data analysis phases. It includes the subject area level research on requirements, re-sources, and scope. It is when the data modeler first starts grasping and document-ing the functionality of this new application. The data modeler can then document and present at this high level to the rest of the project team. Understanding and doc-umenting require participation from the project team and business users, as well as availability to any existing relevant documentation. There are several deliverables from this phase, including a complete list of the application subject areas, an under-standing of how this application fits in with existing applications, an agreement on available resources, the subject area source applications, and reporting requirements if applicable.

Many times we do little if any of this type of analysis at the subject area level. This subject area analysis rarely appears in a project plan, and therefore, there is usually neither time nor money to complete it. For some reason, however, there is always time and money available to fix mistakes in design or code as a result of not fully understanding the subject areas. I find this both fascinating and ironic. It just does not make sense that there are magnitudes more money and resources for fixing problems than for preventing them. What is even more ironic is the relatively small amount of time required to complete this subject area analysis as compared with the subsequent more detailed modeling tasks. Maybe subject area analysis is not given enough attention because we do not fully understand its benefits, which include the following:

Common understanding. In the beginning of a project, there is always a period of time where large gaps in understanding of the application exist. This includes functionality, terminology, reporting, resource, and scope gaps. Subject area analysis fills these gaps and increases common understanding of the application. In this way people with different backgrounds and roles can understand and communicate with each other on the same concepts, and agree on or debate issues. For example, subject area analysis can address the question "Does Customer include potential customers or only existing customers?" Common communication at the subject area level will make the more detailed logical and physical analysis go more smoothly and take less time.

Prevention. By developing a subject area level understanding of the application, there is a strong chance we will be able to identify important issues or concerns that can save substantial time and money later. Topics where prevention can occur include history requirements, functionality limitations, sourcing issues, and so on. An example of a history requirements issue that was brought to the surface at this very early stage of development is the statement, "I didn't know the source system only stored 1 year's worth of orders. I need 3 years' worth."

Scope. At a high level, subject area analysis gives us a complete and accurate understanding of the scope of the new application. This can help determine overlap and gaps that might exist between this new application and existing or other applications under development. For example, "If this application is processing orders, how does it relate to or overlap with this other application that contains order information?"

Prioritization. Understanding the subject areas within a new application can help us prioritize the development activities for each subject area based on issues, concerns, dependencies, and so on. For example, if an Order cannot exist without an Item, perhaps Item should be developed first.

Because the subject area analysis is so important and yet much of the time is overlooked, we need to complete this analysis as accurately as possible within a minimal amount of time. Several tools enable us to do this. This chapter contains five tools to assist with the subject area analysis phase of your project. They should be completed in the order below, which is also the order in which they will be discussed in this chapter:

1. **Subject Area Checklist.** A complete list of subject areas within the new application, along with their definitions and synonyms or aliases. This provides a great starting point for further analysis.

2. **Application Subject Area CRUD Matrix.** Contains the subject area gaps and overlap that can exist between your new application and existing applications. This is a powerful tool for scoping your application.

3. **In-the-Know Template.** Identifies the people and documentation you will need as resources to complete your data modeling deliverables for this new application. This is a straightforward method to gain agreement on the resources you can tap for your data modeling activities.

4. **Subject Area Family Tree.** Contains the source applications for each subject area and several other critical pieces of information. This clarifies where the subject area data will come from.

5. **Subject Area Grain Matrix.** Captures the reporting levels for each measurement or fact subject area using a spreadsheet format. This offers a very easy-to-read document for validating reporting requirements.

These five tools capture, at a minimum, the types of subject area meta data discussed in Chapter 2, "Meta Data Bingo." Take a few moments to recall the Subject Area Meta Data Bingo Card (see Table 5.1).

To obtain an understanding of which of these subject area analysis tools is responsible for capturing which types of meta data, I replaced the priority columns on this Bingo card with the five tools. I put a C in the cells where the tool is responsible for capturing this type of meta data, and an R in the cells that read or use these data. See Table 5.2 for this Subject Area Tool Responsibility Chart.

On this Subject Area Tool Responsibility Chart, the Subject Area Checklist captures the name, alias, and definition information. The other four tools reference the name information captured. In some cases, the alias will be used by the Subject Area Family Tree, when source applications refer to the subject area with a different name than the current application. The Subject Area Checklist also captures the definition. The In-the-Know Template captures resource information, such as stewardship. Each of these tools might also capture other types of meta data that were not necessarily on the Meta Data Bingo Card. The reasons they were not on the card include being mandatory, and thus not up for vote, or being specific to your department or company. For example, the In-the-Know Template also captures documentation resources, which were not mentioned on the Bingo card. The amount of history for both the source and new

Table 5.1   Subject Area Meta Data Bingo Card

CODE	DESCRIPTIVE INFORMATION	HIGH	MEDIUM	LOW	QUESTIONS AND ISSUES
A	Standard enterprise name				
B	Alias				
C	Definition	X			
D	Steward name and department				
E	History requirements				
F	Source				

Table 5.2 Subject Area Tool Responsibility Chart

CODE	DESCRIPTIVE INFORMATION	SUBJECT AREA CHECKLIST	APPLICATION SUBJECT AREA CRUD MATRIX	IN-THE-KNOW TEMPLATE	SUBJECT AREA FAMILY TREE	SUBJECT AREA GRAIN MATRIX
A	Standard enterprise name	C	R	R	R	R
B	Alias	C			R	
C	Definition	C			R	
D	Steward name and department			C		
E	History requirements				C	
F	Source		C		R	

applications are listed on the Subject Area Family Tree. Source information is initially captured on the Subject Area CRUD Matrix and then further refined on the Subject Area Family Tree.

This chapter starts off with a definition of a subject area, which is the level of detail for the subject area analysis phase. We then provide a description of and explain the benefits, format, and usage of each tool. As you read each section, think of how you might need to slightly modify or customize these tools for your specific company or project.

If you visit my Web site, www.wiley.com/compbooks.hoberman, you will find templates for each of the tools in this chapter; additional tools; and more information about tools in this book, including empty templates that you can download.

What Is a Subject Area?

A *subject area* is a concept or term that is both basic and critical to the business. By basic we mean that it is probably mentioned many times a day in normal conversation. By critical we mean that the business would be nonexistent or completely different without this concept. Examples include consumer, customer, employee, and product. Each of these subject areas will be shown in much more detail at the logical and physical phases of design. For example, the consumer concept can be viewed as the logical entities Consumer, Consumer Association, Consumer Demographics, and Consumer Type.

Figure 5.1 is a data model showing the relationships between a subject area, entity, and data element. A subject area such as Product contains one or more entities, such as Product, Product Classification, and Product Component. Each of these entities contains one or more data elements. For example, Product Classification might contain Product Classification Code and Product Classification Description.

It is evident that consumer, customer, employee, and product are subject areas independent of the industry or company in which we work. However, there are many concepts and terms that are considered subject areas that are industry-, company-, and department-specific. For example, when I worked in the telecommunications industry, telephone number was both basic and critical to our business and, therefore, was actually considered a separate subject area. In other industries I have worked in, telephone number was a data element within an entity that was identified during logical data analysis. While working in the manufacturing industry, the concept of a lot number might be considered a subject area. A *lot number* is a code assigned to a product that identifies the place and time the product was manufactured. This also sounds like a data element. After all, it is only a code. Yet because lot number is both basic and critical to the manufacturing industry, it is considered its own subject area.

Figure 5.1 Relationship between subject area, entity, and data element.

TIP

████ Subject areas are not limited to universal concepts, such as customer and product. They can also be specific to an industry, company, or even department, as long as the term meets the subject area definition of being basic and critical.

Subject Area Checklist

As a data modeler, have you ever been in the situation where you were not sure exactly of the optimal place to start your subject area analysis? Have you ever been in the situation where you knew the project team was starting to jump into details a bit prematurely, without an understanding of the big picture? These are two situations that require an understanding of the subject areas and definition of the application. A great starting point is the Subject Area Checklist, which provides already named and defined subject areas. By reusing names and definitions from this list, you can quickly create a big picture for your new application, and raise the level of conversation and debate up to those terms that are most basic and critical to the business.

The Subject Area Checklist is a list of subject area names and definitions, so that you do not have to start from scratch during your subject area analysis phase. It is a very simple yet powerful tool. It contains the major subject areas I have encountered over the years, along with their generic yet useful definitions. A good analogy for the Subject Area Checklist would be packaged software. Instead of starting from scratch, you are starting with something proven and workable. Minor customizations are always expected, but the end result is a more robust solution. Packaged software comes in the box and is implemented after customizing code to the requirements of your company. The Subject Area Checklist comes ready "in the book" instead of "in the box," and, after customizing some of the names and definitions to your needs, it also provides a robust solution.

One significant reason for customizing the names on the Subject Area Checklist would be to increase consistency with existing terminology within your company. For example, if you have enterprise concepts referring to Client instead of Customer, you should continue to use Client within the subject area list for your new application. Using the standard company names means you are being consistent with your department or company at this high level and that you will be consistent with the business in future, more detailed phases.

The Subject Area Checklist provides a starting point to generate the list of subject areas you need for your subject area model. If you do not have much information to start with, or need to encourage project and business teams to get out from the weeds, meaning they are talking at too detailed a level for this point in the project, the subject areas and their definitions within this tool make a great starting point.

NOTE

████ You might find yourself adding to this list of subject areas the more you use this checklist. Feel free to share your new subject area definitions, as well as any

changes you made to the definitions in this section, with the rest of our Web site community, at www.wiley.com/compbooks/hoberman.

The Subject Area Checklist is a very simple tool, which accomplishes a number of very important goals:

Creates a high-level understanding of the subject areas of the application. After completing this checklist, you and the rest of the project team will clearly understand each subject area and know what is within the scope of the application. Knowing these subject areas will make the subject area modeling phase much simpler and easier because when you start the subject area modeling, you will only have to add the relationships between these subject areas to complete the model.

Provides a starting point to the subject area analysis phase. When you have nothing or very little information to start with, this tool provides subject area names and definitions that are common to most of our businesses. Regardless of whether we are in the manufacturing or accounting industries, for example, we all have customers. Customer is one of the subject areas on this list. Also, the definitions are designed to be easily customizable. They can make a good starting point for discussion or debate.

Gets your project team out from the weeds. This is useful when your project team wants to start off the modeling phase diving directly into the data elements. In these situations, it can be very easy to miss key concepts and, therefore, accidentally leave out required information. Starting the application analysis by listing data elements creates a narrow and incomplete view of the project's requirements. In order to step back and really understand the scope of the application, you need to have your team view it from a subject area level. Taking this view allows everyone to see the more complete, bigger picture. Then, after understanding and agreeing on the subject areas that are within the scope of the project, you can dive back into the data element details.

Facilitates entity and data element names and definitions. Having solid names and definitions at the subject area level makes it easier to develop names and definitions at the more detailed levels. If we have a standard name and very good definition for Customer, for example, than we can more easily name and define the entities Customer Location and Customer Association, and the data elements Customer Last Name and Customer Type Code.

Initiates rapport with the project team and business users. Completing the Subject Area Checklist as a group is a very good first data modeling task for you and the rest of the team. It is a quick win, meaning it is not usually very difficult to complete yet has big payoffs. It can help with understanding the content of the new application at a high level and help build rapport with the project team.

Using the Subject Area Checklist

Table 5.3 shows a Subject Area Checklist in a spreadsheet format, with four columns: Name, Synonyms or Industry-Specific Terms, Definition, and Questions. The column

Table 5.3 Subject Area Checklist

NAME	SYNONYMS OR INDUSTRY-SPECIFIC TERMS	DEFINITION	QUESTIONS
Account	General ledger account, accounts receivable, expense account	Structure to facilitate the financial transactions carried out by the company. A formal banking, brokerage, or business relationship established to provide for regular services and financial transactions.	**Can an account exist without an owner? What uniquely identifies an account? Can an account have more than one owner?** These questions will be answered during the subject area modeling phase when we are trying to understand the business rules between the subject areas. However, I have found that account and owner are usually so intertwined that, in many cases, they might be considered the same concept. Understanding their relationship at this point can help come up with a solid definition.
Asset	Machine, part, capital, stock, wealth, supply	Something our company owns that is considered valuable.	**Does this also include purchases we plan on making for the upcoming year?** A question such as this adds the element of a life cycle into these definitions. It is really asking how broad we want to go with this definition. Does it include past, present, and future assets, or only present assets? You can ask questions such as this for each of these subject areas. It will help you refine the definition and possibly introduce new subject areas that were originally overlooked. **Is rented and leased equipment considered assets?** This question tests the scope of the definition.
Associate	Employee, worker	A person who is employed in a full- or part-time capacity by our company, to perform a service or function to our company.	**Clearly distinguish the rules that differentiate an associate and contractor.** There is usually a fine line distinction between the concepts of employee and contractor. Make sure you have documented this fine line.

Term	Synonyms	Question
Carrier	Trucking company, distributor, transporter	A company that physically moves our products from one site to another site.	**Does carrier include both company-owned carriers and externally owned ones? Or just our own carriers?** This question again tests the scope of this subject area.
Company	Corporation, firm, organization, partnership	A government-registered business enterprise that serves a purpose to society and the economy.	**Are our business units or subsidiaries considered separate companies within a larger company, or do we just have one company?** This question is great for very large companies with lots of subsidiaries. It will provide insight into how the business defines these subsidiaries and the relationship to the whole company.
Competitor	Opponent, challenger	An organization that offers customers within the same demographics similar products to those we offer. An organization that competes with us. Organizations whose sale of products can negatively impact our revenues.	**Can we have competitors that are also our customers or suppliers?** This question separates role from entity. What I mean by this is that if the answer to this question is yes, then we need to design for where the same organization can play multiple roles. I like to ask these kinds of questions whenever I recognize concepts that appear similar. It is also a very effective question for scoping out areas for abstraction later, which we will learn about in Chapter 9, "The Abstraction Safety Guide and Components."

continues

Table 5.3 *(Continued)*

NAME	SYNONYMS OR INDUSTRY-SPECIFIC TERMS	DEFINITION	QUESTIONS
Contract	Order, promotion, agreement, invoice, bill of lading, bill of materials, purchase order, policy, statement	A document containing the terms and conditions around the purchase or creation of product.	**What is the difference between a transaction and a contract? Which happens first?** This definition ensures that the concept of an event is different enough from the concept of a record of that event. For example, the event of ordering product is different from the order, which documents that this product has been ordered. The definitions of these two terms need to clearly distinguish their differences.
Contractor	Broker, consultant	A worker for our company that does not meet the Internal Revenue Service (IRS) tax definition of an employee, and is usually paid hourly based on a particular project. One that agrees to furnish materials or perform services at a specified price.	**Clearly distinguish the rules that differentiate an associate and contractor.** We discussed the benefits of this question under associate. **Does this definition need to be a global definition or is this United States definition sufficient?** Sometimes our definitions contain phrases that are only relevant to a particular region or country. In the case of Contractor, mentioning that this does not meet the IRS employee definition limits this definition to the United States.

Term	Definition	Notes
Customer	Patient, claimant, passenger, user, client, consumer The recipient and purchaser of our products. One that acquires goods or services either for direct use or ownership, or for resale or use in production and manufacturing.	**Do customers include only existing customers? In other words, are potential customers who have never purchased anything from us, yet we believe they might one day, considered customers? What about customers who have purchased from us in the past, but have not purchased from us in years?** This question tests the life cycle of this subject area. How broad should our definition be? The definition needs to state which combination of past, present, and future customers are included by this definition. **Explain clearly the difference between a consumer, customer, and client.** This question checks to see if our consumer and customer definitions are unique enough to stand alone.
Department	Cost center, profit center, group, team, division, region, district An internal organization. An area and group of individuals that serve one or more functions to the business.	**Can we have hierarchies within departments?** This question will shed some light on the composite nature of departments and also on the terminology of each of the levels of departments.
Forecast	Plan, budget An estimate of future demand.	**What are the different types of forecasts we have?** This question will be more useful at logical stages of analysis, but it might provide some more specific verbiage for this definition.
Government Agency	Federal organization, state organization, town organization An organization run by the town, city, county, state or country.	**Can a Government Agency also be a customer?** This tests the same multiple roles question mentioned earlier under Competitor.

continues

Table 5.3 *(Continued)*

NAME	SYNONYMS OR INDUSTRY-SPECIFIC TERMS	DEFINITION	QUESTIONS
Interaction	Complaint, compliment, inquiry	An occurrence of a contact. A communication between someone in our organization and someone outside our organization.	**If the same person initiates two interactions with us, is this considered two separate interactions, or one interaction with the same person?** This question tests the relationship between two concepts of which I believe many people do not clearly understand the difference: interaction and the initiator of this interaction. Make sure the definitions of both these terms are clear enough to eliminate confusion and ambiguity.
Inventory	On-hand inventory, available inventory storage	A detailed record of material and products in stock within a site.	**How often does inventory change?** This question might reveal additional documentation required under the transaction subject area or, perhaps, a new subject area for inventory transactions, which includes concepts such as inventory adjustments and balances.
Location	Address	An address of importance to the business. Can be a mailing address, email address, longitude/latitude, and so on.	**What happens if there are two customers with the same address? How about if a customer moves?** This question tests the independence between a customer and its address. Many organizations have too tight of a relationship between these two concepts.
Product	Item, service	Anything we buy, sell, stock, move, or make. Any manufactured or purchased part, material, component, assembly, or product.	**Do products include raw materials? Can a product contain other products? Is a product defined by its packaging or by its content?** These questions will provide more insight into the definition of product and could introduce new product subject areas we need to define in this checklist.

Term	Definition	Notes
Regulatory Body	Standards organization	An organization that ensures our company and industry meet certain quality standards.	**How does this compare with Government Agency?** The definitions between these two terms need to explain the voluntary versus mandatory nature of complying with these two organizations.
Revenue	Accrual, gross margin, gross profit, income	The amount of funds our company earns.	**Clearly explain how the key revenue indicators are calculated.** This might sound like an innocent request, but I have seen the most passionate and aggressive discussions around how key measures are calculated. Be careful not to get too much into the details here, because we are are not yet ready to tackle the individual data elements.
Site	Plant, warehouse, distribution center, office	Facility of importance to the business. An operating unit that manages its own inventory and production independent of other sites.	**Can a site be externally owned?** This tests for how broad a definition of site we need. If the answer is yes, we should expand the definition accordingly. If the answer is no, we may need to add a new subject area for externally owned sites.
Time	Year, quarter, month, week, day, hour, minute, second, nanosecond	A measurable length or interval, such as seconds, minutes, hours, days, weeks, months or years. Can include fiscal, department-specific, and Julian time measurements.	Time is a subject area that you may not want to bring up for definition review at the subject area level. I find that Time as a separate concept causes much confusion with the business, especially in high-level discussions. The business tends to view time more as data elements or attributes of other subject areas. Just assume that time will be there, and do not review it with the team at this point.

continues

Table 5.3 (Continued)

NAME	SYNONYMS OR INDUSTRY-SPECIFIC TERMS	DEFINITION	QUESTIONS
Transaction	Activity, event, balance, adjustment	An individual change or action within our environment.	**What is the difference between a transaction and a contract? Which happens first?** Same question as we had under contract.
Vendor	Supplier, producer	A company or individual that we purchase materials and services from, to complete the manufacturing and distribution and sale of our products.	**Do we treat order and shipment information the same way with vendors, as we do with our customers?** This question will shed light on whether we act as customers with our vendors in the same relationship, in much the same way as our customers act with us.

Name contains the most common name for each subject area. The Subject Area Checklist is listed alphabetically by subject area name. The column Synonyms or Industry-Specific Terms contains all of the other names I have heard and used to represent this same concept. Your company or department might prefer to use one of the synonyms instead of the actual name. For example, I have used the term Customer over and over again, but the standard term in your company might be the synonym Client instead. This column also includes those words that are more specific to a particular industry, or those terms that are a more detailed concept than the subject area term. For example, Order in this column is a more specific term for the Contract subject area.

The column Definition contains the basic definition for each of these terms. The basic definition is designed to be generic enough to be easily customizable, yet detailed enough to provide value. Under the Definition Checklist in Chapter 3, "Ensuring High-Quality Definitions," we have seen the criteria for a good definition. The definitions in Table 5.3 either meet these criteria or provide a starting point so you can easily add to them to meet the criteria. I tried to stay away from generic concepts here, such as alternate identifier and classification. These abstract concepts are important for our abstraction topic in Chapter 9, "The Abstraction Safety Guide and Components," but are not usually used as a subject area starting point.

The column Questions contains some questions that might be worthwhile addressing when refining your subject area definitions. This last column can be a great conversation starter as well, because these questions can spark lively discussion and debate. Your goal for these questions is to more clearly articulate the definition of a subject area by answering questions about what that subject area includes or does not include. For example, are raw materials considered products? This question might cause interesting and exciting discussion between the marketing and manufacturing areas. Use these disagreements and passion to come up with a single solid definition. I have included the rationale behind asking these questions as well. These questions will give you an idea as to the types of questions to ask during this exercise. Knowing the types of questions will help you in coming up with more specific and relevant questions for your particular situation for each of these subject areas.

TIP

The questions I have listed can be used exactly as they are in this checklist, or you can modify and add your own. You can use my initial list as a starting point for your own types of questions.

Remember that in many cases your definitions will be standardized across the enterprise, and hence, your project team might not be the complete audience to review and agree on each of these definitions. You might need to include more people, and the more people you include, the more discussion will occur. You might even want to have several meetings with only a few people each, so that everyone can be heard and there are not too many discussions going on at the same time.

NOTE

The Subject Area Checklist is not a complete list. There will be subject areas unique within your industry, company, or department that are not listed here. For example,

Claim and Premium will be subject areas for the insurance industry but are not on this list. You should add and customize this list to meet your needs. View this list as a starting point.

Subject Area Checklist In Practice

Let's go through each of the steps in using the Subject Area Checklist:

1. **Hand out copies of the Subject Area Checklist and explain its purpose.** You might want to customize this list slightly, adding more subject areas or making the names and definitions more specific. Explain the reasons for going through this exercise, whether to bring people up from the details a bit or to use as a starting point. Do not hand out the Questions column, because it is for your use in asking the most relevant questions. Handing out this column might confuse the participants. See the Subject Area Checklist at www.wiley.com/compbooks/hoberman for an example without this column. Also, as mentioned earlier, come to this Web site to post your own subject area definitions, or read what others have posted.

2. **Ask each participant to review and comment on the list.** Allocate between 15 and 30 minutes for participants to go through the list and write their comments next to each subject area. Ask for comments such as:

   - Do you agree with this definition?
   - Do you disagree?
   - Are there any synonyms or industry-specific terms that should be used as their own subject area?
   - What would you change about this definition or name?
   - What other subject areas would you add, and why?

3. **Discuss as a group.** Carefully facilitate the discussions, because there have been cases where entire days can be spent on a single subject area. Thus, monitor the discussions and limit the amount of time spent on each subject area. OK) Write down unanswered questions or ideas that as a group we did not have time to answer during this meeting. Before this meeting is over, make sure that you schedule the next meeting date to address these questions, perhaps with a subset of the participants.

4. **Publish initial findings.** Distribute the results of this exercise and set a due date for comments by participants. Update the checklist with their comments.

5. **Publish final findings.** After incorporating everyone's comments, send out the final Subject Area Checklist and definitions and congratulate yourself on completing this task.

Subject Area CRUD Matrix

So you have completed the Subject Area Checklist and fully understand which subject areas are within the scope of your new application. You feel pretty good about yourself, and

*rightfully so. You have a list of subject areas along with agreed-on, high-quality defini-
tions. Now that you have this high-level understanding of your application, you can determine how it fits in with existing applications. New questions come to mind: Where are
the subject areas of your application used within the existing application architecture?
How are they used? Does an application create data for this subject area? Update data?
Delete data? Read data? You need to identify at a subject area level on how this new application relates to existing applications, including an understanding of the gaps and
overlap between the new application and the existing applications. This comparison also
produces initial thoughts on where the data for a subject area will be sourced. The Subject Area CRUD Matrix, the focus of this section, captures how existing applications and
your new application use each subject area, with the goal of answering questions such as
these.*

CRUD matrices have been around since early relational database times. CRUD stands
for create, read, update, and delete. These matrices are used to capture how the functions of an application impact the application's data elements. Impacting the data elements includes creating or inserting data, reading data, updating data, and deleting
data. For example, the data element Customer Last Name might be created by the Create New Customer function. After completing this matrix for the data elements, you
can group together the common Creates, Reads, Updates, and Deletes, and these can
be designed and coded for within the same function of this new application. For example, perhaps all of the customer data elements will be created under the Create New
Customer function. In this matrix, the rows represent the data elements and the
columns represent the proposed functions of the application.

The Subject Area CRUD Matrix captures how applications impact subject areas, as opposed to the standard CRUD, which captures how functions within an application impact data elements. The Subject Area CRUD Matrix has a much broader scope. It has
different rows and columns than the standard matrix but captures similar information.
The rows represent all of the subject areas identified on the Subject Area Checklist.
These are the ones within the scope of your application. The columns represent the applications. Applications include your new application as well as existing applications.
The cells play the same role as in the standard CRUD matrix, that is, they represent
how this application impacts this subject area. Impact, as does the standard CRUD matrix, includes creating, reading, updating, and deleting.

The Subject Area CRUD Matrix captures how each of the subject areas within the
scope of your application are impacted by existing applications. This broad understanding of the existing application architecture accomplishes several goals:

Representing the value and usefulness of the new application. By viewing this matrix, you can see which subject areas are unique to this new application. Perhaps
no application today is deleting inactive customers. If there is a D for delete in the
new application and Customer subject area cell, this could be valuable functionality that exists nowhere else today. If there is an R for read in the Customer and Order cells for your new application, and an R for each of these subject areas does
not exist in any other application, this can provide valuable reporting available
nowhere else. If there are several applications that are in the budgeting or estimating phase of development, it could be very important to show the value of your
application on this matrix.

Validating that the application replacement produces no subject area gaps. If your application is going to replace one or more other applications, or even part of an application, you can match the subject areas between applications on this matrix. For example, if you are introducing a packaged piece of software to manage the entire order processing function, this chart will match the subject areas for this packaged software against the three existing legacy applications being replaced. This can ensure that all of the existing subject area functions are accounted for in the new application.

Discovering subject area redundancy. Imagine while using this tool you discover that deletion of inactive customers is currently being done by an existing application? You can save much time and frustration later by uncovering these data overlap issues early. No code has been written yet because it is still very early in the development of the new application. Identifying an overlap issue at the subject area level could impact the scope of the new application or remove the need for the application entirely. You may not want your new application to go away; however, when it has little or no additional functionality, it is best to find out as early as possible.

Identifying initial data sourcing. The Family Tree, which will be discussed shortly, will provide the source information for each subject area. The Subject Area CRUD Matrix will contain all of the applications that create each of the subject areas and, hence, will provide a superset of applications from which to choose for your sourcing. For example, where should you get Item information? It is hoped that the Subject Area CRUD Matrix will have a C for a single application, and therefore, this could be your source. However, there could be another application with an R for Item that might make a more efficient and practical source. Viewing the applications on this matrix can help facilitate these types of decisions.

Using the Subject Area CRUD Matrix

The Subject Area CRUD Matrix has the subject areas as rows and the applications as columns. A value filled in for the intersection of a subject area and application tells us that this particular application impacts this subject area in some way. Table 5.4 is an example of a blank Subject Area CRUD Matrix.

Table 5.4 Subject Area CRUD Matrix

SUBJECT AREA	YOUR NEW APPLICATION	CUSTOMER REFERENCE DATABASE	XYZ APPLICATION	DATA WAREHOUSE
CUSTOMER				
ITEM				
ORDER				
ASSOCIATE				

Normally, you would have a lot more applications as columns and subject areas as rows. Note that the Data Warehouse is listed as one of the columns. This is commonplace for reporting applications, such as data marts. This column will be essential if the data mart is designed within the data warehouse architecture. This can determine what will come from the data warehouse and what will need to come from other applications.

Now, which values do you use to fill in this matrix? As we have seen, there is a key for what to put in each cell to provide us with more specific information on the relationship between a particular application and subject area:

C = Creates the data

R = Reads the data

U = Updates the data

D = Deletes the data

It is pretty simple. The same cell can contain more than one of these values. For example, the Customer Reference Database might create, update, and delete customer data, and therefore, CUD would appear in the cell. Let's practice filling in this matrix.

Subject Area CRUD Matrix In Practice

We will go through two examples, the first being a data mart and the second a packaged operational software replacing a legacy application. In each, we will show the steps to populate the Subject Area CRUD Matrix. Afterward, we will analyze the results and see if there are any surprises in terms of subject area gaps or redundancy.

A New Data Mart

1. List all of the subject areas you have identified in the Subject Area Checklist as separate rows.

SUBJECT AREA
CUSTOMER
ITEM
ORDER
ASSOCIATE

2. List your new application as the first column in this spreadsheet. Fill in the cells according to how the application impacts each subject area, using the key we mentioned previously—that is, C, R, U, or D.

SUBJECT AREA	YOUR NEW DATA MART
CUSTOMER	R
ITEM	R
ORDER	R
ASSOCIATE	R

Note that there is always an R in each cell for data marts, because data marts should only read data and only those subject areas mentioned in the Subject Area Checklist for this data mart should be included.

3. Next, add all of the applications as columns that impact any of the subject areas in some way. For a data mart, definitely include the data warehouse as a separate application, because this can help us identify what we can reuse from the data warehouse. Make sure you have as columns any reference databases, such as Item or Customer applications. I find identifying the rest of the applications to be an iterative task. First ask the advice of business experts or, when available, refer to systems architecture documents to get the initial list of applications. Then, as you fill in values for each subject area and application intersection, you might discover that you do not have a C for a subject area; therefore, you need to add another column to your matrix, which is the application responsible for creating this subject area. I find that this iterative approach works quite well.

SUBJECT AREA	YOUR NEW DATA MART	CUSTOMER REFERENCE DATABASE	XYZ APPLICATION	DATA WAREHOUSE
CUSTOMER	R			
ITEM	R			
ORDER	R			
ASSOCIATE	R			

4. Fill in the values for each of the cells on this matrix using C, R, U, or D.

SUBJECT AREA	YOUR NEW DATA MART	CUSTOMER REFERENCE DATABASE	XYZ APPLICATION	DATA WAREHOUSE
CUSTOMER	R	C	C	R
ITEM	R		C	
ORDER	R		C	
ASSOCIATE	R			R

NOTE

▬▬▬ Once you have created one Subject Area CRUD Matrix, you can always reuse the information in other CRUD matrices. After time, you will be able to fill in the rows very quickly, because of this high amount of reuse.

5. Make any observations on the results, and raise any potential issues. Let's make some observations that can help us in sourcing our subject areas, including identifying potential source systems and source system issues. Making observations at this early point can save analysis and development rework later if we find we are sourcing from the wrong application or trying to resolve a data sourcing issue that could have been caught at the subject area level. Observations we can make on this Subject Area CRUD Matrix include the following:

This data mart probably will get Customer and Associate information directly from the data warehouse. Note that when we get to the data element level, we might find exceptions to this. For example, there might be customer data elements we will need that are not in the data warehouse. At this high level, however, we need to assume that customer information is in the warehouse and can be reused.

Both the Customer Reference Database and the XYZ Application appear to create customer information. This can mean one of three things: we populated this matrix incorrectly, each of these applications is responsible for different aspects of Customer, or we have a sourcing issue. If it is the first of these, we fix the matrix and are done. If it is the second, we should break out Customer into two separate rows, depending on which part of Customer is created by each application. For example, the Customer Reference Database might create customer profile information, whereas the XYZ Application might create customer trending information. If it is the third of these, we should raise this sourcing issue to management as soon as possible. I would be very curious, if we do have a sourcing issue, as to which of these applications is feeding the data warehouse the information. Wouldn't it be interesting if we have just uncovered a sourcing issue that has been hidden for some time because no one has ever viewed the information in this way before? You might be in for a raise if you uncover this!

There is no application that creates information in the associate subject area on this matrix. Therefore, this is an example where you might need to add the application that creates associate information as another column. However, because this is a data mart, and the data warehouse already contains associate subject area information, you may not want to find the actual source because we will be reusing it from the data warehouse. It is hoped that all of the associate information we need will be available in the warehouse.

We have the initial subject area sourcing. In the Family Tree tool, which we will discuss shortly, we probably will document that we will source Customer and Associate information from the data warehouse and item and order information from the XYZ application.

Packaged Operational Software Replacing a Legacy Application

1. List all of the subject areas you have identified in the Subject Area Checklist as separate rows.

SUBJECT AREA
CUSTOMER
ITEM
ORDER
ASSOCIATE

2. List your new application as the first column in this spreadsheet. Fill in the cells according to how the application impacts each subject area, using the key we mentioned previously—that is, C, R, U, or D.

SUBJECT AREA	PACKAGED SOFTWARE FOR ORDER PROCESSING
CUSTOMER	R
ITEM	R
ORDER	C
ASSOCIATE	R

3. Next, add all of the applications as columns that impact any of the subject areas in some way. Note that Ye Old Order Processing System is the application we would like to replace.

SUBJECT AREA	PACKAGED SOFTWARE FOR ORDER PROCESSING	YE OLD ORDER PROCESSING SYSTEM	CUSTOMER REFERENCE DATABASE	XYZ APPLICATION
CUSTOMER	R			
ITEM	R			
ORDER	C			
ASSOCIATE	R			

4. Fill in the values for each of the cells on this matrix, using C, R, U, or D.

SUBJECT AREA	PACKAGED SOFTWARE FOR ORDER PROCESSING	YE OLD ORDER PROCESSING SYSTEM	CUSTOMER REFERENCE DATABASE	XYZ APPLICATION
CUSTOMER	R	R	C	
ITEM	R	R		C
ORDER	C	C		
ASSOCIATE	R	C		C

5. Make any observations on the results, and raise any potential issues. Let's make some observations that can help us in sourcing our subject areas, including identifying potential source systems and source system issues:

The new packaged software does not directly replace the old legacy system. The associate subject area is created within the legacy system, which appears to have been redundant with the XYZ application, which also creates associate information. This could these two applications have both been unknowingly creating associate information. It could also mean these two applications create different areas of associate information, in which case we might be missing new functionality from this packaged software, as the packaged software does not create associate information. I would highlight this difference between the old and new order processing system for confirmation.

This new packaged software will become the only creator for order information. After the old order processing application is retired, the new one will be very valuable because it will be the only creator of order information within the organization.

Using the In-the-Know Template

Do you find yourself writing the contacts for each of your projects on little Post-it Notes and sticking them randomly around your monitor screen? For some projects I have worked on I needed to create a short list or spreadsheet with all of the project members' names, roles, and phone numbers. This became especially useful on teams where there was a high turnover rate, and for very large and distributed teams. After using lists such as this for awhile, I realized that it would be useful to come up with a reusable template to make capturing this project information as complete and efficient as possible.

The In-the-Know Template captures the people and documentation that can provide and validate the data requirements. It is the result of recording the names and roles of people for many projects and standardizing the format to capture the most important types of information about each of the project resources. It also includes where other important resources are located, such as documentation. The documentation includes the location of the documents that are useful for completing the data modeling deliverables, such as business and functional requirements documents. Many times I have tried searching my own memory unsuccessfully for where documents were stored. This is especially common on my first day back from a vacation. I have enough trouble remembering my passwords, so remembering where documents are stored is even more challenging for me. Here is a sample of the types of information captured in this tool:

- Tom Jones has been assigned to your project as the Subject Matter Expert on customer account information. His title is Customer Account Divisional Vice President and he can be reached at. . . .

- The Customer Classification List will help us validate our customer classification data and can be located on our public drive in the customer folder. It is updated twice a year by the. . . .

- The Current Item Report is run quarterly by the Reference Data Team, and we can find the latest copy of this report on the team Web site at www. . . .

The In-the-Know Template captures the people and documentation that can provide and validate the data requirements. Having this information in a standard format accomplishes several goals:

Provides a handy and complete reference list. This template is easy to read and provides all of the types of information necessary to identify people and documentation resources. Even years after the project is in production, this list could still be useful for functional or technical project questions.

Finds gaps or redundancy in your available list of resources. This document will highlight any missing information. For example, if no expert on item information is available, this will be very evident here. If you are missing a key reference document, you will note it here and can bring it to the attention of management.

Acts as a sign off document. For example, if a person is identified as a resource for a particular subject area, the management of that person can be made aware and allocate time accordingly. In this way you will minimize the chances that your customer expert is pulled in another direction when you need the help of that expert.

Using the In-the-Know Template

Table 5.5 is a blank sample of the In-the-Know Template. We will show a filled-in template under "Using the In-the-Know Template" section later in this chapter.

Here is a description of how each of these columns is used:

Subject Area. This is the subject area name. You can take the list of subject areas from the Subject Area Checklist and put them right into this column. You might think that it makes more sense or provides more value to plug in more detailed business terms, such as entities or data elements. However, I have found over the years that the subject area level is almost always the most appropriate level at

Table 5.5 In-the-Know Template

SUBJECT AREA	RESOURCE	TYPE	ROLE/HOW USED	LOCATION/CONTACT

which to capture this information. One of the main exceptions is when the same subject area is broken down into several resources and locations, in which case I might choose to break down the subject area into two or more smaller separate subject areas.

Resource. This is the source for this information. In this template, Resource is broad enough to be anything useful, including people, requirement documents, reports, and so on. Be as specific as possible in this description column. If there is more than one resource for the same subject area, use a separate row in this template for the additional resource. Examples of resources include:

- Bob Jones
- Most current customer classification rollups
- Profitability report for April
- Reference Data Department
- Logistics data mart business requirements document

Type. Provides the category for each of the resources. Because this template can be so generic, it is important to put each of the resources into its most appropriate category. For example, the categories for the examples mentioned previously are put in square brackets:

- Bob Jones [Subject Matter Expert]
- Most current customer classification rollups [Report]
- Profitability report for April [Report]
- Reference Data Department [Organization]
- Logistics data mart business requirements document [Requirements Document]

You can customize the types for your own organization, but I have found this level to be the most useful.

Role/How Used. This provides why the resource is valuable to this project. Why are we bothering to list this resource in this template? The Subject Area CRUD Matrix will help us identify which source system experts we need. For example, the roles for the examples mentioned previously are put in square brackets:

- Bob Jones [XYZ Source System Expert]
- Most current customer classification rollups [Report used to make sure customer reference data hierarchy is correct]
- Profitability report for April [Existing report the users want to expand]
- Reference Data Department [Area that will need to validate all reference data definitions and names]
- Logistics data mart business requirements document [Most current business requirements document for the new application]

Location/Contact. This column contains how to reach the resource. If the resource is a document, this column might contain the path name of the document on the public drive or where to find it on the Web. If the resource is a person, this column might contain the phone number, email address, or mailing address of the person. Thus, for the same examples, the location appears within the square brackets:

- Bob Jones [212-555-1212]
- Most current customer classification rollups [www.customergroupetc.com]
- Profitability report for April [Reporting universe in this folder. . . .]
- Reference Data Department [4th floor of building B; manager is James Smith; phone number 212-555-1212]
- Logistics data mart business requirements document [ftp this document off of this file server. . . .]

In-the-Know Template In Practice

Table 5.6 is a sample of a completed In-the-Know Template. Make sure it is kept up to date after it is filled in to maintain its value to you and the project team.

Table 5.6 Sample In-the-Know Template

SUBJECT AREA	RESOURCE	TYPE	ROLE/HOW USED	LOCATION/CONTACT
Customer	Tom Jones	Subject Matter Expert	Customer Reference Data Administrator	212-555-1212
Customer	Customer classification list	Documentation	To validate and create new customer classifications	S:/customer/custclsfn.xls
Item	Current Item Report	Report	To identify all current item information	www.item.com

Subject Area Family Tree

My wife and I vacationed in England recently and visited many historic castles and estates. I was amazed that the same families have inhabited these buildings for centuries and impressed with how well-documented the lineage was for each family. Huge family tree portraits were completed, capturing the parents, grandparents, and great grandparents, going back hundreds of years. Imagine if the lineage of our data elements within our applications were equally as well-documented! We would be able to select a data element within a data mart, for example, and be able to trace its origin through the data warehouse architecture and all of the source systems until we arrive at its point of entry. Such information would be extremely useful for ensuring we have identified the right data element and fully understand its meaning and history. The Family Tree document captures this application lineage.

A family tree documents lineage. It can trace the origins through the ages and visually show the relationships from child to parent. My family tree would show my parents, grandparents, great grandparents, and so on. A family tree for subject areas captures the source applications for each subject area. Starting with the list of subject areas that came out of the Subject Area Checklist or Subject Area CRUD Matrix, we can trace each subject area from parent to grandparent, or from application to source application, ending at the origin of the data or the strategic source. The *strategic source* is the application responsible for creating or changing the subject area information.

The Subject Area Family Tree is a spreadsheet that captures the source applications and other key meta data for each subject area within the scope of our application. It becomes a necessity when there is more than one source application and sourcing complexities are possible. The Subject Area Family Tree works especially well when our application or destination is a data mart, where this tool can capture both which information currently exists in the data warehouse and which applications from which we will require new information.

There are two family tree documents I use repeatedly during data analysis: the Subject Area Family Tree and Data Element Family Tree. The Subject Area Family Tree is the subject of this section, because we are in the midst of our subject area analysis. As we get more details and understand more about the requirements of the application, we develop the Data Element Family Tree during the logical data analysis phase. The Data Element Family Tree describes the origin and transformations that apply to each data element in the application and builds heavily on the Subject Area Family Tree. In fact, there are times when each subject area on the Subject Area Family Tree is the basis for a separate section on the Data Element Family Tree. The Data Element Family Tree is discussed in depth in Chapter 7, "Logical Data Analysis."

We have two different variations of the Subject Area Family Tree. One provides more granular destination information than the other. Let's call the less granular family tree simply the Subject Area Family Tree and the more granular family tree the Subject Area Family Tree Plus. The Subject Area Family Tree is the standard format, which contains subject area information on both the origin and destination application sides.

The Subject Area Family Tree Plus contains subject area information on the origin side but data element level details on the destination side. It is one step closer to the Data Element Family Tree. I will provide an example of it shortly. The focus of this section is the Subject Area Family Tree.

The Subject Area Family Tree, although rarely more than half a page in length, meets many goals of the subject area analysis phase:

Capturing the source applications of each subject area. The Subject Area Family Tree contains each of the applications that play a role in transporting and shaping the content of each of the subject areas. Not only does this tree list the applications that sourced this subject area, it also identifies any major impacts the application has on this subject area. In the more detailed Data Element Family Tree, these impacts translate into data element level transformations. For example, Customer Account is one of your subject areas on the Subject Area CRUD Matrix. Tracing this subject area to its origin system reveals a more generic Account concept, instead of a Customer Account. This more generic concept is then filtered into the different types of accounts: General Ledger Account, Customer Account, and so on, in the next application after the origin system. Therefore, an impact that this other application had was to filter out all account information except the Customer Account subject area. This is something that would be documented in this tool. In the logical data analysis phase, when we focus on the data element level of detail, this subject area impact translates into many data element level transformations. For example, there might be a filter transformation on an account-type data element that only allows values of CA for Customer Account to pass to the next application.

Keeping the sourcing information neatly organized within a spreadsheet makes validation much easier than sifting through pages in a requirements document. A spreadsheet is an extremely unambiguous way to represent the sourcing requirements. Once the subject area source is validated and agreed on, the Subject Area Family Tree is still useful as a reference. Long after the application is developed and in production, people will still need to refer to this information. The Subject Area Family Tree is a convenient place to capture this information. In fact, if we do not capture this sourcing information here, where would we capture it? The only other place might be in a meta data repository. For now, however, the spreadsheet is a handy reference tool.

NOTE

Note that the Subject Area Family Tree lists the chain of information flow for each subject area. It does not document which source system you eventually choose as your source, only the potential sources. You will need to update this spreadsheet with your final selections, as you will see under the "Subject Area Family Tree In Practice" section.

Determining impact on existing application architecture. The Subject Area Family Tree will identify new interfaces that will need to be developed. These new interfaces impact the upstream applications and, therefore, impact the current application architecture. For example, if the new application we are working on is a data mart, the Subject Area Family Tree will identify which subject areas currently exist within the data warehouse that can be reused, which subject areas will need some type of enhancement, and which new subject areas will have to be brought into the data warehouse. This gives a high-level understanding of the impact from each required subject area.

Estimating work effort. Before starting development, you can gauge pretty accurately how much effort it would take to get the information required. You can judge how many applications are involved and the impact each application will have on your development. This can allow you to create an estimate at the subject area level with the effort to bring this new information into the application. I usually recommend filling in this spreadsheet before finalizing the work estimate. Note that if we are developing a data mart, we cannot complete a subject area level estimate until the Subject Area Grain Matrix, the next tool in this chapter, is also complete. This is because the Subject Area Grain Matrix will identify the number of dimension and fact tables we will need in our initial design.

TIP

▬▬▬ The Subject Area Family Tree should always be completed before finalizing an estimate on your data modeling activities. This is because identifying the source for each subject area will give you an idea of the complexities you will encounter during your design.

Starting the Data Element Family Tree. The Subject Area Family Tree is a great start for the more detailed Data Element Family Tree. I know that if Customer comes from the XYZ application, then all of the Customer data elements should come from this application. The Subject Area Family Tree becomes the high-level view for the more detailed document. It can also be used for prioritizing which subject areas to work on first at the data element level.

Identifying sourcing issues early. By determining the sources at the subject area level, you could potentially save yourself a lot of frustration and time by identifying a sourcing issue at this early stage. For example, let's say your users want 3 years of history for Customer, and by filling in the Subject Area Family Tree, you realize that the source system only keeps 1 year of Customer history. This is a problem that you have discovered with a minimal amount of analysis and time. Identifying these types of problems early on is a great benefit of this tool. It takes a proactive approach to sourcing issues.

Complementing the Subject Area Grain Matrix on reporting levels. If you are developing a data mart, you will also need to complete the Subject Area Grain Matrix, which is discussed in the next part of this chapter. The Subject Area Family Tree complements the Subject Area Grain Matrix but does not replace it. The Subject Area Grain Matrix captures the reporting levels required for each fact subject area within the data mart. Therefore, it is important not to repeat this reporting level information in the Subject Area Family Tree. This document is not designed to capture the levels of reporting required by each measure. It makes things much more complicated if you include the reporting levels in the Subject Area Family Tree. For example, you would list Gross Sales Amount only once in your Subject Area Family Tree and capture all reporting variations of Gross Sales Amount on the Subject Area Grain Matrix. If you listed all combinations of Gross Sales Amount on your family tree, you would have a number of additional data element measurements, such as the following:

- Gross Sales Amount by Month by Customer
- Gross Sales Amount Total Company
- Gross Sales Amount by Day by Customer
- Gross Sales Amount by Customer
- Gross Sales Amount by Customer by Production by Quarter

The family tree captures the source, which complements the Subject Area Grain Matrix, which captures the reporting level required for each subject area.

Using the Subject Area Family Tree

The Subject Area Family Tree contains the origin to destination systems for each subject area in your application. Table 5.7 contains a blank Subject Area Family Tree. The columns in this tool represent a subset from the types of meta data that appear in the Subject Area Meta Data Bingo Card. If types of meta data are chosen on the Bingo card that do not appear in this family tree, it means these types will be captured in other places. For example, stewardship information will not appear on the Subject Area Family Tree but does appear in the In-the-Know Template. We want to make sure we do not repeat any meta data values, or else we will have the same synchronization issues that result when repeating the same data element across entities. Likewise, if types of meta data are chosen as columns on the Subject Area Family Tree that did not appear on the Subject Area Meta Data Bingo Card, we might want to expand our Bingo card with this new information or just assume that this extra meta data is essential and thus does not require a vote on the Bingo card. We also want to make sure the spreadsheet is still readable. Too many columns reduce font size and decrease readability.

In this sample Subject Area Family Tree, we can only trace back a maximum of two applications. The column From Here is the initial origin application, To Here is the destination application for this origin application, and To Arrive Here is our destination application. You can change these names to make them more meaningful to your particular situations.

However, there are situations in which we might want to trace back more than two applications. We then need to add more columns, and hence, the font size decreases and our family tree becomes less user-friendly. Another option is to break down the document into two or more family trees, where the destination of the first family tree document becomes the origin for the second one. Under the section *Source,* I will discuss strategy for determining how many applications to trace back through.

Each of the origin and destination applications contains name, source, definition, and history information.

Table 5.7 Subject Area Family Tree

FROM HERE			TO HERE			TO ARRIVE HERE			
NAME	SOURCE	DEFINITION	HISTORY	NAME	SOURCE	DEFINITION	HISTORY	NAME	DEFINITION	HISTORY	QUESTIONS AND IMPACT

Name

This column contains the names for all of the subject areas within the application. If a subject area is left off this document, there is a good chance it will not be modeled in the subject area modeling phase and thus probably not appear in the logical or physical data model either. Thus, if I leave Account out of this document, it may not be included within the scope of the application. However, we rarely leave out a subject area. Imagine the problems if we did! We need to be more concerned about leaving data elements off the more detailed Data Element Family Tree.

The values in this Name column need to be the agreed-on enterprise name for this subject area. Thus, after using the Definition Checklist described in Chapter 3, "Ensuring High-Quality Definitions," we have a high-quality enterprise definition and corresponding name. This name would go here. You can simply copy the names identified within the Subject Area Checklist or Subject Area CRUD Matrix mentioned previously into this Subject Area Family Tree.

Do we need to have the Name column under each application, or can we have it just once for our destination application? Name is repeated multiple times on the Subject Area Family Tree because of two situations that might arise:

Source systems might call the same subject area a different name. For example, System XYZ might call the enterprise concept of Customer, Client instead. This will rarely happen, because the source systems should also be using the enterprise concepts. If the source applications are fairly old, however, there is a chance this might happen.

Subject areas at a different level of detail might need to be combined to create the final subject area. For example, System XYZ provides Customer Address information and System ABC provides Customer Credit information. These two subject areas combine to form Customer in the system we are modeling. Thus, there can be many origins for one destination. There can also be many destinations for one origin. Thus, names are important whenever there are one-to-many or many-to-many relationships between origin and destination. These many-to-many relationships are sometimes difficult to show in a spreadsheet format.

Source

The Source column contains the source application name for each subject areas. Note that a source application is not just limited to a database but can also be a file or spreadsheet. A very important question to answer at this point is "How far back should we go?" That is, should we list all of the source applications until we reach the point where a user is typing in the information or should we just go back to the immediate source? My advice is to continue following the subject area upstream until you arrive at a reliable and accurate source for this subject area, and then stop.

Let's say we have Customer as a subject area in our family tree for a data mart. If the subject area currently exists in the data warehouse, this should be our reliable and accurate source. Therefore, we should stop here. Thus, for Customer in this example, we only need to go back one application, to the data warehouse. Let's say we have Inventory as a subject area in our family tree. Inventory comes from a Logistics Integration Application, which only gets data once a month. Therefore, unless our requirement is only for monthly data, this integration application is not a reliable source. We need to go further back. The Logistics Integration Application gets its logistics information from the Warehouse Application. This is the place where the warehouse team enters the inventory information. Therefore, this is the most reliable and accurate source and is the place to go for this subject area information.

In determining what is a reliable and accurate source, keep these criteria in mind:

History requirements. Make sure the source system you choose has at least the same amount of history for the subject area as you need in your application. For example, if your application is storing order information and your users request 3 years of order information, you need to make sure your source system has at least 3 years for the initial history load.

How current is the information? If your application requires daily updates, your source system needs to have daily updates. Recently, our initial choice for the sales subject area provided month-end snapshots, when our application was looking for more timely information.

Known data quality problems. Unless there is no alternative, never choose a source that has known data quality problems in your subject area. Source data quality problems raise many issues—not only the potential for poor quality data but several tradeoffs, including whether it is better to be consistent using a poor source or inconsistent with correct information. Try not to put yourself in this situation, because there are no right answers and only mistakes to be made.

System dependencies. In one situation, we chose a source for item information that was already four levels downstream from the actual source. Being this far downstream can cause problems. If any of the applications have problems further upstream, they will affect the delivery of our item information. I know of several cases where item data did not arrive on time because of a dependency on an upstream source. Make sure you take the most immediate accurate source of data. If you need to pull data from a system that is several steps away from the source, make sure there are strong links, which are not going to fail, between these applications.

Future life of the origin application. Make sure the application you are pulling data from, or any of the applications upstream that pass this subject area information, are not going anywhere any time soon. Your source application should be around for a long time.

Definition

Just as we have seen with the Name column, we can have multiple definitions for a single subject area on this tree. The destination definition, or definition that we are modeling, should be consistent with the enterprise definition finalized during the Subject Area Checklist. However, there is a small chance, but it is possible, that one of the source systems might have a definition slightly different from the enterprise definition. Therefore, we need to capture this to make sure we have identified the correct source. We also need definitions when there is not a strict one-to-one relationship between origin and destination, that is, when we have a one-to-many or many-to-many relationship.

History

The History column is the last piece of information we need from each source system at a subject area level. This is the number of years the system has of history on this subject area. For example, the XYZ source system might have 2 years of history. The History column under the To Arrive Here column, meaning for the one you are modeling, is how much history we need. This is a very important distinction. If we want more history than we have in our source system, then we have an issue and must work with the users to agree on less history, at least in the beginning. Finding this history gap at the subject area level could catch a potentially serious problem very early on, before a great deal of time has been invested in this project. It also will help set user expectations.

Questions and Impact

No matter how many columns I have on my Subject Area Family Tree, a must-have column is the one that contains questions and impact information. Because so many people might be looking at this spreadsheet, and this might be the first time the source information has been viewed in this format, there will probably be many questions and comments. Questions and comments must be addressed at this subject area level, because answering a question at this level can save us from problems later. For example, answering a question about the definition or scope of customer in the Subject Area Family Tree can save many questions on the Data Element Family Tree for all of the customer data elements. I could also add notes about impact information within this cell. I could optionally add another column for impact; however, because subject area impact notes only a small percentage of the time, I usually save valuable space by combining them with questions in the same column.

Using the Subject Area Family Tree Plus

The Subject Area Family Tree Plus is a slight variation of the Subject Area Family Tree. It contains the same information for the source applications; however, for the target or application you are modeling, it goes down to the data element level. This is useful when you know the data elements you need for your application but are not quite sure of the exact data elements you will need from the origin applications. A good starting point would be to identify the source applications and their subject areas. Later, during the development of the Data Element Family Tree, the individual data element mapping can be defined. The format looks identical to what we have seen in Table 5.7.

It is the same template except that the values in the To Arrive Here column are data elements instead of subject areas. We will go through an example of this type of family tree as well.

Subject Area Family Tree in Practice

In this section, we review the steps for creating the Subject Area Family Tree and show values filled in for both the Subject Area Family Tree and the Subject Area Family Tree Plus. This detailed example will pertain to a data mart, and therefore, we can show that in some cases the best source for a subject area is the data warehouse. However, these examples can easily be applied to any application under design.

There are several steps to completing the Subject Area Family Tree:

1. **Agree on the columns.** Play Subject Area Meta Data Bingo, discussed in Chapter 2, "Meta Data Bingo." Just use the most important columns to keep the spreadsheet readable. Make sure, as mentioned earlier, that you do not unnecessarily repeat the types of meta data across analysis and design tools.

2. **Fill it in.** You need to coordinate the tasks if multiple people or teams will be filling this in. Start by copying the subject areas from the Subject Area Checklist or Subject Area CRUD Matrix into the destination section of this spreadsheet. Then work your way upstream, filling in the origin applications until you get to a reliable and accurate source. This step is the bulk of the effort in completing the Subject Area Family Tree.

3. **Remove unreliable interim sources.** You want to make sure that your completed Subject Area Family Tree contains only the most immediate accurate source and, therefore, does not show unreliable sources from which you will not be pulling data. This is important to remember because you are documenting where you will get the subject area information from, and not the entire information flow from strategic source onward. Remove those interim sources that you will not be using.

4. **Review.** This could be very iterative.

5. **Maintain.** This becomes a very valuable reference document, therefore, keep it current.

Let's go through an example:

You have started the subject area analysis on a new data mart. You have completed the Subject Area Checklist and know that the following subject areas are included within this mart:

- Customer
- Order
- Product
- Associate
- Time

1. Agree on the Columns

Because you have already read Chapter 2 of this book, "Meta Data Bingo," you are familiar with Meta Data Bingo, which identifies the types of meta data that are important for us to capture. You play Subject Area Meta Data Bingo with your team. After summarizing the results, your final card resembles Table 5.8.

This card tells us that it will be a requirement to capture the meta data types under the High category. The standard enterprise name will be the companywide, agreed-on name for this concept. Definition, which is a requirement to store, is also under the High category. History requirements will identify how many years of history will be required for each subject area. In this way we can compare the history requirements against the source data to make sure we can get at least that much history. Note that source information is also checked off as being high priority and is the point of completing the Subject Area Family Tree.

Alias information will not be captured due to being in the low category. Stewardship information if we decide to capture it will be on the In-the-Know Template. Thus, this step produces a blank Subject Area Checklist, identical to that in Table 5.3.

2. Fill It In

You have copied the subject areas from the Subject Area Checklist into the destination columns and have met with the source system experts from the In-the-Know Template to arrive at an initial Subject Area Family Tree (see Table 5.9).

3. Remove Unreliable Interim Sources

The Transaction Integration Application as a source for Order information appears to be unreliable and is not the preferred source for this information. I observe this based on the following:

Table 5.8 Summarized Subject Area Meta Data Bingo Card

CODE	DESCRIPTIVE INFORMATION	HIGH	MEDIUM	LOW	QUESTIONS AND ISSUES
A	Standard enterprise name	X			
B	Alias			X	
C	Definition	X			
D	Steward name and department		X		
E	History requirements	X			
F	Source	X			

■ It stores only 2 years of history when we need 3 years.

■ It is updated monthly; after talking with the business user, we find we need daily updates.

Thus, we will need to go directly against the Order Entry application, the strategic source, for the order subject area.

Note also that both Associate and Time are already in the data warehouse, which we will need to assume is a reliable source. Many times the data warehouse might contain more abstract structures, such as Party, which contains the Associate concept and probably several other important subject areas as well. We will discuss abstraction in detail in Chapter 9, "The Abstraction Safety Guide and Components."

After removing the unreliable Transaction Integration Application source, we only have a single immediate source for each subject area. Therefore, the updated Subject Area Family Tree document (see Table 5.10) has fewer columns.

4. Review

The next step is to review this Subject Area Family Tree with the team and, it is hoped, leave this review with everyone agreeing on the source information and all of your questions and issues answered. Note that it is important to include both business and source system experts in this review.

5. Maintain

It is very important to maintain your finished Subject Area Family Tree when you are done with your last review. This document will be the starting point for the data element analysis, and you probably will refer back to for many projects to come. Because this information is usually not stored anywhere else, it is important to maintain here.

Subject Area Family Tree Plus in Practice

The Subject Area Family Tree Plus is completed using the same steps as the Subject Area Family Tree, except that the destination side is filled in with data elements instead of subject areas. Note that the Subject Area Family Tree Plus can be built on the Subject Area Family Tree, and a good transition can be made to the Data Element Family Tree during the logical data analysis phase. Rather than go through the same steps, let's just look at this Subject Area Family Tree filled in with data elements instead of subject areas for Customer. See Table 5.11 for a short example.

Table 5.9 Initial Subject Area Family Tree

FROM HERE				TO HERE				TO ARRIVE HERE			
NAME	SOURCE	DEFINITION	HISTORY	NAME	SOURCE	DEFINITION	HISTORY	NAME	DEFINITION	HISTORY	QUESTIONS AND IMPACT
				Customer	Customer Reference Database	The recipient and purchaser of our products.	10	Customer	The recipient and purchaser of our products.	3	Transaction Integration Application consolidates all transactions within the company into a single design. Will need to filter where type code = "ORDER" It is updated monthly.
Order Entry		A contract to buy a quantity of product at a specified price.	4	Transaction	Transaction Integration Application	An individual change or action within our environment.	2	Order	A contract to buy a quantity of product at a specified price.	3	
				Item	Item Reference Database	Anything we buy, sell, stock, move, or make. Any manufactured or purchased part, material, component, assembly, or product.	10	Product	Anything we buy, sell, stock, move, or make. Any manufactured or purchased part, material, component, assembly, or product.	3	

Term	Source	Definition	
Party	Data Warehouse	A person or company that is important to our business in some way.	5
Associate		A person who is employed in a full- or part-time capacity by our company, to perform a service or function to our company.	3
Time	Data Warehouse	A measurable length of seconds, minutes hours, days, weeks, months, or years. Can include both fiscal and Julian time measurements.	10
Time		A measurable length of seconds, minutes hours, days, weeks, months or years. Can include both fiscal and Julian time measurements.	3

Table 5.10 Updated Subject Area Family Tree

	FROM HERE			TO ARRIVE HERE			
NAME	SOURCE	DEFINITION	HISTORY	NAME	DEFINITION	HISTORY	QUESTIONS AND IMPACT
Customer	Customer Reference Database	The recipient and purchaser of our products.	10	Customer	The recipient and purchaser of our products.	3	
Order	Order Entry	A contract to buy a quantity of product at a specified price.	4	Order	A contract to buy a quantity of product at a specified price.	3	
Item	Item Reference Database	Anything we buy, sell, stock, move, or make. Any manufactured or purchased part, material, component, assembly, or product.	10	Product	Anything we buy, sell, stock, move, or make. Any manufactured or purchased part, material, component, assembly, or product.	3	
Party	Data Warehouse	A person or company that is important to our business in some way.	5	Associate	A person who is employed in a full- or part-time capacity by our company, to perform a service or function to our company.	3	
Time	Data Warehouse	A measurable length of seconds, minutes, hours, days, weeks, months or years. Can include both fiscal and Julian time measurements.	10	Time	A measurable length of seconds, minutes, hours, days, weeks, months or years. Can include both fiscal and Julian time measurements.	3	

Table 5.11 Subject Area Family Tree Plus

| | FROM HERE | | | TO ARRIVE HERE | | | |
| | | | | | | | QUESTIONS AND |
NAME	SOURCE	DEFINITION	HISTORY	NAME	DEFINITION	HISTORY	IMPACT
Customer	Customer Reference Database	The recipient and purchaser of our products.	10	Customer Last Name	The last name of the recipient and purchaser of our products.	3	
				Customer First Name	The first name of the recipient and purchaser of our products.	3	
				Customer Home Phone Number	The home phone number of the recipient and purchaser of our products.	3	
				Customer Address City Name	The city of the recipient and purchaser or our products.	3	
				Customer Shoe Size	The shoe size of the recipient and purchaser of our products.	3	

Subject Area Grain Matrix

I have always enjoyed watching science fiction movies. Have you also noticed that there is often a common scene in them in which characters from different planets are in the same room speaking their native languages and no one can understand anyone else. Characters are talking Jupitan and Martian and hundreds of other languages. Then, through the use of a "universal translator" device, everyone can magically understand the languages of everyone else. This little device can translate everything you say into the language of the person you are speaking with, and everything they say into your language. It is an amazing little device. Unfortunately, this is just science fiction. Fortunately, however, such a universal translator device does exist for data warehouse reporting requirements. It is called the Subject Area Grain Matrix.

The Subject Area Grain Matrix is a spreadsheet that captures the levels of reporting for each subject area or fact. It is the spreadsheet view of a subject area star schema design.

This spreadsheet view provides a universal translator between business users and the technical project team, who can understand and validate the reporting requirements through this spreadsheet. Business users might speak the language of reports, whereas technical people might speak the language of data models or star schema designs. The Subject Area Grain Matrix is a common ground, a spreadsheet to which both users and technical people can relate and use as a medium for communication. Note that this is only for reporting applications, such as data marts. Any application that has heavy reporting requirements can take advantage of this tool. Once this spreadsheet is completed, it is a very straightforward process to create a subject area star schema design.

There are two grain matrices I use repeatedly during data mart data analysis: the Subject Area Grain Matrix and the Data Element Grain Matrix. The first is the subject of this section, because we are still in the midst of our subject area analysis. As we get more details and understand more about the requirements of the application, we develop the Data Element Grain Matrix (see Chapter 7, "Logical Data Analysis") during the logical data analysis phase. This matrix describes the reporting requirements for each fact, down to the data element level of granularity. It builds heavily on the Subject Area Grain Matrix.

The Subject Area Grain Matrix can be used for both ad hoc and standard reporting. In ad hoc reporting actions, users have greater access to data and the types of queries they can execute. In standard reporting, predefined queries are included that users can execute with limited access to the data. Standard reports usually are fairly summarized information and usually are formatted to users' requests. Enough details are hidden to make standard reporting more manageable and understandable to the average user. In contrast, ad hoc reporting pretty much provides direct access to the database tables and, therefore, is more complex and requires greater understanding of the underlying structures. For example, a standard report might be the monthly profit report by Customer. An ad hoc report might start out with a similar monthly report, but then the user might want to select different data elements to report on monthly promotions by Customer, monthly complaints by Customer, and so on. Ad hoc reporting is more difficult to predict and, therefore, usually requires more detailed access to the data so that users can summarize and slice the data any way they wish. Standard reporting has a defined level of reporting, which is usually not the lowest level. The Subject Area Grain Matrix can meet both ad hoc and standard reporting needs, usually with separate matrices or with different notation on the same matrix. There are even times when each standard report might require its own Subject Area Grain Matrix or different notation on the same matrix.

The Subject Area Grain Matrix acts as a universal translator for data mart reporting requirements. This common language created by this spreadsheet between business users and the technical team accomplishes several goals:

Permits discussion and agreement on the levels of reporting without showing a data model. Many users with whom I have worked have had difficulty understanding data modeling concepts. This can cause confusion and frustration for users when using a star schema data model to validate reporting requirements. Rather than use the model as a validation mechanism, I prefer to use the Subject Area Grain Matrix. Not too long ago I validated with a business user all of the subject area reporting requirements for a financial data mart, without showing a single data model. I have found that all users are very comfortable with a spreadsheet. As we have seen with the Subject Area Family Tree, the spreadsheet format provides an unambiguous representation for capturing the reporting requirements. Looking at report printouts or paragraphs of text in a requirements document can sometimes lead to lots of questions or incorrect assumptions. A spreadsheet more clearly displays the reporting requirements, making it easier for agreement and validation.

Complements the Subject Area Family Tree. It captures the source information for each subject area, and the Subject Area Grain Matrix captures the reporting requirements for each fact or measurement subject area. These two documents are closely related. Without the family tree, we would never be able to validate whether our reporting requirements are realistic, based on what is available in the existing applications. Without the grain matrix, we would need to add an incredible amount of redundancy to the family tree to capture all possible combinations of fact subject area with reporting levels. For example, if our grain matrix captures that we need to view sales down to an item level, we need to validate this request in the family tree by making sure the source system for sales information goes down to an item level. Likewise, sales might be viewed by item, customer, month, day, and so on. Each of these different ways of viewing sales also would need to appear as a separate row in the family tree document if we did not have the grain matrix to capture all these variations of sales in a single row.

Creates a seamless transition to a star schema. It is very straightforward and easy to translate the Subject Area Grain Matrix into a subject area data model star schema. We will go through these steps in the "Subject Area Grain Matrix In Practice" section later in this chapter.

Starts the Data Element Grain Matrix. The Subject Area Grain Matrix is a great start for the more detailed Data Element Grain Matrix. If I know that all sales need to be reported at the month, item, and customer levels, then I know that all of the sales data elements also need to be reported at these levels. This matrix can also be used for prioritizing which subject areas to work on first at the data element level.

Estimates work effort. Before starting development, you can gauge pretty accurately how many dimension, fact, and summary tables will be required in your design. The Subject Area Grain Matrix, combined with the Subject Area Family Tree, is a quick way to arrive at a rough estimate for data mart development.

TIP

The Subject Area Grain Matrix should always be completed before finalizing an estimate on your data modeling activities. The reason is that identifying the subject area reporting levels provides a rough estimate as to how many tables we will have in our star schema and, hence, how much effort will be required.

Using the Subject Area Grain Matrix

In the Subject Area Grain Matrix, the rows represent transaction subject areas and the columns represent reference subject areas. The rows contain facts or measurements, and thus the columns represent the dimensions. The levels within each dimension are listed as subcolumns under their reference data categories. For example, Time is a dimension that appears as a column category, containing the reporting levels Year, Quarter, Month, and Day. Table 5.12 contains a sample Subject Area Grain Matrix.

Note that we are only listing the reporting levels of each dimension in this spreadsheet, not all of the data elements within each dimension. Thus, for Time we list Year, Quarter, Month, and Day. We do not list Year Code, Year Description Text, Quarter Code, and so on. This data element level of detail will be captured on the Data Element Family Tree, which will be discussed in logical data analysis in Chapter 7.

Note also that this spreadsheet, like the family tree, can have many columns, one for each dimension level. Try to keep the matrix readable and as simple as possible, because too quickly it can become 15 columns long in 6-point type.

Each fact subject area will break down into a number of data element facts on the Data Element Grain Matrix. For example, Shipments might translate into Shipment Gross Dollars, Shipment Weight in Pounds, Shipment Weight in Tons, Shipment Volume, and many others. Capturing the reporting levels at the subject area provides a good starting point for capturing the reporting at the more detailed data element level.

Subject Area Grain Matrix In Practice

Let's go through the steps of completing a Subject Area Grain Matrix and converting it into a subject area star schema.

1. **Agree on the columns and rows.** For the columns, fill in each reference subject area on your Subject Area Checklist or Subject Area CRUD Matrix. Then for each reference subject area, create sub-columns for each dimension level. Copy each transaction subject area into a separate row. This defines both the rows and columns for this matrix.

2. **Fill it in.** A lot of coordination might come into play if there are several different people responsible for completing this spreadsheet. You might want to delegate by transaction subject area or by reference subject area. For example, "John you get all the reporting levels we need for Sales." Also, this step is where we need to distinguish the different types of reporting we will be doing in this data mart. This includes the ad hoc report and each of the specific reports. You can either create separate Subject Area Grain Matrices for each type of reporting or use one matrix with a different notation and a key or legend to identify what each type of notation means. For the example below, we will use one matrix with a key.

3. **Review.** This could be very iterative. Business users must be included in the review and validate each of the reporting levels.

4. **Group rows into common sets.** This is a large step toward star schema design, because those measures that share the same set of reporting levels usually wind up in the same fact table; that is, they share the same grain. It is easy to identify those that share the same grain by putting these rows next to each other.

5. **Convert into initial subject area star schema.** After grouping together the com-

Table 5.12 Subject Area Grain Matrix

SUBJECT AREA	TIME			CUSTOMER		PRODUCT		SALES ORGANIZATION	
	YEAR	QUARTER	MONTH	DAY	CATEGORY	CUSTOMER	BRAND	ITEM	DIVISION	REGION
Shipments										
Debits										
Credits										
Balances										
Production										
Contact										

mon fact subject areas, convert them into a data model containing the fact and dimension subject areas.

TIP

After creating the Subject Area Grain Matrix, I usually do not maintain it because we have the star schema design. The grain matrix is just an interim document to arrive at the data model.

1. Agree on the Columns and Rows

After agreeing on the fact and reference data subject areas, our spreadsheet looks just like our example in Table 5.12.

2. Fill It In

Table 5.13 contains the Subject Area Grain Matrix after it has been initially filled in. Note the different notation used for the ad hoc report versus the production and shipments summary standard reports. Usually in ad hoc analysis, when a dimension is referred to, it is at the lowest level. For example, ad hoc analysis for Product will always be at the Item level. It is very interesting that none of the fact subject areas requires any type of reporting at the Sales Organization level. This could mean we either do not know what reporting we will have at the sales organization level (in which case the review step might shed some light) or do not need sales organization information in this application and, therefore, do not have to continue analyzing this information. Knowing we do not need sales organization information at the subject area level will save lots of time later, because we will not have to analyze each of the sales organization data elements.

3. Review

Reviewing with the business users and technical team reveals no surprises, and everyone understands and agrees to the reporting levels captured. Note how relevant the universal language translator analogy is during this step.

4. Group Rows into Common Sets

See Table 5.14 for grouping together the common rows. Note that it just so happened in this example that the fact subject areas were almost in perfect order. The exception was the Contact Subject Area, which needed to be moved next to Shipments because they both share the same levels of reporting.

5. Convert into Initial Subject Area Star Schema

Your initial star schema design might look very much like what appears in Figure 5.2. I followed several guidelines on this model:

Table 5.13 Filled-In Subject Area Grain Matrix

SUBJECT AREA	TIME				CUSTOMER		PRODUCT		SALES ORGANIZATION	
	YEAR	QUARTER	MONTH	DAY	CATEGORY	CUSTOMER	BRAND	ITEM	DIVISION	REGION
Shipments	AB	AB	AB	A	AB	A	AB	A		
Debits	A	A	A	A	A	A				
Credits	A	A	A	A	A	A				
Balances	A	A	A	A			A	A		
Production	AC	AC	A	A			AC	AC		
Contact	A	A	A	A	A	A	A	A		

A, ad hoc reporting; B, shipments summary report; C, production summary report..

Table 5.14 Filled-In Subject Area Grain Matrix, Common Rows Grouped Together

SUBJECT AREA	TIME				CUSTOMER		PRODUCT		SALES ORGANIZATION	
	YEAR	QUARTER	MONTH	DAY	CATEGORY	CUSTOMER	BRAND	ITEM	DIVISION	REGION
Shipments	AB	AB	AB	A	AB	A	AB	A		
Contact	A	A	A	A	A	A	A	A		
Debits	A	A	A	A	A	A				
Credits	A	A	A	A	A	A				
Balances	A	A	A	A			A	A		
Production	AC	AC	A	A			AC	AC		

A, ad hoc reporting; B, shipments summary report; C, production summary report..

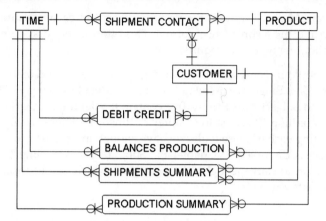

Figure 5.2 Initial star schema design.

I used label names to capture the lowest level that a fact subject area needs. For example, Debit Credit needs time information down to a Day level.

I concatenated the names of the fact subject areas that share the same grain. For example, both debit and credit share the same grain; therefore, the name of this fact subject area is Debit Credit. I would create more meaningful names during the logical data analysis phase.

I used the suffix Summary to indicate a summary subject area. For example, Shipments Summary is the subject area fact table containing the Shipments Summary standard report.

Summary

This chapter focused on five key tools for assisting in the subject area analysis phase of a data modeling effort. They should be completed in this order:

1. **Subject Area Checklist.** A complete list of subject areas within the new application, along with their definitions and synonyms or aliases. This provides a great starting point.

2. **Application Subject Area CRUD Matrix.** Contains the subject area gaps and overlap that can exist between your new application and existing applications. This is a powerful tool for scoping your application.

3. **In-the-Know Template.** Identifies the people and documentation you will need as resources to complete your data modeling deliverables of this new application. This is a straightforward method to gain agreement on the resources you can tap for your data modeling activities.

4. **Subject Area Family Tree.** Contains the source applications for each subject area, and several other critical pieces of information. This clarifies where the subject area data will come from.

5. **Subject Area Grain Matrix.** Captures the reporting levels for each measurement or fact subject area, using a spreadsheet format. This offers a very easy-to-read document for validating reporting requirements.

Each of these tools should be completed in this order, and they are based on the results of Subject Area Meta Data Bingo discussed in Chapter 2, "Meta Data Bingo." The Subject Area Checklist and Subject Area Family Tree contain the definitions that were perfected against the Definition Checklist in Chapter 3, "Ensuring High-Quality Definitions." After completing each of these tools, we have enough information to complete the subject area models discussed in Chapter 6, "Subject Area Modeling." We also have a solid foundation to start the logical data analysis, which will be discussed in Chapter 7, "Logical Data Analysis."

Subject Area Modeling

W̶e were hiking in Arizona several years ago. It was a very hot and dry day. I remember wishing I had brought water or anything thirst-quenching with me, as we walked along the dusty path. The surroundings consisted of pale yellow rocks and cliffs, dotted with countless thorny bushes and cacti. Toward the end of the hike we approached a small tree and stopped us in our tracks. There lay an apple tree in the midst of these desert-like conditions! I was amazed that there were actually huge, golden apples weighing down this tree. As I circled it, I was impressed by how many apples were just within arm's reach. I remember picking apples years before and how I had to really stretch, or stand on someone else, to get the really good ones. And all of these apples looked really good! I pulled one of these low-hanging fruit off the tree, wiped it off on my shirt, and quickly took a large bite out of it. It was juicy and perfect. I still remember how surprised I was to find this delicious fruit so easily accessible. This story literally shows the beauty of low-hanging fruit. With little effort I was able to reap delicious rewards. I consider subject area models also to be low-hanging fruit. With a minimal amount of time and effort, we can model a very broad perspective of the business, gaining understanding and building trust and rapport with the project team.

About This Chapter

After completing the subject area analysis described in Chapter 5, "Subject Area Analysis," we have enough information to create the subject area models. This chapter focuses on three types of subject area models, each being a very powerful validation and scoping tool. I have relied heavily on these three types of subject area models through many challenging projects. All three types share the basic syntax of a subject area model and, therefore, the general purpose and goals of such a model. However, each model also has its own characteristics that lead to additional goals and benefits. These three types of subject area models are:

- Business Clean Slate model

- Application Clean Slate model

- Early Reality Check model

We present these powerful tools in the order in which they appear in this list, which is the order in which they depend on each other. The Application Clean Slate model is dependent on the completion of the Business Clean Slate model. The Early Reality Check model is dependent on the completion of the Application Clean Slate model.

The chapter begins with an overview of the subject area model, including its characteristics and goals, as well as a comparison to the conceptual data model. Then there is a section on reading the business rules. This text focuses on only those business rules that can be captured on the model. Other business rules, such as "Accounts can only be opened the first week of every month," are outside the scope of this text. I have seen many of us over the years develop a sense for one-to-many and many-to-many relationships, and yet we do not know how to read the business rules between them. Therefore, this section describes how to tell the business rule story through the labels and cardinality. Although not a separate tool, knowing how to read the relationships or business rules is a prerequisite to maximizing the value from each of these subject area models.

Afterward, we briefly describe a project scenario involving a consumer response application, which will be the basis for detailed examples of each of the three types of subject area models. Then we review in depth each of these three types of subject area models. We describe each, along with their goals and the modeling situations where they are most effective. Then we will use the project scenario to go through examples of each type of subject area model. First we will create a Business Clean Slate model, then use it to create an Application Clean Slate model, and then use that to create the Early Reality Check model. Thus, we will realize how the models build heavily on each other. It will also be useful and interesting to see the same scenario progress through each of these three models.

What Is a Subject Area Model?

The subject area model is a diagram containing standard data modeling syntax that describes the business in nontechnical terms at a subject area level. It follows the same syntax that we have at the logical and physical data model levels. This syntax is represented with boxes and lines. Boxes represent the concepts, and lines represent the relationships or business rules between these concepts. Boxes on the subject area model are the subject areas that were identified during the analysis phase in the previous chapter, while creating the Subject Area Checklist. Recall that subject areas are concepts that are both basic and critical to the operation of the business. Table 6.1 lists a Subject Area Checklist that will be input to a subject area model example we will describe in this section.

The lines on the subject area model represent the business rules. Business rules are connections that exist and are enforced between two or more concepts. Many of these

Table 6.1 Subject Area Checklist

NAME	DEFINITION
Customer	The recipient and purchaser of our products. One that acquires goods or services either for direct use or ownership, or for resale or use in production and manufacturing.
Credit Account	A structure to facilitate the financial transactions carried out by the company, containing the financial transactions where money is added to the customer's balance.
Debit Account	A structure to facilitate the financial transactions carried out by the company, containing the financial transactions where money is subtracted from the customer's balance.
Order	A contract containing the terms and conditions around the purchase of product.
Product	Anything we buy, sell, stock, move, or make.

business rules can be represented using relationships on our models. These business rules have not been analyzed up to this point. There have not been any tools in the previous chapter that capture these rules. This is because the cleanest and least ambiguous representation for these rules can be shown directly on a data model, and not on spreadsheets or checklists.

TIP

The optimal place to capture subject area business rules is on the subject area model itself, because of the exactness imposed by standard data modeling syntax. There is no room for multiple interpretations.

Examples of business rules for these subject areas might be the following:

- A Customer can own many Credit Accounts.
- A Customer can own many Debit Accounts.
- A Credit Account must belong to either one or two Customers.
- A Debit Account must belong to either one or two Customers.
- There are no restrictions on the number of Debit Accounts or Credit Accounts that a Customer can own.
- An Order must be placed by a single Customer.
- A Customer can place many Orders.
- An Order must be for one or more Products.
- A Product can appear on many Orders.

If we put these boxes and lines on a subject area model it would resemble the model in Figure 6.1.

Note how the subject areas from this Subject Area Checklist have been converted to

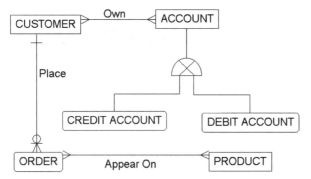

Figure 6.1 Sample subject area model.

boxes on this model. The spreadsheet cell Customer is now the box Customer. It is very interesting to see Debit Account and Credit Account listed as separate subject areas. This means that they are both basic and critical to the organization or department for which we are creating this model. At this point, we might have the urge to question their importance to be considered subject areas. Because we have already done this basic and critical test when creating the Subject Area Checklist, however, we should not do this validation again here. We need to assume that they are valid subject areas. Perhaps this model is for the accounting department, in which case Debit Account and Credit Account are department-specific subject areas.

NOTE

Note the important role of business rules. They are an integral part of the subject area model. They take subject areas that would otherwise be isolated from each other and create dependencies and business logic between them to resemble how the real world works. Just as a logical data model contains relationships that enforce rules between normalized entities, and a physical data model contains constraints that enforce rules between database tables, a subject area model also contains relationships that enforce business rules between subject areas. If we put several experts in a room to review the model in Figure 6.1, they might agree or disagree with these business rules. However, these experts cannot argue about how to interpret the rules in this model. These lines capture the business rules with the same amount of clarity and rigor that we see in the logical and physical data models. They are indisputable syntax for representing the rules. An order must be placed by a single customer. You cannot interpret this relationship in a different way, such as an order can be placed by more than one customer.

Just as in the logical and physical models, these relationships can be one-to-one or one-to-many (subject area models can also include many-to-many relationships and similar to logical data modeling, include subtyping as well):

One-to-one. Although there are no examples of one-to-one relationships in Figure 6.1, they can occur every once in awhile. The reason they are rarer than the other types of relationships is that sometimes one-to-one concepts are really slight variations of the same subject area and, therefore, are shown within a single subject area.

One-to-many. These are the most prevalent in every data model we create, whether at the subject area, logical, or physical levels of detail. An example from Figure 6.1 follows:

- A Customer can place many Orders.

- An Order must be placed by a single Customer.

Many-to-many. Many-to-many relationships show the beauty of keeping concepts at a high level. When converting the subject area model to a logical data model, we will need to create an additional entity to resolve each many-to-many relationship, in some cases called an *associative entity*. On the logical models, we can have many of these associative entities, which sometimes make it difficult to identify the real business entities. The main purpose in life for an associative entity is to store the primary keys from each of the participating entities in a many-to-many relationship, and usually not to provide business value. An associative entity can also have its own data elements and participate in additional business rules. This is more of a logical data modeling concept, which is the focus of Chapter 8, "The Normalization Hike and Denormalization Survival Guide." What is important to keep in mind here is that a many-to-many relationship does not require additional boxes on the subject area model, and therefore, there is less clutter and it is easier to focus on the more important concepts. A many-to-many relationship example from Figure 6.1 would be the following:

- A Customer can own many Accounts.

- An Account must belong to either one or two Customers.

Subtyping. Subtyping is grouping two or more entities that have common data elements or relationships. We will discuss subtyping in Chapter 9, "The Abstraction Safety Guide and Components," when we focus on abstraction. On a subject area model, subtyping is extremely useful. It lets us group together two or more subject areas, called *subtypes*, under a more generic concept called a *supertype*. Connecting business rules to a supertype, removes the need to have redundant business rules connect to each of the subtypes. You will note the subtyping symbol in Figure 6.1 as the semicircle with an X in the middle. This is the Information Engineering symbol for a subtype. Here are our original rules before the Account supertype:

- A Customer can own many Credit Accounts.

- A Customer can own many Debit Accounts.

- A Credit Account must belong to either one or two Customers.

- A Debit Account must belong to either one or two Customers.

- There are no restrictions on the number of Debit Accounts or Credit Accounts that a Customer can own.

Because we used subtyping, Customer relates directly to Account instead of the types of accounts. Thus, Debit Account and Credit Account are separate subject areas that share the common properties of an account. They are both subtypes; Account is the supertype. We can draw the lines, which represent the business rules, directly to Account instead of to both of its subtypes. Thus, in Figure 6.1, our Account-related business rules are now the following:

- An Account can be either a Debit Account or a Credit Account, but not both at the same time.
- A Customer can own many Accounts.
- An Account must belong to either one or two Customers.
- There are no restrictions on the number of Accounts that a Customer can own.

You can see that without the subtyping, we needed to repeat the business rules for both the Debit Account and Credit Account. This can cause additional clutter and confusion on the subject area model. Note that if the business rules are different in any way from Debit Account and Credit Account, we will need to show each rule separately, instead of just one rule for Account.

There are several general goals of a subject area model. There are more specific goals for each of the three types of subject area models we will be discussing shortly, but the following goals apply to all types of subject area models:

Provides broad understanding. The Subject Area Checklist from the previous chapter provides an understanding for each of the subject areas, including their name and definition. What was lacking was how these subject areas relate to each other. Thus, now that we understand what a customer is and what an account is, we must ask what are the business rules, if any, between these two concepts? The subject area model ties together these subject areas and is able to visually show the dependencies and rules between these subject areas. Because we are at the subject area level, it becomes easier to cover very broad areas. We can model entire departments or organizations; external concepts, such as regulatory agencies; or competitors, future architectures, and so on.

Defines scope. By visually showing subject areas and their business rules, we can more easily identify a subset of the model to analyze. Because we can cover such a broad perspective on the subject area model, we can more easily scope down to something more manageable. For example, we can model the entire logistics department, and then scope out of this a particular logistics application that we would like to build.

Provides direction. Because we can cover such a broad area with a subject area model, it can help to determine how planned and existing applications will coexist. It can provide direction and guidance on what new functionality the business will need next. Once I was reviewing a subject area model with a management team in Latin America. This subject area model contained the subject areas and their relationships for their entire business. We were able to look at this model as a team and understand which sections of the business had applications that were working adequately and which sections needed additional application development. Sections that needed work might be a result of heavy manual effort or old legacy applications in need of replacement or enhancement. The senior manager of this team was so impressed with the power of this one-page subject area model that he remarked that it would be our compass for all future development. I think the term compass is an excellent synonym for the subject area model, because it implies that the subject area model is a tool to help us get to a destination. It gives us direction.

A picture is worth a thousand words. Up to this point, our subject area analysis has produced very valuable lists and spreadsheets that help us fully understand different aspects of each subject area, including definition, source, and resource requirements. The subject area model brings together much of this information into a picture. A subject area model can represent visually on a single page what much of the text in a business requirements document captures and what some of the spreadsheets in the previous chapter contain. For example, we can diagram the reporting requirements from the Subject Area Grain Matrix using a subject area model, an example of which we have seen in the previous chapter.

Low-hanging fruit. The subject area model usually takes only hours to develop, and yet it offers a very large payoff in terms of business understanding and creation of a solid foundation for development. Think of the story from the beginning of this chapter where that apple was so easy to pull off the tree and yet tasted so good. I have been in many situations where I was able to build rapport, understand the business from a high level, and set the stage for logical data analysis and modeling, with minimal effort, by using the subject area model.

Comparison to the Conceptual Data Model

As you are reading about the subject area model, a question may have come to mind at some point: "How does this relate to the conceptual data model?" Most of us have heard the term and possibly created Conceptual Data Models (CDMs) at one point or another. A CDM is any high-level view of the business. It can include subject areas but can also contain the following:

- Data elements, including sometimes primary and foreign keys
- Entities, sometimes including associative entities
- Reporting levels for a data mart

When a CDM is purely at the subject area level, it becomes identical to the subject area model, and we can use the terms "CDM" and "subject area model" interchangeably. Because the CDM can encompass different levels of granularity, we can have conceptual data models at purely the entity level, or purely at the entity and key level as well. As soon as we include entities in our model, we have much more complexity and detail. These entity and key models can still be valuable if we have a subject area model to provide a higher level of understanding.

A problem that we sometimes face with a CDM occurs when we combine different levels of granularity into the same model. For example, I have seen a CDM that contained both subject areas and the more detailed entities. Combining levels of granularity can lead to inconsistencies in representing concepts and business rules and, therefore, can limit understanding and cause confusion and frustration. Varying levels on a CDM can also cause accuracy issues, because it is more difficult if not impossible to validate that a CDM containing different levels of granularity is complete and correct. For example, if I am including primary keys on my CDM, how can I be sure before I do any kind of logical data analysis and normalization whether I have the complete and correct list of primary keys defined?

NOTE

The subject area model is a subject area—only view of the business; whereas the conceptual data model can include other levels of granularity, such as entities and keys. When the conceptual data model combines subject areas, entities, and keys on the same model, it forfeits the rigor and consistency that all data models should have. The subject area model, in these cases, provides much more rigor and consistency than the conceptual data model, making it easier to validate and understand.

How to Read the Rules

This book is not an introductory data modeling book and, therefore, we want to avoid spending time on basic modeling concepts. Thus, this section does not go into a detailed explanation of cardinality. Instead, we focus on how to read or interpret the labels and cardinality on the business rules. Many times we might find ourselves defining relationships without understanding their true business meaning. Knowing how to read the business rules will add greater accuracy and clarity to our subject area models. Clearly articulating the business rules provides the following benefits:

Helps business users understand the lines. Reading the business rules and participation can help people with little data modeling background understand and validate these rules. Joe the user may not understand crow's feet (the Information Engineering symbol for many), or lines connecting boxes, but he will understand whether Bob can own five accounts.

Provides a good learning ground in preparation for logical data modeling. If you can explain what the lines mean on a subject area model, you are one step closer to understanding the logical data model. Reading business rules is independent of granularity, and it does not matter whether the boxes represent subject areas or normalized entities.

Tells a story. Remember how isolated each of the subject areas was in the previous chapter? The business rules connect these subject areas and more completely represent the business. The model as a whole tells a story. The subject areas in isolation resemble a book with lots of paragraphs without sequence or order; they are just randomly placed on any page in a book. The ending might become before the beginning, for example. The business rules bring logic and order to the subject areas. It is similar to a book in which the paragraphs have an order and a smooth transition to other paragraphs. Then the book as a whole tells a story, just as the business rules connecting subject areas tell a story and explain the business.

This section goes through a short example on reading the business rules and then provides advice on business rule labels and cardinality.

Reading the Rules In Practice

So let's tell a story. Figure 6.2 contains several different variations of the customer and account business rules.

The first relationship between customer and account is a many-to-many one. The term many-to-many makes no sense to a business user. Reading this relationship might sound like this: "A Customer can own many Accounts. An Account can be owned by many Customers." Note how much more valuable and clear these two sentences sound than just saying we have a many-to-many relationship between Customer and Account. Note also the clockwise direction of reading the relationship labels. Always read the business rules clockwise, regardless of the positions of the boxes and lines on the page—whether vertical, horizontal, or diagonal to each other.

For example, in this second relationship, reading clockwise, a "Customer can own one or more Accounts. An Account must be owned by a single Customer." We use the word "can" because there is optionality on the account side and, therefore, a customer can exist without an account. Rather than saying a Customer can own zero, one, or more Accounts, a clearer story is told by saying, "A Customer can own one or more Accounts." The word "can" implies the "zero." In contrast, "An Account must be owned by a single Customer." We use the term "must" because there is no optionality on the customer side and, therefore, an account cannot exist without a customer. These simple passive words, such as can, might, and may, and active words such as must, create a clearer and easier to understand story. To practice, look at the third example and read the business rule. "A Customer may own an Account. An Account must be owned by a single Customer."

Advice on Labels

Labels are the phrases that appear on the relationship lines. They are very important because they add business context to an otherwise meaningless line. These labels should be as descriptive as possible. Examples of good label names include:

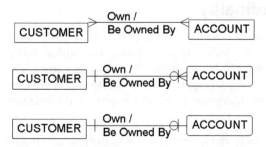

Figure 6.2 Customer and account rules.

- Contain
- Work for
- Own
- Initiate
- Categorize
- Apply to

Always avoid the following words as label names because they tell the reader nothing owing to their generic nature:

- Has
- Have
- Associates
- Participates
- Relates
- Is
- Be

NOTE

You can use these words in combination with other words to make a meaningful label name, just avoid using these words by themselves.

I find myself sometimes using these generic words as labels when I am not paying close enough attention to the relationship. As hard as it might be, replace these generic words with words that are relevant and more descriptive to the particular business rule. If you do not have the level of understanding to know a more descriptive label, refer back to the In-the-Know Template and contact an expert in this area.

As our models become larger, and we have more boxes and lines on the same piece of paper, the labels tend to add clutter to the models, making them almost unreadable. In this case, for the subject area models I usually show only one of the labels. Just make sure, because you are reading clockwise, that you have the label correctly placed so it makes sense.

Advice on Interpreting Cardinality

Cardinality means are there none, one, or many values from each entity involved in a business rule. It means, "How many values of each of these two entities participate in the business rule that connect them?" For example, "A Customer can own many Accounts," means that a customer can participate in the ownership of more than one account. Bob can own five accounts, Mary can own two accounts, and John may have no accounts.

You also need to be very clear as to the words you use to express cardinality. Cardinality can be optional or mandatory. If a relationship is optional, instead of using the word zero, use one of the following:

- Can
- Might
- May

If the relationship is mandatory, use the word must.

The Project Scenario

Now that we clearly understand subject area modeling, we can focus more on the three different types of subject area models. To learn how these models build heavily on each other, it will be useful to carry the same example through all three of these models. In this section we discuss the project scenario that we will use throughout the rest of the chapter.

The Consumer Response Department in your company handles all of the day-to-day interactions with the consumer. The department also runs reports off their current operational application in search of contact trends or patterns. The department is getting increasingly more consumer contacts each day from a variety of media, including snail mail, phone, and email. The department gets over 500,000 contacts a year, and this number is growing at a 25% rate owing to an increase in advertising, an 800 phone number printed on the product packaging, and the company's latest Web site. The department is getting so many contacts that the response staff is spending all of their time answering contacts and little if any time trying to understand trends and patterns. In the past, they had the time to run manually intensive operational reports from their operational application where they enter contact information. But with no time and so many more contacts, they have not been able to run even the most basic reports. They believe a data mart might simplify the reporting they do today and reduce the drain on their current operational application.

In Figure 6.3 we provide a sample report that is frequently run in the Consumer Response Department.

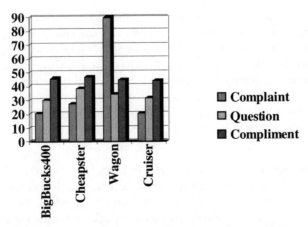

Figure 6.3 Consumer response department sample report.

This report shows how many complaints, compliments, and questions each of these products have received in a particular time period. The user will have the option to ask for more or fewer details on each of these: time, product, and subjects. Subjects include complaints, compliments, and questions. For example, if the users would like to see the actual complaints for the BigBucks400 for this same time period, they can do so.

You have already completed all of your subject area analysis tools for this project in Chapter 5, "Subject Area Analysis." Therefore, you have a strong understanding of the subject areas within this new application, including definition, source, and levels of reporting. You also have captured the people and documentation resources that are available for each of these in the In-the-Know Template. You are now ready to start your subject area modeling, beginning with the Business Clean Slate model.

What Is the Business Clean Slate Model?

Have you ever been in a situation where you had trouble understanding the scope and purpose of an application, because you did not fully understand key business concepts and rules? Many times, before we start understanding an application and its scope, we need to understand the business that this application will be supporting. For example, if we are designing a logistics tracking application, we need to first understand the logistics area. The Business Clean Slate subject area model helps us in understanding a business area.

The Business Clean Slate is a subject area model of a section of the business. The section could be as narrow as a department or part of a department; in contrast, it can be as broad as the entire organization or even the entire industry, including external concepts such as government agencies, competitors, and suppliers. Its only boundaries are the limits defined within the subject area analysis tools in the previous chapter. The Business Clean Slate subject area model focuses on a business area and not on a particular application.

It is called a Clean Slate model because there are no comparisons with any existing models. You are creating a brand new model, and not an enhancement to an existing model. It is based on the premise that we must first understand new concepts in order to understand how they fit into existing concepts. The Business Clean Slate is the model containing these new concepts. It forces you to take a step back and really understand the business before making any architecture or application decisions. You are not limited by any existing applications. The analogy is to a blackboard that you wipe clean and then start from scratch. This model provides a new beginning and fresh perspective.

Many times when we say we are creating a subject area model, we mean the Business Clean Slate model. This is the most common type of subject area model because it represents the starting point for many different types of projects, ranging from trying to understand an area of the business to introducing a large packaged software solution.

The Business Clean Slate model represents a section of the business. Refer back to Figure 6.1 for an example. This could be a subject area model for part of the debit and credit department. This model will be the starting point for the Application Clean Slate model, which will be discussed shortly.

The Business Clean Slate model accomplishes all of the goals mentioned under the subject area modeling section and does the following:

Provides understanding of a business area. This model provides a new way to look at the existing business. It forces us to take a step back and understand how the business operates instead of how an application functions. For example, how does the logistics department work? What are the subject areas and business rules of this department?

Contains a superset of information for the Application Clean Slate model. By understanding the business area, we are in a better position to understand an application that will impact this area. The Business Clean Slate model should be a superset of information by which we can scope out an application. For example, once we clearly understand at a high level how a human resource department functions, we can better determine the content and scope of a human resources application. The Business Clean Slate model is a prerequisite for the Application Clean Slate model.

Builds rapport. This model is usually created either to start an application effort or just to better understand a business area. In either case, it happens very early on in the modeling process. Thus, it helps establish rapport with the business at this early stage. While working for a telephone company, I created a Business Clean Slate model for a group of business managers who had doubts about the abilities of those in the information technology department. I used this Business Clean Slate model as a way to build trust and rapport.

Offers training ground on data modeling concepts. This model is the first and most basic subject area model. Because of its simplicity, and because it contains the standard syntax of boxes and lines found in all data models, it is prime training ground to learn data modeling basics, that is, subject areas or entities, cardinality, and relationships. An understanding of these concepts at the subject area level will make the process of understanding and reviewing a detailed logical data model go much more smoothly.

Using the Business Clean Slate Model

A Business Clean Slate subject area model is most useful for any combination of the following situations:

Understanding a business area. The most popular usage of this model is to gain understanding of an area of the business. Most analyses that data modelers perform are based on an initial understanding of how the business works. The Business Clean Slate model captures how the business works.

Redesigning a business area. There are a lot of buzzwords these days around rethinking business processes: Business Process Reengineering, Process Renewal,

Effect Change Management, and the list goes on. All of these terms imply understanding a process or section of the business and looking for ways to improve it. The Business Clean Slate model is a good starting point for redesigning a section of the business because it helps us understand the current business at a subject area level.

Designing an enterprise model. An enterprise data model must initially be designed at the subject area level. Many times I recommend not going into any more detail than the subject area level because of the complexities and maintenance issues, with hundreds of entities and thousands of data elements. By creating a Business Clean Slate model, we separate ourselves from any planned or existing applications. We can also include concepts outside the scope of the organization, such as government or regulatory bodies. The term top-down implies starting at the highest level and working our way down to more details, and to actual applications. Building an enterprise data model starting with the Business Clean Slate model is a top-down approach.

Starting a new development effort. This model is a very good place to start capturing the subject areas and business rules for a new application. All future subject area and logical data models are based on this initial model. For example, the Business Clean Slate model must be completed before the Application Clean Slate model is completed.

Business Clean Slate Model In Practice

We will go through the five steps in creating a Business Clean Slate subject area model. Then we will apply these steps to the previously described request by the Consumer Response Department for a data mart:

1. **Complete the Subject Area Analysis tools.** This will give us the complete list of standard subject areas, along with definitions, sources, and resources. This involves completing the five tools from the previous chapter:

   - Subject Area Checklist
   - Application Subject Area CRUD Matrix
   - In-the-Know Template
   - Subject Area Family Tree
   - Subject Area Grain Matrix

2. **Put each subject area into a separate box on the model.** This is basically a copy-and-paste activity from the Subject Area Checklist into a data model. At the end of this step we will just have boxes on our model, one for each subject area.

3. **Connect the boxes by identifying the correct business rules.** Rules are identified either in a group setting, or by the designer working independently based on available documentation, and creating a model that then needs to be reviewed by the business experts. When you meet with them, always begin with an overview

of the purpose of a Business Clean Slate model and basic data modeling concepts, including subject areas, relationships, and cardinality.

4. **Review.** Review and agree on, with the relevant parties, the final design or any outstanding issues. Refer to the In-the-Know Template from Chapter 5, "Subject Area Analysis," to decide on who should review and validate this model. Make sure members from the business are present.

5. **Update based on review.** Update this model with any changes that come out of the review. In some cases you might also need to update some of the values in the Subject Area Analysis tools from Chapter 5. If there are substantial changes, meet with the business experts again to review the updated model.

1. Complete the Subject Area Analysis Tools

After meeting with subject area experts within the Consumer Response area, you have completed and had validated all of the five subject area analysis tools mentioned in the previous chapter. Rather than review all of your findings here, let's just list the Subject Area Checklist for this example (see Table 6.2).

Note that there are several subject areas in this checklist that appear to be department-specific ones. I do not think, for example, that Subject and Response would be considered critical, basic concepts in most departments and companies, yet they are considered subject areas in this context.

In addition, the subject areas are listed alphabetically in this checklist. This is one technique you can use to list them. Another option would be to list them in the order that makes the most sense to a business expert, for example, listing reference subject areas first and then transaction subject areas.

2. Put Each Subject Area into a Separate Box on the Model

Figure 6.4 contains a diagram with each subject area in its own box. Recall that these subject areas are the standard names and definitions identified during the analysis phase.

Note that we still do not know how these subject areas relate to each other. At this point, they are just isolated and independent concepts. In addition, they have not been arranged in Figure 6.4 in any particular order. As I mentioned for the Subject Area Checklist, you can position these subject area boxes in a number of different ways, including alphabetically or by what is most comfortable for the business expert.

3. Connect the Boxes by Identifying the Correct Business Rules

Referring to your In-the-Know Template for this Consumer Response example reveals that Stu and Sandy are the business experts who can help you understand the

Table 6.2 Subject Area Checklist

NAME	DEFINITION
Complaint	A contact that involves negative information from consumers about our products. EXAMPLES: Your product, the Widgets Lite, was broken when I took it out of the box. I found your magazine ad offensive. I liked your original formula better than the new formula.
Compliment	A contact that involves positive information from consumers on our products. EXAMPLES: I love your new product, the Widgets Grand. Your latest television ad is ingenious. I admire how environmentally concerned your company is.
Consumer	One that acquires goods or services either for direct use or ownership.
Contact	Interaction with the consumer through a variety of media. It could be a complaint, compliment, or question.
Product	Anything we buy, sell, stock, move, or make. Products we make include advertisements on our products, which can be television ads, magazine ads, Web banners, and so on.
Purchase	A financial transaction between a consumer and a place where our product is sold to acquire our products.
Question	A contact that involves an inquiry from consumers about our products. EXAMPLES: What is the recipe to your Widgets Grand? Where can I get the entry forms for your new sweepstakes? I am doing a book report for school. Can I ask you a few questions on the history of your products?
Representative	An employee of our company who is the point of contact for our consumers. Representatives can answer phones; respond in letter or email; and send out coupons, products, and thank you letters.
Response	The reaction of our company to a contact. We can have a phone conversation, mail coupons, mail product, send thank you letters, and so on.
Subject	Topic that a consumer contacted us about. EXAMPLES: Product breakage Loves product Hates ad

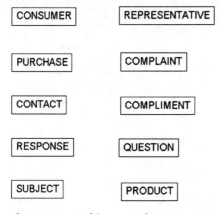

Figure 6.4 Subject area boxes.

relationships between these subject areas. You arrange a meeting with these two experts, and then you summarized their business rules as follows:

- A Contact can be a Complaint, Compliment, or Question.
- A Consumer can initiate many Contacts.
- A Contact must be initiated by a single Consumer.
- A Contact must pertain to a single Subject.
- A Subject can categorize many Contacts.
- A Contact might pertain to a Product.
- A Product can be referenced by many Contacts.
- Products are organized in a hierarchy or tree structure, meaning a product can belong to a single product grouping, and a product grouping can contain one or more products.
- Subjects are also organized in a hierarchy or tree structure.
- A Consumer can make many Purchases.
- A Purchase must be made by a single Consumer.
- A Purchase must consist of a single Product.
- A Product can be the source of many Purchases.
- A Contact can cause many Responses.
- A Response must be produced for a single Contact.
- A Representative can facilitate many Responses.
- A Response must be facilitated by a single Representative.

This leads to the model in Figure 6.5.

Note the use of subtyping in this example. Subtyping is a very good way to group together Compliment, Complaint, and Question so that we do not have to repeat many

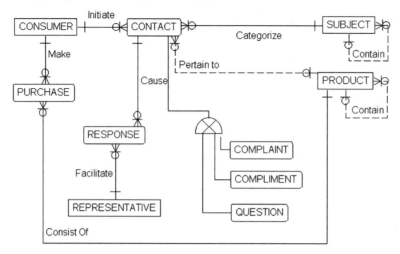

Figure 6.5 Initial Business Clean Slate model.

of the relationships three times. For example, Consumer initiates a Contact. This is much more straightforward and creates much less clutter than relating consumer to each of the types of contacts separately, using three identical relationships instead of one.

Also note the dotted lined recursive relationships on Subject and Product. A *recursive relationship* is one that joins twice to the same entity or table. For example, a Subject might contain other Subjects just as a Complaint might contain different types of Complaints, such as product or advertisement complaints. Relating values in an entity to other values in that same entity is captured with a recursive relationship. The dotted line represents a *nonidentifying relationship,* that is, one in which the foreign key from the parent is not part of the primary key for the child. It becomes a nonidentifying foreign key in the child entity. An identifying relationship is shown using the normal solid line. Even though we are not discussing keys and data elements at all at this level, many data modeling tools enforce these constraints that are of a more detailed level than our subject area models. I usually tell people during a Business Clean Slate model review to ignore whether the line is dotted or solid.

The positions of these subject areas and rules are very important for readability and understanding. We will discuss the proper layout of this model in detail in Chapter 10, "Data Model Beauty Tips."

4. Review

The review step is very important. Make sure all parties involved in the modeling agree and understand that the Business Clean Slate model is accurate and complete. An accurate and complete picture at this point will make the next two subject area models, and the subsequent logical analysis and modeling, go much more smoothly and quickly. As you review this model, remember to tell a story and not to just explain one-to-one and one-to-many relationships. Use the rule reading techniques mentioned previously to make the relationships more meaningful to the business experts.

Examples of the types of questions and issues that might come out of this review include the following:

- Can a Contact be initiated by more than one Consumer?
- We have a very broad definition of Product, which includes advertisements. Is this acceptable?
- Should we subtype further Complaint, Compliment, and Question into more granular subject areas?

Note that some of these questions might have already been answered during the creation of the Subject Area Checklist.

5. Update Based on Review

Do not be surprised when subject area changes come out of this review. Viewing the information in a model format sometimes allows the business experts to see information in new ways and thus to think of things they did not think of before. In fact, be open to updating some of the content on the tools from Chapter 5, "Subject Area Analysis. The reason is that the resources are looking at some of the same subject area information but now the subject areas are connected through business rules to tell a story instead of being just isolated subject areas. Therefore, the business experts might realize there are gaps that existed in previous analysis that went undetected. Also, make sure you resolve all of the issues and questions coming out of the Business Clean Slate model review before proceeding to the Application Clean Slate model.

WARNING

■■■■■■ Resolve outstanding business issues and questions for the Business Clean Slate model before proceeding to the Application Clean Slate model.

What Is the Application Clean Slate Model?

Now that you understand the scope of your business area after creating your Business Clean Slate model, what subset of these subject areas and business rules will be within the scope of your application? As an example, if you have a Business Clean Slate model of the logistics department, how much of this model will be impacted and included by this logistics application? The Application Clean Slate subject area model is where we do this scoping of a business area into an application area.

The Application Clean Slate subject area model is a data model containing the subject areas and business rules for a particular application. It is a subset of the Business Clean Slate subject area model. As an example, after creating the Business Clean Slate model of the human resources department, we can now scope out of this subject area our human resources application. We are not limiting ourselves to a particular type of application here. We can create an Application Clean Slate model for any type of application, including the following:

- Data marts
- Operational applications
- Packaged software

Similar to the Business Clean Slate model, we are using the term Clean Slate because we do not concern ourselves with any existing applications or application architectures at this point. We are creating this model from the Business Clean Slate model, which was created from scratch.

The Application Clean Slate model accomplishes all of the goals mentioned under the subject area modeling section, as well as the following:

Enabling understanding of an application. This model provides the complete picture for an application that is within the scope of the business area of the application. It forces us to take a step back and understand how the application functions within the business. For example, how does the logistics tracking application function within the logistics department? Which of the department subject areas and business rules do this application impact?

Providing input for the Early Reality Check subject area model. Once we understand the subject areas and business rules of the application, we can compare the application's scope to a larger scope, which will become the Early Reality Check subject area model. We compare it to a data warehouse, integration hub, existing application, or enterprise data model. For example, now that we understand the logistics tracking data mart, how does this data mart fit within the rest of the data warehouse architecture? Much of this comparison information might already have been captured in a spreadsheet format on the Subject Area CRUD Matrix or Subject Area Family Tree. These tools would have identified the source applications for each subject area, and these source applications might be the ones requiring comparison in the Early Reality Check model.

Defining application context. This model is shown within the Business Clean Slate model, and therefore, it is very apparent as to which subject areas and business rules are included and which are excluded. By understanding these overlaps and gaps, we can put this application in the context of the rest of the business.

Providing a start for the logical data model. This model is the high-level view of the application logical data model. Each of the subject areas on this subject area model will be broken down into many entities and data elements on the logical data model. The Sales Organization subject area on the Application Clean Slate model might be broken down into the Territory, Region, and Division entities on the logical data model, for example.

The Application Clean Slate subject area model is a scoped down view of the Business Clean Slate subject area model. The best approach for getting the Application Clean Slate model from the Business Clean Slate model is by taking a pencil or marker and outlining on the Business Clean Slate model what is within the scope of the application. For example, Figure 6.6 shows the same model we reviewed in Figure 6.1, except we have now scoped out the requirements for an application.

You can see that I have shaded or outlined the section of the Business Clean Slate model that will become our Application Clean Slate model. We will include Customer, Account, Credit Account, and Debit Account within our scope. Perhaps we are designing a small reference application that manages customers and their debit and credit accounts. In this case, we do not need to concern ourselves with Order and Product; hence these are scoped out of the Application Clean Slate model.

Using the Application Clean Slate Model

An Application Clean Slate model is used mainly in two situations:

New application. Any new application from a sales data mart to an online telephone directory could be designed starting from an Application Clean Slate model.

Prioritizing the application. How do I know which application to work on first? Having an Application Clean Slate model in the context of a Business Clean Slate model can help us visualize the impacted subject areas and business rules and, therefore, can determine the importance and priority of this application.

Application Clean Slate Model In Practice

We will go through the steps in creating an Application Clean Slate model, building on the detailed example that we discussed under the Business Clean Slate model. Note that these steps require less effort than the Business Clean Slate model because these models build on each other, and therefore, no new modeling is required for the Application Clean Slate model. We are just doing a scoping activity:

1. **Complete the Business Clean Slate model.** This will give us the business context in which our application will live. It will also give us a great starting point for

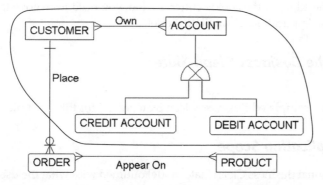

Figure 6.6 Sample Application Clean Slate model.

scoping the application. That is, we do not have to create a brand new subject area model here. We can just use what was done for the Business Clean Slate model. (See the steps in a previous section for completing the Business Clean Slate model.)

2. **Outline application scope.** Scope down the Business Clean Slate model with application requirements. Talk to the business users and reference the important documentation listed in the In-the-Know Template from Chapter 5, "Subject Area Analysis," to fully understand the application at a subject area level. Then use a marker to outline subject areas that are needed on the Business Clean Slate model.

NOTE

■■■■ **If the scope of the application is larger than the Business Clean Slate model, you will need to update it with the additional subject areas and relationships. This usually happens when the application crosses multiple areas of the business, and therefore, the Business Clean Slate model needs to be broadened.**

3. **Review.** Review with the relevant parties and agree on the final design. Refer to the In-the-Know Template from Chapter 5, "Subject Area Analysis," to decide on who needs to review and validate this model. Note that the people who review this model probably will be the same ones who reviewed the Business Clean Slate model. However, the review for the Application Clean Slate model would also include members of the business community who will be using this new application: the business users. Thus, the audience for this model review is both from the business and from the future application.

4. **Update based on review.** Update the Application Clean Slate model with any changes that come out of this meeting. In some cases, if the changes are substantial enough, you might need to schedule another model review. Note that some of the changes might mean also making changes to the Business Clean Slate model and any previous subject area analysis.

5. **Remove the business only subject areas and business rules.** Once everyone agrees on the Application Clean Slate model, you will no longer need the subject areas and business rules that are external to the application. Therefore, just as you use a cookie cutter to make the shapes you want and then remove the excess dough around the edges of the cookie cutter, so, too, you need to remove the edges around the Application Clean Slate model.

1. Complete the Business Clean Slate Model

See Figure 6.5 for the completed Business Clean Slate model for this example.

2. Outline Application Scope

Figure 6.7 is the original Business Clean Slate model outlined with what the users have agreed is within the scope of this application. Note that to determine first the business scope with the Business Clean Slate model and then the application scope with the Ap-

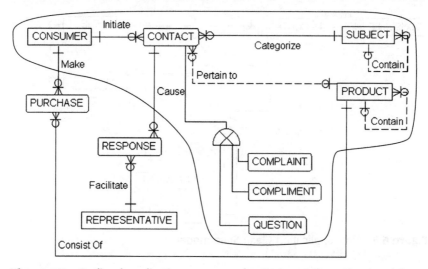

Figure 6.7   Outlined application scope on the Business Clean Slate model.

plication Clean Slate model, will probably require two iterations through the subject area analysis tools mentioned in the previous chapter. The first iteration identifies the subject area information for the business, and the second iteration identifies the subject area information for the application. This second iteration should build on the first iteration and, therefore, should be much shorter in duration.

3. *Review*

Follow the same review process you did for the Business Clean Slate model, except this time make sure you include business users of this application as well. You need to make sure you get more of an application perspective rather than just a business perspective.

Reviewing the Application Clean Slate model involves not just agreeing on the subject areas and business rules but also making sure that we have the application scope correct. Therefore, much of the interaction at this point will focus on scope. Examples of some of the questions and issues that might come up during this review include the following:

■ Are we sure we do not want to include contact responses in our data mart?

■ Are there any interesting reporting trends we can detect by comparing contacts against purchase information? Would purchase information be useful to keep within the scope?

■ How much consumer information do we really need in this data mart?

4. *Update Based on Review*

The feedback you receive on this model can also involve changes to the Business Clean Slate subject area model, and any previous subject area analysis. Remember to have

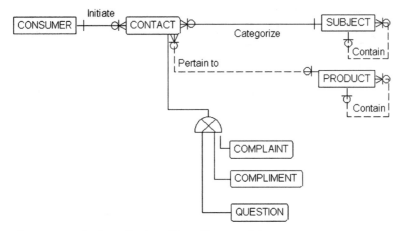

Figure 6.8 Final application Clean Slate model.

another model review if substantial changes come out of this review. Also, there are rare cases—but it does happen—when there is so much debate around subject area and business rules that you will need to go back to the Business Clean Slate model and start again. You will not be ready to discuss application scope until the business is fully understood and represented on the Business Clean Slate model.

5. Remove the Business Only Subject Areas and Business Rules

This is a very easy step. Removing the business only information on this model leaves us with the model in Figure 6.8.

What Is the Early Reality Check Model?

Now that you understand the scope of the application, we need to see how it fits into the larger picture of the application architecture. This is useful for a number of situations, including data warehouse and enterprise application architectures. The model that shows how it fits into this larger architecture is the Early Reality Check subject area model.

The Early Reality Check subject area model is the data model that fits the Application Clean Slate model into the scope of the application architecture in which it will reside. It is called the Early Reality Check model because it provides an overview of how something new fits in with something existing very early in the development process. The term Early is used because we are judging the fit of this new application in our existing environment before any development commences. Therefore, if we discover a problem, we have not invested much time and effort. The term Reality Check is used because our business requirements document will be put to the test in seeing if we have a clean fit at the subject area level; that is, does it match reality? I believe the Early

Reality Check model is the most powerful type of subject area model, and I have had some great successes using it.

The Early Reality Check model has two goals:

To represent the fit with the existing application architecture. This model compares the new application with an existing application environment to see if there are any issues in terms of gaps or redundancy. It makes it easy to display areas for debate and concern. For example, I have used an Early Reality Check model to highlight a serious customer issue we would have had if we had brought a new data mart into our existing data warehouse architecture.

To help estimate the development effort. Because we are showing overlap and gaps a new application will cause within our environment, we can more easily develop a high-level estimate for the development effort. For example, bringing a new data mart into an existing architecture might display either three or five subject areas that overlap. Having overlapping subject areas means there are opportunities to reuse existing structures. Therefore, five subject areas that overlap will probably take less time to develop than would the three areas that overlap.

This type of subject area model is used to determine what currently exists from what does not in analyzing the data needs in a particular area. It is a good tool for gauging work effort in adding the new concepts. I have used two techniques to highlight the overlap between the new application and the application environment:

Colors. I have used green-colored boxes to indicate a complete overlap, yellow to indicate some overlap, and red to indicate no overlap. Boxes without a color indicate that they only exist within the existing application architecture. I have used this color technique on a huge data warehouse integration project where we wanted to know which subject areas from several proposed data marts currently exist in the data warehouse. Colors are great because they jump out at you. You can easily see them on an overhead projector. For example, I can easily see that the Inventory subject area is colored red, and therefore, we have no inventory information in our data warehouse. The problem with colors is that some people might be color-blind. Color printouts also can be expensive and sometimes impossible to get. For example, we cannot show you one in this book, because you would only see it in shades of gray.

Different-sized boxes. This is my preferred technique to show overlap. It can be used in any situation. I will use small boxes to show subject areas that exist in the application architecture but not the Application Clean Slate model, medium boxes to show subject areas that exist in the Application Clean Slate model but not in the application architecture, and large entities to show overlap between the two. You can use different-sized large entities to show varying degrees of overlap. In the example below we will just show a one-size, large entity to highlight the overlap.

The point of these techniques is to be creative. You might think up new, more visual ways to show the overlap that I have never considered. Think of your audience, and then let your imagination run wild.

Using the Early Reality Check Model

The Early Reality Check model can be used in any situation where you are fitting an application into a larger architecture or replacing an application, that is, any situation where you need to have a fit between something new and something that currently exists. For example, the Early Reality Check model can be used for the following situations:

New data mart within current data warehouse architecture. This model will show how the new data mart requirements fit into what currently exists within the data warehouse. I have used this model in this situation several times to help come up with a rough estimate as to how much effort it will require to create a new data mart. For example, seeing five red subject areas means that I need to create these five new subject areas within my data warehouse, because they do not exist in the data warehouse today. If I have only three red subject areas, it will probably take less time to develop and thus be less expensive.

New functionality to an existing operational or data mart application. This model will highlight the new functionality and show how it fits in with current functionality. It is a very good technique for identifying issues and integration challenges very early in the project. Thus, the overlap between the new functionality and existing functionality would highlight the areas that would require minimal effort.

Replacing an old application. This model can show the overlap at a subject area level when you are replacing an existing application with a new one. This is the same technique as replacing existing functionality, except on a larger scale. If we are replacing an order processing application, the Early Reality Check model will highlight which subject areas the existing application impacts and how this compares to which subject areas the new application will impact.

Customization to packaged software. More and more, we will be implementing packaged software, the most popular being Enterprise Resource Planning (ERP) and Customer Resource Management (CRM) applications software. These expensive and very encompassing pieces of software need to be analyzed to see how they fit into the current environment. The Early Reality Check model will allow management to see the impact and overlap caused by introducing packaged software, hopefully before investing lots of money.

Fit within the enterprise data model. We can compare the Application Clean Slate model to our existing Business Clean Slate model for the enterprise and highlight the overlap. This can help us identify inconsistencies with the enterprise, which could lead to model changes for both the new application and the existing enterprise data model.

TIP

Be creative about where you can apply the Early Reality Check model. If you remember you can use it whenever comparing something new with something existing, you will probably think up very interesting and useful ways to apply this type of subject area model.

Early Reality Check Model In Practice

The Early Reality Check subject area model compares two subject area models: the Application Clean Slate model for the application that we have been working on, and the model of the existing application environment. You will probably need to create a subject area model for the existing application environment if you do not currently have one. This environment subject area model will obviously take more time and effort to design; however, once you have completed it, you can refer to it over and over again whenever doing an Early Reality Check model. Here are the steps:

1. **Create the environment subject area model.** You do this only once, and then you have to maintain it. This model is important to have so that an easily understood view of the larger environment exists. To create the environment subject area model, follow the same steps under the Application Clean Slate model, which is your starting point. In most cases, you will need to create an Application Clean Slate model for the environment. However, you can stop at the Business Clean Slate model for enterprise model comparisons.

2. **Create the new Application Clean Slate model.** See steps mentioned under "Application Clean Slate Model In Practice."

3. **Highlight the fit.** Here is where we analyze the fit between your new application and this larger application environment. For example, if I want to bring open orders into my existing data warehouse architecture, which today only contains shipped orders, then I would highlight this overlap. Use one of the techniques mentioned earlier, either different colors or sizes, or come up with your own.

4. **Review.** Review with the relevant parties and agree. Refer to the In-the-Know Template from Chapter 5, "Subject Area Analysis," to decide with whom you should review this model. Make sure members from the business are present. You also need to include experts from the larger application environment. For example, if the environment Application Clean Slate model encompasses the entire data warehouse, make sure you have subject area experts from the data warehouse present at this review.

5. **Update based on review.** Updates that come out of this meeting can lead to changes in these deliverables:

   - New Application Clean Slate model
   - Environment Application Clean Slate model
   - New Application Business Clean Slate model
   - Environment Business Clean Slate model
   - Any of the five subject area analysis tools for both the application and environment analysis

1. Create the Environment Subject Area Model

For this example, we need to fit this new data mart within the scope of the entire data warehouse. You will need to go through the subject area analysis mentioned in

Chapter 5, "Subject Area Analysis," As we did previously in this chapter, instead of looking at the results of all five of the subject area analysis tools, let's just look at the Subject Area Checklist here. See Table 6.3 for the current data warehouse environment Subject Area Checklist, sorted alphabetically.

Using this Subject Area Checklist and following the steps mentioned previously under the Business and Application Clean Slate model, we arrive at the model shown in Figure 6.9.

By this model you can tell that we currently have a small data warehouse. More mature data warehouses would have broader scoped models that would include many more subject areas. This small model will be perfect for our example, however.

2. Create the New Application Clean Slate Model

Follow the steps mentioned under "Application Clean Slate Model In Practice" to arrive at this completed subject area model.

Table 6.3 Data Warehouse Subject Area Checklist

NAME	DEFINITION
Credit	A financial transaction where money is added to the customer's balance.
Customer	The recipient and purchaser of our products. One that acquires goods or services either for direct use or ownership, or for resale or use in production and manufacturing.
Debit	A financial transaction where money is subtracted from the customer's balance.
Employee	A person who is employed in a full- or part-time capacity by our company, to perform a service or function to our company.
Order	An agreement to purchase product at an agreed-on price and quantity.
Product	Anything we buy, sell, stock, move, or make.
Promotion	A document containing the terms and conditions around the discount of product
Transaction	An individual change or action within our environment. EXAMPLES: Debit Credit Order

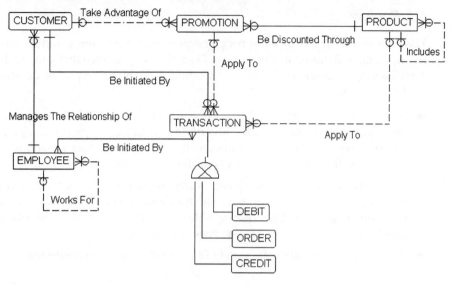

Figure 6.9   Environment Application Clean Slate model.

3.   *Highlight the Fit*

In this example, because I cannot easily show colors, I have used different-sized entities to highlight the overlap. Very large subject areas overlap, very small subject areas belong to the data warehouse and do not overlap, and medium-sized subject areas belong to the data mart and do not currently exist in the data warehouse. Figure 6.10 contains the initial Reality Check subject area model.

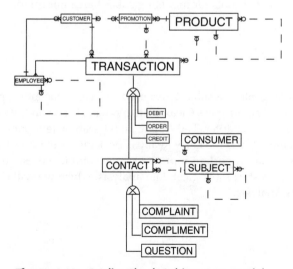

Figure 6.10   Reality Check Subject Area model.

4. Review

This review will involve the most people: experts from the business and the data warehouse, along with future business users. I can almost guarantee that you will have the most exciting discussions during this meeting. Here are examples of questions that might be raised:

- Is the Product hierarchy really the same in both models? The Consumer Application Clean Slate model includes advertisements as well as products we make; however, according to the definition on the checklist, the data warehouse does not seem to include advertisements. Is this a problem?

- The Customer definition on the data warehouse Subject Area Checklist in Table 6.3 has a much broader definition than the definition of the Consumer in the application Subject Area Checklist in Table 6.2. How do these two concepts compare? Are Consumers considered types of Customers?

- Can Contact information accurately fit under the Transaction subtype structure?

5. Update Based on Review

Include everyone's comments, and make any necessary updates in previous subject area model and analysis deliverables. Remember the domino effect: Updates to the Early Reality Check model can impact all previous subject area models and analysis work.

Summary

This chapter explained three power tools for modeling subject area information:

- Business Clean Slate model
- Application Clean Slate model
- Early Reality Check model

Each accomplishes the general goals of a subject area model but also has more specific goals for particular situations. The Business Clean Slate model is based on the subject area analysis tools in the previous chapter. The Application Clean Slate model builds on the Business Clean Slate model, and the Early Reality Check model requires the Application Clean Slate model as an important input. Once we complete these models, we have enough information to start the logical data analysis, which we will discuss in Chapter 7, "Logical Data Analysis."

CHAPTER 7

Logical Data Analysis

A t the beginning of Chapter 5, I mentioned that one of my favorite types of vacations is a road adventure. We would create a high-level map of our destination and identify must-see cities as dots on this map. This map represents our vacation requirements, where the lowest level of detail is the city. These high-level vacation requirements are very similar in purpose and scope to our subject area analysis from Chapter 5, where the lowest level of detail is the subject area. New York City is a must-see place for my vacation, just as Customer is a mandatory subject area for my application. Once we arrived at one of these must-see cities, we would then focus on the detailed vacation requirements. These detailed requirements are at the happening, or activity, level. What are the best places to eat? Are there any good walking tours? What time do the museums open? These detailed vacation requirements are similar in purpose and scope to the logical data analysis phase, which we will discuss in this chapter. My detailed vacation requirement to visit the Metropolitan Museum of Art in New York, for example, is analogous to identifying the application requirement that we will need the Customer Last Name data element within our Customer subject area.

About This Chapter

This chapter transitions our analysis from the subject area to each subject area's data elements. Up to this point in the text, we have been building the foundation of meta data and definition quality required to start any project, and then have performed all of the analysis and modeling at the subject area level. We now have a very strong understanding of each of the subject areas within the scope of our application, including definitions, sources, resources, and reporting requirements. We have enough knowledge about our application at this point to start identifying and capturing the data elements. In other words, we can start getting into the details. Several important questions now need to be answered:

- Which data elements do we need?
- What do they mean?
- Where do they come from?
- What reporting levels do they require?
- Do they contain values that are consistent with their meta data?

Note that some of these questions that we need to answer at the data element level are very similar to those we have answered at the subject area level. Therefore, in this chapter we use some of the tools we used in Chapter 5, "Subject Area Analysis," to build on our logical or data element analysis. Note that I use the terms logical data analysis and data element analysis interchangeably. Table 7.1 compares the tools under subject area analysis and data element analysis.

The Subject Area Checklist provides the list of subject areas within our scope and their definitions. The Subject Area Family Tree contains the source applications for each of these subject areas. Both the Subject Area Checklist and the Subject Area Family Tree provide a starting point for the Data Element Family Tree, which captures the complete list of data elements with definitions, along with their sources and any transformations. For example, the Subject Area Checklist will reveal that Customer is within our scope and this tool will contain an agreed-on definition for Customer. The Subject Area Family Tree will capture from where the Customer subject area will be sourced. The Data Element Family Tree will contain all of the data elements within the Customer subject area, such as Customer Last Name, as well as agreed-on definitions, sourcing, and transformation information. The Data Element Family Tree does both the identifying and sourcing for each data element, and therefore, we do not have a separate Data Element Checklist. Recall that one of the main purposes of the Subject Area Checklist is as a starting point in our analysis, or to bring our project team out from the weeds and the details. Now we are beyond the starting point and ready for the details, and thus, we do not need a separate Data Element Checklist.

The Subject Area Grain Matrix captures the reporting levels for each fact *subject area* within our data mart. The Data Element Grain Matrix captures the reporting levels for each fact *data element* within our data mart. For example, the Sales subject area might

Table 7.1 Subject Area Analysis and Data Element Analysis Tools Comparison

THIS SUBJECT AREA ANALYSIS TOOL ...	PROVIDES A STARTING POINT FOR THIS DATA ELEMENT ANALYSIS TOOL ...
Subject Area Checklist Subject Area Family Tree	Data Element Family Tree
Subject Area Grain Matrix	Data Element Grain Matrix
Application Subject Area CRUD Matrix	
In-The-Know Template	
	Data Quality Capture Template
	Data Quality Validation Template

be reported at the Month and Customer levels of detail, which will be captured on the Subject Area Grain Matrix. The facts within sales, such as Gross Sales Amount and Net Sales Amount, might also be reported at the Month and Customer levels of detail, and this will be captured on the Data Element Grain Matrix. The Subject Area Grain Matrix, as does the Subject Area Family Tree, acts as a starting point for its data element counterpart.

The Application Subject Area CRUD Matrix only exists at the subject area level. This tool puts our application subject areas in the context of the existing application architecture. It provides a very good high-level understanding of the environment and helps drive the completion of the Subject Area Family Tree. Its usefulness is in its simplicity. It is very easy to see sources and dependencies at the subject area level. Such a tool at the data element level would have some usefulness to the enterprise; however, it would be very complex, lengthy, and challenging to maintain. All of the sourcing information we need from our data elements for our current application will be captured on the Data Element Family Tree.

The In-the-Know Template captures the people and documentation resources required to complete and validate all project deliverables. Capturing this information at the data element level would introduce unnecessary redundancy. If we know, for example, that Dennis is the customer expert, what value would it have to list Dennis next to each of the data elements within the Customer subject area? It probably would have some value if the resources vary by data element and not by subject area, for example, if Dennis were the expert on one and Mary the expert on another set of data elements within Customer. However, the only time I have seen this scenario was when different subject areas existed within Customer that needed to be separated into their own subject areas. In this case, Dennis might be the expert on Customer Demographics and Mary on Customer Contact.

At the data element level we need to be concerned about data quality. We need to make sure our data element meta data is consistent with the values that we see in this data element. We do not concern ourselves with data quality at the subject area level. Therefore, the two tools, the Data Quality Capture Template and the Data Quality Validation Template, exist only at the data element level and not the subject area level. These tools capture the meta data and data for each data element for efficient comparison by the business experts.

This chapter focuses on these four logical data analysis tools:

Data Element Family Tree. Contains the complete list of data elements for the application and the sources and transformations for each, along with several other key pieces of data element meta data, including definition and format.

Data Element Grain Matrix. Captures the reporting levels for each measurement or fact so that reporting requirements can be reviewed and validated.

Data Quality Capture Template. Shows the comparison between the meta data and some of the actual data for each data element. This tool is used to arrange sample data and several data query results alongside the corresponding meta data.

Data Quality Validation Template. Provides a review and validation mechanism for the information on the Data Quality Capture Template. Documents how well the meta data and some of the actual data compare for each data element. This tool contains the opinion of an expert about how good or bad the data within each data element actually is.

These four tools capture, at a minimum, the types of data element meta data discussed in Chapter 2, "Meta Data Bingo." Recall the Data Element Meta Data Bingo Card shown in Table 7.2.

To obtain an understanding of which of these logical data analysis tools is responsible for capturing which types of meta data, I replaced the priority columns on this Bingo card with the four data element analysis tools (see Table 7.3). I put a C in the cells where the tool is responsible for Capturing this type of meta data and an R in the cells where the tool needs to Read or use this data.

The Data Element Family Tree captures the bulk of the data element meta data, including name, alias, definition, business purpose, default value, transformations, format, and nullability. This is most of the meta data we see on our logical data models. Because all of these types of meta data are too much to have as columns on a single spreadsheet, usually only a few are listed, such as name, definition, transformations, format, and nullability. What is listed also depends on the results of Data Element Meta Data Bingo. It is possible that several of these types of meta data will not be required to capture for your project based on the Bingo results.

The Data Element Grain Matrix captures the relationships between the facts and their reporting levels. This, of course, is not identified as an item on the Bingo card, because these relationships are non-negotiable meta data we have to capture to complete our model and therefore should not be included in the Bingo voting process.

The Data Quality Capture Template contains the criteria and comparison information between data and meta data, and the Data Quality Validation Template provides proof that the data quality of each data element has been properly reviewed. Sample data values are one source of input for comparing the data and meta data. Other sources include data queries, such as the percentage of nulls found in all values of a data element.

On this Bingo card you will note that none of these data element analysis tools creates or reads keys and index information. This is because we have not yet started our data modeling and, therefore, do not yet have a strong understanding as to which of these data elements will be considered keys or which will be indexed.

This chapter describes each of the logical data analysis tools in the order in which they should be completed:

- Data Element Family Tree
- Data Element Grain Matrix
- Data Quality Capture Template
- Data Quality Validation Template

We will describe each of these four tools and explain the purpose, format, and usage of each. As you read about each tool, think of how you might need to slightly modify or customize them for your specific company or project.

Table 7.2 Data Element Meta Data Bingo Card

	DESCRIPTIVE	FACT			CODE			DATE			ID			TEXT			QUESTIONS
CODE	INFORMATION	H	M	L	H	M	L	H	M	L	H	M	L	H	M	L	AND ISSUES
A	Standard enterprise name	X			X			X			X			X			
B	Alias																
C	Definition	X			X			X			X			X			
D	Business purpose	X															
E	Sample values				X												
F	Default value																
G	Transformation or derivation logic and rules																
H	Format	X			X			X			X			X			
I	Nullability	X			X			X			X			X			
J	Keys and indexes										X						
K	Data quality factors or criteria																
L	Data quality results of factors or criteria																

H, High priority; M, medium priority; L, low priority.

Table 7.3 Meta Data Captured on Logical Data Analysis Tools

CODE	DESCRIPTIVE INFORMATION	DATA ELEMENT FAMILY TREE	DATA ELEMENT GRAIN MATRIX	DATA QUALITY CAPTURE TEMPLATE	DATA QUALITY VALIDATION TEMPLATE
A	Standard enterprise name	C	R	R	R
B	Alias	C			
C	Definition	C		R	R
D	Business purpose	C			
E	Sample values			C	R
F	Default values	C			
G	Transformation or derivation logic and rules	C	C		
H	Format	C		R	R
I	Nullability	C		R	R
J	Keys and indexes				
K	Data quality factors or criteria			C	R
L	Data quality results of factors or criteria				C

If you visit the companion Web site, www.wiley.com/compbooks/hoberman, you will find templates for each of the tools in this chapter; additional tools; and more information about tools in this book, including empty templates that you can download.

What Is the Data Element Family Tree?

You have completed all of the subject area analysis tools for your application, including the Subject Area Family Tree. Now what? You need to identify the data elements within each subject area, along with their sources and any transformations. You need to take the Subject Area Family Tree down to the next level. What you identify at this detailed level will be the data elements that will be used in the remainder of the development. This means that data elements we do not identify in this stage will probably not exist in the final application. Therefore, it is extremely important to organize these data elements in as simple and clear a way as possible to maximize capturing the most complete and accurate information. We need the Data Element Family Tree.

The *Data Element Family Tree* is a spreadsheet that captures the source applications and other key meta data for each data element within the scope of our target application. Note that I refer to the applications we will need to get our data from as the source or origin applications, and the application that we are currently analyzing as the destination or target application. The Data Element Family Tree describes the origin and transformations that apply to each data element in our target application and builds heavily on the Subject Area Family Tree. In fact, there are times when each subject area on the Subject Area Family Tree is the basis for a separate Data Element Family Tree spreadsheet. The types of meta data that are included for the origin and destination data elements include the following:

- Standard enterprise name
- Alias
- Definition
- Business purpose
- Transformations
- Format
- Nullability

Although this is a long list, most of the time we do not include alias and business purpose information on the Data Element Family Tree. It works especially well when our application or destination is a data mart, where this tool can capture which information currently exists in the data warehouse and which does not and thus will be required from other applications.

Starting with the Subject Area Family Tree, we can create the Data Element Family Tree by drilling down into each subject area and identifying its data elements and confirming that they come from the same source application. We can also add derivations or transformations for each of these data elements.

The Data Element Family Tree is usually a fairly large spreadsheet, both in terms of columns and rows; for example, I have created Family Trees over 50 pages long. It meets many of the same goals as the Subject Area Family Tree, along with additional ones:

It provides a complete list of all of the data elements within the application.
The Data Element Family Tree, besides being the detailed version of the Subject Area Family Tree, is also the detailed version of the Subject Area Checklist. This means all of the data elements within the application are listed in the Family Tree along with their source. Many times, the complete list of data elements is not fully identified until we know the source. Identifying a source for a data element, in many cases, can lead to more data elements. For example, let's say Gross Sales Amount is identified as an important data element, and the sources for this data element are List Price and Total Quantity. It is very possible that either one or both of these would also be valuable to have in our application, and therefore, we have new data elements. These new data elements would not have been identified if we did not know the source information. Note that all of the data elements the application needs should be identified in this tree, including data elements you believe will be derived and not stored in the database.

TIP

▬▬▬ **Make sure to include all data elements on your Data Element Family Tree, even those you believe to be derived. This is because at this early stage of analysis, we cannot make judgments as to what is stored in the database and what will be calculated on the fly or in real time while the application is running. We want to make sure we do not miss any data elements because of an incorrect assumption. List all data elements the user needs, independent of how we think they will be stored at this point.**

It captures the sources and transformations of each data element. The Data Element Family Tree builds on the Subject Area Family Tree and, therefore, contains the source applications that play a role in transforming and shaping the content of each of the data elements. This includes identifying any transformations or calculations that help in the creation of these data elements. For example, we might need Gross Sales Amount. The Data Element Family Tree would identify which applications will source Gross Sales Amount and would mention that List Price Amount times Total Quantity gives us the Gross Sales Amount. Therefore, List Price Amount and Total Quantity would be identified as source data elements for Gross Sales Amount, along with the calculation that needs to take place to create Gross Sales Amount.

When we discussed this goal in Chapter 5, "Subject Area Analysis," in the section *Subject Area Family Tree,* we mentioned that keeping the sourcing information neatly organized within a spreadsheet makes validation much easier than if we had to sift through pages in a requirements document. A spreadsheet is an extremely unambiguous way to represent the sourcing requirements. The Data Element Family Tree, because of its level of detail and length, is extremely important to maintain within a spreadsheet, rather than listing it in paragraph form somewhere in a requirements document. A Subject Area Family Tree might contain 10 subject areas, which are neatly organized in a spreadsheet, and the corresponding Data Element Family Tree might contain 100 data elements in a spreadsheet. These 100 data elements described in paragraph form within a requirements document would take up a substantial amount of space and be much more difficult to validate for completeness and accuracy. Which would you rather review, a 5-page spreadsheet neatly organized or a 50-page document written in a sequential paragraph format?

Long after the application is developed and in production, people will still need to refer to this sourcing information. The Data Element Family Tree is a convenient place to capture this information and, hence, becomes a very valuable reference tool for future development.

It determines the detailed impact on the existing application architecture. The Data Element Family Tree will identify the data elements and from where they will need to be sourced. This leads to new interfaces and structures. These new interfaces impact the upstream applications and, therefore, the current application architecture. For example, if the new application we are working on is a data mart, the Data Element Family Tree will identify which data elements currently exist within the data warehouse that can be reused and which will have to be brought into the data warehouse. New source systems that contain the data elements to be brought into the data warehouse will require new interfaces.

It starts the logical data modeling. The Data Element Family Tree provides the complete list of data elements for our application and the key meta data for each of these data elements. Therefore, we have our building blocks for our logical data model. After the logical data analysis phase, we can start assigning data elements to entities and defining appropriate business rules in the form of relationships, building on the subject area models described in the previous chapter. Note that the process for transforming the Data Element Family Tree into a logical data model is discussed in depth in Chapter 7, "Logical Data Analysis."

It identifies data element sourcing issues early. In the Subject Area Family Tree, we were able to identify any high-level sourcing issues. For example, let's say your users want 3 years of history for Customer and, by filling in the Subject Area Family Tree, you realize that the source system only keeps 1 year of Customer history. At the data element level, more specific sourcing issues can arise. For example, the State Code we need in our application is two characters long, yet the source data element for State Code is 20 characters long. This is a potential sourcing issue that we would not catch at the subject area level. However, we still are able to catch this sourcing issue early enough to avoid structure and code rework.

It complements the Data Element Grain Matrix. If you are developing a data mart, you will also need to complete the Data Element Grain Matrix, which is the tool discussed next in this chapter. The Data Element Family Tree complements the Data Element Grain Matrix but does not replace it. The Data Element Grain Matrix captures the reporting levels required for each fact within the data mart. Therefore, it is important not to repeat this reporting level information in the Data Element Family Tree. It makes the spreadsheet much more complicated and ambiguous if you include the reporting levels in the Data Element Family Tree. For example, using the Grain Matrix means we do not have to list Gross Sales Amount by Month, Gross Sales Amount by Week, and Gross Sales Amount by Day, as separate rows in the Family Tree. We will just have a single row, Gross Sales Amount, and capture the different reporting levels on the Data Element Grain Matrix.

Using the Data Element Family Tree

The Data Element Family Tree (see Table 7.4) contains the source systems for each data element in your application. The columns in this tool represent a subset from the types of meta data that appear in the Data Element Meta Data Bingo Card, which are the most common types I have used with this tool. If types of meta data are chosen on the Bingo card that do not appear in this Family Tree, it means they will be captured in other places. We want to make sure that we do not repeat any meta data values across analysis tools, or else we will have the same synchronization issues that result when repeating the same data element across entities. For example, we would need to properly synchronize updates to Customer Last Name if it appears in more than one entity. Likewise, having the definition of a data element located in several different tools

Table 7.4 Blank Data Element Family Tree

| | FROM HERE (SOURCE) | | | | TRANSFORMATION | | TO ARRIVE HERE (TARGET) | | | | |
NAME	SOURCE	DEFINITION	FORMAT	NULL ?	LOGIC		NAME	DEFINITION	FORMAT	NULL ?	QUESTIONS

would cause the same update synchronization issues. We also want to make sure the spreadsheet is still readable. Too many columns reduce the type size and thus decrease readability. Because we can capture many more types of meta data at the data element level, readability becomes much more of an issue here than at the subject area level. I recently saw a Data Element Family Tree in 6-point type! There were so many columns and the type was so small that it was difficult to read and understand.

In this sample Data Element Family Tree, we can only trace back one application for each data element. The column From Here is the origin application, and To Arrive Here" is our destination application. You can change these names to make them more meaningful to your particular situation. If there is more than one source application, we need to trace back and copy the columns under From Here as many times as we need source applications. Remember that the more columns, the less readable the spreadsheet will be. Let's briefly discuss the type of information that goes in each column.

Name

The name column contains the names of all data elements within the application. As mentioned previously, it is extremely important to make sure this column contains the complete list of data elements your application will need. Regardless of whether or not the data element is derived, make sure it is on this list. If a data element is not on this list in the final and agreed-on Data Element Family Tree, there is a very good chance that it will not be in the resulting application. In one data mart we designed, for example, the business user manager questioned us several months after the data mart was in production as to why we did not include a certain data element. We quickly referred back to the Family Tree and were able to show that this data element was not identified as a requirement; that is, it was not listed as a row. The Data Element Family Tree is a very good document for explicitly stating what will and will not be in the resulting application.

TIP

I recommend capturing the actual physical data element database name in the name column. I also sometimes add an extra column on the Data Element Family Tree to capture the business or logical name. Situations in which I do not capture the business or logical name are when the physical database name and definition are enough to clearly understand the data element. If I feel the business or logical name would provide additional understanding and clarity, I would capture it as well.

The one type of information you should never include on the Data Element Family Tree is all of the possible combination of facts and their reporting levels. Gross Sales Amount should appear as a single row, not as the following rows:

- Gross Sales Amount by Day
- Gross Sales Amount by Month by Customer
- Gross Sales Amount Year-to-Date

- Gross Sales Amount by Month by Product
- Gross Sales Amount by Year by Region
- Gross Sales Amount by Week by Customer by Product by Region

All of these names are really the same data element, Gross Sales Amount, with different dimensional levels of reporting. Adding all of these data elements as separate names on the tree document reduces the clarity of this document, and we lose sight of the individual data elements. All of these reporting level variations will be captured on the Data Element Grain Matrix, which we will discuss next.

At one point, I was working on several different data mart projects. In the hope of completing all the projects on time, I asked a functional analyst to complete the entire Data Element Family Tree for his customer data mart. I did not hear from this analyst for several weeks. He finally emailed me a very huge spreadsheet and mentioned that it was very difficult to create and very confusing to read. As soon as I opened the document, I discovered why he found it confusing. He had broken out each fact into every level of reporting combination. There was an incredible amount of redundancy and ambiguity on this spreadsheet. I could tell he put a lot of extra effort into this spreadsheet creating these redundant rows, which we would need to take out of the document. He was very surprised when I mentioned that he should not have included these variations of each fact. Several weeks later, after we also finished the Grain Matrix for this data mart, he agreed that keeping the reporting levels for each fact only on the Grain Matrix was the clearest way to represent this information.

WARNING

Do not include all possible combinations of facts with their reporting levels on the Data Element Family Tree. Doing so will add unnecessary redundancy to the tree and make it difficult to find the real data element. Let the Data Element Grain Matrix capture the relationships between fact and reporting level.

The values in this name column need to be the agreed-on enterprise name for each data element. Thus, after applying the Definition Checklist described in Chapter 3, "Ensuring High-Quality Definitions," we have a high-quality enterprise definition and corresponding name.

Does the Name column need to be under each application, or can we list it just once for our destination application? Just as for the Subject Area Family Tree, there are two situations that arise:

Source systems might call the data element a different name. For example, System XYZ might call the enterprise concept of Customer Last Name, Client Last Name instead. This will happen most frequently in legacy applications, or applications built by third parties. Both legacy and third-party applications might not have followed the same enterprises naming standards you are enforcing today.

A many-to-many relationship may exist between source and target. Two or more source data elements might be needed to create the single target data element within our application. For example, List Price and Total Quantity are both needed to create Gross Sales Amount. Therefore, they will be listed under the source side, and only Gross Sales Amount will be listed under the target side. The values in the column for source will be List Price and Total Quantity; for target, the name will contain Gross Sales Amount. Similarly, we can have List Price as the source for more than one application data element. For example, List Price is needed to create Gross Sales Amount but also Net Sales Amount. Therefore, List Price would appear in the Name column under source; however, both Gross Sales Amount and Net Sales Amount will appear under the target columns. These many-to-many relationships are sometimes difficult to show in a spreadsheet format.

Source

The source column contains the source application name for each data element. Note that a source application can be a database, file, or spreadsheet. Also, almost 100 percent of the time, the source application identified on the Subject Area Family Tree is also the source system for each data element within the subject area. Identifying all of the applications that impact this subject area and agreeing on the application from which to ultimately source this subject area helps us out tremendously with the Data Element Family Tree. Very little, if any, extra analysis is needed to identify the correct source application for each data element. Having said this, as we dive into more details, there are always opportunities to discover something we did not think of at the higher level. We might realize, for example, that even though this is a customer data element and belongs to the Customer subject area, which is identified as being sourced from the XYZ Application, this particular data element cannot be sourced from this same application. The XYZ source system expert might tell us that this data element does not exist in the XYZ application. Therefore, we will need to look elsewhere.

NOTE

There are times when I will not include the Source column on the Data Element Family Tree because I am certain it will be identical to what was discovered on the Subject Area Family Tree, and I want to save valuable real estate on this spreadsheet. To be on the safe side, however, most of the time I will keep the source column at the data element level, just in case exceptions arise and we have a different source application. If you do have a different source, keep in mind to make sure this source meets the reliable and accurate criteria mentioned in Chapter 5, "Subject Area Analysis," under the section *Subject Area Family Tree.*

Definition

The definition for our target data element should be agreed on and meet all the criteria on the Definition Checklist in Chapter 3, "Ensuring High-Quality Definition." This may not be the same definition as that for the legacy or third party software applications, which may not have a definition that matches the Definition Checklist criteria. It is the same situation we have discussed under the section *Name.* Also, because of the many-to-many relationship that exists between source and target, there can be multiple definitions. Although all of the columns are very important to make sure we have identified the correct source data element or data elements, I find comparing a good source and target definition to be the most secure method to help ensure we have the correct source data element.

Format

Format includes both the length and type of each data element. Length includes how long the character or numeric string is; type includes whether the data element is an integer, character, decimal, and so on. Formats that do not match between source and target are the easiest sourcing issues to detect. I can quickly look up and down the columns in this spreadsheet for different lengths and types on the same row. For example, if I noted that the State Code is two characters long on my target side but 20 characters long on my source side, this huge difference would jump out at me. Even someone with no knowledge of the data elements or application should be able to spot this type of inconsistency. Thus, use the format information to quickly identify sourcing problems.

Null?

This column contains the value Y for "Yes, this data element can be null and, therefore, can be blank" and N for "No, this data element is not null and, therefore, must always be filled in." A very quick yet important sourcing inconsistency to detect is when the source application has a Y in this spreadsheet cell but the target application has an N. This means our application expects this data element to always be filled in, but the source application does not expect it to always be filled in. Not detecting this sourcing error at this early point in the process, can lead to many database records "being kicked out" and not loaded because we expected not nulls and we received nulls. I have seen this happen in several situations where we were sourcing from packaged software applications. Developers of these packaged software applications want to make their tools as flexible as possible, and therefore, most of the data elements in their tools can be null.

Transformation Logic

This column contains the business calculations that take place to convert the source data element or elements into the target data element or elements. Business calculations include how to calculate the target data element in terms that a business user can understand and validate. For example, what might appear in the Gross Sales Amount transformation logic cell is:

Multiply List Price and Total Quantity together and round to the nearest penny.

Note that this is not the technical calculation, which optionally can be captured here but definitely will be captured in the Extract, Transform, and Load tool. The Gross

Sales Amount technical calculation for this same transformation to round to two decimal places might look something like this:

*ROUND((LST_PRC * TOTL_QTY),2)*

TIP

If a source data element translates directly into a target data element, with no transformations required, I usually would put some type of default value in this cell, such as "Straight Map" or "Not Applicable." By leaving the cell blank, it might appear as if we have left it incomplete; whereas putting in a default value will document that indeed there is no transformation.

Questions

No matter how many columns I have on my Data Element Family Tree, a must-have column is the one that contains questions and impact information. Because so many people might be looking at this spreadsheet, and this might be the first time the data element source information has been viewed in this format, there will probably be many questions and comments. Questions and comments here include those that have not been addressed at the subject area level. Here are some examples:

- The source State Code is 20 characters long, and we need a 2-character state data element. What is in this source State Code data element? Are just the first two characters populated with what we need?

- Can't seem to find this data element on the source side.

- Is this transformation correct? I took a guess based on the name and definition of the source data element.

- List Price is used to calculate Gross Sales Amount. Do we need List Price as well in our application? Would the users ever want to drill down into List Price?

- The source system can also supply the customer's shoe size. Do we need this data element in our application?

Data Element Family Tree In Practice

In this section we will review the steps for creating the Data Element Family Tree, building on the same example that we discussed in Chapter 5, "Subject Area Analysis," for the Subject Area Family Tree. This example will pertain to a data mart, but these examples can easily be applied to any application undergoing design.

There are several steps to completing the Data Element Family Tree:

1. **Create the Subject Area Family Tree.** Follow the steps outlined in Chapter 5.

2. **Agree on the columns for the Data Element Family Tree.** Play Data Element Meta Data Bingo, discussed in Chapter 2, "Meta Data Bingo." Just use the most

important columns to keep the spreadsheet readable. Make sure, as mentioned previously, that we do not unnecessarily repeat meta data values among data analysis and modeling tools.

3. **Divide this spreadsheet by subject area.** Use the subjects from the Subject Area Family Tree as dividers in the Data Element Family Tree. Each section will contain the data elements for that subject area. Optionally, you can create separate spreadsheets for each subject area. However, I usually prefer to keep the Data Element Family Tree on a single spreadsheet. There are two situations in which I will break up the Data Element Family Tree by subject area across spreadsheets. The first is when we have too many data elements that become unmanageable in a single document. A document that is more than 50 pages long would be considered too large. The second situation would involve different people filling in the spreadsheet for each subject area. For example, if Dennis completes the Customer subject area and Mary the Product subject area, it will be easier to manage changes to this document by keeping the subject areas in separate spreadsheets.

4. **Fill it in.** You need to coordinate this task if multiple people or teams will be filling in the Data Element Family Tree. because it obviously is the most difficult and time-consuming of these steps. There are a number of ways you can populate this spreadsheet. I have successfully used the following approach:

   A. **Initially fill in all application data elements on the target side.** You can use the resources mentioned in the In-the-Know Template. Both a combination of people and documentation should provide enough information to obtain an initial list of data elements. You can organize brainstorming sessions or other types of meetings with your business experts to get this information. You can copy from requirement documents or other important text. The reason I use the word initially in this step is that no matter how confident you are or your team is that you have the complete list of data elements, Step B below will reveal that you were probably missing data elements. I can almost guarantee this.

   B. **Initially fill in all data elements on the source side.** Again refer to the In-the-Know Template. The source system experts and any source system documentation will be very useful in completing these source system columns. As you fill in these columns alongside the application data elements on the target side of the spreadsheet, you will note two types of gaps. An example of the first is when find that you do not have the data element in this particular source system as originally thought. In a case such as this, you will need to tap other source application expertise. I thought I could get Customer Shoe Size from the Customer Reference Database but was mistaken. An example of the second type of gap is when you might find that there are several other source system data elements that appear valuable to have that were not identified by the target application. This is why we used the word initially in Step A.

   C. **Go back to Step A until done.** To fill in gaps on the target side, you will need to go back to the target application experts and ask them if they need these new data elements. I have worked with very knowledgeable source system experts who knew substantially more about what the business needed than did some of the business users themselves. I have also worked with source system experts who *thought* they knew more than the business users themselves. In either case, take these data elements back to the target experts and see if the elements would be useful. You want to avoid the situation where you need to enhance an application interface and lots of structures and code soon after your data mart goes into production. You might need to meet with the source system experts a second time, and hence, we use the term initially in Step B as well. Filling in this spreadsheet is extremely iterative. You need to go back to Step A until you are confident that all issues and questions have been addressed and that you have the complete list of data elements and source information.

TIP

Be open to iteration when completing the Data Element Family Tree. There will be times when a source system expert identifies a data element that your target experts did not consider, and vice versa. Continue with the iterations until all doubt is gone, that is, all questions and issues have been addressed.

5. **Review.** This is usually a fairly quick step, after all the iteration we have done in the previous step. This review meeting involves all source and target system experts in the same room, as opposed to the previous step when they worked independently.

6. **Maintain.** This becomes a very valuable reference document; therefore, keep it current.

Let's go through a detailed example. You have completed the subject area data analysis and modeling on a new data mart. Now you are ready to start the logical data analysis by completing the Data Element Family Tree.

1. Create the Subject Area Family Tree

You have completed all of the subject area analysis tools, including the Subject Area Family Tree (see Table 7.5). Unreliable and inaccurate sources have already been removed, and therefore, the only sources on this spreadsheet are those from which we will get the data. At this point we do not have to perform any more analysis as to what is or is not a valid source, unless we identify data elements that we cannot get from the same application that we identified for their subject area. For example, if all customer data elements should be sourced from the Customer Reference Database but we have found several customer data elements that do not exist in this source application, then we will need to go through the same thought process we went through for each of the subject areas in Chapter 5, "Subject Area Analysis." That is, what are the possible source applications for these customer data elements? Then we select the one that meets the definition as to the most reliable and accurate source for this information.

2. Agree on the Columns for the Data Element Family Tree

Because you have already read Chapter 2 of this book, "Meta Data Bingo," you are familiar with Meta Data Bingo. It identifies the types of meta data that are important for us

Table 7.5 Completed Subject Area Family Tree

NAME	FROM HERE (SOURCE)			TO ARRIVE HERE (TARGET)			QUESTIONS
	SOURCE	DEFINITION	HISTORY	NAME	DEFINITION	HISTORY	AND IMPACT
Customer	Customer Reference Database	The recipient and/or purchaser of our products.	10	Customer	The recipient and/or purchaser of our products.	3	
Order	Order Entry	A contract to buy a quantity of product at a specified price.	4	Order	A contract to buy a quantity of product at a specified price.	3	
Item	Item Reference Database	Anything we buy, sell, stock, move, or make. Any manufactured or purchased part, material, component, assembly, or product.	10	Product	Anything we buy, sell, stock, move, or make. Any manufactured or purchased part, material, component, assembly, or product.	3	
Party	Data Warehouse	A person or company that is important to our business in some way.	5	Associate	A person who is employed in a full- or part-time capacity by our company, to perform a service or function to our company.	3	
Time	Data Warehouse	A measurable length of seconds, minutes, hours, days, weeks, months, or years. Can include both fiscal and Julian time measurements.	10	Time	A measurable length of seconds, minutes, hours, days, weeks, months, or years. Can include both fiscal and Julian time measurements.	3	

to capture. For this particular example, you play Data Element Meta Data Bingo with your team and, after summarizing the results, your final Bingo card is shown in Table 7.6.

This tells us that it will be a requirement to capture the meta data types under the H, or High, category. For all data elements, we will capture the standard enterprise name, definition, format information, nullability, and key data quality measurements. For facts, such as Total Sales Amount and Net Weight, we will also capture business purpose and transformation logic, which is one of the main purposes of the Data Element Family Tree. For codes, such as Cancel Reason Code and State Code, we will also capture sample values, which are extremely important for all codes within our environment. For IDs, such as Customer ID and Product ID, we will also capture key and index information. We will not capture any additional types of meta data for dates, such as Actual Delivery Date and Employee Birthday Date, and for text, such as Customer Comments Text and Order Delivery Instructions Text.

Therefore, we need to capture the following types of meta data:

- Name
- Definition
- Format
- Nullability
- Data quality metrics
- Business purpose (only facts)
- Transformation and derivation logic (only facts)
- Sample values (only codes)
- Keys and indexes (only IDs)

Remember to be very selective when choosing which of these types we would like to have on our Family Tree. Some of this information will be captured in other tools. For example, data quality metrics and sample values will be captured in the data quality tools discussed later in this chapter. The business purpose will need to be captured in another place, because it would not make sense to add this column to the Family Tree if only a very small percentage of the data elements would be using it. Perhaps you could maintain a separate spreadsheet for fact business purposes, or add it directly to the logical data model. If business purpose were required for most or all of the data elements, it would make sense to add it as a separate column to the Family Tree. Keys and indexes will be captured during the logical data modeling.

This leaves us with the following types of meta data for capture on the Data Element Family Tree:

- Name
- Definition
- Format
- Nullability
- Transformation and derivation logic (only facts)

Table 7.6 Summarized Data Element Meta Data Bingo Card

CODE	DESCRIPTIVE INFORMATION	FACT			CODE			DATE			ID			TEXT			QUESTIONS AND ISSUES
		H	M	L	H	M	L	H	M	L	H	M	L	H	M	L	
A	Standard enterprise name	X			X			X			X			X			
B	Alias			X			X			X			X			X	
C	Definition	X			X			X			X			X			
D	Business purpose	X					X			X			X			X	
E	Sample values	X			X												
F	Default value			X			X			X			X			X	
G	Transformation or derivation logic and rules	X					X			X			X			X	
H	Format	X			X			X			X			X			
I	Nullability	X			X			X			X			X			
J	Keys and indexes			X			X			X	X					X	
K	Data quality factors or criteria	X			X			X			X			X			
L	Data quality results of factors or criteria	X			X			X			X			X			

H, High priority; M, medium priority; L, low priority.

We add these types as columns to create a blank Data Element Family Tree (see Table 7.7). We are now ready to fill it in.

3. Divide This Spreadsheet by Subject Area

We take each of the subject areas and use them to divide the spreadsheet into manageable pieces. Our Data Element Family Tree might look like Table 7.8.

Note that I prefer to do reference data before transaction data in the Data Element Family Tree. This is because it usually is easier to identify a reliable and accurate source for reference data than for transaction data. It also usually is more straightforward to define transaction data after having a clear definition of reference data. Therefore, I moved the Order subject area to the end of this Family Tree. We will complete Order after completing all of the reference areas.

Note that I filled in the source column. This is redundant with the information in our Subject Area Family Tree. I put it here to visibly show where each data element is coming from, with the hope of detecting situations where we cannot get the data element from that source system identified at the subject area level. For example, if all of the order data elements will come from Order Entry, listing Order Entry as the source for each will cause an extra validation at the data element level. This might reveal that certain data elements are not available from the Order Entry system. Therefore, we will have a different source listed for some of the order data elements.

4. Fill It In

You are using the iterative approach described previously to fill in this spreadsheet. Recall these steps to take to fill in the tree:

A. Initially fill in all application data elements on the target side.

B. Initially fill in all data elements on the source side.

C. Go back to Step A until done.

On your In-the-Know Template, you have captured that your resources for completing the target data mart side include very detailed reporting requirements, including many sample reports and screen snapshots. You also realize that the target business users mentioned on the In-the-Know Template have minimal experience. Therefore, to complete the target data mart side, you will need to rely more on the documentation than the people. However, you need to make sure that these people have at least the business and reporting requirements knowledge to review and validate the Data Element Family Tree. On the source side, however, the reverse is true. You have very strong source system experts, yet very little documentation. Therefore, when completing the source side of the tree, you will need to rely more on the people than the documentation.

After completing your initial meetings with the data mart and source teams, you are ready to review your findings and decide on areas where iteration will be necessary. So you have completed A and B in the list mentioned previously and are now assessing your approach for C. Table 7.9 shows your initially filled-in Data Element Family

Table 7.7 Blank Data Element Family Tree

FROM HERE (SOURCE)					TRANSFORMATION	TO ARRIVE HERE (TARGET)				
NAME	SOURCE	DEFINITION	FORMAT	NULL ?	LOGIC	NAME	DEFINITION	FORMAT	NULL ?	QUESTIONS

Tree. Note that only a few data elements from each subject area are shown. When we fill these in for real, however, all data elements need to be listed. Note that I have shortened many of the definitions for this example. When you fill these in for real, definitions need to follow the rigor of the Definition Checklist in Chapter 3, "Ensuring High-Quality Definitions."

Here are a number of observations on this initially filled-in Family Tree, some of which will factor into your decisions on where we need iteration:

- Because real estate is very valuable on the Data Element Family Tree, there will be times when text will wrap to the next line, making it difficult to read. For example, look at some of the names under the name column on the target side, such as CUST_REF_DB_ID. This data element spans several lines, making it difficult to read. Play with the column length and type size to maximize readability.

- Note the value of a separate name column for source and target. The source names from the Customer Reference Database appear to be nonenterprise standard names. Therefore, we are able to capture both the F-NAME data element name from the source and the standard name CUST_FRST_NAM from the target. The same is true for the customer identifier. The Customer Reference Database just calls the customer identifier ID. On the target side, however, we will need to distinguish this identifier from other identifiers within our data mart environment. Therefore, we embedded the application name into the name of this data element. Note I also updated the definition on the target side to distinguish it as coming from the Customer Reference Database.

- The name column only contains the physical data element name, and not a business or logical name. You might want to have both logical and physical names on your trees. You need at least the physical name. I have just chosen physical name for this example, because of space reasons.

- There are format differences between the source and target on the customer name data elements. The customer first name is defined as character(15) on the source side and character(20) on the target side. Here is a place where I will need to go back to the data mart users and question the 20-character length in their first-name data element. Values will not be truncated because the target side is larger than the source side. However, we are taking up additional space, which could result in a very large customer table and cause a format inconsistency. The customer last name is more of an issue. It is larger in the source than in the target data mart. We could possibly be truncating up to 10 characters off the last name of a customer, which can cause serious data quality problems as well as inconsistencies as far back as the source application. If the source application sends us the last name value "Rumplestilstonshomaganon," for example, our data mart can only store "Rumplestilstonshomag." Even though it will be a rare case when there will be any type of truncation, there will be times when it happens. Therefore, make this a high-priority item in your next meeting with the data mart users.

- The Product Category data element is null on the source application side but not null on the data mart side. Why is it null on the source side? Was this an oversight? Does it really have null values, or is this data element always filled in but

Table 7.8 Data Element Family Tree Divided by Subject Area

	FROM HERE (SOURCE)					TO ARRIVE HERE (TARGET)				
NAME	SOURCE	DEFINITION	FORMAT	NULL ?	TRANSFORMATION LOGIC	NAME	DEFINITION	FORMAT	NULL ?	QUESTIONS
	CUSTOMER							**CUSTOMER**		
	Customer Reference Database									
	Customer Reference Database									
	Customer Reference Database									
	PRODUCT							**PRODUCT**		
	Item Reference Database									
	Item Reference Database									
	Item Reference Database									

ASSOCIATE

DW
DW
DW

TIME

DW
DW
DW

ORDER

Order Entry
Order Entry
Order Entry

Table 7.9 Initially Filled-In Data Element Family Tree

	FROM HERE (SOURCE)				TRANSFORMATION	TO ARRIVE HERE (TARGET)				
					LOGIC					
NAME	SOURCE	DEFINITION	FORMAT	NULL ?		NAME	DEFINITION	FORMAT	NULL ?	QUESTIONS
		CUSTOMER						CUSTOMER		
ID	Customer Reference Database	The unique way to refer to each customer. A customer's ID will never change or be reused.	Number (8)	N	Straight Map	CUST_ REF_ DB_ID	The unique way to refer to each customer, assigned by the Customer Reference Database application. A customer's ID will never change or be reused.	Number (8)	N	
F-NAME	Customer Reference Database	The first name of the customer. Can be a nickname.	Char(15)	Y	Straight Map	CUST_ FRST _NAM	The first name of the customer. Can be a nickname.	Char(20)	Y	
L-NAME	Customer Reference Database	The last name of the customer.	Char(30)	N	Straight Map	CUST_ LST_ NAM	The last name of the customer.	Char(20)	N	

Field	Source	Definition	Type	Null	Transformation	Target	Definition	Type	Null	Notes
PRO_CD	Item Reference Database	The unique identifier generated for a product.	Char(5)	N	Straight Map	PRO_ITEM_REF_DB_ID	The unique identifier generated for a product.	Char(5)	N	Are these the only 3 levels we can report our products at? I seem to recall a 4th level, but I can't remember its name. (Maxwell)
BRAND	Item Reference Database	The label our customers recognize our products by.	Char(5)	N	Straight Map	PRO_BRAND_CD	The label our customers recognize our products by.	Char(5)	N	
CATE-GORY	Item Reference Database	The internal grouping of our brands.	Char(5)	Y	Straight Map	PRO_CTGY_CD	The internal grouping of our brands.	Char(5)	N	
				ASSOCIATE					**ASSOCIATE**	
NAME	DW	The full name of the associate.	Char(50)	N	Straight Map	ASSOC_NAM	The full name of the associate.	Char(50)	N	
DEPART-MENT	DW	The associate's internal organization name.	Char(30)	N	Straight Map	ASSOC_DEPT_NAM	The associate's internal organization name.	Char(30)	N	
SSN#	DW	The social security number for the associate.	Char(9)	N	Straight Map					Why isn't Social Security Number listed as a requirement? (Francis)

continues

Table 7.9 *(Continued)*

	FROM HERE (SOURCE)			TRANSFORMATION	TO ARRIVE HERE (TARGET)			
NAME	SOURCE	DEFINITION	FORMAT	NULL ?	LOGIC	NAME	DEFINITION	FORMAT	NULL ?	QUESTIONS
			TIME					TIME		
DAY	DW	A full calendar day, defined as 24 hours starting at 12 A.M.	Char(10)	N	Straight Map	DAY	A full calendar day, defined as 24 hours starting at 12 A.M.	Char(10)	N	
MONTH	DW	A full calendar month.	Char(10)	N	Straight Map	MONTH	A full calendar month.	Char(10)	N	
YEAR	DW	A full calendar year.	Char(10)	N	Straight Map	YEAR	A full calendar year.	Char(10)	N	
			ORDER					ORDER		
QUAN-TITY	Order Entry	The number of products on an order.	Dec (15,2)	N	Straight Map	ORD_QUAN-TITY	The number of products on an order.	Dec (15,2)	N	
AMOUNT	Order Entry	The financial cost to the customer for this order.	Dec (15,2)	N	Straight Map	ORD_AMOUNT	The financial cost to the customer for this order.	Dec (15,2)	N	
WEIGHT_POUNDS	Order Entry	The weight in pounds of this order.	Dec (15,2)	Y	Divide the weight in pounds by 2,000 to get the weight in tons: WEIGHT_POUNDS/2000	ORD_WEIGHT_TONS	The weight in tons of this order.	Dec (15,2)	Y	

just not enforced in the source application? A level data element such as Product Category appears to be a data element that should always be populated. You will need to go back to the source experts on this one. If we can ever encounter null values from the source application, we will need to define it as a null data element and update this Family Tree. We also might want to add a question to the Questions column as to why such an important data element can be null.

- There is a product question around the different levels at which product can be reported. Maxwell is probably one of the data mart business users. Remember that the data mart users in this example have limited experience, yet Maxwell's question still needs to be addressed. You will first need to talk with Maxwell to more clearly understand this additional product level. Then you will need to go to the source system experts to inquire about its existence.

- I wonder why Social Security Number was not listed as a requirement from the data mart side. The Associate subject area currently exists in the data warehouse, and therefore, this data element is already easily accessible. Refer back to the data mart documentation or ask the data mart users if they need this data element. The source system expert, Francis, jotted down a question as to whether this data element is needed by the data mart.

- Under Order information, the weight of the order in tons is a derived data element that is calculated by dividing the source application data element, which is in pounds, by 2,000. Note that all derived data elements need to appear on the Data Element Family Tree. I would question whether the data mart users need to see the weight in pounds as well as tons.

5. Review

The next step is to review this Data Element Family Tree with the team and, it is hoped, leave this review with everyone agreeing on the source information and with all of your questions answered and issues resolved. Note that it is important to include both business and source system experts in this review.

6. Maintain

It is very important to maintain your finished Data Element Family Tree when we are done with the last review. This document will be the source for the rest of the data element analysis and the logical data modeling. In addition, it will probably be a valuable reference for many projects to come. Because this information is usually not stored anywhere else, it is important to maintain here.

What Is the Data Element Grain Matrix?

You have completed your Data Element Family Tree and are eager to understand more about the reporting requirements of your data mart. You need an unambiguous way to document the reporting levels for each of the facts identified on the Data Element Family

Tree. You already have completed your Subject Area Grain Matrix, and therefore, you have a good understanding of the levels of reporting for each subject area. Now you need to get more into the details and use this subject area analysis and Data Element Family Tree to create the Data Element Grain Matrix.

The Data Element Grain Matrix is a spreadsheet that captures the levels of reporting for each fact or measurement. It is the spreadsheet view of a star schema design. Both business users and the project team can understand and validate the reporting requirements using this spreadsheet. Business users might speak the language of reports, whereas technical people might speak the language of data models or star schema designs. The Data Element Grain Matrix is a common ground, a spreadsheet to which both the users and technical people can relate and use as a medium for communication. Note that this is only for reporting applications, such as for data marts. Once this spreadsheet is complete, it is a very straightforward process to translate it into an initial star schema design.

NOTE

The Data Element Grain Matrix is only completed for reporting applications, such as for data marts. If you are designing an operational or other nonreporting application, you do not need to complete this tool.

The Data Element Grain Matrix builds on the Subject Area Grain Matrix from Chapter 5, "Subject Area Analysis." Recall that the Subject Area Grain Matrix captures reporting levels at a subject area level, whereas the Data Element Grain Matrix describes the reporting requirements for each fact. For example, a Subject Area Grain Matrix might capture that Sales needs to be viewed at the month level. The corresponding Data Element Grain Matrix would list Gross Sales Amount, Net Sales Amount, Total Sales Weight, and the rest of the sales data elements, also at the month level.

The Data Element Grain Matrix can meet both ad hoc and standard reporting needs, usually with separate matrices or with different notation on the same matrix. There are even times when each standard report might need to be differentiated on the Data Element Grain Matrix. Much of this depends on how this type of reporting was captured at the subject area level. Usually if I have created three Grain Matrices at the subject area level, I will have three at the data element level. I will try to keep a one-to-one relationship between the subject area spreadsheet and the data element spreadsheet.

The Data Element Grain Matrix acts as a common language between business users and the technical team. This tool accomplishes many of the goals mentioned under the Subject Area Grain Matrix from Chapter 5 as well as some additional ones:

Helps validate the levels of reporting without a data model. Many users I have worked with have difficulty understanding data modeling concepts. Using a star schema data model to validate reporting requirements can cause confusion and frustration for a user. Rather than use the model as a validation mechanism, I prefer to use the Data Element Grain Matrix. The spreadsheet format, as we have seen with the Family Tree, provides an unambiguous representation for capturing the reporting requirements.

Complements the Data Element Family Tree. The Data Element Family Tree captures the source information for each data element, and the Data Element Grain Matrix captures the reporting requirements for each fact or measurement. These two documents are tightly coupled. Without the Family Tree, we would never be able to validate whether our reporting requirements are realistic, based on what is available in the source applications. For example, the users might want Gross Sales Amount at a day level, but is it available from the source application at this detailed level? Without the Data Element Grain Matrix, we would need to add an incredible amount of redundancy to the Family Tree to capture all possible combinations of facts with reporting levels. For example, if we did not have the Grain Matrix, then on the Family Tree we would need to have separate rows for Gross Sales Amount by Day, Gross Sales Amount by Week, Gross Sales Amount by Product, and so on.

Leads to new dimensions. If you notice several facts that appear very similar except for a slight variation, such as a unit of measure or currency code, you might want to propose a new dimension for them. For example, looking at the Data Element Grain Matrix you might realize that Order Total Pounds Weight, Order Total Tons Weight, and Order Total Tonnes Weight (metric tons) are all at the same reporting levels and that the only difference between these data elements appears to be their unit of measure. In some cases we might want to add a new dimension, such as a set of columns on the Data Element Grain Matrix called Unit of Measure (UOM), and only capture one data element, that is, Order Total Weight.

Creates a seamless transition to a star schema. It is very straightforward and easy to translate the Data Element Grain Matrix into an initial star schema. We will go through these steps in the example section shortly. This initial design will help us validate the modeling steps we will go through in the next chapter, as well as shed light on where we might need to create summary or aggregate tables.

Using the Data Element Grain Matrix

In the Data Element Grain Matrix, the rows represent facts and the columns represent dimensions and their levels. The levels within each dimension are listed as subcolumns under their reference data categories. For example, Time is a dimension that appears as a column category, containing the reporting levels Year, Quarter, Month, and Day. Table 7.10 contains a Data Element Grain Matrix, with the facts and dimension levels populated in preparation for filling in the levels of reporting for each fact. Note that the rows represent facts, and in this example, each data element within the sales subject area has its own row.

Note that we are only listing the reporting levels of each dimension in this spreadsheet, not all of the data elements within each dimension. Thus, for Time we list Year, Quarter, Month, and Day. We do not list Year Code, Year Description Text, Quarter Code, and so on.

Note also that this spreadsheet, as does the Family Tree, can have many columns, one for each dimension level. Try to keep the matrix readable and as simple as possible, because too quickly it can require 15 columns in 6-point type.

Table 7.10 Sample Data Element Grain Matrix

DATA ELEMENT	TIME				CUSTOMER		PRODUCT		SALES ORGANIZATION	
	YEAR	QUARTER	MONTH	DAY	CATEGORY	CUSTOMER	BRAND	ITEM	DIVISION	REGION
Total Sales Amount										
Total Sales Quantity										
Total Sales Weight										
Sales Shipping Costs Amount										
Sales Gross Profit Amount										
Sales Net Profit Amount										
Sales Total Commission Amount										
Sales Promotions Total Amount										

Data Element Grain Matrix In Practice

In this section we will review the steps for creating the Data Element Grain Matrix. We build on the same example in Chapter 5, "Subject Area Analysis," for the Subject Area Grain Matrix and use the data elements we defined previously in the Data Element Family Tree.

Several steps are involved in completing the Data Element Grain Matrix and converting it into a star schema:

1. **Create the Subject Area Grain Matrix.** Follow the steps outlined in Chapter 5.

2. **Create the Data Element Family Tree.** Follow the steps outlined previously in this chapter.

3. **Add the facts under each subject area.** Take each of the facts that were identified under the Data Element Family Tree and add them as separate rows to the Data Element Grain Matrix, below their respective subject areas.

4. **Initially fill in the subject area reporting levels for each fact.** More than likely, the data element will share the same reporting levels as its subject areas. As a starting point, copy the subject area reporting levels to each of their facts. At this level we also distinguish the different types of reporting, including ad hoc and all the different summary reporting.

5. **Review.** This could be very iterative. Business users must be included in the review and must validate each of the reporting levels. You want to find exceptions here, that is, facts that do not have the same reporting levels as their subject areas.

6. **Group rows into common sets.** This is a large step toward star schema design, because those measures that share the same set of reporting levels usually wind up in the same fact table. That is, they share the same grain. It is easy to identify those measures that share the same grain, if we put these rows next to each other.

7. **Convert into initial star schema.** After grouping together the common fact subject areas, convert them into a data model containing the fact and dimension level data elements. This model can be used to validate the denormalized model created after applying the steps in the next chapter, and also suggest where we might need to add summary tables.

1. Create the Subject Area Grain Matrix

You have done all of your subject area analysis as described in Chapter 5, "Subject Area Analysis," and Table 7.11 contains the completed Subject Area Grain Matrix. Note that there is ad hoc reporting, which is required at all dimensional levels, and a Shipments Summary Report, which is only required at certain summary levels. The notation for representing ad hoc and standard reporting were described in Chapter 5. Note also that we are only showing one fact subject area. More than likely, when we do this for real there will be several subject areas listed.

2. Create the Data Element Family Tree

See Table 7.9 for the Data Element Family Tree we created previously in this chapter.

Table 7.11 Completed Subject Area Grain Matrix

SUBJECT AREA	TIME			CUSTOMER	PRODUCT			ASSOCIATE	
	YEAR	MONTH	DAY	CUSTOMER	CATEGORY	BRAND	PRODUCT	DEPARTMENT	ASSOCIATE
Order	AB	AB	A	A	AB	AB	A	A	A

A, Ad hoc reporting; B, Shipments Summary Report.

3. Add the Facts under Each Subject Area

See Table 7.12 for the listing of all the Order facts under the Order subject area. Note that although pounds and tonnes (metric tons) are added to this matrix, they did not appear on the initial Data Element Family Tree. This could be because when we asked the data mart users whether they would like pounds as well in their data mart, they responded, "Yes, thank you, and can I also have metric tons?"

4. Initially Fill In the Subject Area Reporting Levels for Each Fact

This is a very easy step. Just copy and paste the same reporting levels for each subject area into each of the subject area's facts. See Table 7.12.

5. Review

You have met with the business users of the data mart and, as a result, have made a number of updates to this matrix:

- Weights should not be on the Shipments Summary Report. Therefore, we need to remove B from these weight facts.

- We only need to see Associate levels on the Order Amount data element. This is the data element we will need to use when we want to view associate commissions.

See Table 7.13 for the updated Data Element Grain Matrix.

6. Group Rows into Common Sets

Now that you have finalized what the business users would like to see in terms of reporting levels, we need to start making the transition to the star schema data model. The first step is to group the rows into common sets of reporting levels, as we have done at the subject area level in Chapter 5, "Subject Area Analysis," I also use this step as a place to see if I can identify related facts that might make more sense as a separate dimension. For example, I see three weight data elements in this example: pounds, tons, and tonnes. Would it make more sense to have a Unit of Measure (UOM) dimension with one fact instead of these separate facts? The answer depends on much flexibility we would want on the UOM data elements. Would the users be drilling up and down on different UOMs, such as, "Let me first see total weight by tons; then I want to see it in pounds"? Also would there be new UOMs we would want to store? Keeping UOMs in a separate dimension gives us an added layer of flexibility, as we will learn more about in Chapter 9, "The Abstraction Safety Guide and Components." Let's assume that we have answered these reporting and flexibility questions, and we strongly believe it makes sense to have a UOM dimension. See Table 7.14, with these changes.

Table 7.12 Data Element Family Tree with Facts Listed under Each Subject Area

| DATA ELEMENT | TIME | | | CUSTOMER | PRODUCT | | | ASSOCIATE | |
	YEAR	MONTH	DAY	CUSTOMER	CATEGORY	BRAND	PRODUCT	DEPARTMENT	ASSOCIATE
Order	AB	AB	A	A	AB	AB	A	A	A
ORD_QUANTITY									
ORD_AMOUNT									
ORD_WEIGHT_POUNDS									
ORD_WEIGHT_TONS									
ORD_WEIGHT_TONNES									

A, Ad hoc reporting; B, Shipments Summary Report.

Table 7.13 Updated Grain Matrix after Review

DATA ELEMENT	TIME			CUSTOMER	PRODUCT			ASSOCIATE	
	YEAR	MONTH	DAY	CUSTOMER	CATEGORY	BRAND	PRODUCT	DEPARTMENT	ASSOCIATE
Order									
ORD_QUANTITY	AB	AB	A	A	AB	AB	A		
ORD_AMOUNT	AB	AB	A	A	AB	AB	A	A	A
ORD_WEIGHT_POUNDS	A	A	A	A	A	A	A		
ORD_WEIGHT_TONS	A	A	A	A	A	A	A		
ORD_WEIGHT_TONNES	A	A	A	A	A	A	A		

A, Ad hoc reporting; B, Shipments Summary Report.

Table 7.14 Updated Grain Matrix in Preparation for Star Schema Translation

	TIME			CUSTOMER	PRODUCT			ASSOCIATE		UOM
DATA ELEMENT	YEAR	MONTH	DAY	CUSTOMER	CATEGORY	BRAND	PRODUCT	DEPARTMENT	ASSOCIATE	UOM
Order										
ORD_QUANTITY	AB	AB	A	A	AB	AB	A			
ORD_AMOUNT	AB	AB	A	A	AB	AB	A	A	A	
ORD_WEIGHT	A	A	A	A	A	A	A			A

UOM, Unit of Measure; A, ad hoc reporting; B, Shipments Summary Report.

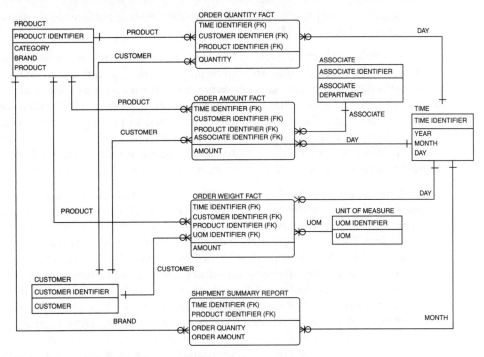

Figure 7.1   Initial star schema model.

7.   Convert into Initial Star Schema

Figure 7.1 contains the initial star schema for this example. Note that there will normally be many more data elements at the fact levels. Note also the use of labels to show the levels of reporting. As mentioned earlier in this chapter, this model is very useful for validating the results of the Denormalization Survival Guide in Chapter 8, as well as for determining where to introduce summary tables into the final physical design.

What Is the Data Quality Capture Template?

After completing the Data Element Family Tree and the Data Element Grain Matrix, you believe you have a very consistent and accurate representation of the data elements and reporting requirements of the application. The data element list appears complete, and each data element has a solid definition and an agreed-on source. For those data elements that are facts, we also have identified their levels of reporting. However, we have gathered this information at a meta data level and probably have not yet seen any actual data. How can we be sure the data matches the meta data? For example, if a data element is defined as not null, are there any actual values that might be null? These questions are starting to haunt you, because you know that the actual data can always reveal a few surprises.

You need to identify the categories that require data checking and to record the data check-
ing results. You need the Data Quality Capture Template.

Many people either avoid data quality checking or do it very late in the development
process. They wait until they are significantly into the application development; then,
when the data found in the tables does not match the meta data on the model, large issues develop. Something has to change when this occurs to make the data consistent
with the meta data. The smallest change is an update to a definition on the data model.
Rarely is this the case. More often, changes are required to data element format, nullability, name, and so on, changes that require restructuring database tables and possibly rewriting some code. This is a very reactive approach to data quality checking.

The better approach, one that is proactive, is to examine the data during the logical
data analysis phase of development. An appropriate place to do so is right after identifying the data elements required in the application, that is, after the Data Element
Family Tree. Therefore, as soon as a data element is identified and defined, we can look
at the data to make sure it is what we believe it to be. If you were completing these
tools in a linear fashion, meaning not starting a tool until finishing the one before, you
would probably start looking at the data after the Data Element Grain Matrix is completed, instead of the Data Element Family Tree. However, if you have the resources to
complete these data element analysis tools in parallel, however, you can do the Grain
Matrix and Data Quality Capture Template at the same time. The challenge is that it is
so early in the development of the application that, in many cases, the data might be
difficult to access, because tables and interface files have not yet been built. You might
need to think up creative ways to get to the data so early in the life cycle. However, the
earlier you can get access to the data, the more quickly you can ensure your meta data
and data are in synch. It will be well worth the effort to get the data at this early point.

TIP

**Validate the data as early as possible in the development of the application. The
earlier you find a data quality problem and address it, the more time and money
you will save the project in rework. You always need to take a proactive approach
to data quality capture and validation.**

Data quality, simply defined, is when the data values match our expectations, which
are based on two main questions:

1. **Does the data match the data from a reliable source?** This means that if I am
   looking at a value of $5.00 in Gross Sales Amount, I would expect to see $5.00 in
   the application that I believe to be a reliable source for Gross Sales Amount. A reliable source is not necessarily the strategic application where the data is initially
   entered. It can be any application that the user trusts. For example, I worked on a
   data mart recently where we were validating the values against another reporting
   application in which the users had a lot of faith. Something to be aware of, however, is that the timing in loading data and amount rounding issues can lead to
   slight variations in the results. For example, if I am comparing Monday's values
   with Tuesday's values, I might get different results. Also, if I round to two decimal places versus rounding up to the nearest dollar, I might get different results.

2. **Does the data match the meta data?** This means that when I see the number 11 as a value in the Customer Shoe Size data element, I would expect this value to be the size of the customer's shoes. I would not expect this value to be the number of children the customer has. In matching data against meta data, we look at not only the definition but other key comparisons as well. These include name, format, nullability, and so on, that is, any type of meta data in which the possibility of finding inconsistencies exists. Note that we are not testing if the data is correct here. Data accuracy is covered in the first question where we are comparing our data against a reliable application source. We are just testing here to see if the data looks like what we would expect, based on all the meta data analysis up to this point.

The Data Quality Capture Template deals with the second of these two questions. It focuses on comparing the data against the meta data. This template is our first tool where we are actually looking at the data. Up to this point, our analysis has focused on defining and getting agreement on the meta data. The Data Quality Capture Template takes all of the meta data up to this point and lays it out against the actual data in four key categories:

Name and Definition. Name and definition data and meta data comparisons require the most effort and analysis. This is because we are checking to make sure each data element name and definition matches what we would expect to see in the values of this data element. For example, if the Customer Age data element has a great definition on the age of the customer but in reality contains the Customer's Shoe Size, we have a conflict between the data and meta data, that is, between the actual values and what we say the actual values mean. To make a robust comparison between the data and meta data for this category, we need a fairly decent sized sample of data values to check against. One or two values usually are not good enough. I have found that between 10 and 25 values usually are an acceptable amount.

Format. This template compares the format defined in the Data Element Family Tree with the format in the actual data. If a State Code is two characters long, the actual data should contain two characters for each of these values. If a description is 1,000 characters long, we should expect to see some values that are fairly close to a 1,000 characters long. If the maximum length of this 1,000-character-long data element is only 50 characters, this would be an example of the data not matching the meta data. Format includes both the length and type of a data element, with type including character, numeric, date, and so on. If the values for a State Code are numeric, but our format is two characters, we might have a data quality issue. This comparison also helps us detect multiple values in the same data element. If in this 1,000-character-long description we are seeing text and then several spaces and then more text, these text blocks might be different pieces of business information; therefore, we might have uncovered multiple values in the same data element.

Nullability. Nullability is a mechanical check. By mechanical I mean that it does not require any analysis, you just need to identify the percentage of nulls in each data element. We check to make sure that if the Data Element Family Tree says a data element is not null (meaning it always must be populated), each of the records we examine are not null and contain a value. For example, if the Customer Last Name data element is defined as not null on the Data Element Family Tree, we should expect to see all values of Customer Last Name to be filled in. This check is also useful for finding completely empty data elements. For example, Order Gross Sales Amount sounds like a very valuable data element to have; however, if it is null 100 percent of the time, then it currently is not valuable.

Lookups. Lookup validations are valuable when we currently have information within our application and are bringing in new information that links to the existing information in some way. For example, if we are bringing in order information to our data warehouse, we would first need to check the Item Identifier on the Order record to make sure all ordered items are valid items from our item reference area.

There are many more than these four categories to look at in terms of data quality, but I have found that these four satisfy the 80/20 rule. That is, for 20 percent of the effort in validating data quality, you can cover at least 80 percent of the data quality errors. These four categories take a relatively minimal amount of time to capture and yet can detect at least 80 percent of the meta data to data quality problems. I will even go a step further and say these four categories will detect 95% of the meta data to data quality problems you will encounter during your development.

There are several benefits to the Data Quality Capture Template:

It compares the data against the meta data. This is the primary purpose of this tool, that is, to make sure the good work you have done up to this point actually matches in reality. I have seen the following many times: Total agreement is finally reached on the definition of a data element; however, when we actually look at the data, we easily detect inconsistencies between the values and definition. This template is designed to detect these inconsistencies. For example, we once agreed on the name and definition for a Company Name data element. When we compared the meta data against the data for this data element, we noticed something very alarming. It looked as if most of the values were really email addresses and not company names at all. This led us to ask more questions about this data element. We learned that, in many cases, the data entry person typed the company's email address into this data element instead of the company name. This is because there was no way to capture email addresses in the source application, and the email address was determined to be more important than the company name.

It provides an early warning to data quality problems. The Data Quality Capture Template is completed before any data is actually brought into your application. Note that we have not even started the logical data modeling yet, and still we are interested in seeing the data. I have found that data quality problems are much smaller problems when they are detected before any actual data are brought in. Because we have not yet written code or designed any tables, corrections at this point have a minor impact. I have also found that detecting data quality problems before data are actually brought into your application puts more of the responsibility on fixing the problem on the source application, rather than on your team. For example, if the item identifiers in your source application do not correctly match the item identifier in your existing item reference data, the source system experts should rapidly take the responsibility to fix this problem. I have found, in some cases, that as soon as poor quality data enter your application, the data become more of your responsibility to detect and correct, instead of just the responsibility of the source application. Taking this proactive approach will avoid this situation.

It separates collection from validation. Many times when we are doing data quality checking we find ourselves overwhelmed by collecting the necessary data and meta data, and then working with experts to validate these data. This tool focuses on only the collection point.

The next tool we will discuss, the Data Quality Validation Template, is used by an expert from the area to make a judgment about whether the sample data and the meta data are in sync.

Using the Data Quality Capture Template

The Data Quality Capture Template is used to format the data and meta data in such a way as to make it easy for validation by a business expert. You can tailor this template to your own particular needs. For example, you might want to add certain meta data to data checks that I do not have listed below. I have only listed the checks that I felt have accounted for most of the data quality issues I have seen. Table 7.15 is an empty Data Quality Capture Template.

There are two main sections to this template: the meta data and the data results. Meta data comes directly from the Data Element Family Tree mentioned previously in this chapter. The meta data columns from the Family Tree can be copied directly into the appropriate columns in this template. The Results columns require having access to the actual data. For the data, we need between 10 and 25 of the rows to examine, and to run simple queries on the entire sample set of data we are provided. Let's look more closely at each of these columns in this tool.

Name

The name column contains the name of the data element. It is useful to have in this template for two reasons: It provides a pointer back to other tools; and, in conjunction with the definition, it can help validate the sample values. If I would like to refer back to the Data Element Family Tree or the Data Element Grain Matrix, knowing the name of the data element would be extremely important. Optionally, I could add some type of cross-reference number that I keep consistent across tools. For example, Gross Sales Amount might be reference number 35 on the Data Quality Capture Template, on the Data Quality Validation Template, and on the Family Tree and Grain Matrix. The name and definition are what we use to make our comparison to the actual data. If the name of the data element is Gross Sales Amount and the sample data shows customer names, we have easily identified a problem.

Table 7.15 Empty Data Quality Capture Template

META DATA				RESULTS				
NAME	DEFINITION	FORMAT	NULL	FIRST 10 TO 25 DISTINCT VALUES	PERCENT NULL	MAXIMUM LENGTH	PERCENT FAILED LOOKUPS

Definition

The definition is the primary meta data piece of information that we need to validate against the actual data. For example, the definition of the TELEPHONE NUMBER data element follows:

> *The phone number of one our customers. Note it does not include the area code, which is stored separately. It also is the pure number, without any formatting information, such as ( ) or —. It contains the actual phone number content, and not its representation.*
> *Examples:*
> *5551212*
> *1234567*

However, the sample rows are as follows:

(718)555-1212
(121)111-1111
444-4444444
(800)5551212

We know that we have a problem. The definition is on one side of the equation, and the actual data values are on the other side of the equation. If they are not equal and do not match, we have a problem.

Format

Format is the length and type of the data element. Examples of format include the following:

- Decimal (12,2)
- Integer
- Character(30)
- Varchar(200)
- Date

Each of these examples should correctly match the actual values we are finding in this data element. Here are some pitfalls to look for:

- Very long character data elements, with a very small percentage of the space being used, for example, a Varchar(2000) data element where we are only using the first 50 characters.
- Code data elements that are exceptionally long, for example, State Code being Varchar(10) instead of Character(2).
- A data element with a numeric-sounding name that has character values, for example, Total Sales Quantity containing text values.
- A date data element containing values other than a date.

Null

Whether or not this data element is defined as null, a Y, or yes, in this column reveals that this data element could be null. That is, it could be empty. An N, or no, reveals that this data element must always be populated, meaning it is not null. We will match this against the actual data, with the goal of looking for two situations:

- Data elements that we believe should not be null, yet we are finding null values.

- Data elements that are completely null, meaning nothing in this data element is populated. These data elements are either future placeholders or a huge mistake.

First 10 to 25 Distinct Values

After looking at between 10 and 25 rows, we should get a good idea of what is in this data element. It also should be distinct values we examine, because the same value might appear in the first 100 rows. This is common with codes. For example, a State Code might have the first 100 rows all with NJ, for New Jersey. Also, there is no guarantee that the 11th or 26th value will not have something very strange that will be in complete contrast to your name and definition. However, this is a risk that we take. Applying the 80/20 rule means there is a relatively small probability that we would have a problem. These sample rows are used to validate against the name and definition meta data, as well as against some of the format criteria, such as, "Does this number data element really contain numbers?"

Percent Null

This is the reality of the null meta data. Which percentages of the values in this data element are null? For example, if we have a Customer Last Name data element that we believe should be not null and 10 percent of the time we find out it is null, we have an issue. Not too long ago I validated a data element that I considered to be one of the most important data elements in a particular subject area, the Gross Sales Amount. This data element was null 100 percent of the time! It is essential that we find these cases as soon as possible. The users might be counting on that data element as an important data element used in many calculations and reports.

Maximum Length

The maximum length is the longest length of all the values within a data element and includes both character and numeric values. For example, a 2,000-character-long data element might have a value whose maximum length is 1,000 characters. It might instead have a maximum length of only 50 characters, in which case we might be wasting lots of space and have a length inconsistency. The same holds true for numeric values. We had a number length of 38 for one of our data elements. Although 38 might not sound huge, think about how large a number that can handle! After checking the maximum length, we discovered that the most it ever held was eight in length. We were very surprised.

Percent Failed Lookups

Percent failed lookups is one of the most frustrating situations we can come across in regard to data quality. It is so frustrating because of all the new data elements very few require a lookup, and these very few, if they have lookup issues, can involve a large investment of time and effort to resolve. We have a really nice-looking set of data elements from the source system and yet out of the 100 data elements on this source system, two need to link to existing structures in our environment. For some reason, one of these two is not linking 5 percent of the time. Now, 5 percent may not seem like a lot of rows; however, if we are looking at millions of transactions, 5 percent quickly adds up. Errors on either the source or current environment side can be the cause of the rows not correctly linking.

Data Quality Capture Template In Practice

Let's go through a detailed example of using the Data Quality Capture Template. We will discuss the steps you can take to complete this template and then build on the example we have been using throughout this chapter. Here are the steps:

1. **Complete the Data Element Family Tree.** See the steps discussed previously in this chapter.

2. **Copy data elements from the Data Element Family Tree.** This is a simple copy-and-paste exercise.

3. **Get access to a reasonable amount of data.** Reasonable is defined as at least a week of data for a transaction subject area with lots of daily records, or a month or more for reference areas with less records.

4. **Run the necessary queries and fill in the template.** Run simple queries to get a sample set of data, and determine null, format, and lookups.

Let's continue with the same example we worked on earlier.

1.   Complete the Data Element Family Tree

You have completed the Data Element Family Tree, and it is shown in Table 7.9.

2.   Copy Data Elements from the Data Element Family Tree

Table 7.16 shows the values copied over into the Data Quality Capture Template. Note that I put the columns in the same order as in the Data Element Family Tree to make it easy to copy and paste.

3.   Get Access to a Reasonable Amount of Data

You needed to come up with a creative way to get this data. By looking at the In-the-Know Template, you have identified Alicia as the technical source system expert. You

Table 7.16 Initial Data Quality Capture Template

	META DATA			RESULTS			
NAME	DEFINITION	FORMAT	NULL	FIRST 10 TO 25 DISTINCT VALUES	PERCENT NULL	PERCENT MAXIMUM LENGTH	PERCENT FAILED LOOKUPS
CUST_REF_DB_ID	The unique way to refer to each customer, assigned by the Customer Reference Database application. A customer's ID will never change or be reused.	Number(8)	N				
CUST_FRST_NAM	The first name of the customer. Can be a nickname.	Char(20)	Y				
CUST_LST_NAM	The last name of the customer.	Char(20)	N				
PRO_ITEM_REF_DB_ID	The unique identifier generated for a product.	Char(5)	N				
PRO_BRAND_CD	The label by which our customer recognize our products.	Char(5)	N				
PRO_CTGY_CD	The internal grouping of our brands.	Char(5)	N				
ASSOC_NAM	The full name of the associate.	Char(50)	N				
ASSOC_DEPT_NAM	The associate's internal organization name.	Char(30)	N				

DAY	A full calendar day, defined as 24 hours starting at 12 A.M.	Char(10)	N
MONTH	A full calendar month.	Char(10)	N
YEAR	A full calendar year.	Char(10)	N
ORD_QUANTITY	The number of products on an order.	Dec(15,2)	N
ORD_AMOUNT	The financial cost to the customer for this order.	Dec(15,2)	N
ORD_WEIGHT_TONS	The weight in tons of this order.	Dec(15,2)	Y

decide to buy her a cup of coffee in exchange for a sample file. You want more than just a single day's worth of data, however. You agree to buy her coffee for an entire week in exchange for one week's worth of data. She agrees and emails you a text file, which you promptly load into a temporary database table.

4. Run the Necessary Queries and Fill in the Template

Below are the queries you ran to fill in the rest of the columns. For each query the syntax used is based on an Oracle database using SQL. I showed the query for the first data element, CUST_REF_DB_ID.

First 10 to 25 Distinct Values

I would run a query similar to the following:

```
Select distinct CUST_REF_DB_ID
from temp_table
where rownum < 11
```

This would give me the first 10 unique rows in this data element. I would do this for each data element and paste the results into these cells. Refer to Table 7.17 for the results of this query.

Percent Null

I would run the following two queries:

```
Select count(*)
from temp_table
where CUST_REF_DB_ID IS NULL
```

```
Select count(*)
from temp_table
```

The first of these queries gives me the total number of values in a data element that are null. The second query gives me the total number of rows in the table. I would then divide the first number returned by the second number returned, multiply by 100 percent, and arrive at the null percentage. I would do this for each data element and paste the results into these cells. Refer to Table 7.17 for the results of these queries.

Maximum Length

I would run a query similar to the following:

```
Select max(length(CUST_REF_DB_ID))
from temp_table
```

This will return the longest length for a data element value. I would do this for each data element and paste the results into these cells. Refer to Table 7.17 for the results of this query.

Percent Failed Lookups

I would run the following two queries:

Table 7.17 Completed Data Quality Capture Template

	META DATA			RESULTS			
NAME	DEFINITION	FORMAT	NULL	FIRST 10 TO 25 DISTINCT VALUES	PERCENT NULL	MAXIMUM LENGTH	PERCENT FAILED LOOKUPS
CUST_REF_DB_ID	The unique way to refer to each customer, assigned by the Customer Reference Database application. A customer's ID will never change or be reused.	Number(8)	N	12345 39385 38595 37584 38494 38393 30349 94847 18238	0	8	0
CUST_FRST_NAM	The first name of the customer. Can be a nickname.	Char(20)	Y	Jane Emily Lori Gary Serena Stu Sandy Jenn Mitch John	9	10	N/A
CUST_LST_NAM	The last name of the customer.	Char(20)	N	Smith Doe Klein Carter Nixon Reagan Bush Clinton Lincoln Washington	0	20	N/A

continues

Table 7.17 (Continued)

NAME	META DATA DEFINITION	FORMAT	NULL	RESULTS FIRST 10 TO 25 DISTINCT VALUES	PERCENT NULL	MAXIMUM LENGTH	PERCENT FAILED LOOKUPS
PRO_ITEM_REF_DB_ID	The unique identifier generated for a product.	Char(5)	N	12452 33855 85958 37580 38447 38936 33490 48476 38111	0	5	95
PRO_BRAND_CD	The label by which our customers recognize our products.	Char(5)	N	DKDKD EIDMD EIFKF DLFPO DD DKFK DLFKD EIEIE PEOE DKDL	0	5	N/A
PRO_CTGY_CD	The internal grouping of our brands.	Char(5)	N	A W D Q S U T E S B	0	1	N/A

ASSOC_NAM	The full name of the associate.	Char(50)	N	Dennis Jones Bill Jones Pete Rose Will Mays Janet Jackson Pete Herman Hank Aaron Gary Carter John Bench M. Jackson	0	45	N/A
ASSOC_DEPT_NAM	The associate's internal organization name.	Char(30)	N	Accounting HR IT Benefits Facilities Sales Marketing Venture Capital Insurance Banking	0	20	N/A
DAY	A full calendar day, defined as 24 hours starting at 12 A.M.	Char(10)	N	01/04/2001 02/14/2001 12/06/2001 10/31/2001 12/25/2001 01/26/2001 01/08/2001 08/27/2001 04/12/2001 03/29/2001	0	10	N/A

continues

Table 7.17 (Continued)

| NAME | META DATA | | | RESULTS | | | |
	DEFINITION	FORMAT	NULL	FIRST 10 TO 25 DISTINCT VALUES	PERCENT NULL	MAXIMUM LENGTH	PERCENT FAILED LOOKUPS
MONTH	A full calendar month.	Char(10)	N	Jan Feb Mar Apr May Jun Jul Aug Sep Oct	0	3	N/A
YEAR	A full calendar year.	Char(10)	N	1999 2000 2001 2002 2003 2004 2005 2006 2007 2008	0	4	N/A
ORD_QUANTITY	The number of products on an order.	Dec(15,2)	N	40 230 50 660 6767670 5454320 4550.89 3493940 20220 293830 2820	0	9.2	N/A

Column	Description	Type	Null	Sample Values			
ORD_AMOUNT	The financial cost to the customer for this order.	Dec(15,2)	N	50000 23020 100 50 45630 49484.45 39387 13059 20000 56000	0	12.2	N/A
ORD_WEIGHT_TONS	The weight in tons of this order.	Dec(15,2)	Y	2 1.4 4 6 5 9 11 13 6.5 8	25	4.2	N/A

```
Select count(*)
from temp_table
where CUST_REF_DB_ID not in (select CUST_ID from CUST)

Select count(*)
from temp_table
```

The first query will return those CUST_REF_DB_ID values that are not in our existing customer reference data. The second query is the same query we ran earlier, so there is no need to run this one again. This query assumes that we already have customer information somewhere in our existing application and are validating the customer identifier from the Customer Reference Database with what is in our existing application. I would then divide this number by the total count, and multiply by 100 percent for a percentage, which I would hope is zero. I would do this for each data element and paste the results into these cells. Refer to Table 7.17 for the results of this query. We will analyze these results in the Data Quality Validation Template in the next section.

What Is the Data Quality Validation Template?

After completing the Data Quality Capture Template, you have a comparison of meta data versus data. You know what the name, definition, format, and nullability should be for each data element, according to the meta data defined in the Data Element Family Tree. You also have a sampling of the data and a number of queries to test nullability, length, and reference key lookup fields. Now we need to interpret these results. What is acceptable? What are the data quality issues? We need business and source system experts involved. We need them to validate the Data Quality Capture Template. We need the Data Quality Validation Template.

When we go to the dentist and x-rays films are taken of different sections of our mouth, we can see the developed x-ray films but do not know how to interpret them. We cannot really make a judgment on the results of the x-ray examination because we do not understand them. The dentist is the expert who can examine this information and determine whether you have a clean bill of health or five cavities. Similarly, we cannot really make judgments on the Data Quality Capture Template. We are probably not experts in this information, and therefore, we need to find one or more experts who can examine this template and be able to make intelligent decisions as to what is and is not a data quality issue. We might, however, be able to identify certain comparisons that obviously do not look right, and be able to ask the expert if there is indeed a problem.

The Data Quality Validation Template captures the thoughts and opinions of the expert on where the data issues are. The format of this template is identical to the Data Quality Capture Template, with the addition of extra columns that contain the expert opinions.

There are several benefits to the Data Quality Validation Template:

It documents whether there is a data quality issue. This is the primary purpose of this tool. To make sure that the meta data and data captured side by side on the

Data Quality Capture Template are of acceptable quality. That is, does the data match the meta data? For example, is it a quality issue if I have a data element named Customer Shoe Size, it has a definition describing that indeed it is the customer's shoe size and I am seeing strange symbols (*, %, and &) in a sample value?

It assigns ownership and responsibility to determining if there is a quality issue. Documenting the opinions of the expert adds more evidence as to whether or not there is a problem. If the expert believes there is not a data quality problem and there actually is one, then the expert is responsible for this mistake. The expert has been named responsible for determining the quality of this data element and, therefore, is responsible for making the right decision. Dennis signed off on the quality of Customer Shoe Size. Therefore, if there is a problem with the quality of this data element, we will need to address this with Dennis.

It separates analysis from collection. Just as we have seen under the Data Quality Capture Template, we are separating collection from analysis and, therefore, can more easily manage each of these.

It highlights problem areas. One of the benefits of any spreadsheet is how easy it can be to highlight information. Cells in a spreadsheet are much easier to find than are paragraphs in a long document. Therefore, if there are data quality issues in your list of data elements, they will be easier to find in a spreadsheet.

Using the Data Quality Validation Template

The experts identified in the In-the-Know Template are provided the Data Quality Validation Template. It is their responsibility to complete this template and return it to you. When they do, each data element will have a specific status about its quality level:

- The data matches the meta data, and therefore, there is no data quality problem.

- The data does not match the meta data, and the data is wrong.

- The data does not match the meta data, and the meta data is wrong.

- The data does not match the meta data, and both the data and meta data are wrong.

- We will need to get more sample data, because I am not sure whether or not there is an issue.

An empty Data Quality Validation Template is shown in Table 7.18.

The meta data and data columns have already been described under the section on *Data Quality Validation*. The validation columns can be filled in with a Y, an N, or a question mark (?). The Y stands for "Yes, the meta data does correctly match the data and, therefore, based on the data sampling, I do not see a data quality problem." The N stands for "No, there is a data quality problem here." The symbol ? stands for "I am

Table 7.18 Empty Data Quality Validation Template

NAME	META DATA			RESULTS					VALIDATION (Y/N/?)				COMMENTS
	DEFINITION	FORMAT	NULL	FIRST 10 TO 25 DISTINCT VALUES	PERCENT NULL	MAXIMUM LENGTH	PERCENT FAILED LOOKUPS		MEANING	NULL	LENGTH	LOOKUP	

not sure if there is a problem; I will need some more information before I can make a determination." The Comments column contains the notes and questions that must be addressed. For example, if there is an N in any of the columns, under Comments the expert might put the reason why there is an issue. If there is a ? symbol in any of the columns, the expert might list the additional information needed under Comments. Let's describe each of the validation columns:

Meaning. Does the name and definition match the sample data we are given? Based on the 10 to 25 rows that we have, does it look like we have consistency? This is one of the validations where there is the possibility of the expert making an error, because we are only looking at a handful of different values.

Null. Does the null column match what we are seeing in the data? This is where we will have data elements defined as not null that might have nulls, and completely null data elements.

Length. Does the length of the character or numeric data elements match what we are seeing in the sample data? This is where we can identify huge discrepancies between allocated length and format and what we are actually seeing. We are only looking at the largest length, and therefore, this check also has room for error.

Lookup. Do we find all cases of this data element matching up correctly against existing data? For example, on order information, are the item identifier values matching up against the corresponding items on our existing item table? Note that this check is done for a very small minority of the data elements, because usually only a few lookup data elements exist.

Comments. Are there any notes or questions on these findings? These might include requests for more information, questions to clarify what the expert is looking at, or more of an explanation about the problems that have been found.

Data Quality Validation Template in Practice

Let's go through a detailed example of using the Data Quality Validation Template. We will discuss the steps you take to complete this template and then go through an actual example. In the detailed example, rather than repeat a very large spreadsheet, we will only focus on the Item subject area. Here are the steps:

1. **Complete the Data Quality Capture Template.** See the steps discussed previously in this chapter.

2. **Identify the expert to validate this template.** Refer to the In-the-Know Template. Usually you can assign validation based on subject area.

3. **Review the findings of the expert.** This is where we will address data quality issues the expert may have raised. The expert should also be in a position to help us resolve these issues. For example, if we are seeing nulls in a data element that

Table 7.19 Item Data Quality Validation Template

| | META DATA | | | RESULTS | | | | VALIDATION (Y/N/?) | | | | |
NAME	DEFINITION	FORMAT	NULL	FIRST 10 TO 25 DISTINCT VALUES	PERCENT NULL	MAXIMUM LENGTH	PERCENT FAILED LOOKUPS	MEANING	NULL	LENGTH	LOOKUP	COMMENTS
PRO_ITEM_REF_DB_ID	The unique identifier generated for a product.	Char(5)	N	12452 33855 85958 37580 38447 38936 33490 48476 38111	0	5	95	Y	Y	Y	?	Are you sure you are doing the lookup properly? Make sure you ignore the last character on each value in this data element when you do the lookup. This last character means something else. Call me if you need more of an explanation.
PRO_BRAND_CD	The label by which our customers recognize our products.	Char(5)	N	DKDKD EIDMD EIFKF DLFPO DD DKFK DLFKD EIEIE PEOE DKDL	0	5	N/a	Y	Y	Y	Y	

PRO_ CTGY _CD	The internal grouping of our brands.	Char(5)	N	A W D Q S U T E S B	0	1	N/a	Y	Y	Y	N	Y	I would like to see this data element defined as a single character. Why waste five characters? This data element will never have values that are longer than a single character.

is not null defined, which is right? Should we change the data element to null, or are values missing?

4. **Make necessary changes and recommendations.** This is where we make any updates based on the recommendations of the expert.

1. Complete the Data Quality Capture Template

Let's use the same Data Quality Capture Template that appears in Table 7.17.

2. Identify the Expert to Validate This Template

You have referred to the In-the-Know Template and identified Mary as the expert for the Item subject area data elements.

3. Review the Findings of the Expert

Mary sends the filled-in Data Quality Validation Template for the Customer subject area back to you (see Table 7.19).

4. Make Necessary Changes and Recommendations

You can see that we have two comments we need to address:

Are you sure you are doing the lookup properly? "Make sure you ignore the last character on each value in this data element when you do the lookup. This last character means something else. Call me if you need more of an explanation." It sounds as if the reason 95 percent of the item IDs were not found on our item reference data was because we were doing the comparison incorrectly. Our next step here would be to change our query to ignore the last character. We would then get back to the business expert to let him or her know if we were successful, or if we still have issues.

I would like to see this data element defined as a single character. Why waste five characters? This data element will never have values that are longer than a single character. I would listen to the request. Because this comment is from the business expert for this subject area, I would change the length. Before I do, however, I would speak with this expert to see whether this data element might increase in length in the future. For example, a few years from now could it be two characters long?

Summary

This chapter focuses on these four logical data analysis tools, which should be applied in this order:

Data Element Family Tree. Contains the complete list of data elements for the application, and the sources and transformations for each, along with several other key pieces of data element meta data.

Data Element Grain Matrix. Captures the reporting levels for each measurement or fact using a spreadsheet format. This offers a very easy-to-read document for validating reporting requirements.

Data Quality Capture Template. Shows the comparison between the meta data and some of the actual data for each data element. This tool is used to validate the most important information within the meta data, including format, null, and description.

Data Quality Validation Template. Documents how well the meta data and some of the actual data compares for each data element. Based directly on the Data Quality Capture Template, this tool contains the opinion of an expert on how good or bad the data within each data element actually is.

After we apply these four tools, we will have a very good understanding of the data elements we need in our application and the overall data quality of each. We are now ready to start our logical data modeling, the topic of Chapter 8, "The Normalization Hike and Denormalization Survival Guide."

PART THREE

Modeling the Requirements and Some Advice

Have you ever started the logical data modeling for a project and fully believed that you have a complete understanding of every data element you were capturing on the model? You will feel this confident after practicing and customizing the tools included in this text up to Chapter 8, "The Normalization Hike and Denormalization Survival Guide." We have built the foundation for application development in Part 1, captured the high-level requirements and data elements in Part 2, and now we are ready to model the data requirements in Part 3. When we think of the ideal data model, we picture one that correctly captures the business requirements in a flexible way, without sacrificing performance and storage factors in the underlying database.

This part of the text focuses on the tools that help ensure our data models meet these criteria. Chapters 8 through 10 present a series of tools for modeling the data requirements in a flexible way, while considering the database performance and storage ramifications. As a bonus, Chapter 11 is also included, which concludes the book with some advice that I learned over the years and continuously follow as a data modeler. Here is the purpose of each of these four chapters:

Create the logical and physical data models. This allows you to accurately represent the business requirements to maximize database performance and storage. Chapter 8, "The Normalization Hike and Denormalization Survival Guide," presents the tools for normalizing and denormalizing your data requirements. The Normalization Hike is a set of rules and guidelines that can lead you to the summit of complete understanding for your application. The Denormalization Survival Guide is a question-and-answer approach to determining where to denormalize your data model. When you are done asking these questions for each relationship, you will have a physical data model at the appropriate level of denormalization.

Incorporate flexibility into the design. This allows maximum flexibility in your design. Chapter 9, "The Abstraction Safety Guide and Components," helps minimize the impact that future data requirements will have on our model and the resulting database design. The Abstraction Safety Guide is a set of three questions that will help you determine where, if at all, you need to abstract on your data models. The Abstraction Components tool is a collection of the most useful of these abstraction building blocks. The components I discuss in Chapter 9 are those you can use in your own application models to replace sections of your models that need more flexibility. These components can exist at the entity, relationship, or data element levels.

Arrange the model for maximum readability and understanding. Chapter 10, "Data Model Beauty Tips," takes your design beyond the immediate application requirements by focusing on tips for improving the visual appearance of the logical and physical data models. These tips are offered at the entity, relationship, and data element levels of detail.

Succeed and excel in the data modeling field. Chapter 11, "Planning a Long and Prosperous Career in Data Modeling," focuses on my advice, which I follow as a data modeler. I have learned this advice over the years, either from my own experiences or from the successes and failures of those around me. Following this advice, which is phrased in the format of a Top Ten list, can help make you become a more successful data modeler.

The Normalization Hike and Denormalization Survival Guide

I t was a crisp fall morning when we drove the 40 miles to our favorite local hike site at the Delaware Water Gap, close to the New Jersey and Pennsylvania border. We decided to try one of the more challenging trails that morning. We quietly worked our way up the steep inclined path, at times getting down on our hands and knees to climb over huge boulders. We could smell the sweet odor from the decaying brown and yellow leaves around us, crunching beneath our feet, as we briskly walked toward our hiking goal—a lookout point. We arrived at this lookout after 3 hours of much effort, breathing heavily as we walked out to the edge of the cliff. We were standing on top of the highest point for as far as the eyes could see. From this height, we could see everything: the highway that took us here, the Delaware River, the surrounding mountains and hills, and several small towns. We worked hard to get to this point, and it was worth the effort. We now have a complete view and appreciation of our surroundings.

As data modelers, we go through a similar trek during every design. We start off at the bottom of a trail, ready for an adventure, with little understanding of the data elements and business rules that lie within the scope of this project. As we progress along the trail—huffing, puffing, and sweating—we get to higher elevations, and our view improves. We normalize—First Normal Form (1NF), Second Normal Form (2NF), Third Normal Form (3NF)—each additional degree of normalization taking us to a higher level of understanding. When we eventually arrive at the Fifth Normal Form (5NF), we have developed a complete understanding and appreciation of the application. The rules and tips for progressing to the lookout point at the Fifth Normal Form are captured in a tool called the Normalization Hike.

After admiring the world from this lookout point for some time, reality sets in. We eventually have to leave this beautiful, well-understood view and work our way back down the trail. There are certain rules in hiking downhill, such as walking heel to toe and maintaining a consistent momentum and pace. Following these rules will lead to safely completing the hike. After reaching 5NF, we also have to succumb to reality and realize that our design is probably going to require some amount of denormalization in order for it to be efficient using current technology. Therefore, there also are certain rules you must follow for your own safety when descending this 5NF lookup point, and denormalizing. These rules will help you make the right denormalization decisions. These rules are described in the tool, the Denormalization Survival Guide.

About This Chapter

Up to this point in the text, we have done a substantial amount of subject area and data element analysis, identifying and documenting key pieces of meta data at both the subject area and data element levels. We have also taken the individual subject areas and connected them together through relationships to create several different types of subject area models. Now we need to connect the data elements together via relationships in much the same way as we connected the subject areas. We understand the subject area view defined in the high-level models and the meaning, nullability, and other information about each individual data element. This chapter focuses on identifying and representing the relationships between the data elements at both the logical and physical levels of design. We take these individual data elements and assign them to the most appropriate entities, according to the dependencies and rules that exist between the data elements.

Normalization is a set of rules that lead to a finished logical data model. Similarly, *denormalization* is a set of rules for arriving at a finished physical data model. I like to visualize the processes of normalizing and denormalizing as an adventure. Figure 8.1 shows the progression of normalization on the ascent of a hike and the progression of denormalization on the descent of the hike. We spend much effort applying the rules of normalization, starting off in a chaotic state at the base of this adventure and then hiking up through each level of normalization until we arrive at the peak. At the peak of this adventure is an unobstructed view of the entire application. We have complete understanding of all of the data elements and their dependencies. Once we have this level of understanding, we can descend the mountain. The descent represents denormalization, and the more we descend the more we denormalize. For operational applications we usually have very little, if any, denormalization; whereas for data marts, we usually have much more denormalization.

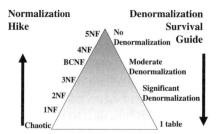

Figure 8.1 The normalization adventure.

Two very important tools that are the subject of this chapter can help you with this Normalization Adventure:

The Normalization Hike. This is a set of rules and guidelines that can lead you to the summit of complete understanding for your application. It requires much effort and persistence to successfully complete this hike through each of the stages of normalization. To complete this tool, you need to apply certain rules, consider certain guidelines and tips, and be aware of several warnings. This tool is not the standard set of normalization rules that we see in other texts. Because I wanted a simpler explanation in this text, I keep the language easy to follow and use practical situations instead of dependency algorithms and mathematical proofs. I also have included special tips and guidelines that have assisted me in completing each level. Consider the Normalization Hike the practical approach to normalization.

The Denormalization Survival Guide. This is a question-and-answer approach to determine where to denormalize your logical data model. The survival guide contains a series of questions that need to be asked for each relationship on our model. There are point values associated with the answers to each question. By adding up these points we can determine whether to denormalize the relationship or keep it normalized. When you are done answering these questions for each relationship, you will have an initial physical data model at the appropriate level of denormalization.

Note that, in many cases, we make the mistake of not going all the way to the top of the Normalization Hike; instead, we look for shortcuts across the lower portions of the mountain. This can lead to a serious lack of understanding of the data elements and functional areas you are modeling and can compromise your physical design. We commit this error over and over again when we model data marts. Many times we go straight to a star schema design, which is usually heavily denormalized into dimension and fact tables, and do not make the effort and take the time to first understand the data elements in 5NF. This is equivalent to going slightly up the normalization side of the mountain before going straight across to the denormalization side where you complete the final physical design by assigning each data element to a dimension or fact table. Always make sure you completely understand the relationships between the data elements by going through all the levels of normalization before descending on the denormalization side.

This chapter focuses on explaining the purposes and techniques used for the Normalization Hike during our logical data modeling phase, and on our Denormalization Survival Guide during our physical data modeling phase. I briefly define normalization before we present the Normalization Hike. I briefly define denormalization before we present the Denormalization Survival Guide. To show how to really use these two tools, we go through a detailed scenario where we create the logical and physical data models for the Dessert Data Mart.

I went back and forth in deciding whether the Normalization Hike and Denormalization Survival Guide belong in their own separate chapters. What ultimately convinced me that they belong in the same chapter was viewing the Normalization Adventure as a single process, where both normalization and denormalization need to occur. In most cases, they are inseparable processes. Normalizing without denormalizing leads to a very well-understood yet, in most cases, only theoretical design. Denormalizing without normalizing leads to a poorly understood and inefficient design. Therefore, it is important to keep these tools within the same chapter to indicate that they are inseparable and part of the larger Normalization Adventure process.

If you visit my Web site, www.wiley.com/compbooks/hoberman, you will find templates for each of the tools in this chapter; additional tools; and more information about tools in this book, including empty templates that you can download.

The Dessert Data Mart

We will be following the same example throughout this chapter. This will allow us to see the same set of data elements progress through the different stages of normalization and denormalization. Many examples that I have seen describing normalization fit into the familiar and overused categories, such as Customer Account. Let's choose a more exciting and entertaining example. Because I am writing this section slightly before dinnertime and am rather hungry, let's choose a food-related example.

Let's say you work for a large restaurant chain. There is a new project underway to report on the popularity of desserts within each restaurant. Management would like answers to questions, such as the following:

What are the best- and worst-selling three desserts each month?
What are the best- and worst-selling three desserts by region each month?
What are the best- and worst-selling three desserts by restaurant each month?
What are the overall best- and worst-selling desserts each year?
Do the restaurant's recommended dessert toppings appear to influence the sale of desserts?
Do the restaurant's recommended drinks for each dessert appear to influence the sale of desserts?
Is there a correlation between the booth location or booth type and the quantity of desserts ordered?

We need to design a data mart for this example. As the data modelers for this data mart, we have already followed the tools in this book up to this point. Therefore, we have completed all of the logical analysis tools discussed in Chapter 7, "Logical Data Analysis." Included is the Data Element Family Tree, which will have major input into this design.

I chose a data mart to design instead of an operational application because we will see more of a drastic change from normalized to denormalized model with a data mart. When we design a data mart, there is usually substantial denormalization and thus more opportunities to make denormalization errors. Another reason I chose a data mart for this example is that data marts tend to be the areas in which we avoid normalization the most and sometimes denormalize too much. There are times when we jump right into the finished data mart star schema design without a good understanding of the included data elements. These two tools will be used with this data mart example to show how we can avoid these problems.

What Is Normalization?

I received a trunk of baseball cards as a present from my parents when I turned 12 years old. I was so excited, and not just because there might be a Hank Aaron or Pete Rose buried somewhere in that trunk but because I loved to organize the cards. I normalized, or categorized, each baseball card according to year, team, number, and so on. Normalizing these cards gave me such a great understanding for the players and their teams that to this day I can answer many baseball card trivia questions. The same normalization or categorization of baseball cards also applies to data elements. Our companies have incredible numbers of data elements spread throughout departments and applications in much the same way those baseball cards lay unsorted in a chaotic state within that trunk. We need to organize or categorize these data elements to completely understand them.

Normalization is a process of removing redundancy and applying rules to better understand and represent the dependencies and participations that exist between data elements. We will define what we mean by dependency and participation shortly.

Normalization consists of several different levels, the most popular being the first three:

- First Normal Form (1NF)
- Second Normal Form (2NF)
- Third Normal Form (3NF)
- Boyce/Codd Normal Form (BCNF)
- Fourth Normal Form (4NF)
- Fifth Normal Form (5NF)

If a design is considered in 5NF, it is also in 4NF, BCNF, and so on. That is, the higher levels of normalization inherit the rules of the lower levels.

There are both business and database benefits to normalizing. The business benefit is that it:

Forces data element understanding. At the logical level it forces us to completely understand each data element and the relationships to each of the other data elements. In our Data Element Family Tree, we developed a very strong understanding of the individual data element. We have agreed on definitions and sample values and other important meta data about the data element, but we are still missing something very important. We do not yet understand or know the detailed relationships between the data elements. At this point, all we know are the groupings of data elements within each subject area. Normalizing the data elements helps us understand how the they relate to each other, just as normalizing my baseball cards gave me a much greater understanding of the players and their teams. For example, we might have a very strong understanding of a Product Category Code and of a Product Brand Code, but what is their relationship to each other and to the rest of the product data elements?

The database benefits are that it:

Maximizes flexibility. Data elements are grouped together based on sharing the same dependency and participation characteristics. This creates logical groupings of data elements that correspond to business concepts, such as Customer, Account, and Product. Thus, these logical groupings can represent and enforce the same rules and flexibility that exist in the business concepts. A customer can own one account, five accounts, or no accounts, without requiring design changes to the database. This encourages application growth and makes the database easier to maintain.

Minimizes redundancy. Nonkey data elements are stored in only one place, and therefore, there is less redundancy. Having less redundancy leads to less data quality issues and faster inserts, updates, and deletes. It also saves on space. Is it quicker and the result less prone to error to update Customer Last Name if it exists in one entity or in five entities?

Maximizes reuse. The data elements are in their most appropriate entity. That is, each data element is with other data elements that share some of the same characteristics. For example, all the account data elements might belong to the same entity and all the order data elements might belong to the same entity. These distinct groupings of data elements are easy to identify and reuse. If I needed to reuse account information, I would find this information much easier to identify and understand all the account data elements existed within their own entity than if the account data elements shared the same entity as the customer data elements.

What Is the Normalization Hike?

The *Normalization Hike* is a set of rules and guidelines that can lead you to the lookout point of a beautiful vista, where you completely understand each data element and their relationships to other data elements. It requires much effort and persistence to successfully complete this hike. To arrive at the lookout point, you need to apply certain rules, consider certain guidelines and tips, and be aware of warnings. The rules include the standard rules of normalization we have come to memorize and love but that are phrased in practical and easy-to-understand terminology. For the most part, the guidelines, tips, and warnings come from experience during my own design work.

Before a set of database tables can be created, there must be a complete understanding of the data elements and their relationships to each other. The Normalization Hike will progress through each stage of normalization to help us in determining the relationships and proper place for each data element.

Although the normalization rules become increasingly more rigorous as we progress through each level, there are two common themes by which each level abides in determining where data elements belong: dependency and participation. Dependency means that the one or more data elements that make up the primary key for an entity only have one possible value for each of the nonprimary key data elements within that entity. This is called functional dependency. For example, if the Customer entity is identified by the Social Security Number, then for each Social Security Number value we can have only one value for each of the customer data elements. Thus, let's assume that these are the data elements in the customer entity:

- Social Security Number
- First Name
- Last Name
- Shoe Size
- Height
- Date of Birth
- Favorite Ice Cream Flavor

If Social Security Number is the primary key, then a Social Security Number of 123-45-6789 would have only one value for First Name, Last Name, and so on. Thus, First Name for this Social Security Number might be "Bob"; however, it cannot be "Bob" and "Mike" for the same Social Security Number value 123-45-6789. Therefore, these data elements are all dependent on the Social Security Number data element. Normalization ensures we have identified and represented all of these dependencies correctly within our set of data elements. Combining the dependent data elements with their data element or elements they depend on leads to buckets of data elements called entities. Each entity will be identified by a primary key, which is the data element or elements that the rest of the data elements will functionally depend on. In this example, we might have a Customer entity identified by the Social Security Number data element containing the list of customer data elements mentioned previously.

After we understand the dependency factor, we turn our attention to participation. Participation is represented through the relationships between entities. *Participation* means the number of instances or occurrences that each entity contributes to a relationship with other entities. Participation also includes the mandatory or optional involvement of each entity within a relationship. For example, here are some of the relationships in which a customer might participate:

A Customer can own many Accounts. Therefore, our customer Bob can own both a checking and a savings account. The word can implies optionality, meaning Bob also can exist without any accounts.

A Customer must be serviced by one Associate. Our associate Nancy is Bob's contact at our company. Our customer Bob must only have one contact, which is Nancy. Bob cannot exist within our scope unless he is assigned an associate. This shows mandatory participation.

A Customer can purchase many Products. Bob can purchase the Widgets 9000 and the Widgets Lite. Again, the word can implies optionality, so that Bob can exist without making any purchases.

A Customer can visit any of our Web pages. Bob can visit one or more of the pages on our Web site. Be alert to whether relationships are optional or mandatory. The word can is an optionality giveaway again.

A Customer includes Competitor. Bob is one of our good customers, yet he also provides certain services to the public that overlap with our services and, therefore, is also our competitor. Bob also can exist without being a competitor of ours.

Through each stage of normalization, we use participation and dependencies to build entities and their relationships.

There are several goals of the Normalization Hike:

To describe the levels of normalization in a succinct and practical way. The Normalization Hike provides a less technical and theoretical explanation of normalization than your standard book. For example, this tool avoids words such as determinate and join dependency.

To offer normalization guidelines, tips, and warnings. The hike provides useful pointers for each stage of normalization. For example, looking for data elements that are fairly long codes can help detect situations where multiple pieces of business information are being stored within the same data element.

To provide the visual image. The Normalization Hike is a progression we go through whenever we do a design. Just as in any long hike with a challenging destination, the more we progress along the trail, the greater our understanding and appreciation and the more sweat and effort goes into arriving at the final normalized logical design. This visual image is very effective in explaining the value of normalization and the effort it requires. It is also a good visual image for showing how we sometimes take shortcuts along the mountain. These shortcuts involve only going up a few levels of normalization before trekking across the mountain and denormalizing. This shortcut on the Normalization Hike shows how much understanding we miss by not normalizing completely up to 5NF.

To become the starting point for the Denormalization Survival Guide. Once we have hiked up to the lookout point and have a fully normalized data model, we need to start working our way down and denormalizing. The Normalization Hike makes sure we have gone up as high as we can go before descending using the Denormalization Survival Guide.

Using the Normalization Hike

We will apply the Normalization Hike to the Dessert Data Mart example described previously in this chapter. Starting in a chaotic state, we will introduce additional rigor and integrity into the Dessert Data Mart, hiking through each level of normalization until we arrive at the lookout point in 5NF. We will briefly explain each level of normalization as we go through this example. As mentioned previously, however, we do not want to spend too much time on the standard normalization rules mentioned in many of the introductory data modeling texts.

WARNING

In order to describe normalization in a simple way, the Normalization Hike must sometimes be imprecise in technical details. For example, it does not distinguish functional from existence dependencies, determinates, decomposition operators,

and so on. I listed a few references in the suggested reading list that treat normalization in a more formal and rigorous manner.

The Normalization Hike focuses on tips, guidelines, and warnings to correctly and efficiently progress through each level of normalization. One tip that is worthwhile to present now that you will see used throughout this section is the use of sample values to check normalization rules.

TIP

Always use sample values to test the rules of normalization against your design. I find this is the easiest way to make sure my structure meets the normalization criteria. For example, Bob Jones appears in the same record as his checking account. What dependencies does this create between Bob and his account? If Bob's checking account disappears, do we also lose Bob? It becomes a much more visual method to determine if we are violating any of the levels of normalization.

Starting with Chaos

We have all built puzzles at one time or another. When we first open the puzzle box and spill out the pieces onto our work area, we can be overwhelmed by what lies in front of us. We have hundreds, maybe even thousands, of tiny pieces in one large pile. This large pile is in a state of chaos. As we pick up each puzzle piece to examine, we understand the characteristics that make it unique. What we lack at this point, however, is how these puzzle pieces connect with each other. We begin this intense and challenging process of fitting together the pieces. After much effort, we complete our masterpiece, with each puzzle piece in its proper place.

The term chaos can be applied to any unorganized pile of lots of little things, including data elements. We have a strong understanding of each individual data element, because we have finished all of the data analysis tools mentioned in Chapter 7, "Logical Data Analysis." For example, we already have the complete list of data elements and know their definitions and transformations from the Data Element Family Tree. What is lacking at this point is how all of these data elements fit together. How do the data elements relate to each other? We understand each piece of the puzzle but do not yet understand the connections between the pieces. For example, how do the customer address and telephone number data elements relate to each other? Just as we need to determine the appropriate place for each piece within our puzzle, we need to determine the appropriate place for each data element within our design.

This chaotic state where we do not yet understand the connections or relationships between our data elements is our starting point for the Normalization Hike. To get to the chaotic state, all we need is the completed Data Element Family Tree with our list of data elements and their meta data.

Chaos in Practice

For our Dessert Data Mart, out of all the completed data element analysis tools from Chapter 7, "Logical Data Analysis," the chaotic state only requires the Data Element

Family Tree. This Dessert Data Mart Family Tree appears in Table 8.1. Note that on this Family Tree, I did not show the source system meta data, because it will not be used for this example and I wanted to save space and reduce clutter. You will also note that the definitions are kept very brief. The full-blown Dessert Data Mart Data Element Family Tree will have complete sourcing information and will follow the rigor of the Definition Checklist from Chapter 3, "Ensuring High-Quality Definitions." Also be aware that this Family Tree is divided by subject area, and the assignment of data elements to subject areas will become very helpful during the initial part of the 1NF.

First Normal Form (1NF)

The first normal form is the first level where we start removing redundancy and increasing the flexibility of our design. I believe that there are three activities required to go from chaos to 1NF. They go somewhat beyond the standard definition of 1NF, which is simply the removing redundancy step that appears as the third activity in this list. I include these three activities with 1NF because I feel that they should all happen as soon as we start the normalization process:

Make the leap to a prenormalized model. This is the most significant change that we will make during the entire Normalization Hike. We transition from spreadsheet to model. Each of the isolated data elements on the Data Element Family Tree are assigned to entities that follow the dependency and participation guidelines mentioned previously. The best method I have used to achieve this initial model is to create an entity for each subject area on the Family Tree. I could also use the Application Clean Slate subject area model discussed in Chapter 6, "Subject Area Modeling," as my starting point. Once I have this subject area model, I simply copy and paste each of the data elements listed on the spreadsheet rows under each subject area to their respective box on the model. Then, after all of the data elements appear in one of the subject area boxes on the model, I identify an initial primary key. This is one or more data elements that I believe will uniquely identify a row within this subject area. For example, if Customer were one of my subject areas, I would have all 20 customer data elements within the Customer entity on my initial model. I would then review each of these customer data elements for the one or more of them that uniquely identify the subject area concept of a customer. This would then become my initial primary key for a customer. I like the term prenormalized for such a model, because no normalization rules have been applied to this model yet and it is our starting point for applying all of these rules.

Resolve many-to-many relationships. Wherever there are many-to-many relationships on our model, we need to replace them with associative entities. *Associative entities* are entities that, at a minimum, contain the data element foreign keys from the two entities that made up the many-to-many relationship. For example, if a Customer can own many accounts and an Account can be owned by many customers, we have a many-to-many relationship. We would need to add an associative entity, such as Account Ownership, between Customer and Account.

Table 8.1 Dessert Data Mart Data Element Family Tree

| | FROM HERE (SOURCE) | | | | | TO ARRIVE HERE (TARGET) | | | |
NAME	SOURCE	DEFINITION	FORMAT	NULL ?	TRANSFORMA-TION LOGIC	NAME	DEFINITION	FORMAT	NULL ?	QUESTIONS
BOOTH						**BOOTH**				
						BOOTH LOCATION CODE	The unique number assigned to a booth within a restaurant.	Char(3)	N	
						SMOKING SECTION INDICA-TOR	Determines whether the booth is located within the restaurant's smoking section. Y = It is in the smoking section. N = It is not in the smoking section.	Char(1)	Y	
						BOOTH CAPACITY	The maximum number of people that can sit at a booth. Does not include high chairs for babies.	Number	Y	

continues

Table 8.1 (Continued)

FROM HERE (SOURCE)						TO ARRIVE HERE (TARGET)				
NAME	SOURCE	DEFINITION	FORMAT	NULL?	TRANSFORMA-TION LOGIC	NAME	DEFINITION	FORMAT	NULL?	QUESTIONS
		BOOTH					BOOTH			
						BOOTH TYPE CODE	The code corresponding to one of several types of booths, including bar, benches, and table.	Char(1)	N	
						BOOTH TYPE TEXT	The description corresponding to one of several types of booths, including bar, benches, and table.	Char(20)	N	

CHECK			
CHECK IDENTI-FIER	The unique number assigned to each check. This is usually the number preprinted on the upper right-hand corner of each check.	Number	N
CHECK AMOUNT	The total amount of the order that the customer needs to pay for the meal. Does not include sales tax or gratuity.	Dec(6,2)	N

continues

Table 8.1 (Continued)

| FROM HERE (SOURCE) | | | | | TO ARRIVE HERE (TARGET) | | | |
NAME	SOURCE	DEFINITION	FORMAT	NULL ?	TRANSFORMA-TION LOGIC	NAME	DEFINITION	FORMAT	NULL ?	QUESTIONS
CHECK						CHECK				
						GRATUITY AMOUNT	The total amount of the tip that the customer leaves for the server or servers.	Dec(6,2)	Y	
						CHECK DATE AND TIME	When the check was paid. Note this is not the time when the customers sat down. It is only when payment was received for the meal.	Date	N	

DESSERT			
DESSERT CODE	The unique code assigned to each dessert. This value is independent of time, meaning the same dessert offered each October will have the same dessert code.	Number	N
DESSERT OFFERED DATE RANGE	A range of days that this dessert will be offered to customers. Desserts are offered either continuously, on a seasonal basis, or as a special.	Char(21)	N

continues

Table 8.1 *(Continued)*

FROM HERE (SOURCE)					TO ARRIVE HERE (TARGET)			
NAME	SOURCE	DEFINITION	FORMAT	NULL ?	TRANSFORMA-TION LOGIC	NAME	DEFINITION	FORMAT	NULL ?	QUESTIONS
			DESSERT					**DESSERT**		
						DESSERT NAME	The full name of the dessert that appears on the menu.	Char(30)	N	
						DESSERT DESCRIP-TION	The text that appears under the name on the menu describing the dessert.	Char(20)	Y	
						DESSERT CATE-GORY CODE	This includes all of the categories to which the dessert belongs. It is in a list format separated by commas. For example, the dessert Banana Split might have this value: Indulgent, Frozen, Big.	Char(200)	N	

DRINK NAME	The restaurant's recommended drink that goes with this dessert. It could be hot or cold.	Char(30)	Y
TOPPING NAME	The restaurant's recommended toppings that go with this dessert. Examples include hot fudge and powdered sugar.	Char(30)	Y
DESSERT PRICE AMOUNT	The price of this dessert. This is the list price from the menu, not including tax.	Dec(6,2)	N

continues

Table 8.1 (Continued)

	FROM HERE (SOURCE)				TO ARRIVE HERE (TARGET)				
NAME	SOURCE	DEFINITION	FORMAT	NULL ?	TRANSFORMA-TION LOGIC	NAME	DEFINITION	FORMAT	NULL ?	QUESTIONS
	RESTAURANT					RESTAURANT				
						RESTAU-RANT IDENTI-FIER	The unique identifier for a restaurant	Number	N	
						RESTAU-RANT REGION CODE	The code within a region of the United States. Example: NE = Northeast	Char(2)	N	
						RESTAU-RANT REGION NAME	The name of the region within the United States. Example: Northeast	Char(30)	N	
						RESTAU-RANT OWNER 1 NAME	The owner of the restaurant.	Char(30)	N	
						RESTAU-RANT OWNER 2 NAME	The second owner, if applicable, of the restaurant.	Char(30)	Y	

RESTAURANT OWNER 3 NAME	The third owner, if applicable, of the restaurant.	Char(30)	Y
RESTAURANT MAXIMUM CAPACITY NUMBER	The maximum number of people that can fit in the restaurant at any one time. The Health Department determines this number. It includes both customers and employees.	Number	N

Start removing redundancy. There are two simple rules we need to apply at this early point of normalization:

1. **Move repeating data elements to a new entity.** A repeating data element is one which appears at least twice in the same entity. Most of the time these data elements can be easily identified by looking for a sequence number in the name. For example, let's say that in our Customer entity we have these data elements:

   - ADDRESS LINE 1 TEXT
   - ADDRESS LINE 2 TEXT
   - ADDRESS LINE 3 TEXT

   To remove these repeating data elements, we need to create a new entity, called Address, which has a many-to-many relationship to the Customer entity. In this new entity will be an address line data element, with a composite primary key consisting of the customer identifier and an address sequence number. This sequence number will indicate whether this line is the first or fourth line of the address. Also notice that in creating a new entity we have increased our flexibility. We are not just constrained to three lines of address information but can represent one or more lines of address information. In creating a new entity where the primary key is the key of the original entity, we are not necessarily reducing redundancy; however, we are increasing flexibility. We are introducing new records instead of columns, yet there is still the same amount of redundancy. For example, 10 Main Street will be repeated for each Customer that lives at 10 Main Street because the customer identifier is part of the address table entity. Thus, in this short example, removing repeating data elements has led to more flexibility with the same amount of redundancy.

2. **Separate multivalued data elements.** Multivalued means that we are storing at least two separate business concepts within the same data element. For example, a name data element might contain both a first name and last name, which could be considered two separate business concepts. Another example might be Gross Sales, which contains both the gross sales amount and weight. Enforcing class words (described briefly in Chapter 7, "Logical Data Analysis," and in more detail in Chapter 9, "The Abstraction Safety Guide and Components") keeps the multivalued data elements to a minimum. For example, it would not allow Gross Sales to be a separate data element. It would require a separate data element for each class word, and therefore, we would have Gross Sales Amount and Gross Sales Weight.

TIP

Enforcing class words on the Data Element Family Tree minimizes the opportunities that multiple data values will be stored within the same data element. This is because the class word indicates a single data element category, such as Name, Code, Date, Amount, and so on. Therefore, there is less of a chance there will be more than one type of value in this data element. There is a greater chance we will find multiple values in the Gross Sales data element than in the Gross Sales Amount data element.

The optimal way to explain how to perform these normalization activities is through our example, in which we can highlight and fix situations that violate these rules.

First Normal Form in Practice

Let's apply each of these activities to our Dessert Data Mart example. After all of these activities are applied, we will have our model in 1NF. Figure 8.3 shows our data model in 1NF. You might want to refer to this figure after each of these activities.

We need to start by taking our Data Element Family Tree and using it to create a prenormalized data model for the Dessert Data Mart. We follow these steps and create subject areas boxes on our model and copy and paste the data elements from the rows in the Family Tree to their respective subject areas on this model. We then assign one or more data elements to be the primary key for each of the subject areas. Let's assume the subject areas are identified by the following data elements:

DESSERT can be identified by DESSERT CODE and DESSERT OFFERED DATE RANGE.

RESTAURANT can be identified by RESTAURANT IDENTIFIER.

BOOTH can be identified by RESTAURANT IDENTIFIER and BOOTH LOCATION CODE.

CHECK can be identified by the CHECK IDENTIFIER.

Our prenormalized model for the Dessert Data Mart is shown in Figure 8.2. Note that this model is exactly like our Application Clean Slate subject area data model with the addition of data elements, including a primary key for each subject area.

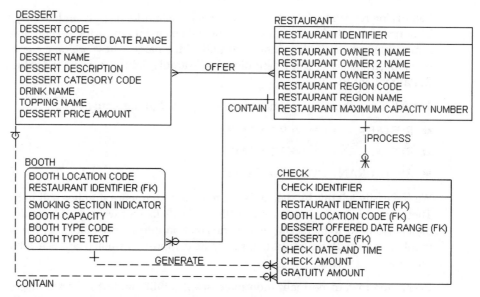

Figure 8.2 Dessert data mart prenormalized model.

You can see from this model that we have some work ahead of us. Many of the data elements within the same subject area do not appear to be at the same level of detail with the same participation and dependencies. Thus, we will need to do some normalizing. For example, in the dessert subject area, there is not just information about the dessert but also on which drinks and toppings go best with the dessert. As we work our way up the Normalization Hike, we will be identifying and correcting these situations.

CAUTION

Never stop your data modeling at the prenormalization stage. I have seen several situations where after entities with primary keys have been defined, tables have been created and the data modeling has been considered complete. This translates into never doing the Normalization Hike and missing out on some valuable opportunities for flexibility and efficiency. It might sound obvious not to stop at the prenormalization stage. However, sometimes because of time constraints, or people believing any workable primary keys on entities is enough design work, we are led to make this very poor and regrettable decision.

Let's do the second activity, which is to resolve many-to-many relationships. This is a very straightforward task. There is one many-to-many relationship that needs resolving on this example, which is the relationship between Dessert and Restaurant.

The third and final activity for 1NF is to remove some redundancy by applying the following two rules:

- Move repeating data elements to a new entity.
- Separate multivalued data elements.

Identifying repeating data elements is a very quick rule to apply and an easy normalization violation to fix. Look for the same data element appearing several times in the same table, usually with a number as part of the name. These are data elements that semantically share the same definition. For example, Table 8.2 shows the values for the Restaurant entity.

The following three data elements are all repeated in this entity:

- RESTAURANT OWNER 1 NAME
- RESTAURANT OWNER 2 NAME
- RESTAURANT OWNER 3 NAME

We can easily tell this by seeing the incrementing sequence number within the name. Therefore, this model is not yet in 1NF. 1NF tells us that we cannot have this redundancy. We need to break out owner information into its own table, with a sequence number and the Restaurant Identifier as its composite primary key. See Table 8.3 for this new Owner entity.

Every step toward normalization increases flexibility and, it is hoped, decreases redundancy. For example, by moving owner name to another table, we have built in the

Table 8.2 Sample Values for the Restaurant Entity

RESTAURANT IDENTIFIER	RESTAURANT REGION CODE	RESTAURANT OWNER 1 NAME	RESTAURANT OWNER 2 NAME	RESTAURANT OWNER 3 NAME	RESTAURANT REGION NAME	RESTAURANT MAXIMUM CAPACITY NUMBER
123	NE	Bob Jones	Paul Smith	Mary Doe	Northeast	50
124	NE	Bill Barker	James Pierce	Bob Jones	Northeast	200
125	SW	Mary Doe			Southwest	175
126	SE	Mary Doe	Mike Myers		Southeast	100

Table 8.3 Sample Values for the New Owner Entity

RESTAURANT IDENTIFIER	OWNER SEQUENCE NUMBER	OWNER NAME
123	1	Bob Jones
123	2	Paul Smith
123	3	Mary Doe
124	1	Bill Barker
124	2	James Pierce
124	3	Bob Jones
125	1	Mary Doe
126	2	Mary Doe
126	1	Mike Myers

flexibility to handle one owner, two owners, and even 10 owners for a single restaurant; we are not limited to only three owners. There could be more than three owners for restaurants 123 and 124, but we did not have the room to capture them in the prenormalized design. In this new Owner entity, however, if Steve Smith becomes an owner of 123 as well, we can easily add him as another row.

It is important to note, however, that our redundancy of the owner name did not go away. Instead of repeating Mary Doe in the third and first owner columns for one and two restaurants, respectively, we repeated her name three times in the single owner name data element on the Owner entity. We are repeating her name in new rows instead of columns because we have no other information about the owner except for the name. If we also had an owner identifier, for example, we would be able to store the owner name only once and use an associative entity to relate owner identifiers to restaurant identifiers.

TIP

If you see at least two data elements within the same entity that have the same name, with the exception of a different sequence number, you have identified repeating data elements that violate 1NF. For example, ADDRESS_LINE_1_TEXT, ADDRESS_LINE_2_TEXT, and ADDRESS_LINE_3_TEXT, are repeating data elements that need to be moved into another entity.

Let's turn our attention to multivalued data elements. There are several in this example. The Owner Name is a multivalued data element because it contains the first and last names of the owner. We should put the first and last name into separate data elements. As mentioned previously, see Figure 8.3 for the completed 1NF model.

Several other multivalued data elements are left to resolve, two of which are in the Dessert entity. See Table 8.4.

There are two multivalued data elements in this entity, DESSERT OFFERED DATE RANGE and DESSERT CATEGORY CODE. We need to break up each of these into separate data elements or entities to avoid redundancy and increase flexibility.

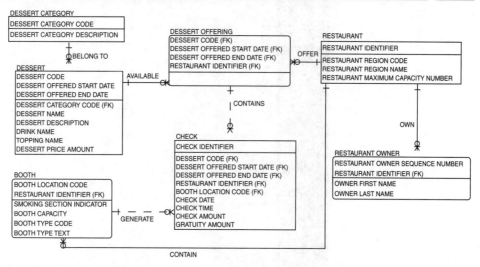

Figure 8.3 Dessert data mart in First Normal Form.

DESSERT OFFERED DATE RANGE contains the start and end dates for this dessert, which represent two separate data elements. Therefore, we need to break up these data elements. We can separate them into DESSERT OFFERED START DATE and DESSERT OFFERED END DATE. If we kept these two dates together in the same data element, we would cause much inefficiency, including a very complicated update and retrieval mechanism.

DESSERT CATEGORY CODE contains more than just a code. It contains the full set of all categories for this data element. We need to break it out into a separate entity. Note that this is one of the more difficult multivalued situations to detect, that is, when you have a data element that does not appear to be an issue by looking at its name. When we read the definition and start looking at its values and format, we see the issue. If the length and format of the data element seem to be mismatched, we can more easily detect a potential multivalued data element. A 200-character-long code, such as Dessert Category Code, should raise eyebrows. Recently, I was reviewing the data quality of an innocent-looking seven-character-long data element. It was defined as a code. This may not sound unusual, but we knew that normally this concept was only four characters long, not seven characters long. After doing some research into the values of this data element, we learned that there were some interesting values in the three extra characters. We discovered that the data entry people were inserting a sub-code concept within this data element. We had identified a multivalued data element.

TIP

Sometimes multivalued data elements are difficult to detect. A good question to ask yourself for each data element is, "Does the length and format of this data element make sense?" For example, the following three situations would all raise my eyebrows and cause me to do a bit of investigation to see if there were more than one concept hiding inside:

Table 8.4 Sample Values for the Dessert Entity

DESSERT CODE	DESSERT OFFERED DATE RANGE	DESSERT NAME	DESSERT DESCRIPTION	DESSERT CATEGORY CODE	DRINK NAME	TOPPING NAME	DESSERT PRICE AMOUNT
AB	10/1/1999– 10/31/1999	Scary Sundae	Lots of licorice, bats, and hot fudge over broom-shaped cookies	Holiday, Cookie, Medium	Spooky Hot Chocolate	Hot fudge	$2.95
BC	1/1/1996– 12/31/2002	Banana Split	Three large scoops of ice cream with two fresh bananas and an unbelievable number of toppings, including hot fudge and strawberry	Fruit, Frozen, Large		Hot fudge	$4.95
EE	6/1/2001– 9/1/2001	Summer Refresher	Lots of different types of fruits, all put into a blender	Fruit, Health, Seasonal, Small		Cherries	$1.95

- A code data element with a very long character data type
- A numeric-sounding data element with a character data type
- A name data element more than 30 characters long

Here are some of the values for the data element CHECK DATE AND TIME from the Check entity:

4/1/2001 11:36 A.M.

5/9/2001 9:00 A.M.

2/6/2001 5:34 P.M.

3/10/1999 7:00 P.M.

1/14/2000 6:55 P.M.

Note that we have both date and time information in these data elements. If we felt it necessary to separate date from time, now would be the opportunity to do this.

TIP

The word *and* is usually a giveaway that we have multiple pieces of information in the same data element. I consider these freebies when I see them on a design, because they are so obvious to detect and so easy to fix.

Second Normal Form

As we progress up toward higher elevations of normalization, we come to more rigid rules our model must satisfy. In 2NF, we apply just one rule. 2NF = 1NF + the following rule:

Remove nonkey data elements not dependent on the whole primary key. Nonkey data elements are all data elements except for primary, foreign, or alternate keys. For example, nonkey data elements within the Dessert entity in the 1NF model in Figure 8.3 are:

- DESSERT NAME
- DESSERT DESCRIPTION
- DRINK NAME
- TOPPING NAME
- DESSERT PRICE AMOUNT

However, DESSERT CATEGORY CODE is a foreign key back to Dessert Category and, therefore, is a key data element and not included in our test for 2NF.

"Dependent on the whole primary key" means that each nonkey data element relies on the entire primary key and not just one part of it; that is, there are no partial key dependencies. For example, if we have the nonkey data element CUSTOMER SHOE SIZE, which exists within the Customer entity where both a customer identifier and account identifier make up the primary key, we have a partial key dependency. CUS-TOMER SHOE SIZE depends on both the customer and account, which is not a true relationship. It should depend only on the customer. We would need to redefine the customer primary key or move the customer shoe size into another entity. Making the CUSTOMER SHOE SIZE partially dependent on the account number means that for each account Bob owns, we will be repeating Bob's shoe size. 2NF removes this redundancy.

TIP

For 2NF, just examine those entities having two or more data elements that make up their primary key. In this way you can quickly narrow down the number of entities to check for this rule.

Second Normal Form In Practice

Figure 8.4 shows our data model in 2NF. Only entities with two or more data elements in their primary key will be impacted by 2NF. Entities with a composite primary key in our Dessert Data Mart include:

- Booth
- Dessert
- Dessert Offering
- Owner

We select each of these entities and determine whether there are any partial key dependencies. Let's examine some of the sample values from Booth in Table 8.5.

It appears that BOOTH CAPACITY, BOOTH TYPE CODE, and BOOTH TYPE TEXT are really are dependent only on the BOOTH LOCATION CODE and not the RESTAURANT IDENTIFIER. Therefore, we have a partial dependency. Characteristics of the booth are independent of the restaurant. AB will be a four-person table no matter which restaurant we are in. Therefore, we need to separate the booth characteristics from the SMOKING SECTION INDICATOR, which appears to depend on both the booth and the restaurant.

Similarly, if we look at the DESSERT OFFERED START DATE and DESSERT OFFERED END DATE parts of the Dessert primary key, we will note that the nonkey data elements, such as DESSERT NAME and DESSERT DESCRIPTION, depend more on the dessert code than on when the dessert was active. Thus, we need to move these begin and end dates to the association entity between Restaurant and Dessert. Dessert Offering and Owner contain data elements that are fully dependent on the primary key, and therefore, these two entities are already in 2NF.

Third Normal Form

When we hear the term normalization, we usually think of 3NF. This is the level of normalization at which many of us stop. That is, we might consider the peak of the Normalization Hike to be 3NF instead of 5NF. 3NF + 2NF + the following rule:

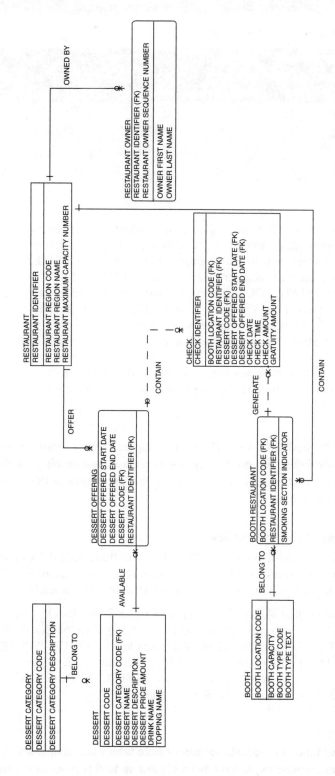

Figure 8.4 Dessert data mart in Second Normal Form.

Table 8.5 Sample Values for the Booth Entity

BOOTH LOCATION CODE	RESTAURANT IDENTIFIER	SMOKING SECTION INDICATOR	BOOTH CAPACITY	BOOTH TYPE CODE	BOOTH TYPE TEXT
AB	123	Y	4	T	Table
BC	123	Y	6	E	Bench
AD	321	N	2	T	Table
AE	456	Y	8	T	Table

- All nonkey elements must be directly dependent on the primary key and not directly dependent on any other data elements within the same entity, with the exception of alternate keys. For example, if I have both the STATE CODE and STATE NAME within my Customer Address entity, STATE NAME is really directly dependent on STATE CODE and not on whatever the primary key is in the Customer Address entity. Therefore, although this might be in 2NF, it is not in 3NF. To substantially reduce redundancy, we need to break up STATE CODE and STATE NAME into their own entities, with a foreign key back to the Customer Address entity. For example, instead of repeating the term New York for each customer that lives in New York, we will have New York just once within the new state entity, with pointers back to the customer entity for each New York resident.

TIP

We can test for both 2NF and 3NF within a single sentence: Every nonkey data element is totally dependent on the key, the whole key, and nothing but the key. 2NF is captured in the first two phrases and 3NF in the last phrase of this sentence. This can save us some time.

Third Normal Form in Practice

Figure 8.5 shows our data model in 3NF. To get to this finished 3NF model, a couple of areas on our Dessert Data Mart data model will require some refinement. Let's start by examining some of the sample values from the 2NF Booth entity in Table 8.6.

We can observe that the BOOTH TYPE TEXT is really directly dependent on the BOOTH TYPE CODE and not on the BOOTH LOCATION CODE. Whenever the BOOTH TYPE CODE has the value T, for example, the BOOTH TYPE TEXT will have the value Table. It does not matter to which particular booth we are referring. Therefore, we need to move BOOTH TYPE CODE and BOOTH TYPE TEXT into their own entities, with a foreign key to the BOOTH entity.

TIP

Applying 3NF tends to separate lookup or code tables into their own entities. Codes and their descriptions might have been hidden up to this point in the Normalization

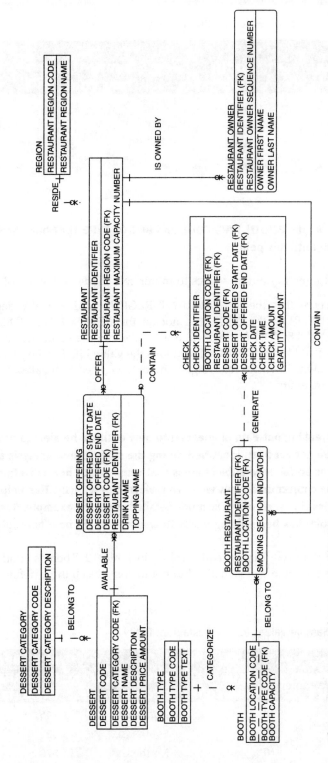

Figure 8.5 Dessert data mart in Third Normal Form.

Table 8.6 Sample Values for the Booth Entity

BOOTH LOCATION CODE	BOOTH CAPACITY	BOOTH TYPE CODE	BOOTH TYPE TEXT
AB	4	T	Table
BC	6	E	Bench
AD	2	T	Table
AE	8	T	Table

Hike. For example, **BOOTH TYPE CODE** and **BOOTH TYPE TEXT** have been hidden within Booth until this point.

Let's look at some Restaurant values from our 2NF model in Figure 8.4. See Table 8.7.

We can observe that the RESTAURANT REGION NAME really depends on the RESTAURANT REGION CODE and not on the RESTAURANT IDENTIFIER. The RESTAURANT REGION NAME will always contain the value Northeast whenever the RESTAURANT REGION CODE contains the value NE. It is not dependent on the restaurant to which we are referring. Therefore, we need to break out the region out into a separate entity.

WARNING

Whenever breaking out data elements into new entities, be alert to new subject areas that have not yet been identified during the subject area analysis and modeling we have done so far. New subject areas that come out of normalization need to be added to the subject area tools we have reviewed previously. This helps keep our high-level view in synch with our more detailed view. For example, Region, which up to this point has been hiding inside Restaurant, might be a new subject area.

Refer back to the 1NF Dessert entity values in Table 8.2. There is another normalization issue in this table that is in 2NF but not in 3NF. Recall these definitions:

Table 8.7 Sample Values for the Restaurant Entity

RESTAURANT IDENTIFIER	RESTAURANT REGION CODE	RESTAURANT REGION NAME	RESTAURANT MAXIMUM CAPACITY NUMBER
454	NE	Northeast	145
326	SE	Southeast	322
789	NE	Northeast	678

- DRINK NAME—The restaurant's recommended drink that goes with this dessert. It could be hot or cold.

- TOPPING NAME—The restaurant's recommended toppings that go with this dessert. Examples include hot fudge and powdered sugar.

It appears that although DRINK NAME and TOPPING NAME are both dependent on the primary key of DESSERT CODE, they are not dependent on just this. They are also dependent on the restaurant that offers these desserts. The definitions of these two indicate that the restaurant recommends the drink or topping to accompany this dessert. Therefore, these two data elements need to move from the Dessert entity to the association entity between Dessert and Restaurant, Dessert Offering. This was a tricky one to catch. We needed to fully understand the meaning of these data elements to catch this 3NF violation.

Boyce/Codd Normal Form

Most of us normally stop at 3NF. Some of us stop because we do not fully understand the levels of normalization after 3NF. In his book entitled, *Data Modeling Essentials*, Graeme Simsion says, "The higher normal forms are frequently misunderstood by practitioners and hence ignored, or cited to support unsound modeling practices." We need to understand these higher levels of normalization, however, because these higher levels present additional opportunities to normalize and help us continue to reduce redundancy and increase flexibility. Even though the next three levels of normalization may cause changes only a small percentage of the time, some flexibility and efficiency opportunities are still waiting to be discovered.

We have already checked all nonkey data elements to make sure they are dependent on the whole primary key (3NF). BCNF means applying the same level of rigor to the remaining data elements: the alternate keys. If we have a data element that by itself is an alternate key, by definition it is dependent on the whole primary key. However, having two or more data elements in the alternate key creates the potential that one or more could be dependent on a subset of the primary key (overlapping keys), instead of on the whole primary key. These cases could be in 3NF but not in BCNF. Therefore, BCNF + 3NF + the following rule:

Each data element is totally dependent on the key, the whole key, and nothing but the key. Note that it is the same as 3NF, except it includes all data elements and not just nonkey data elements. We need to examine any composite alternate keys. For example, let's say for a shoe store we are using the last name and shoe size of the customer as a composite alternate key to the customer table. Shoe size is part of this alternate key that does not depend directly on the primary key to this customer table. Therefore, this example is in 3NF but not in BCNF. To make this example valid in BCNF, we will need to break up this alternate identifier and possibly create a new entity or redefine the alternate identifier for the table.

Boyce/Codd Normal Form in Practice

Figure 8.6 shows our data model in BCNF. Let's assume that we have a composite alternate key defined on our Check entity on our 3NF model in Figure 8.5. It includes the following data elements:

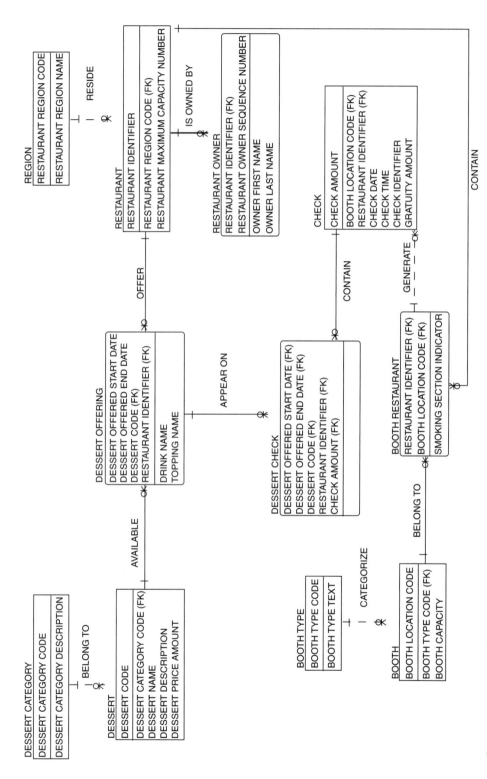

Figure 8.6 Dessert data mart in Boyce/Codd Normal Form.

- BOOTH LOCATION CODE
- RESTAURANT IDENTIFIER
- CHECK DATE
- CHECK TIME

These four make a very good alternate key for a check. However, we need to be very alert here as to what is considered a check. It appears that there also are dessert-related data elements associated with the check. It might be possible (probably unlikely, however) that a new check identifier is generated for each new dessert on the same order. Therefore, the alternate key defined earlier is for a check, but the CHECK IDENTIFIER appears to be unique for both the check and a dessert. Therefore, we need to move the dessert related data elements into their own entity for this alternate key to be fully dependent on the primary key. Note that the relationship between Check and Dessert Offering may be rather farfetched, because I doubt most restaurants would create a separate check for each dessert on the same order; however, it nicely illustrates BCNF.

Fourth Normal Form

The Fourth Normal Form is when we break down entities with three or more foreign key data elements as part of their primary key into two or more separate entities with relationships. The catch with 4NF is that we can only break down those entities where there are no constraints between the data elements within the primary key. Therefore, 4NF + 3NF + the following rule:

Break up entities with three or more foreign key data elements in their primary key that have no constraints between them, into two or more entities. Well, what does this mean? First, it means that we only need to concern ourselves with those entities with three or more identifying relationships coming into an entity. This is usually a very small percentage of the total number of entities on our model. Next, we ask ourselves, "Are there any constraints between these three or more data elements that make up the primary key to this entity?" For example, let's say we have the entity Employee Skill Objective, which captures the relationships between an employee and his or her skills and objectives. Let's say that the primary key to this entity is Employee ID, Skill ID, and Objective ID, making it fall under scrutiny for 4NF. The question now is, "Are there constraints between these three data elements?" In other words, can an Employee have any Skill set with any set of Objectives? If Bob the employee can have the skill of being a good juggler and be assigned a set of data modeling objectives for the year, there are no constraints between these three data elements. Note that there could be constraints between any two of these data elements—for example, a data modeling objective requires the skills of data modeling—as long as there is no constraint on all three. If only employee names starting with the letter D can have the skill of data modeling and have data modeling objectives, then we have constraints between all three data elements and need to keep the entity intact for 4NF.

Fourth Normal Form in Practice

At the end of this section, in Figure 8.8, is our data model in 4NF.

Many times when we go through this normalization process, we discover additional ways to minimize redundancy and sometimes to increase flexibility. For example, currently we have only a single recommended topping and drink for each dessert within each restaurant. See the entity Dessert Offering in Figure 8.6. Let's say the business user would like the additional flexibility to allow more than one recommended drink and topping for a given dessert. If we want this added flexibility, we should separate them into their own relationship. This new relationship allows us to define any number of recommended drinks and toppings for a given dessert. This updated model is shown in Figure 8.7.

This more flexible business rule could not have been better timed, because we are about to apply 4NF and the entity Drink Dessert Combination meets the criteria to be scrutinized under 4NF. Thus, this expanded business rule not only shows how we uncover new avenues for flexibility and less redundancy with increased normalization but also will provide a good test for 4NF. Are there any constraints between toppings, drinks, and dessert offerings? For example, must we always recommend hot fudge as the topping and coffee as the drink for the banana split dessert? If cases such as this are possible, then we cannot break up this entity and it meets the definition of 4NF (but maybe not 5NF—stay tuned!). If we do not have constraints between all three of these foreign keys, we can split up the entity, as shown in the new entities Dessert Drink and Dessert Toppings in Figure 8.8.

Fifth Normal Form

If you understood 4NF, then 5NF is a breeze. In fact, almost all of the time, when a model is in 4NF it is also in 5NF. The only exception is when there are constraints between the three or more identifying foreign keys. In this case, you need to break up the entity according to the different constraints that exist between the data elements. This helps us represent additional business rules and relationships on the model. Therefore, 5NF + 4NF + the following rule:

Break up entities with three or more foreign key data elements in their primary key that have constraints between them, into many-to-many relationships required for all of the constraints. Thus, in 4NF we broke out three identifying foreign keys into two separate many-to-many relationships with the original entity. In 5NF, if there are constraints, we break out the data elements into all possible many-to-many relationships. That is, we represent the relationships between all of the identifying foreign keys. The best way to understand this is to go through an example.

Fifth Normal Form in Practice

For example, if we always wanted to relate hot fudge as the topping, coffee as the drink, and the banana split as the dessert, then we need to show how all three relate. Just to demonstrate 5NF, let's assume that we have constraints between all three. In Figure 8.9, I show the original Drink Dessert Combination structure from Figure 8.7 broken out into three separate many-to-many relationships, representing the constraints between all three of the identifying foreign keys. For the examples that follow in the remainder of this chapter, let's assume we do not have constraints on these data elements, and therefore, our fully normalized data model is our 4NF design in Figure 8.8.

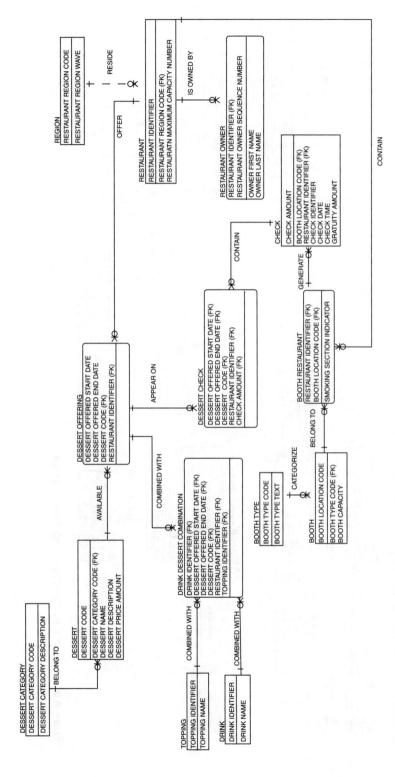

Figure 8.7 Dessert data mart with expanded business rule.

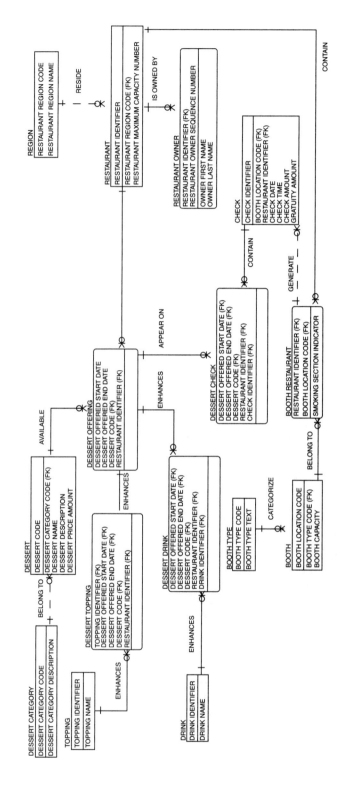

Figure 8.8 Dessert data mart in Fourth Normal Form.

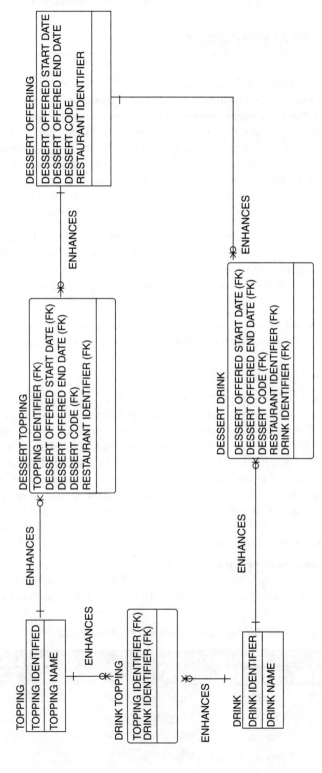

Figure 8.9 Drink, dessert, and topping constraints in Fifth Normal Form.

What Is Denormalization?

In her book entitled *Handbook of Relational Database Design*, Barbara von Halle has a great definition for denormalization: "Denormalization is the process whereby, after defining a stable, fully normalized data structure, you selectively introduce duplicate data to facilitate specific performance requirements." *Denormalization* is the process of combining data elements from different entities. By doing so, we lose the benefits of normalization and, therefore, reintroduce redundancy into the design. This extra redundancy can help improve retrieval time performance. Reducing retrieval time is the primary reason for denormalizing. Let's say we denormalize the customer name into the Purchase entity. Some of the values from this entity are listed in Table 8.8.

If we need to retrieve the name of the customer who purchased Widgets The Revenge, we can do so very quickly on the same record as where this item is mentioned. We do not have to join to a separate Customer table and lookup a customer identifier to find the name information. By repeating the data elements, we can more rapidly get access to our data.

My favorite word in von Halle's definition is selectively. We have to be very careful and selective where we introduce denormalization because it can come with a huge price even though it also can decrease retrieval time. The price for denormalizing can take the form of these bleak situations:

Update, delete, and insert performance can suffer. When we repeat a data element in two or more tables, we can usually retrieve the values within this data element much more quickly. However, if we have to change the value in this data element, we need to change it in every table where it resides. Thus, in the list of values from Table 8.8, if Bob Jones would prefer to be called Robert Jones, we need to update all of his purchase records with this change. In this case, we would need to update the CUSTOMER FIRST NAME data element three times, where we change the value Bob to Robert. This takes more time to make these changes than just having the customer name within the customer entity and making the change from Bob to Robert only once.

Sometimes even read performance can suffer. We denormalize to increase read or retrieval performance. Yet if too many data elements are denormalized into a single entity, each record length can get very large and there is the potential that a

Table 8.8 Sample Values from Denormalized Purchase Entity

CUSTOMER FIRST NAME	CUSTOMER LAST NAME	ITEM	PURCHASE DATE	AMOUNT
Bob	Jones	Widgets	1/1/1999	$ 50.00
Mary	Beth	Widgets Lite	4/4/1999	$155.00
Bob	Jones	Widgets The Revenge	6/15/2000	$ 75.00
Bob	Jones	Widgets II	2/15/2001	$250.00

single record might span a database block size, which is the length of contiguous memory defined within the database. If a record is longer than a block size, it could mean that retrieval time will take much longer because now some of the information the user requests will be in one block, and the rest of the information could be in a different part of the disk, taking significantly more time to retrieve. A Shipment entity I worked on recently suffered from this problem. It contained a very large number of data elements and therefore crossed database blocks causing a very inefficient design.

You may end up with too much redundant data. Let's say the CUSTOMER LAST NAME data element takes up 30 characters. Repeating this data element three times means we are now using 90 instead of 30 characters. In a table with a small number of records, or with duplicate data elements with a fairly short length, this extra storage space will not be substantial. However, in tables with millions of rows, every character could require megabytes of additional space. For example, in our data warehouse fact tables and large dimension tables, such as Customer, we can waste a significant amount of space denormalizing. Although space might be relatively inexpensive, and it is getting increasingly inexpensive, a lot of something inexpensive suddenly can become rather expensive!

It may mask lack of understanding. The performance and storage implications of denormalizing are very database- and technology-specific. Not fully understanding the data elements within a design, however, is more of a functional and business concern, with potentially much worse consequences. We should never denormalize without first normalizing. When we normalize, as mentioned in the previous sections in this chapter, we increase our understanding of the relationships between the data elements. We need this understanding in order to know where to denormalize. If we just go straight to a denormalized design, without reaching the summit of the Normalization Hike, we could make very poor design decisions that could require complete system rewrites soon after going into production. I once reviewed the design for an online phone directory, where all of the data elements for the entire design were denormalized into a single table. On the surface, the table looked like a fairly accurate primary key. However, I started grilling the designer with specific questions about his online phone directory design:

- What if an employee has two home phone numbers?
- How can we store more than one email address for the same employee?
- Can two employees share the same work phone number?

After receiving a blank stare from the designer, I realized that denormalization was applied before going through the effort of the Normalization Hike, and therefore, there was significant lack of understanding of the relationships between the data elements.

It might introduce data quality problems. There are always opportunities to mess up the data within our applications. During design, we can prevent certain data quality problems through the Data Quality Capture Template and Data Quality Validation Template mentioned in Chapter 7, "Logical Data Analysis." However, by having the same data element multiple times in our design, we substantially increase opportunities for data quality issues. From Table 8.8, if we update Bob's first name from Bob to Robert we need to update his first name in all three occurrences of the CUSTOMER FIRST NAME data element. If we update his first name to Robert in two of these three CUSTOMER FIRST NAME values, we have created a data quality issue. There are always hardware, network, and software situations that sometimes arise that could lead to inconsistencies in values between these three CUSTOMER FIRST NAME values.

It could stunt the growth of the application. When we denormalize, it can become harder to enhance structures to meet new requirements. If we were to add a new customer data element to the Customer entity, we probably can add it relatively painlessly and start populating it with information soon afterward. However, if Customer was denormalized into the Purchase entity, as we saw in Table 8.8, adding a new customer data element becomes much more complicated. Let's say we add the CUSTOMER SHOE SIZE data element to the Purchase entity. We need to make sure we populate this data element correctly for each customer name, thereby increasing the risks of data quality problems and the need for manual intervention to get a valid structure. With a substantial amount of extra effort to add new requirements, denormalized structures can turn people off from expanding an application, thereby limiting its potential.

With these very large risks of decreased performance, too much redundancy, lack of understanding, more data quality issues, and introduced limitations on future growth, we need to make denormalization decisions very "selectively." We need to have a full understanding of the pros and cons of each opportunity we have to denormalize. This is where the Denormalization Survival Guide becomes a very important tool. The Denormalization Survival Guide will help us make the right denormalization decisions, so that our designs can survive the test of time and minimize the chances of these bleak situations from occurring.

What Is the Denormalization Survival Guide?

You have finished the Normalization Hike for the design of the Dessert Data Mart. Your design completely meets the rigor of 5NF. This is quite an accomplishment. You are feeling very good about yourself, because you have taken the time and effort to fully understand all of the participation and dependency rules that exist between the data elements. However, reality suddenly sets in. "This is a logical data model I've created. What will my physical data model look like?" You realize you will have to leave your lookout point at the top of this mountain of normalization, your view of complete and clear understanding, and probably descend to some level of denormalization. To arrive safely at this denormalization point will require some guidance. You need to know where to introduce denormalization and where to leave the physical data model in a normalized state. You want to make sure any denormalization you introduce will not cause the bleak situations mentioned in the previous section, and yet will provide the benefits of quicker data retrieval. You are starting to get a bit anxious. You believe your next promotion at work is tightly tied to developing an efficient physical design for the Dessert Data Mart that en-

compasses the flexibility of normalization with the performance of denormalization. You are starting to break into a cold sweat, until you realize that there is a tool that can help you with these decisions. You smile, and refer to the Denormalization Survival Guide.

The Denormalization Survival Guide is a question-and-answer approach to determining where to denormalize your logical data model. The Survival Guide contains a series of questions in several different categories that need to be asked for each relationship on our model. There are point values associated with answers to each question. By adding up these points, we can determine whether to denormalize each specific relationship. If our score is 10 or more after summing the individual scores, we will denormalize the relationship. If our score is less than 20, we will keep the relationship normalized and intact. When you are done asking these questions for each relationship, you will have a physical data model at the appropriate level of denormalization.

The questions within the Denormalization Survival Guide belong to several areas that we will review in detail:

- Type of relationship
- Participation ratio
- Parent entity size
- Commonality or usage
- Placeholder factor
- Change factor

There are several goals of the Denormalization Survival Guide:

Maximizing the benefits of denormalization and minimizing the costs. The tradeoffs that can come with denormalization have been mentioned previously. Whenever we denormalize, we potentially gain something but also potentially lose something. The purpose of the Denormalization Survival Guide is to make sure we maximize our gains and minimize our losses. Therefore, if using the guide dictates that we should denormalize Account into the Customer entity, it will be because the benefits of denormalization will outweigh the costs.

Providing consistent criteria for denormalization. We are applying the same set of questions and point values to each relationship. Therefore, there is a consistency that we will use in deciding when to denormalize. If two relationships have similar answers, either both will be denormalized or both will remain normalized. This consistency leads to greater reuse and understanding. It leads to greater reuse of entities and tables because if a new application requires both Customer and Account information, there is a very good chance the denormalization questions we ask for Customer and Account will produce the same resulting structure as has been produced at other times in the past when we analyzed the Customer Account relationship. Therefore, we should have a similar structure and be able to reuse this physical structure in other places. In addition, because we will start to see the same structures in multiple places, we will more easily be able to learn and understand new structures. For example, if Customer and Account are denormalized into a single entity, we will quickly be able to understand the meaning of the

Customer and Account information in other applications that also have it stored in the same single entity.

TIP

■■■■■ **Although you can use the questions and point values discussed in this section exactly as they appear in this chapter, you might want to consider some customization. I will point out specifically where you should be extra alert for customizing to your particular situation as we go through each question. You might have different questions you would like to ask or might assign different point values, depending on how important each question is in relation to the others. Use the questions and point values given subsequently a guide or starting point for your own specific Denormalization Survival Guide. Point values might also change, depending on the type of application you are designing. For example, a data mart might have slightly different scores for each of these questions than an operational application. The point values and questions in this chapter are applicable for a data mart design.**

Denormalization Survival Guide Questions

In this section we will go through each of the questions in the Denormalization Survival Guide and introduce a handy template for recording the scores for each of these questions for each relationship. The questions are:

- What type of relationship?
- What is the participation ratio?
- How many data elements are in the parent entity?
- What is the usage ratio?
- Is the parent entity a placeholder?
- What is the rate of change comparison?

These questions can be answered in any particular order. Your total score will not change if you answer the questions in a different order. I find it easier to choose the same order for asking these questions every time for each relationship.

WARNING

■■■■■ **Even with a highly customized Denormalization Survival Guide, you need to be aware that the denormalization questions attempt to impose an art on a science, which can increase the risk of making a denormalization mistake. The guide will provide the right answers most of the time. There are enough questions asked across a wide range of topics so that there will be a very good chance you will have the optimal level of denormalization.**

An important concept to fully understand is that there is a parent and a child in every relationship on our design. The parent is on the "one" side of the relationship, and the child is on the "many" side of the relationship. For example, if a Customer can purchase many Items, Customer would be the parent and Item would be the child. Remember that the entity containing the foreign key for the relationship is the child. Item would contain the foreign key back to Customer, and therefore, Item is the child. I will use the terms parent and child quite often in our survival guide questions.

In addition, the higher the scores, the greater the chance we will be denormalizing the relationship. If our score is 10 or more after summing the individual scores, we will denormalize the relationship. If our score is less than 10, we will keep the relationship normalized and intact. I have found that the number 10 works for me in distinguishing the normalization–denormalization border. As mentioned previously, feel free to change this number in your own situations as you get more comfortable with this tool.

What Type of Relationship?

This question addresses the type of relationship we are analyzing. What relationship does the parent entity have to the child entity? We need to choose one of three options (the points for each option are listed in parentheses):

Hierarchy (20 points). A hierarchy relationship (also known as a "Contains" or "includes" relationship) is very common among reference data. Examples include:

- Customer Group contains Customers.
- Product Brand contains Products.
- Year contains Months.
- Order Header contains Order Lines.
- Fruit includes Apple.
- Customer includes Current Customer.

   Usually there is a very strong dependency from child to parent in a hierarchical relationship. In data marts, for example, the users usually select information from both child and parent entities in the same query. It is for this reason that if your relationship is a hierarchy, you get 20 points because we are leaning toward denormalizing these concepts into a single entity. In addition, the "includes" implies a subtype relationship between two entities. We will discuss subtyping more in depth in the next chapter. Subtyping is a way of grouping entities in which the grouping entity or supertype could be considered the parent and the entities that are being grouped or subtyped could be considered the children. Because of the strong relationship between subtype and supertype, there is a very high probability that the two will be denormalized on the physical data model. Hence, we have a high score of 20 points.

Peer (−10 points). Peer is a relationship where both child and parent entities have an independent existence. Examples include:

- Sales Person services Customers.
- Consumers purchase Products.
- Teacher instructs Students.
- Printer requires Paper.

Denormalizing entities that have an independent existence means that one of these entities will now become dependent on the other entity. There is a good reason for keeping independent entities in separate tables. It keeps the design consistent with the business rules and definitions that explain this independence.

Definition (−20 points). Definition is when the parent entity determines the meaning of the child entity. Definition relationships are either relationships from transaction to reference data, or associative entities. Examples include:

- Customer defines Customer Account.
- Account defines Customer Account.
- Product defines Order Line.
- Time defines Sales Report.

Many-to-many relationships are the more prominent on operational data models. For data marts, however, transaction-to-reference data in the form of fact table-to-dimension table relationships are the more prominent. In many-to-many relationships, the associative table that is introduced to resolve the many-to-many relationship is considered the child, and both tables that participate in the many-to-many relationship are considered the parents. In transaction-to-reference relationships, the transaction table is the child and the reference table is the parent. Usually the child table is very large and very volatile, meaning there are lots of rows and lots of changes to these rows. Because the parent table is usually much less volatile and much smaller, we tend to keep these two entities normalized in separate tables. Hence, we have the low score of −20.

What Is the Participation Ratio?

This question addresses the participation of each of the entities in this relationship. In other words, for a given parent entity value, roughly how many children entity values would I have? The closer to a one-to-one relationship between parent and child, the greater the chance we will denormalize. This is because a relationship with a one-to-10 ratio will have, on average, 20 percent of the redundancy of a relationship with a one-to-50 participation ratio. To determine the ratio, assume the parent is a "one" and ask yourself, on average, how many children can you have for this parent? A Car contains four tires; therefore, we have a one-to-four ratio. We need to choose one of three options for this question (the points for each option are listed in parentheses):

Up to a one-to-five ratio (20 points). In this option we will have the least amount of redundancy if we denormalize the parent entity into the child entity. Hence, if this option is chosen, your relationship will get 20 points. Examples include:

- A Car contains Tires.
- An Employee can declare Dependents.
- An Ice Cream Sundae includes Toppings.

Up to a one-to-100 ratio (−10 points). In this option we would have an average amount of redundancy if we denormalize. Examples include:

- A Company contains Employees.
- An Employee services Customers.
- A Year includes Months.

Over a one-to-100 ratio (−20 points). In this option we would have lots of redundancy by denormalizing. Therefore, the low score indicates we would prefer to keep the structure in its normalized state.

- An Item can appear on an Order Line.
- A Year includes Days.
- A Consumer can purchase Products.

How Many Data Elements Are in the Parent Entity?

This question addresses the redundancy in terms of extra space from parent entity data elements we will need in the child entity if we denormalize the parent entity into the child entity. If there are less than 10 parent data elements, it means there will not be lots of data elements added from the parent entity; therefore, not a lot of redundancy will be introduced by denormalizing. Thus, we get 20 points. If there are between 10 and 20 data elements, we get −10 points because there is a fairly substantial amount of redundancy. If there are more than 20 data elements from the parent, denormalizing will cause a lot of redundancy. Thus, we get −20 points, because a more normalized structure might make the most sense. Avoid including the primary key of the parent entity in counting the number of data elements that will be introduced if we denormalize, because the parent primary key will be in the child entity regardless of whether we denormalize. That is, if we keep the design normalized, the parent primary key will appear as a foreign key in the child entity. If we decide to denormalize, the parent primary key would probably also appear in the child entity.

TIP

For this question, also keep in mind the length of each of the data elements. For example, adding 20 one-character data elements introduces less redundancy than does adding five 50-character data elements. Thus, when answering this question, also consider the length.

Less than 10 data elements (20 points). The parent entity contains less than 10 data elements, and therefore, there will be less redundancy in denormalizing this relationship. Examples include:

- A Year includes Days.
- An Ice Cream Sundae includes Toppings.
- Customer Group contains Customers.
- Product Brand contains Products.

Between 10 and 20 data elements (−10 points). The parent entity contains a fairly substantial amount of data elements, between 10 and 20. Examples include:

- Consumers purchase Products.

- Teacher instructs Students.

- Printer requires Paper.

More than 20 data elements (−20 points). The parent entity contains a large number of data elements. Examples include:

- Customer defines Customer Account.

- Account defines Customer Account.

- Product defines Order Line.

Note that there is something very interesting here. The previous question determines the number of rows that might be redundant. For example, if we fold Car up into Tire, we will be repeating all the car records four times, one for each tire. This question determines the number of additional data elements that will need to be added. These two questions go hand in hand. A large participation ratio and a high size range will mean there is a very low score, which means the entities will probably stay in a normalized state. A very low participation ratio and a very low size range will mean a very high score, indicating a denormalization option. If there is a low participation ratio and high size range, or high participation ratio and low size range, participation and size cancel each other out and thus will have no influence on the denormalization decision. For example, a Year can include many Days; therefore, we have a high participation ratio. However, that year will have a low size range of probably not more than three data elements. Therefore, we get −20 points for the high participation ratio but 20 for the low size range. Adding 20 and −20 gives us zero. Thus, these two questions cancel each other out and have no impact on our decision to denormalize this relationship.

What Is the Usage Ratio?

When users need information from the child, do they often include information from the parent? Likewise, if users need information from the parent, do they often include information from the child? In other words, how tightly coupled or correlated are these two entities? I consider this question to be the most important in designing data marts, because in our data warehouse dimensions users can ask for more or fewer details within a subject area or dimension, which usually spans multiple normalized entities. Therefore, if the data elements from two entities will appear together on many user queries and reports, the information will be retrieved more quickly if it is within the same table instead of joining multiple tables. Because of the importance of this question, I have assigned it more weight than the other questions. After all, if very little correlation between two entities exists, why would we want to denormalize them?

Strong correlation with each other (30 points). This means that the two entities have data elements that will be queried on or created together. Examples include:

- Customer Group contains Customers.

- Product Brand contains Products.

- Fruit includes Apple.

Weak or no correlation with each other (−30 points). This means the two entities are usually reported or created separately. Examples include:

- Consumers purchase Products.
- Teacher instructs Students.
- Printer requires Paper.

Is the Parent Entity a Placeholder?

Are we going to add more data elements or relationships to the parent entity in the near future? If the answer is no, then there is a stronger tendency to denormalize. This is because we would not need to worry about the extra space and redundancy new parent data elements would cause that we have not considered. Also, we do not have to worry about integrity and the enforcement of new business rules against the parent. It also means that we will not impact the child entity with parent entity changes, thereby minimizing database maintenance problems. If the answer is yes, then we are going to add data elements in the near future and thus have a strong tendency to keep the two entities separate because of future maintenance and redundancy issues.

Note that when answering this question, you should take into account potential new or changed business rules as well as new data elements. We recently had a one-to-one relationship between two entities that we were prepared to fold up into a single entity, when we realized we needed to have a placeholder for a new business rule that would be introduced in the near future. This new business rule made it apparent that we should keep the two entities normalized and separate.

Yes (−20 points). This means we will be having new data elements or relationships in the near future. This point value could change based on how soon in the near future these additions will take place and how encompassing and huge these additions will be. For example, if we expect 15 new data elements in the parent table within 3 months, you might want to make this −40 instead of −20. Likewise, if it turns out it that only one new data element will be added a year from now, we can change the −20 to a −5.

No (20 points). This means we do not foresee new data elements or relationships in the near future. I usually leave this point value at 20, which is in line with the other point values.

What Is the Rate of Change Comparison?

This question addresses whether the two entities have a similar number of inserts and updates within the same time period. If one of the two entities changes very seldomly, whereas the other entity changes very often, there is a strong tendency to keep them normalized in separate tables. This is because we will be performing lots of updates on a larger denormalized table that contains a percentage of data elements that rarely change. This can cause performance and synchronization data issues, especially in data warehousing where we have many large tables and where updates can cause a significant amount of time being wasted. Therefore, the two entities have a different rate of change, and we assign −20 points to aim toward keeping them normalized. If the two entities have roughly the same rate of change, it would make more sense to denormalize them into the same entity; therefore, we receive 20 points.

Same (20 points). This means that the two entities change at roughly the same rate. Examples include:

- A Year includes Months.
- A Car contains Tires.
- An Employee can declare Dependents.

Different (−20 points). This means that one of the two entities changes much more often. Examples include:

- Product defines Order Line.
- A Company contains Employees.
- Customer Group contains Customers.

A very good way to keep the scores for each relationship is through a spreadsheet. Table 8.9 is a format that works very well. The first column contains each of the six questions. The second column contains the different answers and their point values. The third column contains the points, and their sum appears at the end. We will use this template for each relationship on the Dessert Data Mart example in the next section.

Table 8.9 Denormalization Survival Guide Questions Template

QUESTION	OPTIONS	POINTS
What type of relationship?	Hierarchy (20) Peer (−10) Definition (−20)	
What is the participation ratio?	1-1 to 1-5 (20) 1-5 to 1-100 (−10) 1-100 and up (−20)	
How many data elements are in the parent entity?	Less than 10 (20) Between ten and 20 (−10) More than 20 (−20)	
What is the usage ratio?	Strong correlation with each other (30) Weak or no correlation with each other (−30)	
Is the parent entity a placeholder?	Yes (−20) No (20)	
What is the rate of change comparison?	Same (20) Different (−20)	
TOTAL POINTS		

Using the Denormalization Survival Guide

Let's decide on where to introduce denormalization into our 5NF Dessert Data Mart model from Figure 8.8. Here are the steps we need to go through to use the survival guide:

1. **Prioritize the relationships on the model.** We want to apply the Denormalization Survival Guide to the relationships that have the greatest probability of being denormalized first. This is because if we pick the relationships that have the least amount of being denormalized first, our decisions can impact the relationships that would make the most sense to denormalize. We prioritize the relationships by assigning each to one of four categories. If there are several relationships within each category, I tend to start with those with the most similar set of primary keys, as these have a greater chance of being denormalized. You can take a marker or pen and circle on your model each relationship as to which category it belongs. Here are the four categories:

   - **One-to-one relationships.** These are relationships where one entity value is related to only one entity value from the other entity, and vice versa. For example, a Customer can own a maximum of one Account, and an Account can only belong to a single Customer. You can easily find one-to-one relationships on your model by examining the cardinality on each relationship. Although most 5NF models do not have these types of relationships, they have the highest probably of being denormalized when they do occur, This is because one-to-one relationships should introduce little if any redundancy when denormalized. Take a marker and circle the two entities and their one-to-one relationship. Note that subtyping constructs capture one-to-one relationships.

   - **Reference-to-reference relationships.** These are relationships between reference entities. For example, a Customer can be serviced by one Employee, and an Employee can service many Customers. This one-to-many relationship is a reference-to-reference relationship. Group these on the model as well. There is also a fairly good chance that these types of relationships will be denormalized, especially if they are relatively small tables whose values change at roughly the same pace.

   - **Transaction-to-transaction relationships.** These are relationships between two entities that contain transaction data. These relationships can range from very detailed tables to highly summarized tables. An example of a detailed transaction relationship is between Order and Order Line. An Order can contain multiple Order Lines, and an Order Line must belong to a single Order. This transaction-to-transaction relationship may or may not be denormalized, depending on the answers to the questions, especially the two questions focusing on the size of the parent entity.

   - **Transaction-to-reference relationships.** Although this category of relationship has the lowest probably of being denormalized, it still is worthwhile to consider. This is when there is a relationship between a transaction and reference entity. For example, a Customer can place many Orders, and an Order must be placed by a single Customer. Because the size and rate of change are usually quite different between the transaction and reference entity, these relationships remain normalized most of the time.

2. **Pick a relationship.** Identify the most relevant relationship to start with from the previous exercise. Remember to follow the order of the groups mentioned previously. If there are several relationships within each category, start with the ones with the most similar set of primary keys. You can even number these relationship groups according to the order in which you will do them. For example, if you have three one-to-one relationships on your model, you can randomly label one of these 1, the other 2, and the last 3. Your fourth relationship will be from the reference-to-reference category.

3. **Answer the questions on this relationship.** Go through the complete set of questions on this relationship. When you are done, add up your scores to get your final score. To make it easier, you might want to fill in the spreadsheet template mentioned previously.

4. **Denormalize if score is equal to or greater than 10.** If, after adding up the point scores for all the questions for a relationship, the total score is equal to or greater than 10, you should denormalize the relationship. After you fold together these two entities, you might need to reevaluate the next relationship to work on. Folding up the tables can lead to new relationships that we did not originally group.

5. **Go back to step 2 until done.** Continue picking a relationship, answering the questions, and determining whether to denormalize over and over again until all relationships have been considered. Once your have applied the Denormalization Survival Guide to each relationship, your physical data model is now complete.

Let's go through each of these steps starting with our 5NF Dessert Data Mart in Figure 8.8.

1. Prioritize the Relationships on the Model

There are no one-to-one relationships on the Dessert Data Mart logical data model, and therefore, we need to start grouping relationships in the reference-to-reference category. We first identify and number, all of the reference-to-reference relationships.

Here is the order in which we will review each of the reference-to-reference relationships:

1. Dessert Category to Dessert
2. Booth Type to Booth
3. Region to Restaurant
4. Restaurant to Restaurant Owner

Then we need to number all of the transaction-to-transaction relationships. We number them starting with where we left off with the reference-to-reference relationships:

5. Dessert Offering to Dessert Topping

6. Dessert Offering to Dessert Drink

7. Dessert Offering to Dessert Check

Then we complete grouping these relationships by numbering the transaction-to-reference relationships:

8. Topping to Dessert Topping

9. Dessert to Dessert Offering

10. Drink to Dessert Drink

11. Check to Dessert Check

12. Restaurant to Dessert Offering

13. Restaurant to Booth Restaurant

14. Booth to Booth Restaurant

15. Booth Restaurant to Check

To demonstrate the Denormalization Survival Guide, for repetitive purposes let's limit ourselves to only the first relationship in each of these three categories:

- Dessert Category to Dessert
- Dessert Offering to Dessert Topping
- Topping to Dessert Topping

See Figure 8.10 for the Dessert Data Mart Model marked up with the first of these three relationship chunks, Dessert Category to Dessert, to which we will now apply the guide.

2. Pick a Relationship

Let's start with number one on our list. We can start with any of the reference-to-reference relationships. I just picked this one because it was the first on the list.

3. Answer the Questions on This Relationship

Let's fill in the questions template for this relationship. I am including Steps 4 and 5 within this step as well, because we are looking at multiple relationships instead of just a single relationship. Applying these questions to each relationship in this example led to making our last denormalization decision in the model shown in Figure 8.12. Optionally, you might want to go through this exercise yourself and then see if your design is similar to the completed denormalized design in Figure 8.12.

For purposes of showing the thought process, I also have been using the Points column to make any notes that are worthwhile to mention for the particular question and relationship. Note that the answer to each of these questions is in boldface type in the

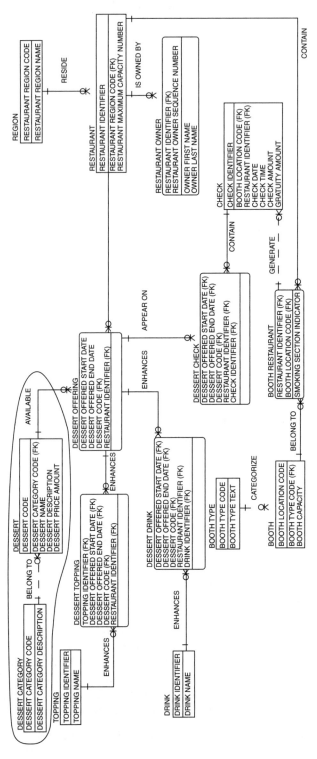

Figure 8.10 Dessert data mart model with first relationship highlighted.

Options column. Because there would need to be many discussions and references to documents to correctly answer some of these questions, I made some assumptions for this example. Let's get started! See Table 8.10.

Because our total score is greater than 10, we denormalize. Again note that I am including Steps 4 and 5 with Step 3 in this example. Step 4 is when we make the decision whether or not to denormalize, depending on the total of the points from each question. Step 5 is finding the next relationship to which to ask the questions. See Figure 8.11 for this change to the model by denormalizing the Dessert Category to Dessert relationship. Now let's select the next relationship from the list (see Table 8.11).

Because the total score is greater than 10, we denormalize. See Figure 8.12 for this change. Let's answer the questions for the next relationship. See Table 8.12.

With such a low score, we keep this relationship normalized. Therefore, Figure 8.12 contains our denormalized design so far. You can continue applying these questions to the remainder of the relationships. As you get more practice using the Denormalization Survival Guide, you will develop a sense for which relationships will be normalized or denormalized, probably before even answering all of the questions. However, if we rely on just a sense or gut feeling, we usually wind up making inconsistent denormalization decisions. Therefore, although it is very good to have a sense of whether

Table 8.10 Sample Reference-to-Reference Relationship: Dessert Category to Dessert

QUESTION	OPTIONS	POINTS
What type of relationship?	**Hierarchy (20)** Peer (−10) Definition (−20)	20—It is easy to look at the label "Belong To" and identify it as a "contains" relationship.
What is the participation ratio?	**1-1 to 1-5 (20)** 1-5 to 1-100 (−10) 1-100 and up (−20)	20—There are probably not more than five desserts within each category.
What is the size range of the parent entity?	**Low (20)** Medium (−10) High (−20)	20—We do not even need to concern ourselves with the Dessert Category Code data element, because this already exists in the child entity as a foreign key.
What is the usage ratio?	**Strong correlation with each other (30)** Weak or no correlation with each other (−30)	30—I can see most queries at the dessert level also including dessert category code and/or description.
Is the parent entity a placeholder?	Yes (−20) **No (20)**	20—I am making an assumption here.
What is the rate of change comparison?	Same (20) **Different (−20)**	−20—Desserts probably change much more frequently than their categories.
TOTAL POINTS		90

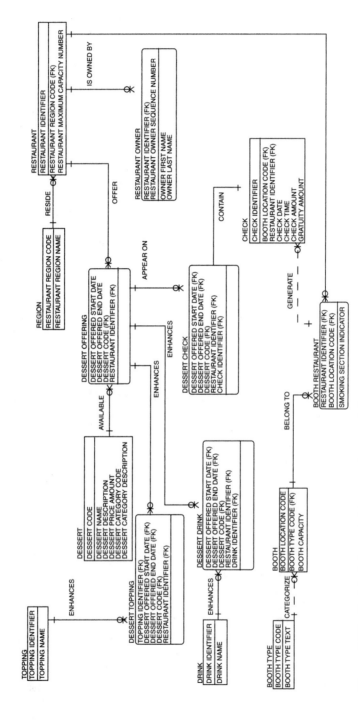

Figure 8.11 Updated dessert data mart data model.

Table 8.11 Sample Transaction-to-Transaction Relationship: Dessert Offering to Dessert Topping

QUESTION	OPTIONS	POINTS
What type of relationship?	Hierarchy (20) **Peer (−10)** Definition (−20)	−10
What is the participation ratio?	**1-1 to 1-5 (20)** 1-5 to 1-100 (−10) 1-100 and up (−20)	20—Hopefully there are not more than five toppings on any dessert!
What is the size range of the parent entity?	**Low (20)** Medium (−10) High (−20)	20
What is the usage ratio?	**Strong correlation with each other (30)** Weak or no correlation with each other (−30)	30
Is the parent entity a placeholder?	Yes (−20) **No (20)**	20
What is the rate of change comparison?	**Same (20)** Different (−20)	20
TOTAL POINTS		100

Table 8.12 Sample Reference-to-Transaction Relationship: Topping to Dessert Offering

QUESTION	OPTIONS	POINTS
What type of relationship?	Hierarchy (20) Peer (−10) **Definition (−20)**	−20
What is the participation ratio?	1-1 to 1-5 (20) 1-5 to 1-100 (−10) **1-100 and up (−20)**	−20
What is the size range of the parent entity?	**Low (20)** Medium (−10) High (−20)	20
What is the usage ratio?	Strong correlation with each other (30) **Weak or no correlation with each other (−30)**	−30
Is the parent entity a placeholder?	Yes (−20) **No (20)**	20
What is the rate of change comparison?	Same (20) **Different (−20)**	−20
TOTAL POINTS		−50

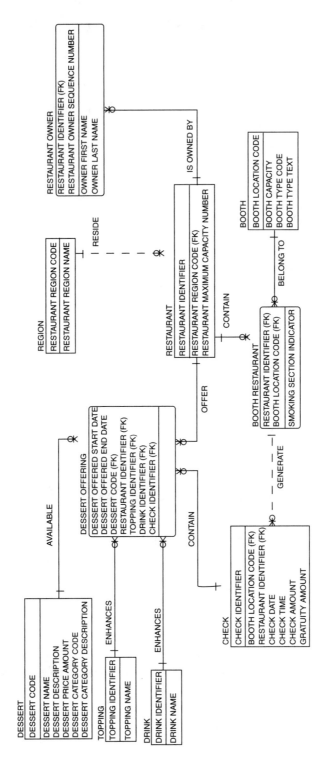

Figure 8.12 Updated dessert data mart data model.

a relationship must be normalized or denormalized, validate this sense or feeling against the Denormalization Survival Guide questions.

Summary

This chapter focused on two tools that will assist us in the Normalization Adventure, where we ascend a mountain toward total understanding with a 5NF data model and then descend toward an effective denormalized design:

The Normalization Hike. A simple explanation of normalization. Also included are special tips and guidelines that have assisted me in progressing through each level of normalization.

The Denormalization Survival Guide. A question-and-answer approach to determining where to denormalize your logical data model. When you are done answering these questions for each relationship, you will have an initial physical data model at the appropriate level of denormalization.

Using the Dessert Data Mart as an example, we have completed both logical and physical designs using these two tools within this chapter. Over the remaining chapters we will introduce several tools to enhance both the logical and physical designs. In Chapter 9, "The Abstraction Safety Guide and Components," we will focus on the powerful tool of abstraction.

The Abstraction Safety Guide and Components

We usually plan our annual weekend getaway to the beach in May or September. By traveling this time of year, we avoid the crowds and higher hotel room rates between the peak season from Memorial Day to Labor Day. However, saving some money and avoiding millions of beach lovers does come with a price. The weather is usually much more difficult to predict in May or September than it is in July or August. In May or September it can be chilly and breezy or a beautiful sunny warm beach day. There is an unknown factor that requires us to be flexible in our packing and weekend activities. If the weather is a bit cold, we will wear sweatshirts and maybe go for a bike ride. If the weather is hot and sunny, we will put on some suntan lotion and relax at the beach. We need to plan for the unknown.

This same unknown factor can exist within the requirements that drive our data model designs. If we believe the data requirements can change or expand in the near future, we should plan accordingly. Failure to design with some flexibility can lead to costly structure and development rework. Abstraction is a very good technique to build flexibility into our data models to plan for the unknown factor and minimize future rework.

About This Chapter

The tools we applied in Chapter 8, "The Normalization Hike and Denormalization Survival Guide," helped us create the logical and physical data models that meet current application requirements. The Normalization Hike ensured we have a logical data model that meets the rigor of Fifth Normal Form. The Denormalization Survival Guide helped us selectively introduce denormalization into our completed physical data model to quicken data retrieval in the resulting application. So, are we done with our modeling work? Can we pack up our data modeling tools and go home? Well, because there are still a few chapters to go in this text, the answer must be "No, we're not done yet!"

Data modelers are one of the few individuals in our organizations who need to see beyond the application requirements as they exist today. We need to make sure the data model we create for a specific application fits nicely into the larger enterprise data model or enterprise definitions, if this enterprise view exists. We also need to have the foresight to know where certain sections of our data model might be susceptible to expanded or enhanced data requirements that were not envisioned in the current application data requirements,—in other words, the unknown. One of the functions of the modeler is to minimize future design rework, which requires designing flexible structures.

The tools we have discussed and practiced up to this point in the text have focused on completely capturing current application requirements. We now turn our attention to abstraction, which helps us build flexibility into the sections of the design that we believe will need to handle expanded requirements that were not anticipated today. Abstraction handles the unknown factor beyond capturing the current application requirements.

Abstraction is a method to bring flexibility to your logical and physical data models by redefining and combining some of the data elements, entities, and relationships within the model into more generic terms. For example, instead of having separate Customer and Employee entities, there might be situations where it would be valuable to have the generic Person entity, which groups both customers and employees together. We will discuss in detail abstraction in the subsequent sections.

There are several very good books and Web sites on using already designed and built abstract data models and customizing them for your own needs. I believe, however, that we need to always first start with a strong understanding of our own application requirements and environment before we try applying a generic design. Therefore, we will not spend time on these prebuilt abstract models here. Instead, in this chapter, we focus on two very important abstraction tools that build on and complement the analysis and design tools we have spoken about up to this point in the text, which have helped us understand and correctly model our applications:

Abstraction Safety Guide. This is a set of three questions that will help us determine where, if at all, we need to abstract on our data models. It helps introduce consistency in deciding where to abstract, makes sure we do not miss any opportunities for abstraction, and helps us avoid overabstraction.

Abstraction Components. The more we abstract, the more we realize that the same rather tiny abstraction building blocks or components keep appearing in our designs, with very slight variations. The Abstraction Components tool is a collection of the most useful of these abstraction building blocks, which are not complete reusable generic models that you can customize for your own use. As mentioned previously, there are generic models for almost any industry you can think of. But you need to first understand your application before you can successfully apply these generic models. The components we discuss in this chapter are those we can use in our own application models to replace sections of our models that need more flexibility. These components can exist at the entity, relationship, or data element level. For entities, we discuss the six most prevalent abstract entities; for relationships, the three most powerful abstract relationships; and for data elements the basic building block of any data element: the classword.

This chapter starts off with an explanation of abstraction. We will go through several examples of abstraction and discuss its benefits, costs, and best uses. Then I will explain the concept of abstracting entities called subtyping. I will discuss the purpose of subtyping and review the four different variations of subtyping. Then I will focus on the Abstraction Safety Guide. I will explain this tool, including its purposes and how and where it should be used, and give a detailed example of its use. An explanation along with examples will then be shown for each Abstraction Component. We will practice using each of the entity, relationship, and data element abstraction components and show how they build and depend on each other.

If you visit my Web site, www.wiley.com/compbook/hoberman, you will find templates for each tool in this chapter; additional tools; and more information about tools in this book, including empty templates that you can download.

What Is Abstraction?

Abstraction is the removal of details in such a way as to make applicable to a wide class of situations, while preserving the important properties and essential nature from concepts or subjects. By removing these details, we remove differences. Therefore we change the way we view these concepts or subjects, including seeing similarities that were not apparent or even existent before. We have all seen abstract paintings, which appear to simplify their subjects and blur the differences between the objects on the paintings. We can view abstraction on data models in a similar way. Abstraction is the process of combining entities, relationships, and data elements into a more generic structure.

By abstracting two or more entities, relationships, and data elements that we believe to share certain properties, we can more easily handle new concepts that are similar to the current concepts that we have abstracted. Therefore, abstraction in our data modeling is based on the belief that if we have two or more concepts that appear similar, there is a chance we might have additional concepts that are similar in the near future. If there are two of something similar, there will be a greater chance that we will have a third one, as opposed to having only one of something and wondering if there would be a second one. For example, we might abstract Customer and Associate if we believe new types of concepts might appear soon that are different variations of what Customer and Associate represent. For example, Regulatory Body might be a new concept that has something in common with both Customer and Associate.

TIP

When there are two or more concepts on our model that share certain properties, there is a chance that there might be additional concepts that are similar to these that might come up in the near future. Therefore, abstraction is most valuable and useful when there are already two or more common data elements, entities, and relationships in the current model.

Let's go through a slightly more detailed example. Let's say you are creating a data model for the owner of a tuxedo shop. Being a good data modeler, you have used all the analysis and design tools in the text up to this point, and have just completed both the Normalization Hike and Denormalization Survival Guide. One of the main entities on your design is Customer. The Customer entity on your data model includes a number of data elements, including the following:

- Customer waist size
- Customer leg length
- Customer neck size
- Customer arm length
- Customer shoulder width

The owner of the tuxedo shop is very happy with your design, and his application is developed based on this model. You receive a phone call from the owner of the shop 2 months later, asking where he can store the customer's shoe size. You explain to him there is no place to put the shoe size, because that was not part of the original requirements. There is a long silence. The owner of the shop explains that he is expanding his business and many of his customers who rent tuxedos will also require shoes. You explain how much money and time it would take to make this change to his application. Again there is a long silence. And then you hear a few clicks as the owner hangs up the phone in disgust.

To paint a brighter picture, let's say after completing the Normalization Hike, you realize that all of the data elements around leg, waist, neck, arm, and shoulder measurements are really just a person's apparel measurements. Instead of listing each measurement as a separate data element, you abstract this concept in your data model to just two data elements:

- Customer Measurement Number
- Customer Measurement Type Name

The Customer Measurement Number data element includes any size value, such as:

- 42
- 17½
- 34

Each of these values has a type, which is captured in Customer Measurement Type Name, such as:

- 42 = Arm length
- 17½ = Neck size
- 34 = Leg length

Note that I used Number and Name to end the names of these two data elements because these are valid class words that we will discuss in more depth under the data element components section toward the end of this chapter. A Customer can have one or more of these measurements. Then, when we get the phone call from the tuxedo shop owner requesting where shoe size should be stored, we simply add a new row in the Measurement Type table called Shoe size. The owner can now enter his shoe size values with this shoe size type. This flexibility in our design has led to effortlessly supporting this new requirement. You have made the tuxedo shop owner so happy that he gives you a free Armani Tuxedo as a token of his appreciation.

We can see the flexibility and power abstraction offers.

Benefits of Abstraction

Abstraction offers the following benefits:

Provides greater flexibility. Flexibility is the primary benefit of abstraction. We are able to design our structures to better handle the unknown. New situations can arise that we did not originally anticipate. When we use abstraction, these situations may require few, if any, changes to our data model, and therefore, we can keep the database and code intact. Recall the example where we had Measurement Number and Measurement Type Name data elements. These two data elements allow us to handle any new types of measurements, such as the customer's shoe size. In a recent design, I decided to use abstraction in the part of the model that captured sales organization information. I abstracted all of the relationships between salespeople and their positions. Even though we did not immediately need all possible combinations of relationships, my abstracted model would handle them if they arose. Sure enough, shortly after the sales organization subject area went into production, we had the need to add a new type of relationship. Our sales organization structure was able to handle this new requirement without any changes to the data model and, hence, keep the database structure and code intact.

Reduces analysis and design time. Once we are familiar with abstraction, we can apply it to areas of our model in parallel with completing the Normalization Hike. This means that instead of spending extra time making sure we have all of the requirements complete and accurate, we can build in abstraction to cover all possible situations that might arise. In the example mentioned previously, instead of taking the time to capture all of the additional types of measurements for a tuxedo fitting, we can simply add the measurement number and type data elements and have all possible measurements automatically covered within your model. Within 2 weeks, I was able to create a model showing the entire manufacturing industry by using a substantial amount of abstraction. Instead of spending significant amounts of time analyzing each data element, I abstracted to make sure any possible requirement was handled within the model.

WARNING

Note that abstracting before completely understanding the requirements does reduce time but also reduces a complete understanding of the application. Be very selective when abstracting during the normalization process. If you abstract after fully normalizing your design, you will have complete understanding of the requirements and still achieve the flexibility of abstraction.

Encourages greater understanding of entities, relationships, and data elements. When we abstract after completing the Normalization Hike, the first step is to identify those areas that might make good candidates for abstraction. This means we need to completely understand what is common across the entities, relationships, and data elements. To know what is common means understanding completely each of the concepts that you might want to abstract. We need to understand what Customer Arm Length and Customer Shoulder Width have in common to determine if they are good candidates for abstraction.

Costs of Abstraction

Abstraction might sound as if it can do everything from cure the common cold to ensure world peace (slight exaggeration). However, the benefits come with a price because abstraction also does the following:

Hides business concepts on the model. When we just have Measurement Number and Measurement Type Name in our data model, we can no longer see the individual tuxedo fitting measurements. Customer Arm Length is no longer a data element we can clearly identify and explain but is only a value within the Measurement Number data element. When we abstract we lose the actual business data element name. The data model, however, still contains the same information. These measurements become row values instead of individual data elements. Six months after we create the tuxedo data model with abstraction, someone might ask us, "Hey, what does Measurement Type mean?" What sounded like a great idea when we were doing the data model, might no longer make sense. Therefore, there is a task we need to do even more rigorously than before. We need to have definitions that follow the strictness of the Definition Checklist described in Chapter 3, "Ensuring High-Quality Definitions." For abstractions that produce types or codes, we need to list all or most possible values in their definitions. This is because these values used to be the data elements on our design. For example, this might be the definition for Measurement Type Name:

> *The kind of length, width, weight, or amount that defines a characteristic of our customer.*
>
> *EXAMPLES:*
>
> *01 = Customer Waist Size*
>
> *02 = Customer Legs Length Size*
>
> *03 = Customer Neck Size*
>
> *04 = Customer Arm Length*
>
> *05 = Customer Shoulder Width*

In this way, down the road when you or someone else needs to understand what Measurement Type Name encompasses, all of the values of this code within the definition can be viewed. You can also use meta data helper tables to capture this important name and definition meta data. These helper tables will be discussed subsequently. Just remember that you need to capture the meaning of the values somewhere.

Leads to indulgence. Like anything that makes us feel good (such as eating chocolate or sitting in the sun), abstraction can be taken to an extreme and abused with unfavorable outcomes. Too much chocolate can give us a stomachache or toothache. Too much sun can result in painful sunburn. Too much abstraction can give us a design totally meaningless in understanding and impossible to develop. Let's say we continue to abstract the tuxedo data model. Eventually, we will wind up with a single entity called Thing with a recursive relationship, as shown in Figure 9.1. Imagine the power of this entity! We can represent anything with this entity. In fact, we can represent an entire Enterprise Resource Planning (ERP) application using this single entity! However, imagine explaining this model to someone in our business area. Imagine trying to write the code that uses this entity. Now the Thing concept is a bit of an exaggeration; however, I have seen an item data model where abstraction was taken to the point where it was difficult to find anything business-related on the model. It was also very difficult to walk a business user through this model. All of the item components familiar to a user, such as brand and size, were no longer visible on the model. Everything was defined in very abstract structures.

Removes rules. When we abstract, we can lose the ability to see and validate business rules on our logical data model and enforce relationships through the database between tables on our physical data model. We can no longer view on the model the relationship between Position and Person within our sales organization area if we abstracted this relationship. This relationship will also not be able to be enforced within our database. We tend to use programming code to enforce the business rules or relationships instead of using constraints in the database. I have seen many data quality problems caused by relying on code to stop bad data rather than database constraints.

However, these data quality problems can be avoided by using meta data helper tables. These entities are a good option to maintain the rules in the database when using abstraction. These entities enforce relationships between the abstract tables as well as provide definition and other meta data readily available directly in the model and database. For example, we use an abstract association structure to relate any two entities to each other, instead of specifying each of the

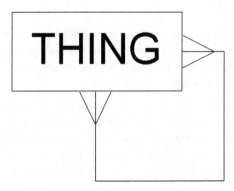

Figure 9.1 The Thing abstraction.

relationships between the entities. The association structure can now handle all types of relationships but cannot enforce rules such as, "I can have relationships between Customers and Associates, and between Suppliers and Associates, but I cannot have relationships between Customers and Suppliers." This is where the meta data helper table comes in. This table will contain the types of entities that can share relationships, and then have two foreign keys into the association table so that only certain types of relationships can be allowed. This helps enforce business rules without giving up abstraction. Later in this chapter, I will show you part of a data model containing a meta data helper table.

Lengthens development time. Although analysis and design time can be decreased using abstraction, development time can be increased. It takes longer to write code and logic against row values than against columns. For example, it would be more complex and take longer to write the code to populate or select information out of the Measurement Number and Measurement Type Name data elements than it would be if we had the specific measurement data elements at our disposal. We would need to have more complicated query statements, including possibly nested query statements, where the inner most query retrieves the type while the outer query returns the value for this type. Without abstraction, our queries would be much simpler and easier to create. For example, without abstraction, returning the name and leg length of all of the customers with a waist size of 42 would look like this:

```
SELECT CUSTOMER_FIRST_NAME, CUSTOMER_LAST_NAME, CUSTOMER_LEG_LENGTH
FROM CUSTOMER
WHERE
CUSTOMER_WAIST_SIZE = '42'
```

It is very easy and straightforward to create this query. In contrast, using abstraction to get the same results might look like this:

```
SELECT CUSTOMER.CUSTOMER_FIRST_NAME,
CUSTOMER.CUSTOMER_LAST_NAME,
MEASUREMENT_TYPE.CUSTOMER_LEG_LENGTH
FROM CUSTOMER, MEASUREMENT_TYPE
WHERE CUSTOMER.CUSTOMER_IDENTIFIER = MEASUREMENT_TYPE.CUSTOMER_IDENTIFIER
AND MEASUREMENT_TYPE.MEASUREMENT_TYPE_NAME = 'Customer waist size'
AND MEASUREMENT_TYPE.MEASUREMENT_NUMBER = '42'
```

Note that we need to do an additional table join on the customer's identifier. Also, abstract queries can be much more complicated than this example, especially if we have a separate code table or lookup table for the different measurement type names (for example, 01 = Customer Waist Size).

Increases reporting difficulty and complexity. There are some reporting tools on the market today that have a very difficult if not impossible time extracting data from abstract structures. There have been several cases where I introduced abstraction into the logical and physical data models and then had to reverse this decision because the reporting tool, and the query language in general, had difficulty retrieving information from these structures.

Using Abstraction

Abstraction is most useful in any situation where two conditions are present:

The design needs to last forever. Abstraction is very useful when the data model you are working on is for an application that is for a critical component of a systems architecture or the source application for very important and strategic information. These types of applications are expected to last a very long time, and therefore, it is important to design with flexibility in mind. I reviewed the model for an integration hub not too long ago. It was a critical component to the marketing department of a large company. Many source applications fed this integration hub. Many other applications depended on data from this integration hub. This integration hub has a very normalized physical design. Its business rules are clearly understood, and there is minimal redundancy in the database. Despite a clear understanding and minimal redundancy, enhancements to this integration hub require months of effort and cost lots of money. There was such a large investment because the data model had to be changed, and therefore the database and usually a substantial amount of programming code also had to be changed. One of the main reasons for this huge effort to make modifications is the lack of abstraction within the design of this integration hub. A hub, as any other integrated application, is very important to the business and is usually the heart of a systems architecture. Therefore, it needs to be designed with flexibility using abstraction, or else every little change will become a huge development effort. Inevitably, the integration hub will be slowly replaced by something more flexible, but only after spending lots of money and time.

Requirements can change. There are applications whose requirements can slowly change with the passage of time. This is not necessarily the fault of incomplete business or functional requirements. Rather, the applications are anticipated to grow and meet the needs of more individuals and departments and, therefore, will be required to handle additional types of information. You can imagine, in the integration hub example mentioned in the previous paragraph, how new requirements would naturally emerge. With new source systems, and new target systems, there will always be another data element or business rule that is requested to become part of the design of the integration. There is no way to predict all future requirements in the initial application design. Therefore, there is a need for flexibility and abstraction.

Applications that can benefit from using abstraction owing to their need to last "forever" and the realization that their requirements that can change quite often include the following:

Data warehouses. Data warehouses represent the infrastructure behind our data marts and we would consider the data warehouses to be a critical component of our reporting architecture. These types of applications take lots of data in from a variety of sources and send lots of data out to many data marts. The data warehouse is the heart of our reporting architecture, and is not expected to disappear any time soon. Therefore, we need to design the data warehouse with flexibility in mind. An example of using abstraction within a data warehouse was a customer structure I modeled that used abstraction to represent different ways of classifying customers. Regardless of whether we wanted to classify customers by size, industry, or location, this classification structure would flexibly handle any customer grouping scenario. This abstract structure would receive customer information from several different source applications, and pass this customer information to several different data marts. Keeping customer classification within an abstract structure means that when new types of classifications are passed from source applications, we will not need to make any changes to the data warehouse design. We would just add a new row to a classification type entity and we are done.

Meta data repositories. With the current state of the meta data repository market, many of us are currently not sure what to do about a meta data repository. Most of our companies seem to fall into one of three categories:

- Using a meta data repository that does not meet all of your requirements
- Considering purchasing a meta data repository
- Considering building your own meta data repository

A small percentage of companies have meta data repositories that are used often and provide all required functionality. Most of us who have repositories probably belong to the first category, and not all of our requirements are being satisfied. This is most likely due to an inflexible design. If you belong to the second or third category, you need to be aware that the data model behind the repository needs to be flexible enough to handle new types of meta data requirements and, therefore, must be able to last a very long time. This translates into being able to accommodate new meta data requirements. For example, let's say you suddenly want to store the new type of meta data of subject area stewardship information within your repository. Can you do it? Or, do you need to change the data model and, therefore, the structure and code of the repository to accommodate this new requirement? If the repository needs changing every time new types of meta data need to be added, eventually someone who is paying the bills for these enhancements will realize that it is no longer worth the extra effort. Then the repository will die a slow death.

The more information we have to store and retrieve, the more valuable repositories become. Therefore, we want more and more people to use repositories to retrieve and store valuable business and technical meta data. Because we cannot predict all possible types of meta data that might be requested, we need a meta data repository data model that uses abstraction to be flexible enough to handle new requirements. Therefore, repositories require an abstract structure to have a long and meaningful life. I have seen the data models to a number of packaged meta data repositories, and even though some of the models have hundreds of entities, somewhere in their design should be a set of four abstract tables similar to Figure 9.2. Please note that I changed the names of these entities to avoid specifically referring to any actual packaged software entity names.

The Object entity includes any piece of meta data in our organization. Examples of some of the values of Object include:

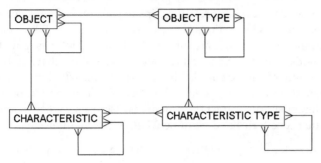

Figure 9.2 Meta data repository abstract model.

- Customer Last Name
- Product Classification
- Vendor
- Customer to Sales Representative relationship
- Order Data Model

Objects can relate to other objects and hence the recursive relationship. For example, the Customer Last Name data element can belong to the Customer entity. The Object Type entity categorizes the meta data, examples being:

- Entity
- Data element
- Relationship
- Data model

Object Types can also have relationships to each other, shown with its recursive relationship. For example, Entities can contain Data Elements. All of the types of meta data mentioned in the bingo tools from Chapter 2, "Meta Data Bingo," would be object types. The Characteristic entity contains all of the descriptive information about the meta data, such as definition, format, nullability, and version information. For example:

- Customer Last Name is the surname of the customer.
- Customer Last Name is 30 characters in length.
- Order Data Model was last changed on March 2, 2001, 5 P.M. by Bob Jones.

Characteristics can also have relationships to each other, shown through its recursive relationship. Characteristic types contain the descriptive information about the characteristics, such as:

- Definition
- Format
- Version

Characteristic Types can also have relationships to each other by way of a recursive relationship, such as Definitions always require a Version. Take a moment or two to let your imagination run rampant, and try to identify types of meta data that this abstract model will not support. I can almost guarantee that any type of meta data you can think of can be handled by this structure. Whether we have business, functional, or technical meta data, this design will support it. Be aware that this meta data repository abstract data model is also useful when evaluating packaged meta data repositories to determine whether they will meet your needs.

Packaged software. In determining whether to purchase a packaged piece of software, it is a good idea to compare your needs against the data model of the packaged software to see if you will be satisfied with the functionality. Although it can sometimes be very difficult to get the data model from the software company (I have heard "That's proprietary!" way too many times), if it is critical to purchasing the product, most software vendors will provide it to you. Do not just compare your existing normalized logical data model with their packaged software data model. This will only help you answer the question, "Does this piece of software meet my current needs?" You want to know if it will meet some of your future needs as well. Therefore, apply abstraction according to the Abstraction Safety Guide, which we will discuss shortly, to your normalized model. Then match your abstract model against the packaged software model to see how flexible the packaged software model really is. You will quickly find out whether this product will meet your current and future needs or whether it will limit your functionality and not be worth the investment. For example, if you are evaluating a packaged meta data repository, compare the data model for the packaged meta data repository with the one in Figure 9.2 to see if it can handle all possible types of meta data within your organization.

Recently, I analyzed several data elements within a consumer contact database that was purchased as a packaged piece of software. I was shocked when I noted email addresses within the Company Name data element. When I brought this up to the functional analyst as a potential data quality issue, he responded that they always store their email address there. He must have noticed a surprised look on my face, so he added that there are no other places to put email addresses in the packaged software and thus they decided to use one of their least populated data elements for this information, which was the Company Name. This could be a very good example of an inflexible design that is the result of a data model with not enough abstraction to handle an obvious future requirement.

Reference databases. Many of our companies have separate applications for specific reference subject areas. The most popular examples are Item and Customer databases. These applications need to handle a variety of changing requirements and pass this information on to many downstream applications. There might always be new item brands or different ways of classifying items. Using abstraction allows us to handle these types of changes without making changes to the design. Making changes to a design for a reference database not only impacts the reference database but also potentially impacts all of the applications downstream that receive information from the reference database. Thus, you want to minimize making changes to reference databases and, hence, the usefulness of abstraction. I have seen both item and customer applications with abstraction applied to increase flexibility. I have seen an item model where an abstract classification structure was used to handle any way of classifying products, such as by brand or by size. I have seen a customer model where an abstract association structure was used to handle any possible relationships between customers.

What Is Subtyping?

Subtyping is simply abstracting the common properties across entities, while maintaining the parts of each entity that are not common and unique to each entity. We are abstracting or categorizing entities that have data elements and relationships in common with each other. Everything that is common across entities is moved up to the abstract entity, called the supertype, and everything that is not common across entities stays in their original entity, called the subtype.

A relationship defined between the supertype and two or more subtypes groups these subtypes together. The subtype entities inherit all of the properties from the supertype entity, meaning any data elements or relationships at the supertype level also belong to the subtype entity. For example, Checking Account and Savings Account might have much in common, such as Account Number and Account Balance Amount. Whatever they have in common might be moved to the abstract supertype entity, Account; whereas, everything that is not in common, such as an Interest Rate Number for the Savings Account and a Maximum Free Checks Per Month Quantity for the Checking Account, would remain in their original entities. Account Number and Account Balance Amount are two of the data elements that are inherited to the Checking Account and Savings Account subtypes.

Subtype relationships are exhaustive or nonexhaustive, and overlapping or nonoverlapping:

Exhaustive. This is when all of the subtypes mentioned under a supertype make up the complete set of subtypes for that supertype. All possible subtypes under a supertype are specified. For example, Checking Account and Savings Account might be the only two types of accounts a bank may offer. Therefore, if both of these subtypes are listed under Account we have the complete list of subtypes, and this subtype relationship is considered exhaustive.

Non-exhaustive. This is when we do not have the complete list of subtypes under a supertype. We know that one or more subtypes are missing from this supertype. Unless we can guarantee that we have the complete set of subtypes under a supertype, we need to assume that the relationship is nonexhaustive. If Checking Account and Savings Account are the only two subtypes under Account, and we believe that there are several more types of accounts that are missing, such as Money Market Account and Brokerage Account, then the subtype relationship is nonexhaustive.

Overlapping. This is when the same supertype value can include two or more subtype values. We mentioned previously that a subtype inherits the data elements and relationships from its supertype. There is usually a one-to-one relationship between supertype and subtype, which is considered nonoverlapping and discussed shortly. In some cases, there can be a one-to-many from supertype to its subtypes, meaning the same supertype instance or value can be equal to one or more subtype instances or values. For example, returning to our account example, if the same Account can be both a Checking Account and Savings Account, it would be considered overlapping subtypes.

Nonoverlapping. This is when the supertype and subtype have a one-to-one relationship, and therefore, the supertype value can only include one of the subtype values. Nonoverlapping is much more common than the overlapping subtyping relationship. Thus, if an Account can be either a Checking or Savings Account but not both, it would be considered nonoverlapping.

Therefore, there are four possible types of subtypes we can have:

- Exhaustive and overlapping
- Exhaustive and nonoverlapping
- Nonexhaustive and overlapping
- Nonexhaustive and nonoverlapping

See Table 9.1 for an example of each. You will see one of the ways to represent subtyping on your model in a detailed example provided subsequently in this chapter.

An exhaustive and overlapping subtype means that the subtypes represent the complete list for the supertype and that the same supertype value can play the role of more than one of the subtypes. For example, Course is the supertype and Lecture and Workshop are the subtypes. Lecture and Workshop represent the complete set of subtypes for Course; there can be no other subtypes. Also, the same Course can overlap and be both a Lecture and Workshop. This means the same course can have data elements and relationships that cross the Lecture and Workshop subtypes.

TIP

 Note how important context or scope is in determining whether the subtypes are exhaustive or overlapping. What is considered exhaustive for a department, for example, might not be exhaustive for the department's organization. Also, what is considered exhaustive for a department today might not be exhaustive for that same department a year from now. For example, if a bank only has checking and savings accounts today but expects brokerage accounts some time shortly, a sub-

Table 9.1 Examples of Subtype Criteria

		OVERLAPPING		NONOVERLAPPING	
Exhaustive	Supertype	Course		Associate	
	Subtype	Lecture	Workshop	Male	Female
Nonexhaustive	Supertype	Person		Phone Call	
	Subtype	Student	Instructor	Compliment	Complaint

type relationship with just checking and savings account entities will be exhaustive today but nonexhaustive shortly. Therefore, make sure you have defined the right context before determining which combination of exhaustive and overlapping to use.

An exhaustive and nonoverlapping subtype means that we have the complete set of subtypes, but this time the subtypes do not overlap with each other. Associate is the supertype and Male and Female are the subtypes. Male and Female represent the complete set of subtypes for an associate; there can be no other subtypes other than these two. Also an Associate can be either a Male or a Female but not both; therefore it is nonoverlapping.

A nonexhaustive and overlapping subtype means that we do not have the complete set of subtypes, and the subtypes overlap. Person is the supertype to Student and Instructor. Student and Instructor represent two of the subtypes for Person; however, there are other subtypes that are not shown here, such as Tutor or Instructor Assistant. Student and Instructor can also overlap, because the same person can be both a Student and Instructor.

A nonexhaustive and nonoverlapping subtype means that the subtypes do not represent the complete list for the supertype and that the same supertype value can only play the role of one of the subtypes. For example, a Phone Call can be a Compliment or a Complaint. It is nonexhaustive, meaning that there can be other types of Phone Calls that are not shown here, such as Questions. It is nonoverlapping meaning that a Phone Call can be a Compliment or Complaint but not both for the same Phone Call. If somebody calls with a complaint, they cannot also provide a compliment during that same phone call. If someone does call up with both a complaint and a compliment during the same phone call, we would need to consider this two distinct phone calls because we have enforced a nonoverlapping subtype in this example.

WARNING

Although they provide additional information about the subtype relationship, exhaustive and overlapping distinctions are very limited to capture with the current data model and database toolset. I am currently not aware of any modeling tools or notation that can represent all four different subtype combinations. Most notation that I have seen supports either exhaustive or nonexhaustive, or overlapping and nonoverlapping, but not all four. Also, subtyping does not exist in the physical database, and therefore, usually each relationship between supertype and subtype is treated as a separate physical database constraint, or if denormalized, a type code can be used to distinguish the subtypes from each other.

What Is the Abstraction Safety Guide?

The Abstraction Safety Guide is a set of three questions to help us determine where we should abstract. We can apply these three questions to the entities, relationships, and data elements on our model. As mentioned previously, we do not want to abstract for the sake of abstracting. Doing so will create a level of vagueness and confusion that will compromise the understanding we have worked so hard to create on our normalized logical data model. Thus, we want to use abstraction very selectively. These three questions will help us determine the optimal usage of abstraction. The Safety Guide will make sure we take advantage of abstraction where there is true value and will help us avoid the dark side of abstracting everything until all we have left is the single and meaningless Thing entity in Figure 9.1.

Here are the three questions:

- Does this data element, entity, or relationship have something in common with one or more other data elements, entities, or relationships?
- If yes, are there concrete situations that would warrant an abstract structure?
- If yes, will the extra development effort now be substantially less than that in the future?

The first question addresses commonality, the second question purpose, and the third question effort. Let's go into more detail about each of these.

Commonality

The first of these three questions asks, "Do we have a match anywhere on our model?" Did we find two or more entities, relationships, or data elements that appear to share a common trait? The detective work comes in when we scan our model in search of anything that might appear to match something else. Remember playing the card game Concentration when you were a child? You would put a deck of picture cards face down on a table and then turn over two to see if they match. It is the same concept on the data model. For example, we can take the concepts on a data model and list them in much the same way as the Concentration cards on the table. See Table 9.2.

Which of these concepts match? I noticed a few date data elements that might make a good abstraction candidate. The Order Date, Ship Date, and Actual Delivery Date have in common that they are dates around the order life cycle process. In addition, Carrier, Supplier, and Vendor are all entities that share the common trait that they might be external companies. Product Size, Product Brand, and Product Dimension all appear to be different ways of classifying or categorizing a product.

Let's list these in a table format to more easily see their similarities. This format is a useful way to view and validate that we have grouped together similar concepts. See Table 9.3.

Table 9.2 Can You Find a Match?

Order Date	Supplier	Actual Delivery Date
Carrier	Ship Date	Vendor
Product Size	Product Brand	Product Dimension

Table 9.3 Commonality

SIMILAR CONCEPTS	REASONS THEY ARE SIMILAR
Order Date Ship Date Actual Delivery Date	These are dates around the order life cycle.
Carrier Supplier Vendor	All are external companies.
Product Size Product Brand Product Dimension	All are ways of classifying products.

Purpose

Now that we have found several potential candidates for abstraction, for each of these we need to ask, "Are there concrete situations that would warrant an abstract structure?" In other words, is there value in abstracting? Many times when we abuse abstraction and overabstract, we avoid asking this question. We usually find a match and then abstract without regard for the usefulness of the abstraction. "Somebody will use this flexibility someday" might be how we rationalize the abuse of abstraction. However, because these abstractions result in loss of understanding and clarity in the model, as well as extra development effort, we cannot be so generous in abstracting where there is no immediate or short-term benefit. Let's add a purpose column to each of these similar concepts. See Table 9.4.

Note the question-and-answer approach I chose to take in determining if each of these similar concepts is worth abstracting. When we abstract, we gain the ability to have additional "types" of something. Thus, if we were to abstract the different order life cycle dates from the first row in Table 9.4, we would be able to represent additional types of dates, such as in-transit and originally scheduled dates.

TIP

In determining the value of abstraction, ask the business expert questions starting off similar to this: "Would your application need additional types of....?", and fill in the end of this question with what you are considering to abstract. For example, "Would your application need additional types of order life cycle dates?" It might also be helpful to give some examples of concepts not on the model today that might be useful to have. By asking this type of question, you expand what is covered by abstraction from more of what is currently on the model to new types that did not exist before. Thus, not only would we be able to represent multiple Order Dates by abstracting the order life cycle data elements but we would also be able to represent new types of order life cycle dates by having this abstraction on the model.

Table 9.4 Purpose

SIMILAR CONCEPTS	REASONS THEY ARE SIMILAR	VALUE IN ABSTRACTING
Order Date Ship Date Actual Delivery Date	These are dates around the order life cycle.	Would you want to store additional types of order life cycle dates in the future? The business expert replies: "Yes, we might need to handle several additional types of in-transit shipment dates in the near future."
Carrier Supplier Vendor	All are external companies.	Do you need to represent additional types of external companies? The business expert replies: "We already have the complete list of external companies defined. I do not think we will have other external companies for quite a few years." You are thinking to yourself, "But how can they be sure?"
Product Size Product Brand Product Dimension	All are ways of classifying products.	Do you need to represent additional types of product groupings or classifications? The business expert replies: "Yes, I believe there will be several volume product groupings in the near future."

After filling in the purpose column, we can review the reasons and make intelligent decisions as to what has value in abstracting. Both the dates and the product groupings appear like very good candidates for abstraction. However, the reason for abstracting external companies is not as solid. It appears the modeler might be looking for an area to abuse abstraction. In real life, we will never see our question, "But how can they be sure?" documented officially, but how often do you think people think it? Thus, we should not pursue abstracting external companies in this case. It will not be valuable in the near future, and therefore, we should not sacrifice understanding on the model by abstracting these data elements.

Effort

The final question is around the effort involved in implementing the abstract structure. After determining that there is value in having such an abstract structure, we now need to answer the question, "Is the extra development effort now substantially less than the development effort down the road will be?" This is a very tricky question, because it depends on whom you ask. If you ask the data modeler (probably yourself) or anyone from the data administration team, the answer will probably be a resounding, "Yes, it is worth the effort now." This is because we are looking ahead for the next requirement that can take advantage of these abstract structures. We are looking beyond just the current application. However, the individual or department that pays the bills for the current application is the one who really needs to answer this question. Unfortunately, in many cases, the bill payer is usually just concerned about the particular application at a point in time and may not see the value of such an abstract structure.

I have conceded to several arguments or discussions in the past because of people focusing on the very short term and the cost right now, instead of the much higher cost in the future. Sometimes the only way to convince someone of abstracting a valuable concept is to not abstract it and then use the "I told you so" argument to use abstraction the next time around. If you need to sacrifice an abstraction structure, carefully document any redesign work required in this application in the future owing to its inflexible design that could have benefited from abstraction.

What I have found very valuable is to quantify in terms of money and time how much could have been saved by abstracting instead of implementing an inflexible solution. Then use these facts showing this rework to more easily gain commitment the next time abstraction is considered valuable but determined to be not worth the effort. It is better to invest a little extra effort now rather than a lot later. You can add an effort column to our spreadsheet documenting roughly how much effort will be involved. You can break this up by team or function. For this example I will just use a single number, which includes all design and development effort. Note that I removed the external company abstraction because we learned in the previous step that it does not provide any value. See Table 9.5.

I usually list the effort in weeks, but you can list it in any time duration that makes the most sense for your application. By using the three questions in this example, you can see the value of the Abstraction Safety Guide:

Identifies all areas to abstract. We want to make sure we do not miss any abstraction opportunities. Having a step dedicated to brainstorming for all possible matches helps ensure we completely find any areas to abstract.

Prohibits overabstracting. We want to avoid abstracting because it looks cool or elegant or we think it might be useful one day. Avoid the "build it and they will come" mentality. If we abuse abstraction, it becomes more difficult to convince people to abstract the next time around. You might get comments such as, "We never used that association type concept you build into our last design. It only

Table 9.5 Effort

SIMILAR CONCEPTS	REASONS THEY ARE SIMILAR	VALUE IN ABSTRACTING	EFFORT
Order Date Ship Date Actual Delivery Date	These are dates around the order life cycle.	Would you want to store additional types of order life cycle dates in the future? The business expert replies: "Yes, we might need to handle several additional types of in-transit shipment dates in the near future."	1 week
Product Size Product Brand Product Dimension	All are ways of classifying products.	Do you need to represent additional types of product groupings or classifications? The business expert replies: "Yes, I believe there will be several volume product groupings in the near future."	2 weeks

confused us. I do not want to use any more nebulous concepts on our designs." In addition, as mentioned previously, overabstracting causes unnecessary loss of business information on the model and extra effort and complexity in development. The Safety Guide makes sure the only abstraction used will be that which provides some benefit and value.

Factors in future rework. Is it worth the effort now, or can it wait? Will it take the same amount of effort later? If you have a strong reason why abstraction would be useful, I would assume that it is worth the effort, answer this question with a yes, and model with the abstraction. In abstracting, it is sometimes better to ask for forgiveness than for permission in weighing the costs.

Provides consistency. By applying the same three questions to every situation where abstraction can be used, we build a level of consistency with regard to abstraction in our models. Let's say there are five entities that each capture a different way of categorizing a product. All five of these entities might be abstracted into a single classification abstract structure. There is a very good chance that on all of the data models that contain these five product entities we will see the same abstract classification structure on all of the data models that contain these five product entities. This consistency leads to making quicker abstraction decisions over time, and helps people who are reading the models come up to speed more rapidly. For example, you might hear a functional analyst say during a model review, "Oh, I've seen that classification concept on the last model. I understand what that is."

Using the Abstraction Safety Guide

Let's put the Abstraction Safety Guide in the context of the normalization and denormalization steps from the previous chapter:

1. **Apply the Normalization Hike.** Usually before we do any kind of abstraction we first need to have a fully normalized model. Therefore, the first step is to go through the Normalization Hike mentioned in Chapter 8, "The Normalization Hike and Denormalization Survival Guide." Note that as you get more comfortable applying both the Normalization Hike and the Abstraction Safety Guide, you might find yourself applying some levels of abstraction during the Normalization Hike. As long as you fully apply the Abstraction Safety Guide, it is fine to introduce abstraction at this early point. In fact, introducing abstraction at this point in the design can provide us with the abstraction benefit of saving analysis and design time, because we do not need to consider all possible alternatives. Returning to the example mentioned previously, we do not need to analyze all possible types of customer measurements from the tuxedo store. We just need to capture the measurement number and measurement type name, and then we can handle any type of customer measurement.

WARNING

Never abstract without some amount of normalization first. Without doing the proper data element analysis first, you will be abstracting before developing an understanding of the business. You will have very generic concepts that mean nothing

to a business user and will have be much difficulty in mapping business concepts to these abstract structures.

2. **Apply the Abstraction Safety Guide.** This is where we will ask the three questions of commonality, purpose, and effort:

   - Does this data element, entity, or relationship have something in common with one or more other data elements, entities, or relationships?

   - If yes, are there concrete situations that would warrant an abstract structure?

   - If yes, will the extra development effort now be substantially less than that in the future?

3. **Document in detail.** As mentioned previously, it is extremely important to have very rigorous definitions that follow the Definition Checklist from Chapter 3, "Ensuring High Quality Definitions," whenever we are applying abstraction. This is because abstraction removes business concepts from the model and replaces them with very encompassing but generic structures. For example, if on a data model you noticed the data element Measurement Type Code, would you really know what this data element means? If you follow the Definition Checklist, you will find yourself listing all possible values (or most of the values) for each of the code data elements. Therefore, in the definitions of abstract data elements, such as the Measurement Type Code, we will list all of the possible types of measurements, such as:

   EXAMPLES:

   01 = Customer Waist Size

   02 = Customer Legs Length Size

   03 = Customer Neck Size

   04 = Customer Arm Length

   05 = Customer Shoulder Width

   In some situations, where it may not be clear from the code value, you might even want to include brief descriptions of each of the values. For example, if the code A = Alliance, what does Alliance mean? The tuxedo fitting examples mentioned, however, appear self-explanatory and probably do not require any other descriptive information. I have spent some time reviewing a product data model that used abstraction heavily. Although abstraction was used very appropriately, there were very few definitions on the model. This made the understanding level of the model very low, and you really could not walk through the data model without also having access to some actual values from the database. Looking at the actual data was the only way you could see that the Classification Type Code can represent the brand of the product.

4. **Apply the Denormalization Survival Guide.** Once we have applied abstraction to our fully normalized logical data model, we can look for areas to denormalize following the Denormalization Survival Guide mentioned in Chapter 8, "The Normalization Hike and Denormalization Survival Guide."

Note where abstraction fits within these steps. I would recommend abstracting during and after the Normalization Hike. In the beginning, when you are still getting comfortable with abstraction, you should first finish the Normalization Hike and then apply the Abstraction Safety Guide. However, you want to make sure you apply abstraction before you denormalize. We abstract before denormalizing for two reasons:

Once you denormalize it becomes more difficult to find common entities, relationships, and data elements to abstract. If we had denormalized Product Size, Product Brand, and Product Dimension into the same entity, it would become more difficult and sometimes impossible to realize that these three concepts are all classifications and thus could be abstracted. It is easier to identify common concepts to abstract when your design most accurately represents the business, which is the fully normalized data model.

We can potentially avoid denormalizing structures that already have been abstracted. For example, if we were to abstract Product Size, Product Brand, and Product Dimension into a generic grouping concept, we would not even need to consider whether we should denormalize these three concepts. Because we should only introduce denormalization very selectively, we eliminate a number of situations where we need to consider denormalization. This saves us time in applying the Denormalization Survival Guide because there are potentially less relationships to consider, and it also helps us maintain some of the flexibility that abstraction offers us that denormalization does not.

NOTE

It is important to be aware of the distinction between normalization and abstraction. When we normalize, we assign the business data elements to their most appropriate entities to remove redundancy and increase flexibility of *existing* concepts. When we abstract, we redefine business concepts to increase flexibility of introducing *new* concepts. For example, if a Customer can have two or more home phone numbers, we will normalize home phone number into its own entity and define a one-to-many relationship between the entities Customer and Customer Home Phone Number. This reduces the redundancy of having Customer Home Phone 1 Number, Customer Home Phone 2 Number, and so on, in the Customer entity. Normalizing home phone number lets us represent any number of home phone numbers for a customer without any design or development changes. However, if we abstract Customer Home Phone Number into Customer Phone Number, we can now handle additional types of phone numbers that we could not previously, such as fax, cell, and pager phone numbers. Redefining concepts to handle new types of information is abstraction, which is different from normalization where we are building flexibility into existing concepts.

NOTE

It is also necessary to be aware of the differences between denormalization and abstraction. Denormalization is combining entities and introducing redundancy to

hopefully decrease retrieval times. Abstraction is combining entities (also data elements and relationships) to increase flexibility. You are not increasing redundancy through abstraction, and you are also not decreasing retrieval time. In fact, it probably would take longer to retrieve data from an abstract structure owing to looking for row values instead of directly accessing a data element. Likewise, denormalization does not give us added flexibility. Abstracting Product Size, Product Brand, and Product Dimension into a classification structure gives us the flexibility to represent any other types of classification without design changes. Denormalizing Product Size, Product Brand, and Product Dimension within the Product entity allows us to retrieve these three data elements faster when viewing product reference data than if these data elements were in separate tables.

I often am asked, "So, is abstraction considered logical or physical?" In other words, would we incorporate abstraction on our logical data model or only on our physical data model? I consider abstraction to be a logical construct because it is used to increase the flexibility of our design, which is one of the reasons we create a logical data model. In addition, a physical data model is created for performance or storage reasons. Abstraction is not incorporated into a design for any physical performance or storage purposes but only for flexibility.

Abstraction Safety Guide In Practice

For this exercise, we will be creating abstract logical and physical data models for customer, supplier, and associate information. Let's assume that we have completed all of the subject area and data element analysis tools discussed up to this chapter. Now it is time to incorporate abstraction using the steps previously outlined.

1. Apply the Normalization Hike

Table 9.6 lists all of the data elements that appeared on our Data Element Family Tree for this example. These data elements are the only ones we will need for this model. Rather than list the complete Family Tree here, I decided to list each of the data element names under its respective subject area.

We are also given the following business rules:

- An Associate can be assigned to many Customers.
- A Customer can contact many Associates.
- An Associate manages the relationship with many Suppliers.
- A Supplier can contact many Associates.

In other words, we have many-to-many relationships between Customer and Associate, and between Supplier and Associate. Note that I could have made these relationships more specific, such as an Associate can manage many Customers, an Associate can interact with many Customers, an Associate can visit many Customers, and so on;

Table 9.6 Data Element List

CUSTOMER	SUPPLIER	ASSOCIATE
First name	Company name	First name
Last name	Contact first name	Last name
Address line	Contact last name	Address line
City	Address line	City
State	City	State
Zip code	State	Zip code
Phone number	Zip code	Phone number
Fax number	Phone number	Pager number
Tax identifier	Fax number	Social Security Number
First order date	Credit Rating	Email address
Dun & Bradstreet Number	First Purchase Order Date	Hire date
(DUNs)	Dun & Bradstreet Number (DUNs)	Clock number

however, we can demonstrate the Abstraction Safety Guide by keeping it at this simpler many-to-many relationship level.

I will not go through the Normalization Hike steps here because they were discussed in detail in Chapter 8, "The Normalization Hike and Denormalization Survival Guide." See Figure 9.3 for what this model looks like after applying the Normalization Hike, which culminates with the Fifth Normal Form model. Note that I took the liberty of creating surrogate, or meaningless, primary keys for each of the entities in this example.

2. Apply the Abstraction Safety Guide

We now need to ask the three questions of the Abstraction Safety Guide:

- Does this data element, entity, or relationship have something in common with one or more other data elements, entities, or relationships?
- If yes, are there concrete situations that would warrant an abstract structure?
- If yes, will the extra development effort now be substantially less than that in the future?

But where should we start? Because we have a fully normalized model with entities, relationships, and data elements, we can start at any of these three levels. Which one would be the best? I usually recommend starting with data elements for three reasons:

Data elements within each entity already have something in common. We know that on a normalized model all of the data elements within an entity have something in common with each other. That is, they are all fully dependent on the primary key of the entity. Therefore, it becomes more straightforward to find poten-

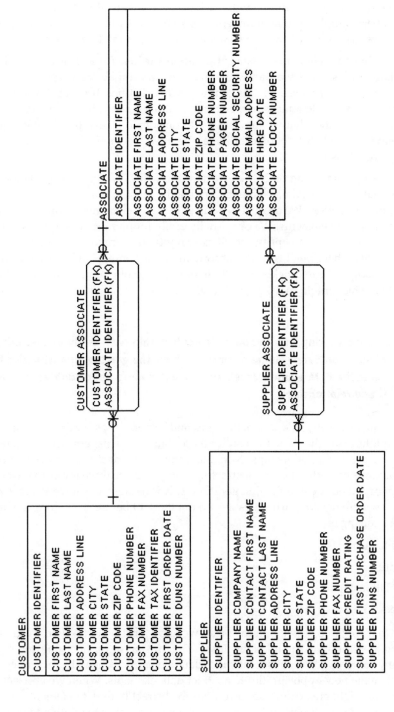

Figure 9.3 Fifth normal form model.

tial abstraction candidates. Two phone numbers within the same entity already have something in common with each other: They are already customer phone numbers, supplier phone numbers, and so on. Two phone numbers in different entities may or may not have something in common with each other.

Abstracting data elements creates other opportunities for abstracting entities and relationships. Once we start with data elements and abstract where appropriate, we can more easily see what is common across entities. If we abstracted several data elements into a measurement type abstract concept in two distinct entities, these two entities that we may not have considered abstracting before might now seem like good abstraction candidates, because they both share the measurement type relationship.

Abstracting data elements is the low-hanging fruit. Out of entities, relationships, and data elements, data elements provide the most opportunities for abstraction for the least effort. We are just looking at the data elements within each entity for common data elements. We can usually easily pinpoint several good abstraction candidates within an entity, which can provide us immediate benefits in terms of flexibility. Therefore, I consider abstracting data elements to be low-hanging fruit. For example, I can quickly identify two phone number data elements within an entity, which might make a good candidate for abstraction.

TIP

I recommend starting with the data elements within each entity in answering the three Abstraction Safety Guide questions. I have the greatest opportunities for abstraction at the data element level, and it creates more opportunities for abstracting entities and relationships.

After data elements, let's abstract entities and relationships. Entities are next because they might open the door to abstract more data elements, entities, or relationships. Then we abstract relationships. Note that after abstracting each of these, there might still be some opportunities for abstracting at any of these three levels that were not apparent or did not exist in the first iteration. This is because when we abstract we sometimes open up new opportunities we did not think of before. Therefore, the final order for abstracting is:

1. Data elements
2. Entities
3. Relationships
4. Back to number one

Note that we have iteration in the order we apply abstraction. When we are done applying abstraction to the relationships, we again start at number one and see if there are any more opportunities to abstract data elements. When abstracting entities, we might create new opportunities to abstract data elements. When we abstract relationships, we might create new opportunities to abstract both data elements and entities. If we do find new opportunities to abstract data elements, we might add an abstracted structure and then find more opportunities to abstract entities and relationships.

Let's start with the data elements and choose the entities in this order:

- Customer
- Supplier
- Associate

Note that there is no particular order for choosing the entities to start with when looking for data elements to abstract. We are looking at each entity individually and, therefore, are not concerned with the dependencies and relationships between the entities at this point.

Abstracting Data Elements

Let's start with the Customer data elements. If you refer back to Table 9.6, you will note that most of the data elements in the customer column seem to be profile information, such as contact and identifier data elements. Let's revisit the three questions for data elements and complete the same templates we used from the previous example:

Does this data element have something in common with one or more other data elements? I usually categorize the data elements within each entity into common concepts, such as phone, address, or name. You might want to highlight with different-colored markers each of these concepts within an entity. All of the phone data elements might be highlighted in yellow, the name data elements highlighted in blue, and so on.

If yes, are there concrete situations that would warrant an abstract structure? This is where you need to look into your crystal ball and determine if there is value in abstracting. A good way to do this is to speak with business experts identified on the In-the-Know Template for a subject area and ask them if flexibility is needed in this area. They may not relate to the word flexibility, so I have usually found the best way to ask them this question is to phrase it in business terminology, such as "You already have two types of phone numbers. Do you think you will ever have other types?" Thus, ask the business expert the question in business terms instead of in generic terms, such as flexibility. As mentioned previously, I like to reinforce the words "additional types" in my questions with the business user, supplemented by some actual examples, if possible.

If yes, will the extra development effort now be substantially less than that in the future? I usually always answer yes here, unless told otherwise. Remember that it is better to ask for forgiveness than permission, and we are data modelers who know from experience that it is always better to put the extra effort in now to save time and money 6 months from now, especially if there is value and need in abstracting.

So let's try to answer the first question by grouping the concepts that are similar. See Table 9.7 for how the data elements break down, using the table format we discussed previously.

We have identified four areas on abstraction to consider. Note that these are areas and that there could be more than one abstraction structure within each area. This answers

Table 9.7 Commonality on Customer Data Elements

SIMILAR CONCEPTS	REASONS THEY ARE SIMILAR
First name Last name	Both are names.
Address line City State Zip code	All of these data elements capture the address information for a customer.
Phone number Fax number	Both are phone numbers.
Tax identifier Dun & Bradstreet Number (DUNs)	Each is a different way of identifying the customer.

the first question on commonality. Now we need to consider the purpose of each of these. See Table 9.8.

Note how useful the business expert is in answering the business questions. She can be the judge in determining whether or not it is valuable to abstract. Make sure the business expert you ask these questions of is represented on the In-the-Know Template from Chapter 5, "Subject Area Analysis," as a very knowledgeable resource and a forward thinker in the area of your application.

Also please realize that we are not normalizing, we are abstracting. Note that we could have broken out address into its own table and supported multiple addresses for the same customer. However, this was not a requirement from the users. Our business rule when we completed the Normalization Hike was that we have only one address for a customer. If there could have been two or more addresses, this would have been already normalized into a separate entity. We are not normalizing here. We are looking to handle future types of address information. Thus, note the use of the word type under the value column in this table.

Note how many kudos you are getting for asking the right questions. You are doing preventive maintenance by asking these questions. Anyone from the business who is paying the bill for this application and hopes to reap the benefits should be very thankful that you are asking these questions to help increase flexibility in their application, and avoid future rework.

It looks as if both the phone and identifier concepts are worth pursuing in terms of abstracting. Let's look at the effort of each of these in Table 9.9.

Note how little effort most of these abstraction changes really require. This is the effort for all development. Optionally, you might want to compare the effort to abstract with the effort to make any types of changes after the application is in production. A comparison can also be useful if the effort to incorporate abstraction is relatively high, for example, 2 months as opposed to the 1 week mentioned in Table 9.9.

Also note we have ruled out the other concepts that were deemed not useful to abstract. Therefore, we will abstract these two concepts. Why waste the effort in deter-

Table 9.8 Value on Customer Data Elements

SIMILAR CONCEPTS	REASONS THEY ARE SIMILAR	VALUE IN ABSTRACTING
First name Last name	Both are names.	Would you want to store additional types of names for your customer, for example, a nickname or middle name? The business expert replies: "There is never a need to capture or report on any customer name except first name and last name."
Address line City State Zip code	All of these data elements capture the address information for a customer.	Would you ever need to represent additional types of address information, such a longitude and latitude? What about addresses outside of the United States? The business expert replies: "No. I do not believe we will ever have that need."
Phone number Fax number	Both are phone numbers.	Would you want to store additional types of phone numbers in the future? The business expert replies: "Yes, that's a great idea. As a matter of fact, I was going to ask you if there was a place for the customer's pager number. Thanks for suggesting this!"

Tax identifier
Dun &
  Bradstreet
  Number
  (DUNs)
	Each is a different way of identifying the customer.	Would you want to store additional types of identifiers for your customers?
		The business expert replies: "Another great suggestion! Yes, there are many times when we would like to store other industry standard identifiers for our customers. You know your stuff!"

Table 9.9 Effort on Customer Data Elements

SIMILAR CONCEPTS	REASONS THEY ARE SIMILAR	VALUE IN ABSTRACTING	EFFORT
Phone number Fax number	Both are phone numbers.	Would you want to store additional types of phone numbers in the future? The business expert replies: "Yes, that's a great idea. As a matter of fact, I was going to ask you if there was a place for the customer's pager number. Thanks for suggesting this!"	1 week

Tax identifier
Dun &
  Bradstreet
  Number
  (DUNS)
	Each is a different way of identifying the customer.	Would you want to store additional types of identifiers for your customers?
		The business expert replies: "Another great suggestion! Yes, there are many times when we would like to store other industry standard identifiers for our customers. You know your stuff!"
			1 week

mining how long it will take to design and develop an abstract concept that was not deemed valuable? See Figure 9.4 for this model updated with the abstracted Customer structure. Note the flexibility this gives us.

Note that Phone Number and Fax Number are now abstracted into the Customer Phone entity. To capture Eric's phone and fax numbers, we get Eric's Customer Identifier, which is 123, and then add two rows to the Customer Phone entity. The result would resemble Table 9.10.

The Customer Phone Sequence Number are in increment of one for each new phone number for the same customer. Thus, Eric's next phone number will have a sequence number equal to three. The Customer Phone Type could be a short code, such as 01, 02, and 03, or could be a short word, such as Phone or Fax. If we choose to use a short code, we might decide to have an additional meta data helper table to store the codes and descriptions around phone type. For example, 01 = Phone, 02 = Fax, 03 = Cell, and so on.

Let's say Customer 123 has many phone numbers. See Table 9.11 to see how flexible this structure really is in accommodating all of these different phone number types.

This structure can support many types of phone numbers. Note also that we might need to capture more information now that our structure is so flexible. We might want

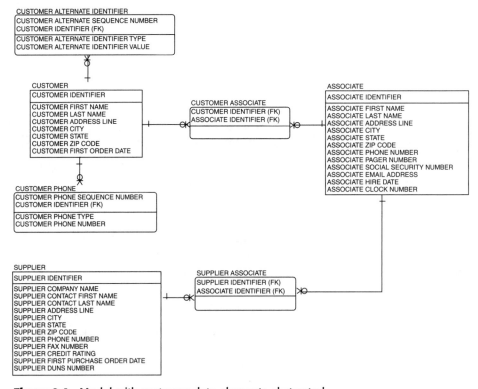

Figure 9.4 Model with customer data elements abstracted.

Table 9.10   Sample Customer Phone Entity Values

CUSTOMER IDENTIFIER	CUSTOMER PHONE SEQUENCE NUMBER	CUSTOMER PHONE TYPE	CUSTOMER PHONE NUMBER
123	1	Phone	555-555-1212
123	2	Fax	555-555-1212

to add a primary indicator, so we know which of Eric's home phone numbers is the one we should call him at first. We also might want to add an office–home indicator, so that we do not have to specify whether the phone type is work or home under the Customer Phone Type data element. I will not add these additional data elements here but be aware that extra codes or indicators might be needed when you abstract.

TIP

Be alert for extra data elements you might need to add when you are abstracting. Because of the flexibility we gain, we also sometimes need to add indicators or other descriptive data elements, for example, the office–home indicator in the Customer Phone entity just discussed.

Just as we abstracted phone number information, we can also abstract customer alternate identifiers. Alternate identifiers are ways of identifying the entity, other than the primary key. Alternate identifiers for the customer currently include tax number and DUNs number. As we learned by asking the value question mentioned previously, however there may be more alternate identifiers that we do not know about yet. Let's take a look at sample values for the Customer Alternate Identifier entity in Table 9.12.

Just as we observed with Phone number, we add an incredible amount of flexibility by using the abstract alternate identifier concept. A year from now we might have several additional types of identifiers. See Table 9.13 for sample values showing how flexible this structure really is.

Table 9.11   Sample Customer Phone Entity Values

CUSTOMER IDENTIFIER	CUSTOMER PHONE SEQUENCE NUMBER	CUSTOMER PHONE TYPE	CUSTOMER PHONE NUMBER
123	1	Work Phone	555-555-1212
123	2	Home Fax	555-555-2121
123	3	Pager	555-555-1234
123	4	Cell	555-555-2345
123	5	Home Phone	555-555-7890
123	6	Work Fax	555-555-4545
123	7	Home Phone	555-555-7788
123	8	Home Phone	555-555-3456

Table 9.12 Sample Customer Alternate Identifier Entity Values

CUSTOMER IDENTIFIER	CUSTOMER ALTERNATE SEQUENCE NUMBER	CUSTOMER ALTERNATE IDENTIFIER TYPE	CUSTOMER ALTERNATE IDENTIFIER VALUE
123	1	Tax	999-99-9999
123	2	DUNs	12345

We can represent any type of alternate identifier, including several of each of these if that is possible. Note that replacing the Customer Alternate Identifier Type data element with a Customer Alternate Identifier Type Code might be the best option here. This is because many of these values seem rather long, for example "Customer's identifier for themselves," and if any of these descriptions ever change we would need to update the description in every row in which it appears. Using the type code provides a buffer layer against these types of changes. For example, "01 = Customer's identifier for themselves." The alternate identifier concept will be discussed as one of the abstraction components subsequently in this chapter, because it comes up so often.

Let's now look at the Supplier data elements from Table 9.6. Breaking them up into groups of similar concepts is shown in Table 9.14.

Note that all three of these are identical to the ones from customer. The more you abstract, the more you recognize common types of abstraction. Even though there are three names instead of two, it is still the same abstract concept. I will discuss the most common pieces of abstraction under the Abstraction Components section subsequently in this chapter. Also note that we only had one identifier, the DUNs number. Therefore, there were no other data elements in Supplier that were common with this one and we did not need to mention it on this commonality spreadsheet.

Now let's look at the value in abstracting these concepts. See Table 9.15. Observe the "nice to have" comment. Every once in a while you will have identified data elements

Table 9.13 Sample Customer Alternate Identifier Entity Values

CUSTOMER IDENTIFIER	CUSTOMER ALTERNATE SEQUENCE NUMBER	CUSTOMER ALTERNATE IDENTIFIER TYPE	CUSTOMER ALTERNATE IDENTIFIER VALUE
123	1	Tax	999-99-9999
123	2	DUNs	12345
123	3	Social Security Number	999-99-9999
123	4	System XYZ	abc
123	5	Customer's identifier for themselves	widg
123	6	International ID	457423

Table 9.14 Commonality on Supplier Data Elements

SIMILAR CONCEPTS	REASONS THEY ARE SIMILAR
Company name Contact first name Contact last name	All are names.
Address line City State Zip code	All these data elements capture the address information for a supplier.
Phone number Fax number	Both are phone numbers.

that have something in common, and the flexibility this abstraction provides will never be used or will not used for a very long time. The name data elements from Supplier fit into this category. It appears that the business expert is interested in this abstraction only if it requires no extra effort. We will have to wait until the effort discussion to make our decision here. When I get the "nice to have" comment, I tend to lean toward not abstracting, even if the development effort is small. This is because we always lose business terms on the model when we abstract, and I would not want to give up the business understanding if there were no value for the flexibility in the short term.

Table 9.15 Value on Supplier Data Elements

SIMILAR CONCEPTS	REASONS THEY ARE SIMILAR	VALUE IN ABSTRACTING
Company name Contact first name Contact last name	All are names.	Would you want to store additional types of names for your supplier, for example, a nickname or middle name for the contact, or a different company name? The business expert replies: "We might have this need some time next year. I'm not sure, though. I might be interested in this if I can get it with little effort."
Address line City State Zip code	All of these data elements capture the address information for a supplier.	Would you ever need to represent additional types of address information, such as longitude and latitude? The business expert replies: "No."
Phone number Fax number	Both are phone numbers.	Would you want to store additional types of phone numbers in the future? The business expert replies: "Yes, just like with customer, we might need to store the supplier's cell phone number. There might be a few more types as well."

Let's look at the effort for these in Table 9.16.

Note that the name abstracting concept will take 2 weeks of effort. This might be too much effort to invest in a concept that may never provide any benefit, or if it does provide benefit, it will not be for at least a year. Therefore, talk to the business expert; however, I believe we should not abstract this concept, because of the loss of business understanding I mentioned earlier.

It is interesting that abstracting phone number for supplier will take only 3 days instead of the 1 week required to abstract the phone number for customer. This is because we have already invested the time to abstract phone number within our customer area. It is hoped that we would be able to reuse meta data and development from customer phone number for supplier. This should shorten the length of time to complete.

Our model updated with these changes appears in Figure 9.5.

Note that we gain the same flexibility with Supplier Phone as we have seen with Customer Phone in Table 9.9.

Moving on to Associate, we see several different data elements but similar abstract concepts as we saw in Customer. See Table 9.17 for the commonality among these data elements.

We have identified four areas on abstraction to consider. This answers the first question. Observe that the email address is grouped with the phone numbers. In looking for common concepts, we realize that both email address and phone numbers are ways of contacting associates. Therefore, this is a more encompassing and complete concept than just having phone information grouped together and leaving off the

Table 9.16 Effort On Supplier Data Elements

SIMILAR CONCEPTS	REASONS THEY ARE SIMILAR	VALUE IN ABSTRACTING	EFFORT
Company name Contact first name Contact last name	All are names.	Would you want to store additional types of names for your supplier, for example, a nickname or middle name for the contact, or a different company name? The business expert replies: "We might have this need some time next year. I'm not sure, though. I might be interested in this if I can get it with little effort."	2 weeks
Phone number Fax number	Both are phone numbers.	Would you want to store additional types of phone numbers in the future? The business expert replies: "Yes, just like with customer, we might need to store the supplier's cell phone number. There might be a few more types as well."	3 days

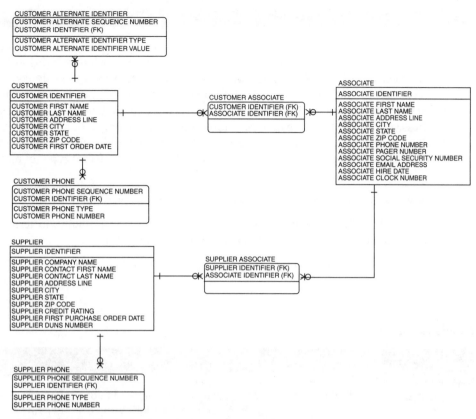

Figure 9.5 Model with supplier data elements abstracted.

Table 9.17 Commonality on Associate Data Elements

SIMILAR CONCEPTS	REASONS THEY ARE SIMILAR
First name Last name	Both are names.
Address line City State Zip Code	All of these data elements capture the address information for an associate.
Phone number Pager number Email address	All are ways to communicate with an associate.
Social Security Number Clock number	Each is a different way of identifying the associate. For example, a clock number is a unique identifier assigned to each associate who needs to punch in for their start time and punch out for their end time every day using a time clock.

email address. This gives us flexibility to represent any way of communicating with the associate, and not just by phone. In the environment of ever-changing technology in which we live, abstracting for ways to communicate with somebody could prove very useful in the short term, because there is no doubt that new ways of communicating will come along. If the business expert felt we could have different types of addresses, we would add the address information with the phone number and email address, with the hope of abstracting all of these including the address. However, the business expert believed firmly that we would not need different types of addresses, so address will not be included as part of this abstraction.

Now we need to consider the purpose of each of these. See Table 9.18.

It looks like the phone and identifier concepts are worth pursuing in terms of abstracting. Let's look at the effort of each of these in Table 9.19.

Our model updated with these two changes appears in Figure 9.6.

Table 9.18 Value on Associate Data Elements

SIMILAR	REASONS THEY ARE SIMILAR	VALUE IN ABSTRACTING
First name Last name	Both are names.	Would you want to store additional types of names for your associate, for example, a nickname or middle name? The business expert replies: "There is never a need to capture or report on any associate name except first name and last name."
Address line City State Zip code	All of these data elements capture the address information for an associate.	Would you ever need to represent additional types of address information, such a longitude and latitude? What about addresses outside of the United States? The business expert replies: "No."
Phone number Pager number Email address	All are ways to communicate with an associate.	Would you want to store additional types of communication mechanisms in the future? The business expert replies: "Yes, that's a great idea. I would not have considered grouping the email address in with the phone number, but you are right. It makes sense. They are all ways of communicating with our associates. I believe we will have other ways in the future."
Social Security Number Employee internal identifier	Each is a different way of identifying the associate	Would you want to store additional types of identifiers for your associates? The business expert replies: "Another great suggestion! Yes, there are many times when we would like to store other industry standard identifiers for our associates."

Table 9.19   Effort On Associate Data Elements

SIMILAR	REASONS THEY ARE SIMILAR	VALUE IN ABSTRACTING	EFFORT
Phone number Pager number Email address	All are ways to communicate with an associate.	Would you want to store additional types of communication mechanisms in the future? The business expert replies: "Yes, that's a great idea. I would not have considered grouping the email address in with the phone number, but you are right. It makes sense. They are all ways of communicating with our associates. I believe we will have other ways in the future."	1 week
Social Security Number Clock number	Each is a different way of identifying the associate.	Would you want to store additional types of identifiers for your associates? The business expert replies: "Another great suggestion! Yes, there are many times when we would like to store other industry standard identifiers for our associates."	1 week

Let's look at some sample values from the Associate Communication Medium entity to highlight its flexibility (see Table 9.20). Widgets 9000 might be a new technology for communication coming out shortly. We have now finished reviewing each of the data elements. Now let's move on to the entities.

Abstracting Entities

Now let's look a little closer at our three entities: Customer, Supplier, and Associate. Do they have anything in common? Let's fill in a similar set of templates at the entity level. Let's start with the first question and see if there is anything common across these entities. See Table 9.21.

Note that these all represent the Who. We will learn more about the Who concept under entities. They all are people or organizations that are important to the business. Also be aware that the data elements helped open the door for entity abstraction opportunities. Because we know that these entities share certain contact and identifier relationships from abstracting the data elements, we can more easily see what these three entities have in common.

Let's look at the value template in Table 9.22. There are two questions that we asked the business expert to determine if abstraction is worthwhile in this situation. The first question follows the same general format as our previous questions. In other words, are there additional types of this concept that might come up in the future? The second question is only specific when we are abstracting entities using the subtype concept. If a customer can also be a supplier, or a supplier can also be a customer, the

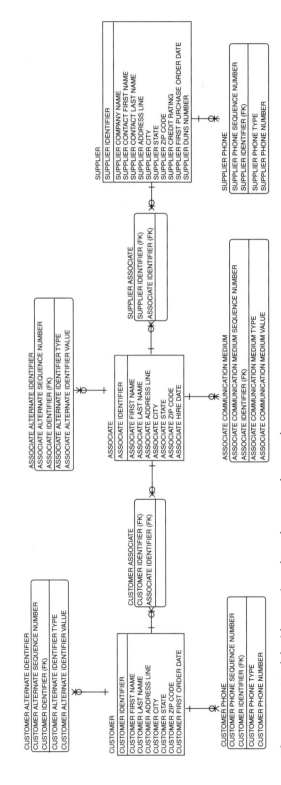

Figure 9.6 Model with associate data elements abstracted.

Table 9.20   Sample Associate Communication Medium Entity

ASSOCIATE IDENTIFIER	ASSOCIATE COMMUNICATION MEDIUM SEQUENCE NUMBER	ASSOCIATE COMMUNICATION MEDIUM TYPE	ASSOCIATE COMMUNICATION MEDIUM VALUE
789	1	Work Phone	555-555-1212
789	2	Fax	555-555-2121
789	3	Pager	555-555-1234
789	4	Cell	555-555-2345
789	5	Work email address	Bobemail@workemail.com
789	6	Home email address	Bobemail@homeemail.com
789	7	Widgets 9000	abcde

concept of overlapping subtypes could be very relevant and make us lean toward using abstraction to reduce redundancy.

Let's look at the effort template in Table 9.23.

Abstracting these three entities appears to add a considerable amount to the development. We need to decide if this is worth the effort. Abstracting entities that have a lot in common (not just data elements but also business rules) gives us a substantial amount of flexibility. Even if the effort were slightly more than other types of abstraction, it might be worth it to abstract these structures.

Let's assume that it is worth the effort to abstract these entities. Our model updated with this change appears in Figure 9.7.

Note that the Party supertype now has all of the common data elements from each of the Customer, Supplier, and Associate subtypes. Instead of repeating these name and address data elements three times, we now have them only once in the Party entity. If another subtype comes along, for example, a Regulatory Company, we already have the name and address data elements in place and ready to be used. Abstracting these entities up to the Party level sets the stage for abstracting the relationships, which we will do in the next step. Note also that we did not lose the business concepts of Customer, Associate, and Supplier. They all still exist in Figure 9.7, with any common data elements or relationships moved up to the Party level.

Table 9.21   Commonality on Entities

SIMILAR CONCEPTS	REASONS THEY ARE SIMILAR
Customer Supplier Associate	They are all something of importance to the business. They all contain contact and identifier information.

Table 9.22 Value on Entities

SIMILAR CONCEPTS	REASONS THEY ARE SIMILAR	VALUE IN ABSTRACTING
Customer Supplier Associate	They are all something of importance to the business. They all contain contact and identifier information.	Would you want to represent different types of concepts other than Customer, Supplier, and Associate? Would you ever have the same organization or person play more than one role? The business expert replies: "I believe we might have several new types shortly. I would eventually like to include our regulatory body and several of our competitors within this application."

Abstracting Relationships

After abstracting data elements and entities, we now turn our attention to the relationships. Refer to Table 9.24 for the answer to the commonality question for the relationships.

Note how easy it is to identify these relationships as common. We have already abstracted the entities into the Party concept, and therefore, we know that these relationships are nothing more than relationships between additional types of parties.

How valuable is abstracting these relationships? See Table 9.25.

The question really is not directed only at only Supplier, Associate, and Customer, but also at any of the new subtypes that we might add under Party. Therefore, abstracting the relationships could be even more valuable than the question phrased under Value. For example, the new concept of Regulatory Body would be able to take advantage of all of the common structures we have abstracted to date. Note the advantages of abstracting the communication medium and alternate identifier concepts. We gain additional flexibility, including the ability to capture email addresses and unlimited numbers of alternate identifier values and types for all subtypes.

Table 9.23 Effort On Entities

SIMILAR CONCEPTS	REASONS THEY ARE SIMILAR	VALUE IN ABSTRACTING	EFFORT
Customer Supplier Associate	They are all something of importance to the business. They all contain contact and identifier information.	Would you want to represent different types of concepts other than Customer, Supplier, and Associate? Would you ever have the same organization or person play more than one role? The business expert replies: "I believe we might have several new types shortly. I would eventually like to include our regulatory body and several of our competitors within this application."	3 weeks

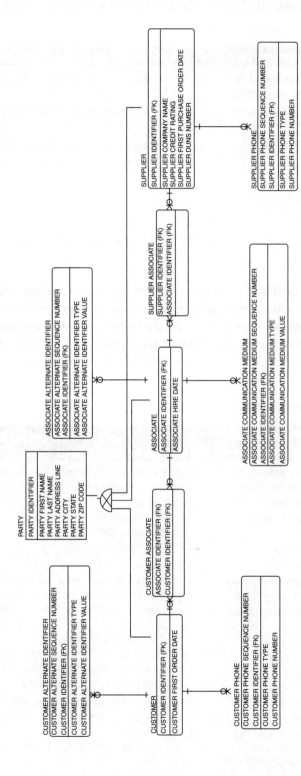

Figure 9.7 Model with entities abstracted.

Table 9.24 Commonality on Relationships

SIMILAR CONCEPTS	REASONS THEY ARE SIMILAR
Supplier-to-associate relationship Customer-to-associate relationship	They are all relationships between parties.
Phone and communication Media relationships	They all handle ways to communicate with parties.
Alternate identifier relationships	They are all abstract alternate identifier concepts for parties.

Refer to the effort template in Table 9.26.

Figure 9.8 shows our model updated with these relationship abstract changes.

NOTE

■■■■■ **Abstracting a combination of data elements, entities, and relationships increases the power of abstraction exponentially. For example, abstracting email address up to the party concept instead of to just the customer level dramatically increases the power of abstraction, because we now can represent any number of email addresses or other modes of communication for any of the subtypes of Party.**

Table 9.25 Value on Relationships

SIMILAR CONCEPTS	REASONS THEY ARE SIMILAR	VALUE IN ABSTRACTING
Supplier-to-associate relationship Customer-to-associate relationship	They are all relationships between parties.	Would you want to represent additional types of relationships other than the existing ones? The business expert replies: "We possibly would want to have relationships between associates, and maybe a few others if you give me some time to think about it."
Phone and communication media relationships	They all handle ways to communicate with parties.	Would you want to have email addresses for Customers and Suppliers? Are there other modes of communication we would want to represent for Customers, Suppliers, and Associates that we do not capture today? The business expert replies: "It would be nice to have the option to store email addresses for suppliers and customers. There also might be other modes that I did not think of that we might have in the near future."
Alternate identifier relationships	They are all abstract alternate identifier concepts for parties.	Do you want to store more than one type of identifier for a supplier, that is, in addition to the DUNs number? The business expert replies: "I believe we might need to shortly."

Table 9.26 Effort On Relationships

SIMILAR CONCEPTS	REASONS THEY ARE SIMILAR	VALUE IN ABSTRACTING	EFFORT
Supplier-to-associate relationship Customer-to-associate relationship	They are all relationships between parties.	Would you want to represent additional types of relationships other than the existing ones? The business expert replies: "We possibly would want to have relationships between associates, and maybe a few others if you give me some time to think about it."	1 week
Phone and communication media relationships	They all handle ways to communicate with parties.	Would you want to have email addresses for Customers and Suppliers? Are there other modes of communication we would want to represent for Customers, Suppliers, and Associates that we do not capture today? The business expert replies: "It would be nice to have the option to store email addresses for suppliers and customers. There also might be other modes that I did not think of that we might have in the near future."	1 week
Alternate identifier relationships	They are all abstract alternate identifier concepts for parties.	Do you want to store more than one type of identifier for a supplier, that is, in addition to the DUNs number? The business expert relies: "I believe we might need to shortly."	1 week

Go Back to Number One

This is the step where we iterate back to Step 1, looking for additional data elements to abstract. This iteration makes sure we do not miss any opportunities for abstraction that might have appeared after abstracting other data elements, entities, or relationships. Can you find any other opportunities on Figure 9.8? Let's assume Figure 9.8 is our completed abstracted logical data model.

3. Document in Detail

What's a Communication Medium Type anyway? You might know what this term means because you modeled it today and it is fresh in your mind. But what will happen a month from now when you look at this term? How will users react when they see this term for the first time? That is why definitions are even more important for abstract concepts. When you abstract, the rows tell the meaning instead of the columns. It becomes very important to document well. Always apply the rigor of the Definition Checklist described in Chapter 3, "Ensuring High-Quality Definitions."

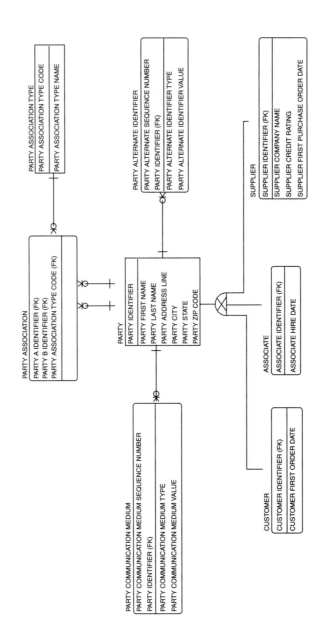

Figure 9.8 Model with relationships abstracted.

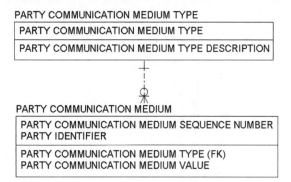

Figure 9.9 Meta data helper table for communication medium.

We mentioned the concept of meta data helper tables previously in this chapter. These tables can capture not only additional business rules that abstraction tends to remove but also some of the definitions and names that abstraction can remove. For example, Party Communication Medium Type would contain the description for each of the type values. Having it stored this way can also make it easier for the report user to access the meta data. See Figure 9.9 for an optional meta data helper table for Party Communication Medium.

The Party Communication Medium Type table provides the codes and values for each communication medium. Table 9.27 shows some of these sample values. Note that we now have the names for each code stored within the database. These names can be used whenever users want to know the meaning of one of the codes. We can also add the definition and other types of meta data to clarify this abstraction concept.

4.   Apply the Denormalization Survival Guide

The abstract logical data model we have just completed is for a reporting application. Therefore, we will probably need to introduce some amount of denormalization. We can apply the rules in the Denormalization Survival Guide to the logical abstract model to arrive at the physical data model in Figure 9.10.

Table 9.27 Sample Party Communication Medium Type Values

PARTY COMMUNICATION MEDIUM TYPE	PARTY COMMUNICATION MEDIUM TYPE DESCRIPTION
01	Work Phone
02	Fax
03	Pager
04	Cell
05	Work email address
06	Home email address

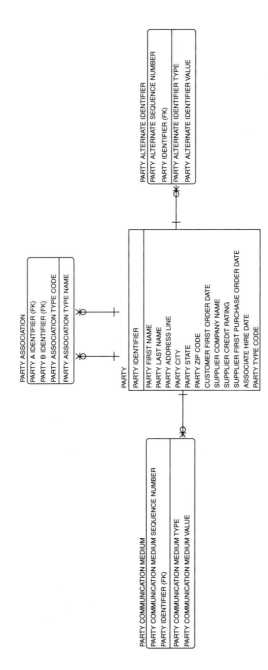

Figure 9.10 Finished abstracted physical data model.

Note that subtypes usually get denormalized into the supertype when creating a physical data model for a reporting application. Following the guidelines on the Survival Guide will ensure you will make the right decision about converting logical subtypes into physical structures.

Also be aware that the Party Type Code data element has been introduced to distinguish between each of the types of subtypes on the model. For example, a type of 1 could be customer, 2 could be associate, and 3 could be supplier. This type code could be a very efficient way to enforce only particular values for a Party. For example, if we want to allow just 1, 2, and 3 as values for customer, associate, and supplier, respectively, we could prohibit any other types of Parties from being added. However, because we want flexibility for additional types of Parties, we may not want to enforce this restriction.

I am always impressed with how simple the model appears. If we waited to abstract until we were done with the physical data model, our model would look very different. It would be substantially more complex, and we would not be able to easily identify areas for abstraction.

What Are the Abstraction Components?

Abstraction Components are small abstract model pieces that can be used over and over again in many modeling situations, independent of industry or organization or even subject area. After using abstraction a number of times during the data modeling phase, you will start to see trends in the abstraction constructs that appear. Answering the questions from the Abstraction Safety Guide will lead to the creation of these common abstract patterns containing data elements, entities, and relationships. Once you are aware of these Abstraction Components, you can follow the Safety Guide and use them frequently in your designs. These Abstraction Components have several goals:

Create designs faster. By knowing that these Abstraction Components exist and when to use them, you can simply apply the Safety Guide and replace business structures with them on your model. For example, there is an abstraction component concept for alternate identifiers, which we discussed in our detailed example for the Abstraction Safety Guide. As soon as you apply the Abstraction Safety Guide and identify several alternate identifiers in your logical data model, you can use the alternate identifier abstract structure in your design. This can drastically decrease modeling time because you do no have to create new abstract structures. Note that you also can reuse definitions and other types of meta data from these components. For example, once you define the Alternate Identifier entity, you should be able to reuse the definition of this entity wherever Alternate Identifier is reused.

Speed up development. If you continually reuse the same designs, there is a very good chance that you also will be able to reuse other parts of the software lifecycle. You potentially will be able to reuse some of the code and reporting and mapping and population logic. For example, if you have programming code to populate the alternate identifier structures for customer, you can probably reuse a large portion of this code to populate the alternate identifier structures for supplier.

Improve consistency across data models. By using the same abstraction components over and over again you increase the consistency across your models. This leads to greater understanding and integration between your applications. For example, if the alternate identifier abstract concept is structured the same in three different models, someone very familiar with only one of the models would be able to understand this concept in all three models. This helps reduce the loss of business meaning that abstraction can introduce. After the alternate identifier concept is explained to someone once, he or she will understand alternate identifier everywhere it appears.

Offer generic but useful structures. These components are at a high enough level where they can be used by all industries and all companies within these industries. Both an insurance and a manufacturing company should be able to take advantage of the alternate identifier structure. However, these components are not abstract to the level of being meaningless. For example, if I wanted to make Thing an abstraction component, I would be able to use it everywhere but it will not be really useful anywhere, because it is too vague.

There are a number of very useful Abstraction Components that I have used in my designs. We can discuss them in the context of whether they are components at the entity, relationship, or data element levels.

Using Entity Abstraction Components

There are only six Abstraction Components I have used at the entity level, and they are abstract concepts all of us have been taught while in grade school. They are the basic questions of any person, place, idea, or thing in our environment and surroundings. We might call these questions more sophisticated names on our data models, but at the core of each of these sophisticated names exist six simple questions that translate into these six entity abstraction components:

- Who?
- What?
- When?
- Where?
- Why?
- How?

In the sections that follow, we will define each one of these and go through an example.

Who?

Who are the people and companies that interest us? A sample of a Who subtyping structure is shown in Figure 9.11. These subtypes are listed to help you answer the commonality question in the Abstraction Safety Guide. If you have two or more of these similar

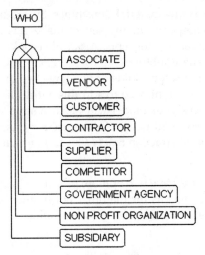

Figure 9.11 Sample Who component.

entities on your model, you might need to add this entity abstraction component. If your business expert believes your model will need to support additional types of Who in the near future, you will have a future use for this abstract structure and should document this in the Abstraction Safety Guide Template for the second question: the value question. Note that, in some cases, there could be multiple levels of subtyping. For example, instead of going directly from Who to Customer, Vendor, Associate, and so on, we could have first subtyped from Who down to Person and Organization, and then Person down to Customer, Associate, and so on. If you choose to do this, however, be aware that, in some cases, the subtypes will be overlapping and thus will be both people and organizations. As long as you document this overlapping situation, your multilevel subtyping structure will be correct and accurate.

This Who concept is limited to situations that have two or more people or organization entities on the same model. Note that Who, just as for the other entity questions, is never automatically applied to a model. We first need to complete the Abstraction Safety Guide on each of these.

I have seen Who called many different names over the years:

- Party
- Involved Party
- Business Party
- Person
- Organization

What?

What are the products and services that interest us? Note that we did not ask, "What are the products and services that we sell?" This is because the What includes everything that is product- and service-related, such as raw materials, machines, by-products, interim products, and end products that a company can buy, sell, or make. It is very encompassing, as are all of these entity abstraction concepts. A sample of a What subtyping structure is shown in Figure 9.12. These subtypes are listed to help you answer the commonality question in the Abstraction Safety Guide. If you have two or more of these or similar entities on your model, you might need to add this entity abstraction component. If your business expert believes your model will need to support additional types of What in the near future, you will have a future use for this abstract structure and should document this in the Abstraction Safety Guide Template for the second question: the value question.

This What concept is limited to situations that have two or more product or service entities on the same model. Note that What, just as for the other entity questions, are never applied to a model before completing the Abstraction Safety Guide.

I've seen What called a number of names:

- Product
- Service
- Item
- Component
- Offering

When?

When do we do business? A sample of a When subtyping structure is shown in Figure 9.13. These subtypes are listed to help you answer the commonality question in the Abstraction Safety Guide. If you have two or more of these or similar entities on your model, you might need to add this entity abstraction component. If your business expert believes your model will need to support additional types of When in the near fu-

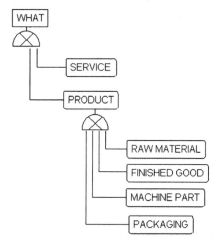

Figure 9.12 Sample What component.

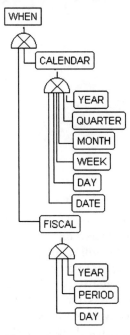

Figure 9.13 Sample When component.

ture, you will have a future use for this abstract structure and should document this in the Abstraction Safety Guide Template for the second question: the value question. Note that in some cases, there could be multiple levels of subtyping. For example, instead of going directly from When to Month, Day, Year, we could have first gone down to Calendar or Fiscal, and then broken down each of these into further subtypes. The When includes the times and dates for anything that happens within our business, including ship dates, insurance claim dates, months used to report on profitability, and so on.

This When concept is limited to situations that have two or more time-related entities on the same model. Note that When, just as for the other entity questions, is never automatically applied to a model. We first need to complete the Abstraction Safety Guide on each of these.

I've seen When called a number of names:

- Time
- Time Period
- Date

Where?

Where are the locations for the places that interest us? A sample of a Where subtyping structure is shown in Figure 9.14. These subtypes are listed to help you answer the

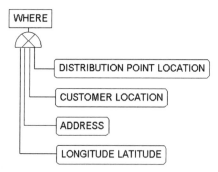

Figure 9.14 Sample Where component.

commonality question in the Abstraction Safety Guide. If you have two or more of these or similar entities on your model, you might need to add this entity abstraction component. If your business expert believes your model will need to support additional types of Where in the near future, you will have a future use for this abstract structure and should document this in the Abstraction Safety Guide Template for the second question: the value question. Note that, in some cases, there could be multiple levels of subtyping. For example, instead of going directly from Where to an address, we could have first gone down to the type of address, such as Longitude/Latitude or street address, and then to each of these subtypes.

This Where concept is limited to situations that have two or more location concepts on the same model. Note that Where, just as for the other entity questions, is never automatically applied to a model. We first need to complete the Abstraction Safety Guide on each of these.

I've seen Where called a number of names:

- Location
- Address
- Site

Why?

Why do we stay in business? A sample of a Why subtyping structure is shown in Figure 9.15. These subtypes are listed to help you answer the commonality question in the Abstraction Safety Guide. If you have two or more of these or similar entities on your model, you might need to add this entity abstraction component. If your business expert believes your model will need to support additional types of Why in the near future, you will have a future use for this abstract structure and should document this in the Abstraction Safety Guide Template for the second question: the value question. The Why includes all of the events that happen within our organization. Look at the model in the figure for some examples.

This Why concept is limited to situations that have two or more event or transaction concepts on the same model. Note that Why, just as for the other entity questions, is

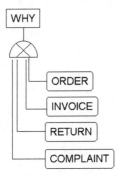

Figure 9.15   Sample Why component.

never automatically applied to a model. We first need to complete the Abstraction Safety Guide on each of these.

I've seen Why called a number of names:

- Transaction
- Event
- Happening
- Occurrence

How?

How do we receive and record the events that keep us in business? A sample of a How subtyping structure is shown in Figure 9.16. These subtypes are listed to help you answer the commonality question in the Abstraction Safety Guide. If you have two or more of these or similar entities on your model, you might need to add this entity abstraction component. If your business expert believes your model will need to support additional types of How in the near future, you will have a future use for this abstract structure and should document this in the Abstraction Safety Guide Template for the second question: the value question. The How includes the medium and documents and contracts that record the transactions in our business.

This How concept is limited to situations that have two or more documents and contracts concepts on the same model. Note that How, just as for the other entity questions, is never automatically applied to a model. We first need to complete the Abstraction Safety Guide on each of these.

I've seen How called a number of names:

- Document
- Agreement
- Contract

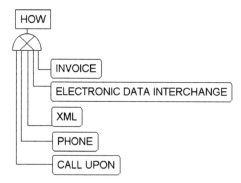

Figure 9.16 Sample How component.

Using Relationship Abstraction Components

In this section we discuss a number of the common types of relationships we can have between entities. You will find that the more you abstract entities, the more you will be able to abstract their relationships. The three most common types of abstract relationships I have found include:

- Association
- Classification
- Alternate identifier

Let's explain each of these and provide examples.

Association Abstraction Component

This abstraction component is extremely powerful. It lets you represent any relationship between any two entities. See Figure 9.17 for the association component. I used the Thing entity; however, you can substitute any entity name for Thing, such as Party, Customer, or Employee. Substituting Employee would allow us to represent the additional types of relationships between any two employees, for example, a management relationship, a functional counterpart relationship, a team relationship, and so on.

In the association entity you should label one key A and one B. We do this because we have no idea whether the relationship between two Things is going to be a parent and child relationship or a peer relationship. For example, an employee management relationship would be a parent and child relationship, where Bob reports to Mary. However, a peer relationship would capture that Bob and Mary are on the same team, and therefore, which should be the parent? By adding the A or B to the foreign key, we try not to assume the type of relationship that exists between the two entities.

I often use meta data helper tables to support validation. We could have added several extra entities to support validation, only allowing certain types of relationships.

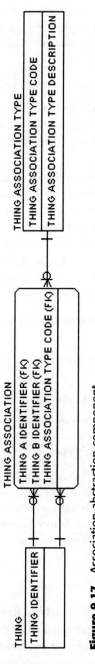

Figure 9.17 Association abstraction component.

For example, refer to Figure 9.17. We can ensure that only the types of relationships listed in the Employee Type entity have relationships between them. Only those types will be allowed. Thus, a management relationship might only allow relationships between managers and people who are not managers, for example. This can help replace the integrity and constraints that we lost when going to this more abstract structure.

I have used this association concept in several areas:

Location. It captures the relationship between any two locations. Thus, I can show the relationship between a warehouse and a retail store location. I could also show the relationship between manufacturing plant and the warehouse locations to which products are shipped.

Sales Organization. It can represent the relationships between any two people within the sales area, for example, the "works for" relationship. It can also represent the relationships between people and their positions. For example, Mitch is both National Sales Manager and President of the Northeast Division. This would be two separate rows or records in the association table.

Time. It captures the relationship between the different time intervals. For example, a Year contains Months would be one type of relationship and a Month contains Days might be another type of relationship.

When would you use this association component? It works best when these conditions are met:

- You have already abstracted entities into supertypes, such as Party, Person, Organization, and so on, and

- You have lots of relationships between the subtypes, and

- You believe there will be more relationships in the future. More relationships can come from existing subtypes or when you add new subtypes and thus have new relationships to these new subtypes.

In the example we discussed previously in this chapter, we had a Party supertype with the Customer, Employee, and Supplier subtypes. There were several relationships between these subtypes; after applying the Abstraction Safety Guide, we realized there could be more relationships in the future. Therefore, to save redundancy and clutter on the model, and to be able to handle additional types of relationships in the future, we added the association component.

NOTE

New subtypes can mean new relationships. Even if there are only a few subtypes, and you believe that you have captured all of the relationships between the subtypes, by creating a supertype concept you are adding the flexibility to have more subtypes in the future. This being said, we can expect to have more relationships between the subtypes in the future. For example, if I add the Competitor entity as another Party to our existing Customer, Employee, and Supplier entities, I might also

want to add new relationships. I might want to add a relationship between Competitor and Supplier, for example. Because I have built in the flexibility to handle new subtypes, it would also be very useful to build in the flexibility to handle new relationships between these subtypes.

Association also works well when you need to build flexibility into your business rules. For example, you know within the next month or so you might want to add several new types of relationships between Employee and Customer. You can do so seamlessly with the association concept, without worrying about impacting the database and application with new relationships and constraints.

Classification Abstraction Component

The classification abstraction component is very effective whenever you need to group things into categories. For example, I have seen classification used extensively within the product subject area. It gives me the flexibility to classify products by brand, size, ingredients, and so on. See Figure 9.18 for the classification component.

A Thing can belong to multiple classifications. In many cases when we are classifying entities, we need to allow for entities to belong to multiple classifications. For example, a Product might belong to both the Brand and Size classifications.

Note that there are even less meaningful business-related structures on the model. In the association concept we were replacing relationships. Here we are replacing relationships and the reference code entities, such as Brand Code and Size Code. Therefore, we are losing even more business readability on the model.

I have used this classification concept in several areas:

Product. As mentioned, to capture brand, package type, size, and so on, for each product.

Customer. Classification can group customers by size (small, medium, large), status (existing, inactive, potential), and type of business (retail, distributor, exporter).

When would you use this classification component?

- When your entities have groupings or categories you need to represent. That is, the commonality question from the Abstraction Safety Guide.

- When there are potentially more categories coming shortly that you cannot predict. That is, the value question from the Abstraction Safety Guide.

NOTE

Note the difference between association and classification. Association relates any two entity values. For example, Bob works for Mary. Classification groups these values together and does not relate them directly. For example, Mary belongs to the management classification.

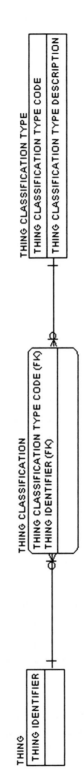

Figure 9.18 Classification abstraction component.

Alternate Identifier Abstraction Component

The alternate identifier component is very useful whenever there is more than one way of uniquely referring to an entity. Usually all identifiers that relate to the external environment of the company are prime candidates for alternate identifiers. We have seen this concept earlier in this chapter where Employee had two unique identifiers, a Social Security Number and a Clock Number. See Figure 9.19 for this component.

Note that a Thing can have many alternate identifiers. There are usually several different ways to refer to a Thing, so we need to design in this flexibility.

I have used this alternate identifier concept in several areas:

Product. There are many industry- and company-specific identifiers for a product.

Person. Any type of person, such as an Employee, Customer, and so on, will have at least two alternate identifiers.

Organization. Any company will usually have a number of alternate identifiers assigned by government, industry standards, your company, or any other outside and external organization.

When would you use this alternate identifier component?

- When there is currently more than one way to refer to an entity, that is, the commonality question from the Abstraction Safety Guide.

- When there are potentially more ways to refer to entities that you believe are coming shortly and that you cannot predict, that is, the value question from the Abstraction Safety Guide.

Using Data Element
Abstraction Components

In this section we discuss abstracting data elements to the level of a class word. We begin with a definition and explanation of a class word and then discuss each of the data element Abstraction Components.

What Is a Class Word?

The data element class is the domain category to which a data element belongs, for example, name, code, date, and so on. The data element class word is a single word describing this class or category. The class word appears as the last word on the data element name. It is a single word that is usually the most critical component of the data element name. Of all the thousands of data elements in our companies, they will all fit into roughly a dozen different class word categories. For example, all of the following data elements belong to the Name class word:

- Customer Last Name
- Associate First Name

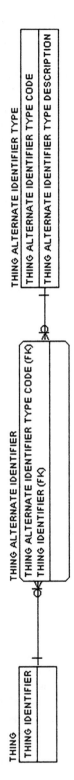

Figure 9.19 Alternate identifier abstraction component.

- Company Name
- Product Abbreviated Name
- City Name
- User Password Name

There are many benefits to using class words. They do the following:

Make normalization easier. By enforcing that every data element must end with a valid class word, we minimize the chances that there will be more than one piece of information within the same data element. For example, Gross Sales as a data element name might contain both the Gross Sales Amount and the Gross Sales Weight. There is nothing about the name that limits it to only a single value. Gross Sales Amount, where Amount is the class word, helps minimize having multiple values within this data element. However, using class words does not eliminate the situation where we can have multiple values within the same data element. For example, Customer Name ends in the class word Name but we might have both first and last names stored within this data element. Therefore, the class word does not prevent multivalues in the same data element but does reduce the occurrence of multivalues.

Improve naming consistency. By agreeing to end each data element name with a valid class word, we are increasing the consistency between application models and increasing consistency with the enterprise model, if one exists. Thus, class words should be a part of any data element naming strategy. Someone familiar with a naming strategy can quickly understand models by recognizing data element names or the components of data element names, such as the class words.

Allow for the assignment of common format, length, and other meta data. The class word Name can have a certain definition, format, length, and perhaps several other characteristics. This can save time in defining common characteristics for each data element. We only need to assign a data element the Name class word and then we know a lot about that data element. For example, we know its definition, that it cannot be more than 30 characters long, and that it almost always contain only letters.

Facilitate searching repositories or data dictionaries. I can more easily find data elements by searching on their class word. For example, if I am looking for the data element containing the middle name for a customer, I can do some sort of wild-card search, which includes the Name class word. For example, "CUS%NAM" might bring back a number of data elements, with a good chance that one of them will be the customer's middle name.

What Are the Class Words?

Over the years, I have used the class word concept at many companies. Although each company might have several class words that the other companies did not need or have included within another class word, there was a common theme across all of these companies. Below is this common, all encompassing class word list. It is divided into class words based on the traits and characteristics of each one. For example, the

Quantity class word implies that addition and other mathematical operations can be applied against these values. However, the Number class word is just a number, and we are not permitted to apply mathematical operations to these values. As you review each, try to think of data elements that do not fit cleanly into any of these class word categories. I would imagine it would be difficult to identify data elements that do not belong to any of these categories.

Quantity. The quantity class word represents any additive amount other than currency. This can include weights, quantity, and dimensions. Here are some examples:

- Total Order Quantity
- Patient Weight Quantity
- Total Shipments by Month Quantity
- House Width Quantity
- Ice Cream Flavor Quantity

Amount. This class word represents monetary or currency data elements. Examples include:

- Invoice Amount
- Account Balance Amount
- Employee Annual Salary Amount
- Stock Price Amount
- Item List Price Amount

Number. This represents any number that is nonadditive. Examples include:

- Social Security Number
- Telephone Number
- Examination Score Percent Number
- Percent Returned Orders Number
- Average Temperature in July Number
- Rate Conversion Factor Number

Identifier. This represents the primary key for a set of data elements. These usually are, but do not have to be, limited to surrogate or nonintelligent keys, such as counters. Examples include:

- Employee Identifier
- Claim Identifier
- Web Page Identifier
- Account Identifier
- Check Identifier

Name. This is a way to refer to or designate a person, place, or thing. Examples include:

- Employee First Name
- Company Name
- Automobile Manufacturer Name
- Ice Cream Flavor Name
- Product Name

Code. This is a shortened form for a long description or a symbol to represent a single other data element. Examples include:

- Account Type Code
- State Code
- Employee Status Code
- Cancel Reason Code
- Consumer Response Code

Description. This is one or more sentences or phrases that describe something in detail. Examples include:

- Claim Description
- Product Full Description
- Contact Full Notes Description
- Address Description
- Cancel Reason Description

Date. This is any date or timestamp. Examples include:

- Order Date
- Actual Delivery Date
- Employee Hire Date
- Record Receive Date
- Expiration Date

A few of these class words might appear to overlap in meaning. Here is the difference between the class words that most often cause confusion:

Difference between Code and Identifier class words. A Code is used to represent a single description in shortened form. An Identifier is used to represent the primary key to an entity with multiple data elements. The Code can also be a primary identifier when there is only a single description in the entity.

Difference between Number and Identifier class words. Most identifiers are numbers. The class word Identifier is the priority class word over Number. This is because Identifier is more descriptive than Number. If a number is not an identifier, it becomes the Number class word, or else it becomes the Identifier class word.

Whenever you have two or more data elements that appear to have the same class word, you have addressed the commonality question of the Abstraction Safety Guide. Because you will find many data elements that end in the same class word, the value question from the Abstraction Safety Guide will be critical in determining when to introduce abstraction based on the class word. What usually happens is that there is something else the data elements have in common in addition to the class word. The class word provides a very good starting point for looking for these other hints that there is something else in common. For example, we have seen in a previous example in this chapter that having several telephone number data elements may mean there is a potential abstract structure.

Summary

In this chapter we explained abstraction, subtyping, and class words, and focused on two very important abstraction tools:

Abstraction Safety Guide. This is a set of three questions that helped identify where we need to abstract on our data models. It helped introduce consistency in our abstraction practices, made sure we did not miss any opportunities for abstraction, and prevented overabstracting.

Abstraction Components. This is the set of the most useful Abstraction Components. These components can exist at the entity, relationship, or data element levels. We discussed six entity Abstraction Components, three relationship Abstraction Components, and eight data element Abstraction Components. Using these components reduces the time it takes to complete a data model and increases the consistency between your designs.

This chapter presented tools that help improve the efficiency and flexibility of your data models; whereas, Chapter 10, "Data Model Beauty Tips," focuses on the appearance of your data models. Chapter 10 offers guidelines on the layout or arrangement of entities, relationships, and data elements on the data model.

CHAPTER 10

Data Model Beauty Tips

The day after returning from a vacation usually involves scanning and recycling mounds of junk mail, doing loads of laundry, and dropping off rolls of vacation film for processing. When the processing is completed, I organize these vacation photographs in an album. I like to have my photos appear chronologically in the album, along with other paper memories, such as airline ticket stubs, maps, and restaurant menus. The first page in the album contains photos from our first day of vacation, and the last page from our last day of vacation. Thus, I need to take all of the photos and lots of paper souvenirs and arrange them in the album by when they occurred. For example, if on our vacation we went hiking on Monday and shopping on Tuesday, I would put Monday hiking pictures and maybe a hiking trail map before the Tuesday shopping pictures. By arranging the pictures by time sequence, I can easily walk through the album with family and friends and have them understand the activities and adventures from our vacation. Therefore, the layout of the photos within the album is extremely important for understanding and clarity.

The same understanding and clarity occurs when I am walking business users and functional analysts through a data model, where the entities, relationships, and data elements have been laid out properly for maximum understanding and readability. Both the photo album and data model tell a story. The photo album tells the story of a vacation; the data model tells the story of a particular set of data requirements. This story is more easily told and understood with the proper sequence or arrangement. This arrangement is accomplished with the help of some valuable tips, which help improve and beautify your data models. This chapter discusses a number of these Data Model Beauty Tips.

About This Chapter

After finishing Chapter 8, "The Normalization and Denormalization Survival Guide," we have completed our initial application logical and physical data models. Chapter 9,

"The Abstraction Safety Guide and Components," introduced the Abstraction Safety Guide, which took our design beyond the immediate application requirements, where we focused on flexibility and future needs. This chapter also takes our design beyond the immediate application requirements, by focusing on improving the visual appearance of the logical and physical data models. Improving the appearance of the models is achieved through five categories containing a number of data modeling beauty tips:

Logical Data Element Sequence Tips. These tips propose ordering or sequencing of the data elements within each entity on your logical data model. This sequencing is done to improve the readability and understanding of the data elements within each entity. For example, positioning Customer First Name directly before Customer Last Name would be easier to review and understand than would positioning Customer First Name in the middle of all the customer data elements and Customer Last Name toward the end of the customer data elements.

Physical Data Element Sequence Tips. These tips are more of memory storage and performance tips than they are visual tips. It is important to include these tips in this chapter, because we need to be aware that the optimal sequence of data elements in the logical data model is usually not the same as the one in the physical data model. From a physical perspective, ordering the data elements a certain way can potentially save space in the database and reduce data retrieval times. Therefore, it is less of a priority to sequence the data elements for maximum readability and understanding on the physical data model. Instead, we focus more on data element length, nullability, and composite alternate and primary keys. For example, a Customer Comments Text data element that is 255 characters long and empty most of time should appear later in the list of customer data elements than the Customer First Name data element, which is 20 characters long and always filled in. Larger, emptier data elements listed toward the end of each entity can save valuable storage space.

Entity Layout Tips. These tips focus on the optimal layout of each entity on both the logical and physical data models, which is purely for purposes of readability and understanding. It is amazing how much of a difference the positions of the entities can impact a data model review. When the entities are correctly positioned, the review is much easier and more intuitive than if no thought were given to their placement. Without focusing on placement, more time will be spent during the review trying to find entities than trying to understand them. A proper entity layout on the model not only saves time spent locating entities on the model but can uncover design issues that otherwise would remain hidden.

Relationship Layout Tips. These tips focus on rearranging relationship lines that overlap and relationships that go through entities instead of around them to the entities they connect. These tips are usually stressed in Data Modeling 101, that is, introductory data modeling. Over the years, however, we start to forget these pointers (just as we begin to forget a lot of other things as we mature [sigh]). We need to remind ourselves how important it is to properly lay out these relationship lines. Just moving a relationship line slightly up or down on the model can make the difference between confusion and clarity. I recently completed a data model where there were several instances of poorly placed relationships. Luckily, I was able to catch these situations on my model and correct them before the model review.

Attention-Getting Tips. These tips focus on ways to draw attention to specific parts of the logical and physical data models. There are times when we need to highlight data elements, entities, or relationships on our design. One reason for highlighting might be that we may only want to show a portion of the model that might have outstanding issues or certain reporting needs. We may not want to look at all of these data elements but only a small subset of them, especially when entities have 20 or more data elements.

I recommend applying these tips in the order in which they appear, because we can first focus on each of the entities and arrange their data elements appropriately. At this point it does not matter where the entities and relationships are placed on the model. Next, we can lay out the entities in their most appropriate spots. Then when we move relationships around, the entities are already fairly fixed; therefore, we will not compromise an entity movement that reduces understanding for a relationship movement. In this chapter we discuss each of these five categories of tips and reinforce them through a number of examples.

If you visit my Web site, www.wiley.com/compbook/hoberman, you will find the templates for each of the tools in this chapter; additional tools; and more information about tools in this book, including empty templates that you can download.

What Are Logical Data Element Sequence Tips?

Many times we complete a data model without taking the time to appropriately arrange the data elements within each entity. There is a certain order that will make it easier for you as the modeler, and your business and functional audience as the reviewers, to agree on and validate the model. Usually right after completing the Normalization Hike and Abstraction Safety Guide, we are ready to present our model to the functional analysts and business users to make sure we have correctly and accurately captured the data requirements of the application. Before we do, however, we need to make sure the reviewers have a clear picture of the data elements within each entity. When we walk through the model, we need to clearly tell the story captured on the model, a story that is easier to discuss and grasp if the data elements appear in the right sequence. To help present this clear picture, we need to order the data elements in a sequence that makes business sense. For example, let's look at the following two Customer entities in Figure 10.1, each of which contain the same set of data elements.

Which of these two Customer entities would be easier to validate and understand? The first appears to have no order to its data elements, which can make validating and reviewing difficult. For example, can you quickly look at the data elements in this entity and verify that all of the customer address data elements are there? Are any data elements missing? It would not be quick or intuitive to do this validation. However, can you look at the data elements in the second Customer entity and validate that we

CUSTOMER

CUSTOMER IDENTIFIER
CUSTOMER FAX NUMBER
CUSTOMER FIRST NAME
CUSTOMER FIRST ORDER DATE
CUSTOMER DUNS NUMBER
CUSTOMER ZIP CODE
CUSTOMER PHONE NUMBER
CUSTOMER CITY
CUSTOMER ADDRESS LINE
CUSTOMER TAX IDENTIFIER
CUSTOMER LAST NAME

CUSTOMER

CUSTOMER IDENTIFIER
CUSTOMER TAX IDENTIFIER
CUSTOMER DUNS NUMBER
CUSTOMER FIRST NAME
CUSTOMER LAST NAME
CUSTOMER ADDRESS LINE
CUSTOMER CITY
CUSTOMER ZIP CODE
CUSTOMER FIRST ORDER DATE
CUSTOMER PHONE NUMBER
CUSTOMER FAX NUMBER

Figure 10.1 Customer entity with two different data element sequences.

have all of the customer address data elements listed? The state clearly appears to be missing on the second Customer entity. It is not as clear that the state is missing on the first Customer entity. I applied several Logical Data Element Sequence Tips to the second example that makes it more understandable.

Logical Data Element Sequence Tips provide a handy reference as to the optimal logical order of the data elements within each entity. These tips provide the following benefits:

Greater understanding of the model among business and functional people. By looking at the previous customer example, we can easily see that it is more understandable when there is a sequence to the data elements that makes sense. The ordering guidelines are a result of many model reviews with business users and functional analysts and what made the most sense to them. By putting myself in their shoes, so to speak, I was able to come up with a standard approach for the optimal way to list or sequence the data elements. As you review the Logical Data Element Sequence Tips, you will see how common sense plays a role in the data element ordering.

Quicker detection of errors and issues. We have seen that it was easier to identify the missing state data element on the organized version of Customer. Ordering the data elements correctly is less work for the eyes and brain in identifying problem areas or questions. Without this ordering, the errors and issues would be hidden, making them much more difficult to detect and resolve. Recently, I was able to detect several redundant time-related data elements because they were grouped together following these tips. This allowed me to remove this redundancy from a fairly large transaction table, reducing confusion and saving space.

Greater consistency within and between models. By following the same approach in listing the data elements within each of the logical entities, we gain a level of consistency across entities, both within and between models. This consistency gives us the same benefits we have seen with consistency throughout this text, which includes the quick rate at which persons will understand a new model because they are seeing the same order as on a model that is familiar to them. For example, if business users have seen address information in the same place in the

Customer entity, they should expect to see address information in the same place in the Supplier or Associate entities. This can speed up and improve the efficiency of model walk-throughs, because there will be less time spent looking for data elements and more time spent reviewing and validating data elements.

Easier to copy data elements between entities. By knowing where to look in each entity for the particular data elements, it becomes quicker and easier to reuse these data elements across entities. For example, if I would like to copy the Customer address data elements to a new entity I am designing, I will know quickly where to look within the Customer entity.

TIP

These benefits have greater payoffs the more data elements we have within an entity. An entity with 50 data elements would benefit more from the appropriate data element sequence than an entity with five data elements. The more data elements within an entity, the more complicated and difficult it can be to review and understand these data elements, as well as to ask questions and raise issues.

Let's review the tips to list the data elements within each logical entity.

Using the Logical Data Element Sequence Tips

There are seven Logical Data Element Sequence Tips. I will describe each and then go through a detailed example. Although you will get the same results regardless of the order in which you apply these tips, I recommend applying them in the order in which they appear. I have listed them in this order to more efficiently put each data element in the proper sequence. Thus, applying the tips in this order is the fastest approach and will result in fewer mistakes. Here are the tips:

1. **Primary key.** Always list the primary key first within each entity. This usually happens by default, because most modeling tools will always put the primary key as the first data element or elements in the entity. If there is a composite primary key, meaning more than one data element makes up the primary key of the entity, list the data elements within the key in their order of access or usage. For example, if Customer Last Name and Customer Shoe Size make up the primary key for Customer, and we learn that Customer Last Name is accessed much more often than Customer Shoe Size, we need to list Customer Last Name first in this composite primary key.

2. **Alternate keys.** An alternate key is a unique identifier for an entity, but it is not defined as *the* unique identifier for the entity. That is, it is not the primary key. Because of their importance, these alternate keys should be listed next, directly under the primary key. Most of the time, these alternate keys are data elements that have business significance to the users. Many times, our primary keys are internally system-generated identifiers that are irrelevant for business use. The alternate keys, however, usually contain what the business users and functional analysts would consider unique for this concept or entity. For example, we might

have an internally system-generated identifier for the Item entity, but we kept the Stock Keeping Unit (SKU) as an alternate key. SKUs have business significance and, therefore, are very important to the users and analysts. For composite alternate keys, follow the same guidelines we discussed under primary keys, meaning list them in the order of access from most to least used. If there are multiple alternate keys within a table, list them in order of importance to the business users and functional analysts. For example, if we have both an SKU and another item alternate identifier, and the SKU is accessed or entered more frequently, we would list it before the other item alternate identifier.

3. **Foreign keys with corresponding natural foreign keys.** Natural foreign keys are foreign keys from the source application or foreign keys from the business user's perspective. For example, having the Customer Social Security Number on an order record might represent a natural foreign key because the business user might view Social Security Number as the unique way of identifying a customer. However, we might also have a Customer Identifier assigned by our application as a foreign key in the order entity. In some cases, we might keep both the natural foreign keys and foreign keys in the same entity. When we do this, we need to make sure that these data elements are listed together so that the model reviewers know that these data elements represent the same concept. For example, in data warehousing, there are times when we might have both date data elements and time identifier foreign key data elements that reference the Time dimension. The date data elements might be natural foreign keys, and the Time Identifier is a foreign key. If we have three date data elements within our entity and one pointer or foreign key back to the Time dimension, we need to list this Time Identifier beneath the natural foreign key date data element to which it corresponds. This pairs together the two data elements so that we know they are the same concept. The modeling tools of today do a relatively poor job in automatically relating the natural and foreign keys, and therefore, it is up to us to manually group these together and list them directly under the alternate keys.

4. **Rest of foreign keys.** Next, list the rest of the foreign keys, which are all internal foreign keys, in order of their importance to the business users and functional analysts. Order of importance means the order in which the users need to see the data elements. For example, if we have foreign Customer and Item identifiers in the Shipment Line entity, which of these two would be entered or accessed more often? That is the key that would be listed first.

5. **System data elements.** These are the internally system-generated data elements created by applications and are of no value to a business user. That is, these data elements are not used in any kind of data entry or analysis. These elements should always go at the end of each of the entities, because they are not important for business understanding. Examples include System Update Date and Last Changed User Identifier.

6. **Remaining data elements grouped by concept.** I am using the term concept here in the same way we used it under abstraction. *Concept* is a grouping of data elements that means one idea or subject to the business. For example, concepts might include address, phone, identifier, name, and so on. After grouping the data elements into concepts, list the concepts in order of importance within the entity. If

the name concept is used more often than the address concept, list the name concept first.

7. **Remaining data elements within each concept, grouped by either chronology or class word.** The best order to list each of the data elements within each concept is usually based on chronology or class word. Ordering by chronology means by time or the sequence of when these data elements should be entered or analyzed. For example, if we have a number of address data elements, ordering by chronology means listing the city data element before the state data element, and the state data element before the zip code data element, and so on. It is the order in which they occur within the business. My first choice for grouping the data elements is by chronology, then by class word. Class words were explained in the previous chapter when we discussed abstracting data elements. Grouping by class word would mean grouping all dates together, grouping all names together, grouping all codes together, and so on. I prefer grouping by chronology, because it is more intuitive to the business experts than grouping by class word. When the chronology is too difficult to determine or is unknown, however, I will order by class word.

NOTE

▬▬▬ **Some people prefer to order data elements alphabetically within an entity. I frown on this approach, because it usually produces a data element sequence that requires more effort to understand and validate. For example, Address City Name would appear before Address Line Text if we listed them alphabetically, which does not make sense. In addition, this approach is not amenable to adding data elements.**

Let's apply these seven tips to a detailed example.

Logical Data Element Sequence Tips In Practice

Figure 10.2 is the Order entity with the data elements not yet arranged in any logical sequence. Let's apply the Logical Data Element Sequence Tips to this example. You will notice that throughout this example I needed to make some assumptions because we are not reviewing all of the meta data around this example, only this single Order entity based on the names of the data elements. Figure 10.3 is the Order entity with all of these tips applied.

1. **Primary key.** The first step involves making sure the primary key is listed first in the entity. Because most data modeling tools automatically list the primary key first, the only change we sometimes need to make is to rearrange the data elements within a composite primary key in their order usage. For example, if Item Identifier would be accessed more often than Order Identifier, we should rearrange these two data elements within the primary key. Refer to Figure 10.3.

2. **Alternate keys.** Each modeling tool has its own notation for distinguishing the alternate keys within an entity. The modeling tool I used to create the data models

ORDER

ORDER
ORDER_IDENTIFIER: NUMBER(12) NOT NULL ITEM_IDENTIFIER: NUMBER(12) NOT NULL (FK)
EXTRACT_FILE_BATCH_NUMBER: INTEGER NOT NULL SOURCE_SYSTEM_ORDER_IDENTIFIER: VARCHAR(8) NOT NULL (AK1.1) ORDER_STATUS_CODE: VARCHAR(4) NOT NULL DELIVERY_ADDRESS_POSTAL_CODE: CHAR(10) NULL ORDER_TYPE_CODE: VARCHAR(2) NOT NULL ORDER_ENTRY_DATE: DATE NOT NULL (AK2.1) DELIVERY_ADDRESS_CITY_NAME: VARCHAR(20) NULL ACTUAL_DELIVERY_DATE: DATE NULL ORDER_CUSTOMER_COMMENTS_TEXT: VARCHAR2(2000) NULL DELIVERY_ADDRESS_LINE_TEXT: VARCHAR(30) NULL ORIGINAL_DELIVERY_DATE: DATE NULL REVISED_DELIVERY_DATE: DATE NULL CUSTOMER_IDENTIFIER: NUMBER(12) NOT NULL (FK) (AK2.2) UNIT_CODE: VARCHAR(2) NOT NULL (AK1.2) DELIVERY_ADDRESS_STATE_CODE: CHAR(2) NULL TIME_IDENTIFIER: NUMBER(12) NOT NULL (FK) CANCEL_DATE: DATE NULL SALESPERSON_IDENTIFIER: NUMBER(12) NULL (FK) ACTUAL_SHIP_DATE: DATE NULL ORDER_QUANTITY: DECIMAL(15,2) NULL

Figure 10.2 Entity before logical data element sequence guidelines have been applied.

throughout this text uses AK in parentheses after the data element name to indicate this data element makes up a complete alternate key or part of a composite
alternate key. There are two numbers after AK. The first number is a sequence
number for the alternate key. Thus, if there are three separate alternate keys
within the same entity, data elements belonging to the first alternate key will start
with a 1, those belonging to the second alternate key with a 2, and those belonging to the third alternate key with a 3. In this example, we have two sets of alter-

ORDER

ORDER
ITEM_IDENTIFIER: NUMBER(12) NOT NULL (FK) ORDER_IDENTIFIER: NUMBER(12) NOT NULL
SOURCE_SYSTEM_ORDER_IDENTIFIER: VARCHAR(8) NOT NULL (AK1.1) UNIT_CODE: VARCHAR(2) NOT NULL (AK1.2) ORDER_ENTRY_DATE: DATE NOT NULL (AK2.1) CUSTOMER_IDENTIFIER: NUMBER(12) NOT NULL (FK) (AK2.2) ACTUAL_DELIVERY_DATE: DATE NULL TIME_IDENTIFIER: NUMBER(12) NOT NULL (FK) SALESPERSON_IDENTIFIER: NUMBER(12) NULL (FK) ORDER_TYPE_CODE: VARCHAR(2) NOT NULL ORDER_STATUS_CODE: VARCHAR(4) NOT NULL ACTUAL_SHIP_DATE: DATE NULL ORIGINAL_DELIVERY_DATE: DATE NULL REVISED_DELIVERY_DATE: DATE NULL CANCEL_DATE: DATE NULL ORDER_QUANTITY: DECIMAL(15,2) NULL DELIVERY_ADDRESS_LINE_TEXT: VARCHAR(30) NULL DELIVERY_ADDRESS_CITY_NAME: VARCHAR(20) NULL DELIVERY_ADDRESS_STATE_CODE: CHAR(2) NULL DELIVERY_ADDRESS_POSTAL_CODE: CHAR(10) NULL ORDER_CUSTOMER_COMMENTS_TEXT: VARCHAR2(2000) NULL EXTRACT_FILE_BATCH_NUMBER: INTEGER NOT NULL

Figure 10.3 Entity after logical data element sequence guidelines have been applied.

nate keys. The first alternate key includes Source System Order Identifier and Unit Code. The second includes Order Entry Date and Customer Identifier. I listed the data elements within each alternate key by importance. See Figure 10.3 for the alternate keys placed in their most appropriate spot within this entity, which is immediately after the primary key.

3. **Foreign keys with corresponding natural foreign keys.** Many of the modeling tools of today do a relatively poor job of associating natural foreign keys and foreign keys. If I have many dates in my table, I would not be able to identify the one that is associated with a time foreign key. Therefore, we need to pair together the natural foreign keys and foreign keys so that we can clearly see which data element the foreign key references. It is important to note, however, that most of the time we should not have both natural foreign keys and their foreign keys within the same entity. We would only have this redundancy if the natural foreign key represented something important to the business that we could not easily get from another entity. Let's assume that in the example we are going through, Actual Delivery Date is the natural time foreign key in our Order entity. Therefore, if Actual Delivery Date contains 04/20/2001, the Time Identifier foreign key in the Order entity might contain the value 123, which points back to a record in the Time dimension containing the same date, 04/20/2001. See Figure 10.3 for this grouping applied to this example.

4. **Rest of foreign keys.** Next, we list all foreign keys that were not paired previously with natural keys. This provides a quick reference of all the other entities on the data model to which this entity is related. Note that the FK notation distinguishes foreign keys on the model. See Figure 10.3 for the movement of the foreign key, Salesperson Identifier, to immediately following the Time Identifier.

5. **System data elements.** These are the data elements created by applications to help with auditing, record-keeping, and troubleshooting purposes. These data elements could be very useful to the technical team but provide no value to the business user. Therefore, they should always go at the end of each of the entities. Note that I am suggesting we apply this step at this point in the guide and not as the last tip, because the next few steps deal with the remaining data elements, all of which fit somewhere in the middle of the entity. Therefore, as long as we know these system data elements go at the very end of the entity, we should put them there so we do not have to include them with the other data elements in the next few steps. See Figure 10.3 for this model with the system data element, Extract File Batch Number, at the end.

6. **Remaining data elements grouped by concept.** In this step we are preparing to sort the remaining data elements by assigning them to concepts. In this example, we have the following data elements left and unsorted:

- Actual Ship Date
- Cancel Date
- Delivery Address City Name
- Delivery Address Line Text
- Delivery Address Postal Code
- Delivery Address State Code

- Order Customer Comments Text
- Order Quantity
- Order Status Code
- Order Type Code
- Original Delivery Date
- Revised Delivery Date

Grouping these data elements together into concepts would give us the spreadsheet in Table 10.1. Note that I listed all of the data elements, even if we only have one per concept. Note that a business expert from the In-the-Know Template in Chapter 5, "Subject Area Analysis," would have to help me prioritize these concepts in terms of importance. It is really up to the business experts as to the order of the concepts, so whatever they prefer should be the order you choose.

TIP

As you become more aware of the importance of data element sequence, you will probably find yourself making sequence decisions during your data modeling, as opposed to afterward, as we are doing in this example. It is fine to apply certain sequence logic during your design instead of afterward, as long as you use these seven tips as a validation to make sure you have the optimal order when you are done.

See Figure 10.3 for the updated entity, with concepts by importance.

7. **Remaining data elements within each concept, grouped by either chronology or class word.** Refer to Table 10.2 for our data elements grouped either chronologically or by class word for each of these concepts. You will note that I made some assumptions about the meanings of these data elements for the purposes of this

Table 10.1 Data Elements Grouped by Concept

CONCEPT	DATA ELEMENTS
Order Codes	Order Status Code Order Type Code
Order Life Cycle Dates	Actual Ship Date Cancel Date Original Delivery Date Revised Delivery Date
Order Measurements	Order Quantity
Address	Delivery Address City Name Delivery Address Line Text Delivery Address State Code Delivery Address Postal Code
Order Description	Order Customer Comments Text

Table 10.2   Data Elements Grouped by Chronology within Concept

CONCEPT	DATA ELEMENTS
Order Codes	Order Type Code Order Status Code
Order Life Cycle Dates	Actual Ship Date Original Delivery Date Revised Delivery Date Cancel Date
Order Measurements	Order Quantity
Address	Delivery Address Line Text Delivery Address City Name Delivery Address State Code Delivery Address Postal Code
Order Description	Order Customer Comments Text

example. In reality, we would have a Data Element Family Tree completely filled in and thus would understand that Order Type Code happens before Order Status Code.

See Figure 10.3 for this model updated with this data element chronology. We now have the optimal logical sequence for our data elements within this entity. We need to apply these steps to all the entities within our model. As mentioned previously, the more you become familiar with these tips the more you can apply them during your modeling instead of afterward to save time.

What Are Physical Data Element Sequence Tips?

Just as there is an ideal logical data element sequence for model readability and understanding, there is also a physical data element sequence to improve the efficiency of storing and retrieving the information. When we order the data elements within each entity in the logical data model, we do not necessarily have the optimal order for the data elements within each table in the database. This is a very important point. We need to have a set of rules for ordering the data elements on the physical data model to optimize the storage and performance of the resulting structures. Physical Data Element Sequence Tips provide a handy reference as to the optimal physical order of the data elements within each entity. Following these Physical Data Element Sequence Tips provides these benefits:

Space savings. Ordering the data elements following the Physical Data Element Sequence Tips maximizes the amount of space that can be saved in the database. For small tables, meaning a minimal number of data elements and rows, it may not make sense to apply this sequence because the savings might not be worth the effort. For large tables, such as reference tables like Customer or Order, however, every character we save could save us megabytes. Every character we save in a table containing one million rows saves one megabyte. You will note that the maximum amount of space to save comes from the longest length data elements that are usually empty or almost empty a very high percentage of the time. For example, a data element that is 255 variable characters long and empty half of the time would be a good candidate to list last in the list of data elements within an entity, because we would save any unused space from this data element.

Faster retrieval. If the data elements that belong to the composite alternate and primary keys are ordered within their keys according to how they are accessed, retrieval times can be much quicker. For example, if Order Entry Date and Customer Identifier from our Order entity are alternate keys that are used most often by first accessing the Order Entry Date and then the Customer Identifier, storing them in this sequence will reduce retrieval times because their access matches how they are indexed within the database. This is one case in which the logical and physical sequence should be identical. That is, the order of the data elements within the composite keys should be the same in both the logical and physical data models.

TIP

▬▬▬ **Applying the Physical Data Element Sequence is only useful when character strings are defined as variable length instead of fixed length.** *Variable length* **means that only the space that is filled in with data is actually used, as opposed to** *fixed length* **where even if there is nothing filled in, space will still always be reserved. A downside of variable-length data elements, however, is that updating them can be expensive in terms of performance if their values need to be split among different sections of the disk during updates because space was no longer available. For example, if Smith is stored in the variable-length data element Customer Last Name, and then we update Smith to Smithfield, a possibility exists that the field portion of the name might be stored in a separate part of memory from the Smith portion of the name.**

Let's review the steps to list the data elements within each physical entity.

Using Physical Data Element Sequence Tips

These rules can vary slightly, depending on your database software. In general, here is how we order the data elements:

1. **Primary key.** Just as we did under the Logical Data Element Sequence Tips, we list the primary key first because it will be used quite often during development and support activities. If we have a composite primary key, we should list the most used data element first. So far, this is identical to the first logical sequence tip.

2. **Alternate keys.** Just as we did with our logical sequence, we list alternate keys next. Composite alternate keys require listing the data elements within this alter-

nate key in order from most to least used, which again is identical to our Logical Data Element Sequence Tips. Listing the alternate keys in the order of usage improves data retrieval times, because the user will be accessing the composite key in the same order this composite key has been indexed and thereby retrieving data faster.

3. **Not nulls from shortest to longest.** In applying these physical tips, our goal changes from increasing understanding to saving space and increasing performance. Therefore, we list those data elements that we believe to always be filled in, from shortest to longest length. Thus, a Customer Shoe Size data element that is two characters long will be listed before the Customer Last Name data element that is 20 characters long. This is because if we have a long variable-length data element where only the first few characters are filled in, and there is no used space after this data element in this entity, we would have the potential to save the unused space from the long variable-length data element. Let's look at some examples in Table 10.3. I used the letter X to represent an empty space; the X is not a blank space.

Note that this space savings is only applicable when the data element is defined as variable length and no data elements within the same entity after Customer Last Name are filled in. As soon as we have another value after Customer Last Name all the space savings is lost, because the memory needs to be allocated up to the last data element that is filled in. Note also that, using this reasoning, if we reversed the order of Customer Shoe Size and Customer Last Name, we would not have saved any space because shoe size would have been filled in and thus any empty spaces in Customer Last Name could not be reused. Note also that the amount of memory that could be saved varies by the memory allocation algorithms of the different database software packages.

4. **Nulls from shortest to longest.** The same reasoning and examples we just applied for not null data elements can equally be applied for null data elements. If Customer Shoe Size and Customer Last Name were both null, we could apply the same reasoning mentioned previously. The reason we distinguish nulls from not nulls is because for nulls the entire data element value can be blank or empty; whereas, for not nulls, something needs to be filled in. Therefore, we get the greatest potential space savings by listing those data elements that can be completely blank—that is, the null data elements—toward the end of the data element sequence.

Table 10.3 Sample Values for Customer Last Name and Shoe Size

CUSTOMER SHOE SIZE (2 CHARACTERS)	CUSTOMER LAST NAME (20 CHARACTERS, VARIABLE LENGTH	SPACE SAVINGS (IN CHARACTERS)
10	SmithXXXXXXXXXXXXXXX	15
13	HobermanXXXXXXXXXXXX	12
X9	JonesXXXXXXXXXXXXXXX	15
12	JacksonXXXXXXXXXXXXX	13

Physical Data Element Sequence Tips In Practice

Let's start with the same example we used under the Logical Data Element Sequence Tips, which is the Order entity in Figure 10.2. From here we apply these four rules:

1. **Primary key.** This is the same as we have under Logical. Therefore, it is identical to Figure 10.3.

2. **Alternate keys.** This is the same as we have under Logical. Therefore, it is also identical to Figure 10.3.

3. **Not nulls from shortest to longest.** This is a very easy step. We order the not null data elements within each entity from shortest to longest. If you are unsure of how format length compares, ask your database administrator or refer to the database documentation. Ordering by not null length in our example is shown in Figure 10.4.

NOTE

Applying the physical sequence is a mechanical and straightforward set of steps that requires no business or technical knowledge. Just apply the rules in this order, and you will be saving the maximum amount of space possible within your database.

4. **Nulls from shortest to longest.** This is also a very easy and straightforward step. Follow the same rules from Step 3, except we are only ordering the null data elements. This is shown in Figure 10.4.

```
ORDER
┌────────────────────────────────────────────────────────────────┐
│ ITEM_IDENTIFIER: NUMBER(12) NOT NULL (FK)                        │
│ ORDER_IDENTIFIER: NUMBER(12) NOT NULL                            │
├────────────────────────────────────────────────────────────────┤
│ CUSTOMER_IDENTIFIER: NUMBER(12) NOT NULL (FK) (AK2.2)            │
│ TIME_IDENTIFIER: NUMBER(12) NOT NULL (FK)                        │
│ ORDER_TYPE_CODE: VARCHAR(2) NOT NULL                             │
│ UNIT_CODE: VARCHAR(2) NOT NULL (AK1.2)                           │
│ ORDER_STATUS_CODE: VARCHAR(4) NOT NULL                           │
│ EXTRACT_FILE_BATCH_NUMBER: INTEGER NOT NULL                      │
│ SOURCE_SYSTEM_ORDER_IDENTIFIER: VARCHAR(8) NOT NULL (AK1.1)      │
│ ORDER_ENTRY_DATE: DATE NOT NULL (AK2.1)                          │
│ ACTUAL_DELIVERY_DATE: DATE NULL                                  │
│ ACTUAL_SHIP_DATE: DATE NULL                                      │
│ ORIGINAL_DELIVERY_DATE: DATE NULL                                │
│ REVISED_DELIVERY_DATE: DATE NULL                                 │
│ CANCEL_DATE: DATE NULL                                           │
│ SALESPERSON_IDENTIFIER: NUMBER(12) NULL (FK)                     │
│ DELIVERY_ADDRESS_STATE_CODE: CHAR(2) NULL                        │
│ ORDER_QUANTITY: DECIMAL(15,2) NULL                               │
│ DELIVERY_ADDRESS_POSTAL_CODE: CHAR(10) NULL                      │
│ DELIVERY_ADDRESS_CITY_NAME: VARCHAR(20) NULL                     │
│ DELIVERY_ADDRESS_LINE_TEXT: VARCHAR(30) NULL                     │
│ ORDER_CUSTOMER_COMMENTS_TEXT: VARCHAR2(2000) NULL                │
└────────────────────────────────────────────────────────────────┘
```

Figure 10.4 Entity after physical data element sequence guidelines have been applied.

NOTE

■■■■■ You might need to tailor the Physical Data Element Sequence Tips to your particular database software. Feel free to customize these tips to maximize how much you can save within your own environment.

What Are Entity Layout Tips?

The placement of the entities on our data model can make a very big difference in its readability. During the design of my first few data models, I remember the only data model beauty tip I applied was minimizing the number of relationship lines crossing each other. Although it is important to clearly lay out the relationships, as we will see shortly, it is even more important to lay out the entities in their most appropriate places. Entity Layout Tips require an understanding of what these entities mean and how they relate to each other to determine their best position on the model.

I use only one but powerful tip for laying out entities on the model:

Position child entities under the parent entities, or position child entities toward the center of the model. This simple statement will dramatically improve the layout of the entities on the model. The parent entity, as we discussed previously in this text, is the entity that participates in the relationship as the driver or independent entity in the relationship. The parent entity is the "one" side of the relationship; the child entity is the "many" side of the relationship. The child entity is the dependent or weaker of the two entities in the relationship. Thus, if a Customer can place many Orders, Customer is the parent entity and Order is the child entity. Laying out the parent and child entities in this way produces a number of options, including all those in Figure 10.5.

The main benefits to laying out the entities appropriately follow:

Easier readability on the model. By laying out the entities in their most appropriate places, we make it easier to walk through and review the models. It is simpler to tell the story within the data model and clearly read the relationships from parent entity to child entity.

Quicker detection of errors and issues. Just as we have seen with the properly laying out of the data elements, laying out the entities properly can more quickly find errors and issues. You might more rapidly notice circular relationships, for

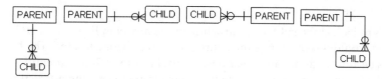

Figure 10.5 Different entity layouts for parent and child.

example. Circular relationships exist when parent contains child, child contains its child, and its child contains the original parent. Laying out the entities according the Entity Layout Tips can more easily identify this type of situation and many others.

Greater consistency. By laying out the entities using the Entity Layout Tips, we increase consistency within our data model and between data models. I would know generally where to look on the model to find Customer and where to look to find Order.

Let's review the different situations or uses that can take advantage of the Entity Layout Tips.

Using Entity Layout Tips

The Entity Layout Tips can be used when any two entities share a relationship. In any relationship, there are always a parent entity and a child entity. Therefore, the proper layout by applying these tips is to place the parent entity above or toward the outside of the model from the child entity. This translates into placing the child entity beneath the parent entity, or toward the center of the model; whereas, the parent entity is toward the border of the model. Although these tips can be applied to any relationship, we will discuss examples of the following types of relationships in the next section:

- Subtyping
- Reference-to-transaction relationships
- Reference-to-reference hierarchical relationships
- Associative entities

Entity Layout Tips In Practice

Here are the situations in which the Entity Layout Tips are most useful:

Subtyping. Always place the supertype above the subtype, or the subtypes toward the center of the model. See Figure 10.6. This is one of the subtyping structures we discussed in Chapter 9, "The Abstraction Safety Guide and Components," when we reviewed the Entity Abstraction Component, Who. I rearranged the entities to create an example in which there does not appear to be any order to where the subtypes are placed. Note how hard it is to understand the relationships between the supertype and subtype. Note that it is even harder to determine that Who is the supertype.

You might look at the subtyping structure in the model in Figure 10.6 and think that you would never arrange the entities in such a chaotic fashion. The larger our models become and the more relationships we have to each of our entities (especially the subtypes), however, the more prone we are to creating a structure that is

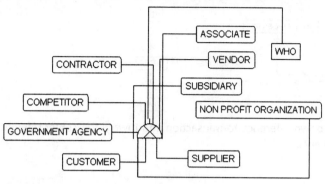

Figure 10.6 No order to subtype placement.

difficult to interpret and understand. The two ways to organize the subtypes, that is, top down and toward the center, are shown in Figure 10.7. Both approaches would correctly display the parent–child relationship.

I usually choose one approach over the other because of the particular modeling situation with which I am faced. For example, if I have only a few subtypes, I might choose the top-down approach. If I have many subtypes where I could use up too much space if I organize them top down, I might use the toward-the-center approach. Another factor in choosing the approach would be the number of relationships to the supertype and subtypes. For example, if the supertype has lots of relationships and the subtypes have few if any relationships, I might choose to arrange the subtyping structure in a top-down fashion along the bottom of the model. This will allow the relationships of the supertype to

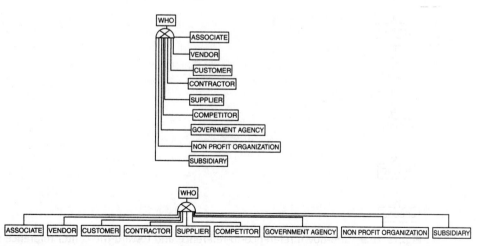

Figure 10.7 Top-down and toward-the-center subtype placements.

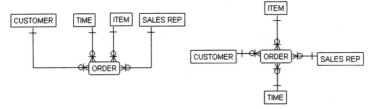

Figure 10.8 Top-down reference-to-transaction and toward-the-center reference-to-transaction placements.

more clearly connect to their other entities without getting entangled with the subtypes.

Reference-to-transaction relationships. You will note a common theme throughout all these examples: they follow the same approach as either top down or toward the center. See Figure 10.8 for examples of reference-to-transaction relationships. Note that the toward-the-center option is usually preferred when data modeling data marts. This option matches the typical data mart data model layout where the transaction entity is a fact table and the reference entity is the dimension table. The dimension tables are around the border of the model and the fact tables are toward the center, giving us a structure that looks like a bicycle hub and spokes.

TIP

I usually will not place the child entity above the parent entity using the toward-the-center approach unless all other sides of the child entity already have parent

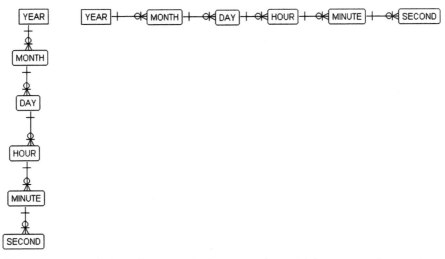

Figure 10.9 Top-down reference-to-reference and toward-the-center reference-to-reference hierarchical placements.

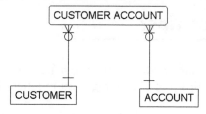

Figure 10.10 Associative entity, no placement.

entities related to it. For example, in Figure 10.8, Time appears under Order only because there already are parent entities on all sides of Order. If there were just three parent entities relating to Order, they would be placed on either side and on top of the child entity, but not beneath it.

Reference-to-reference hierarchical relationships. Examples of top-down and toward-the-center reference-to-reference hierarchical relationships are shown in Figure 10.9.

Associative entities. Associative entities should always appear somewhere between the two parent entities. Figure 10.10 shows a layout that you want to avoid. This layout makes it difficult to identify which of these entities is the associative entity and misleads the reader into believing that the Customer Account entity is the most important of the three entities modeled. That is, the Customer Account entity appears to be the parent entity in this relationship, which we know is not the case. We need to treat the associative entity like a connector between the two parent entities. See Figure 10.11 for two toward-the-center approaches. Note that you could use the top-down approach as well, but it does not show the connection between the two parent entities as clearly as the toward-the-center approach.

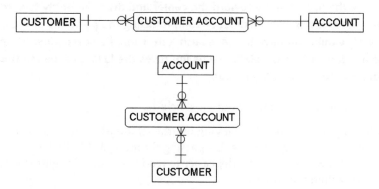

Figure 10.11 Associative entity, toward-the-center placement.

What Are Relationship Layout Tips?

Where we place the relationships on our data model can make a big difference in the readability of the model. There are two tips that I encourage you to follow for relationships:

Minimize crossing lines. This is Data Modeling 101, meaning a very basic and fundamental data modeling beauty tip. If you can avoid it, try not to let your relationship lines cross. There are times when you cannot help but cross the lines, especially when you have more than two relationships coming into two or more interconnected entities. But try to minimize crossing lines wherever possible.

Never let lines pass through entities. This means that you have an entity that just happened to be placed on a relationship line but does not participate in that relationship. Entities on either side of this entity participate in this relationship, giving the false appearance that this entity is somehow attached to and therefore participates in this relationship. Lines passing through unrelated entities are sometimes difficult to detect, and it is very annoying and embarrassing when they are detected during model reviews. Spend the extra effort to find and correct these situations before reviewing the model with anyone. Sometimes I try to find these situations by looking for places where there is no cardinality appearing at the intersection of an entity and relationship. If I find a situation where there is no cardinality, I have probably found a case where the relationship line passes through to another entity. The problem usually is easily fixed by moving the entity in the middle slightly up or down so that it no longer crosses the line. Optionally, move the relationship so it no longer hits the entity. Remember to make these changes without compromising the entity layout techniques discussed previously.

TIP

Give the entity layout priority over the relationship layout. For example, if the only way not to have two relationships cross is to move the child entity above the parent entity, or move the parent entity toward the center and the child entity toward the border, keep the crossing lines instead of compromising the positions of the entities. Very rarely would you have to make such a decision, however. Most of time, slightly moving the entities or relationships improves the layout of the relationship without compromising the entity layout.

The benefits of the Relationship Layout Tips include:

Easier readability on the model. By laying out the relationships to minimize crossing lines and eliminating relationships passing through entities that are not part of the relationship, we make the model easier to read and more straightforward to tell the story within the structures.

Quicker detection of errors and issues. Just as we saw with properly laying out the data elements and entities, laying out the relationships can allow you to find errors and issues more quickly. For example, you might more rapidly notice entities that should be related but are not, or entities that are but should not be related.

Using Relationship Layout Tips

You should apply the two Relationship Layout Tips of minimizing crossing lines and avoiding relationships passing through unrelated entities everywhere on your model. In the next section, we go through two examples of how to apply these tips.

Relationship Layout Tips In Practice

Figure 10.12 shows an example of a model that violates the Relationship Layout Tip to minimize crossing lines. Figure 10.13 shows this tip applied to Figure 10.12 to create properly laid out relationships. The trick is to minimize the number of crossing lines, not always to eliminate the crossing lines.

Figure 10.14 contains an example of a relationship line passing through an entity, which violates the second Relationship Layout Tip. Figure 10.15 shows a case in which this tip is applied and the problem fixed.

What Are Attention-Getting Tips?

Once we sort the data elements in their most appropriate logical and physical sequence and properly lay out the entities and relationships, we might want to highlight certain data elements, entities, or relationships that need to stand out for the audience. There are three ways to do this:

By color. If you have easy access to a color printer or you are reviewing the data model through your computer or a projector, color might be the best option. When everything else on the model is black and white, a red or blue object really stands out. If you need to show multiple types of information, color works very well. For example, if blue represents a new data element and red represents a new data

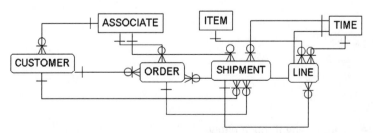

Figure 10.12   Too many crossing lines.

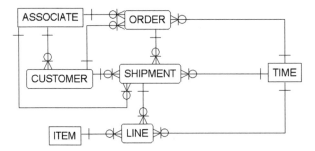

Figure 10.13 Minimal number of crossing lines.

element in which we have an outstanding issue, these distinctions are easier to view using different colors. Colors also can indicate severity. A red data element might be a more important issue than a blue data element, for example. Not being able to show colors in this book is an example of the biggest drawback to using colors: It is not possible to show colors in every media.

By size. Most modeling tools will let you increase the size of one or more data elements within an entity, leaving the remaining data elements their default size. This can be a very good approach when the color option is not feasible. It could also be the optimal approach when you only want to show two different scenarios. For example, you can use 18-point type to indicate a new data element and 10-point type for an existing data element.

By style. Using a combination of italics, boldface, and underlining can also be a very good way to highlight data elements on the model. This works especially well when there are multiple types of information you are looking to show and when color is not the best option. For example, italics could mean a new data element ready for review, italics plus boldface a new data element with an outstanding issue, and underlining a data element that has been reviewed and is considered to be complete.

You can use any one of these or a combination of any of the three: color, size, and style. Combining these three can highlight the data elements, entities, or relationships even

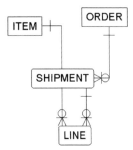

Figure 10.14 Line passing through entity.

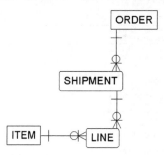

Figure 10.15 Fixed line passing through entity.

more. For example, a red data element would stand out much more if it were red in 18-point type and boldface.

NOTE

━━━ **A disadvantage of highlighting data elements, entities, and relationships on your model is that you will eventually have to remove the highlighting. Once an issue has been resolved and the data element, entity, or relationship has been completely reviewed and agreed on, you will need to change the formatting back to the default formatting for the model. In this way, when new items require highlighting they will still stand out. Please make sure you remove the highlighting when you are done. I have reviewed models where the formatting was never changed back to the default. This caused confusion, for example, people thinking there was an outstanding issue with a data element that long ago had been resolved.**

The benefit of following the Attention-Getting Tips is:

Highlights those objects requiring discussion. By highlighting a subset of data elements, entities, and relationships we can limit discussions to only these objects. If we have a large data model, we can use highlighting to scope out only a very small set of information for discussion. For example, if we need to discuss an issue on order address, which of the entities in Figure 10.16 would be easier to focus on?

Let's review the uses for these Attention-Getting Tips.

Using Attention-Getting Tips

There are several very good uses of highlighting the entities, relationships, and data elements:

Looking at only new structures, not existing ones. This is when you build on to an existing structure. For example, if we are adding certain logistics data elements to an existing logistics structure, we might want to highlight these new data elements in some way to make it easier to review and validate them, instead of looking at data elements that already exist and, it is hoped, have already been

ORDER

ORDER
ITEM_IDENTIFIER: NUMBER(12) NOT NULL(FK)
ORDER_IDENTIFIER: NUMBER(12) NOT NULL
SOURCE_SYSTEM_ORDER_IDENTIFIER:VARCHAR(30) NOT NULL(AK1.1)
UNIT_CODE:VARCHAR(2) NOT NULL(AK1.2)
ORDER_ENTRY_DATE: DATE NOT NULL(AK2.1)
CUSTOMER_IDENTIFIER: NUMBER(12) NOT NULL(FK)(AK2.2)
ACTUAL_DELIVERY_DATE: DATE NULL
TIME_IDENTIFIER: NUMBER(12) NOT NULL(FK)
SALESPERSON_IDENTIFIER: NUMBER(12) NULL(FK)
ORDER_TYPE_CODE: VARCHAR(2) NOT NULL
ORDER_STATUS_CODE: VARCHAR(4) NOT NULL
ACTUAL_SHIP_DATE: DATE NULL
ORIGINAL_DELIVERY_DATE: DATE NULL
REVISED_DELIVERY_DATE: DATE NULL
CANCEL_DATE: DATE NULL
ORDER_QUANTITY: DECIMAL(15.2) NULL
DELIVERY_ADDRESS_LINE_TEXT: VARCHAR(20) NULL
DELIVERY_ADDRESS_CITY_NAME: VARCHAR(20) NULL
DELIVERY_ADDRESS_STATE_CODE: CHAR(2) NULL
DELIVERY_ADDRESS_POSTAL_CODE: CHAR(10) NULL
ORDER_CUSTOMER_COMMENTS_TEXT: VARCHAR2(2000) NULL
EXTRACT_FILE_BATCH_NUMBER: INTEGER NOT NULL

ORDER
ITEM_IDENTIFIER: NUMBER(12) NOT NULL(FK)
ORDER_IDENTIFIER: NUMBER(12) NOT NULL
SOURCE_SYSTEM_ORDER_IDENTIFIER:VARCHAR(30) NOT NULL(AK1.1)
UNIT CODE: VARCHAR(2) NOT NULL(AK1.2)
ORDER_ENTRY_DATE: DATE NOT NULL(AK2.1)
CUSTOMER_IDENTIFIER: NUMBER(12) NOT NULL(FK)(AK2.2)
ACTUAL_DELIVERY_DATE: DATE NULL
TIME_IDENTIFIER: NUMBER(12) NOT NULL(FK)
SALESPERSON_IDENTIFIER: NUMBER(12) NULL(FK)
ORDER TYPE_CODE: VARCHAR(2) NOT NULL
ORDER_STATUS_CODE: VARCHAR(4) NOT NULL
ACTUAL_SHIP_DATE: DATE NULL
ORIGINAL_DELIVERY_DATE: DATE NULL
REVISED_DELIVERY_DATE: DATE NULL
CANCEL_DATE: DATE NULL
ORDER_QUANTITY: DECIMAL(15.2) NULL
DELIVERY_ADDRESS_LINE_TEXT: VARCHAR(30) NULL
DELIVERY_ADDRESS_CITY_NAME: VARCHAR(20) NULL
DELIVERY_ADDRESS_STATE_CODE: CHAR(2) NULL
DELIVERY_ADDRESS_POSTAL_CODE: CHAR(10) NULL
ORDER_CUSTOMER_COMMENTS_TEXT: VARCHAR2(2000) NULL
EXTRACT_FILE_BATCH_NUMBER: INTEGER NOT NULL

Figure 10.16 Address data elements requiring discussion.

reviewed. An example we have seen in Chapter 6, "Subject Area Modeling," when we discussed the Early Reality Check subject area data model, was to use colors to highlight the new data mart structures and not the existing data warehouse structures. By doing so, you are able to detect the impact these new structures will have on the data warehouse architecture.

Showing the most important structures. This is when you want to really show those structures that are key business or technical concepts. I usually highlight those data elements that are used frequently by the business (such as Order Quantity and Customer Last Name) as well as those required for much usage by the technical team (such as Last Update Date and system identifiers for data elements). I found this very useful for entities when I wanted to show the critical entities (such as Customer and Associate) as compared to the less critical entities (such as Customer Type and Associate Alternate Identifier).

Highlighting issues and questions. These are structures that have problems that need to be resolved before the data model can be considered finished. For example, if we cannot agree on the calculation for Gross Sales Value, I might highlight this data element to show we have an outstanding issue. If I am unsure whether a relationship should go from Customer to Order or from Customer to Shipment, I might highlight these relationships on the model.

Establishing reporting requirements. There are times when we are designing a data mart and we only want to show certain data elements, entities, and relationships on the reports. Perhaps the remaining structures will only be used for detailed analysis. Perhaps they will be shown on a future report. But we only want to highlight the structures that will be shown on the current reports. I have used this approach recently in a customer data mart to highlight those entities that belong in the first-phase reporting environment. It worked very well because only a small percentage of the data elements were in the reporting environment; therefore, they stood out. It does not work as well when most of the data elements are in the reporting environment.

NOTE

Think up a few new uses for style, size, and color highlights. The ones mentioned in this section were uses that I am familiar with and have successfully used. There are many others yet to be discovered. Try to think up some new ones specific to your department or project.

Attention-Getting Tips In Practice

Let's go through both size and style attention-getting examples. Let's say we are adding the address data elements to our order entity. We will need to distinguish the currently existing data elements from the new address data elements, so that we can more easily hone in on and review only the new information. See Figure 10.17 for what this model might look like using two different sizes, the default size for existing data elements and a larger size for new data elements. You can see that using different sizes works well when there are only two possibilities. That is, either a data element is new or it exists. If we are representing multiple possibilities, just using size could be confusing. Imagine using five different sizes on the same model! It would not provide the highlighting benefits mentioned previously.

Figure 10.17 is an example of using different sizes. Let's say that this Order entity is for a data mart. Some of the data elements in this entity will be shown in the report-

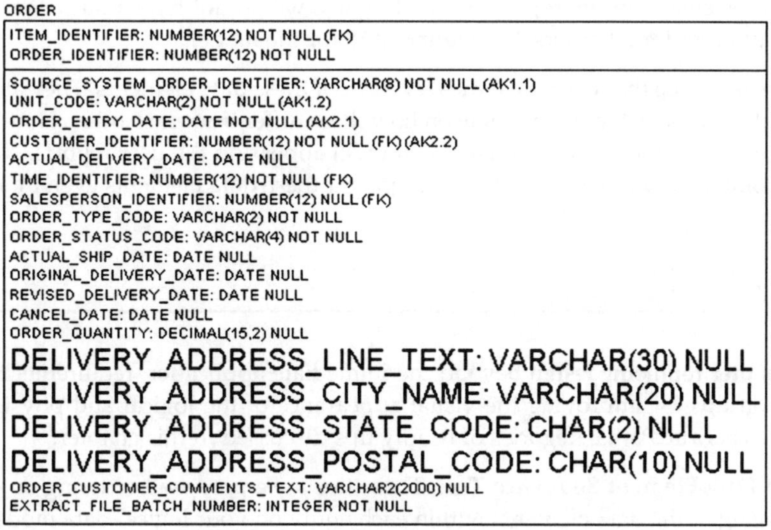

```
ORDER
ITEM_IDENTIFIER: NUMBER(12) NOT NULL (FK)
ORDER_IDENTIFIER: NUMBER(12) NOT NULL
─────────────────────────────────────────────
SOURCE_SYSTEM_ORDER_IDENTIFIER: VARCHAR(8) NOT NULL (AK1.1)
UNIT_CODE: VARCHAR(2) NOT NULL (AK1.2)
ORDER_ENTRY_DATE: DATE NOT NULL (AK2.1)
CUSTOMER_IDENTIFIER: NUMBER(12) NOT NULL (FK) (AK2.2)
ACTUAL_DELIVERY_DATE: DATE NULL
TIME_IDENTIFIER: NUMBER(12) NOT NULL (FK)
SALESPERSON_IDENTIFIER: NUMBER(12) NULL (FK)
ORDER_TYPE_CODE: VARCHAR(2) NOT NULL
ORDER_STATUS_CODE: VARCHAR(4) NOT NULL
ACTUAL_SHIP_DATE: DATE NULL
ORIGINAL_DELIVERY_DATE: DATE NULL
REVISED_DELIVERY_DATE: DATE NULL
CANCEL_DATE: DATE NULL
ORDER_QUANTITY: DECIMAL(15,2) NULL
DELIVERY_ADDRESS_LINE_TEXT: VARCHAR(30) NULL
DELIVERY_ADDRESS_CITY_NAME: VARCHAR(20) NULL
DELIVERY_ADDRESS_STATE_CODE: CHAR(2) NULL
DELIVERY_ADDRESS_POSTAL_CODE: CHAR(10) NULL
ORDER_CUSTOMER_COMMENTS_TEXT: VARCHAR2(2000) NULL
EXTRACT_FILE_BATCH_NUMBER: INTEGER NOT NULL
```

Figure 10.17 Use of size to highlight new data elements.

```
ORDER
┌─────────────────────────────────────────────────────────────┐
│ ITEM_IDENTIFIER: NUMBER(12) NOT NULL (FK)                     │
│ ORDER_IDENTIFIER: NUMBER(12) NOT NULL                         │
├─────────────────────────────────────────────────────────────┤
│ SOURCE_SYSTEM_ORDER_IDENTIFIER: VARCHAR(8) NOT NULL (AK1.1)   │
│ UNIT_CODE: VARCHAR(2) NOT NULL (AK1.2)                        │
```

ORDER_ENTRY_DATE: DATE NOT NULL (AK2.1)

```
CUSTOMER_IDENTIFIER: NUMBER(12) NOT NULL (FK) (AK2.2)
```

ACTUAL_DELIVERY_DATE: DATE NULL

```
TIME_IDENTIFIER: NUMBER(12) NOT NULL (FK)
SALESPERSON_IDENTIFIER: NUMBER(12) NULL (FK)
ORDER_TYPE_CODE: VARCHAR(2) NOT NULL
ORDER_STATUS_CODE: VARCHAR(4) NOT NULL
```

ACTUAL_SHIP_DATE: DATE NULL

ORIGINAL_DELIVERY_DATE: DATE NULL

REVISED_DELIVERY_DATE: DATE NULL

CANCEL_DATE: DATE NULL

ORDER_QUANTITY: DECIMAL(15,2) NULL

DELIVERY_ADDRESS_LINE_TEXT: VARCHAR(30) NULL

DELIVERY_ADDRESS_CITY_NAME: VARCHAR(20) NULL

DELIVERY_ADDRESS_STATE_CODE: CHAR(2) NULL

DELIVERY_ADDRESS_POSTAL_CODE: CHAR(10) NULL

```
ORDER_CUSTOMER_COMMENTS_TEXT: VARCHAR2(2000) NULL
EXTRACT_FILE_BATCH_NUMBER: INTEGER NOT NULL
```

Figure 10.18 Use of style to highlight new data elements.

ing environment and some will be hidden or shown at a later date. Let's use large type in italics to show those data elements that will be shown in the report and with which we have at least one issue. Let's use a large boldface style to show those data elements that will be shown in the report and with which we do not have issues. We will use the default font for all others. See Figure 10.18 for the model.

You can easily see that we have issues for three of these data elements. They all appear to be dates. Perhaps there is an issue on how these differ from each other. Note that the boldface data elements have no issues and will appear on the user reports. Note also how I combined type size and style to highlight these data elements even more.

Summary

This chapter took our design beyond the immediate application requirements by focusing on tips for improving the visual appearance of the logical and physical data models. There are five categories of beauty tips discussed in this chapter:

Logical Data Element Sequence Tips. These tips are a proposed ordering or sequencing of the data elements within each entity on your logical data model.

Physical Data Element Sequence Tips. These tips are less of visual tips and more of storage and performance tips.

Entity Layout Tips. These tips focus on the optimal layout of each entity on the data model.

Relationship Layout Tips. These tips focus on rearranging relationship lines that overlap and relationships that appear to go through entities instead of around them to the entities they connect.

Attention-Getting Tips. These are tips focusing on highlighting data elements, entities, or relationships on our design.

Applying these beauty tips to our data model concludes our work on the logical and physical designs. The next chapter concludes this text with advice for the data modeler.

CHAPTER 11

Planning a Long and Prosperous Career in Data Modeling

I travel fairly often. Being a frequent traveler increases my odds of making the occasional vacation blunder. I have learned from many of my mistakes, in the hope of preventing them from occurring again. To eliminate these mistakes, thereby maximizing the likelihood that I will have an enjoyable and memorable travel experience, I follow advice that I have developed over time. Some of this advice, which I definitely learned the hard way, I would like to share with you now:

Don't overplan. I once went on a vacation where every minute of every day was neatly planned. I knew exactly what I would be doing several hours from now, where I would eat lunch, what I would be doing tomorrow, and so on. It was so well planned that when an unexpected event occurred that required modifying the plans, we were left in a stressful situation. We were so rigid in our planning that we had no room for any deviation at all. Even if something entertaining came along that we would have liked to do, it would have been very stressful to change all of the future planned activities to accommodate it. This has taught me to plan just enough to make sure I do not miss important events or activities, and never to overplan.

Don't overpack. I recently returned from a vacation with an entire extra suitcase that I had never even opened! I had to lug this heavy suitcase to a number of different destinations, and I never wore any of the clothes in it. Since this eye-opening and aggravating experience, I have been questioning and challenging myself on every piece of clothing that I pack. "Do I really need this shirt? I already have four shirts packed." I need to resist my own tendency to overpack. I now believe in packing the minimum when I travel.

Don't take too many pictures. I never want to find myself spending most of my vacation taking pictures or video, because then I miss experiencing the real vacation. One of my first vacations with a video recorder involved taking over 7 hours of video, which I have never even watched! That's 7 hours when I was trying to *record* my vacation, instead of actually *being* on vacation. I now substantially limit the amount of photographs I take, so that I can increase the enjoyment of being on vacation.

Try laughing instead of panicking. Looking back on a vacation, some of the best memories and stories were those that could have been very stressful situations. A flat tire in a town where no one spoke English, a rental car with a stick shift transmission when I only knew how to drive an automatic, hotel reservations magically disappearing, and so on. These situations require a special attitude. Whenever I am on the border of panic or frustration, I remind myself that I am on vacation and even this potentially stressful situation is an experience and memory that is part of my vacation, and that I will laugh about in the near future. I usually try to savor even these potentially disastrous experiences.

I try to follow my own advice while on vacation. I also try to follow my own advice while data modeling. This advice has helped me survive and prosper in many different and difficult industries and assignments. This data model advice, as the vacation advice, has been learned the hard way through experience and mistakes. This last chapter contains my advice on data modeling to help you also survive and prosper in the data model industry.

About This Chapter

This concluding chapter focuses on the modeler rather than the model. Up to this point in the text, we have been discussing tools to improve the efficiencies and resulting designs of our logical and physical data models. We have applied analysis and modeling tools from the subject area down to the detailed data element levels. Now we turn our attention to the person behind the model. There is certain advice that could prove very valuable to data modelers to help them succeed and excel in the industry. This chapter focuses on my advice that I follow as a data modeler. I have learned these lessons over the years from my own experiences and from the successes and failures of those around me.

Here is my Top Ten list of advice for the data modeler (in no particular order):

1. Remember: Flexibility, Accuracy, and Context.
2. Modeling is only a small piece of your job.
3. Try on other hats.
4. Be aware of the 95/5 rule.
5. Data modeling is never boring.
6. Stay sharp.
7. Try not to get emotionally attached to your model.
8. Let your imagination soar.
9. Theory alone is too expensive.
10. Become a great storyteller.

In this chapter, we discuss each of these in more detail and give examples.

NOTE

You may not agree with some of this advice. That's ok. We seem to be bombarded with advice regarding every aspect of life—advice on money, happiness, health, and the list goes on. Some we agree with, and some we don't. The advice presented in this chapter is advice that I strongly believe will be valuable for the data modeler.

The Top Ten List of Advice for the Data Modeler

The Top Ten list is a collection of 10 pointers to help you have a long and successful data modeling career. Each has a significant amount of experience behind it. There are many war stories that have led to this advice being included here. As you read through these pointers, some of them might hit home more than others. You can focus on those pointers that have the most relevance to your current assignment or position.

You might have some other advice or pointers that are not listed in this chapter, based on your own experiences. I recommend that you keep a list of your most valuable advice and continually remind yourself of that advice daily. Sometimes it is useful to write the most important pointers on Post-it Notes and place them around your workstation. This will be a constant reminder to follow this advice. Many times advice sounds great and motivates us for a short time, but then we forget and keep doing things the way we have always done them. Reading the advice on a regular basis until it becomes part of your daily routine helps with maximizing its effectiveness.

TIP

As you read this chapter, think of some other data modeler tidbits or pointers that you would consider good advice. Usually there are very valuable pointers each of us have, which lie somewhere in the far recesses of our minds, and it is a good idea to write them down somewhere and remind ourselves of them daily. You might even want to share them with your coworkers.

The main benefit of following all of this advice is to make you a better data modeler. All of the tools in this book up to this point have focused on creating a better data model. Practicing these tools, in turn, will help you become a better data modeler. Being armed with these tools sometimes is not enough. The attitude, experience, and guidance that you bring to the table are just as important.

1. Remember: Flexibility, Accuracy, and Context

As data modelers, flexibility, accuracy, and context are the three most important words in our language. They almost guarantee a successful data modeling activity. If these three characteristics are not represented somewhere during our design work, there will be some useful functionality lacking from our resulting logical and physical data model.

Flexibility means designing your model so that it can handle data requirement enhancements with few, if any, changes. Chapter 9, "The Abstraction Safety Guide and Components," focused on the Abstraction Safety Guide and a number of Abstraction Building Blocks. The use of abstraction automatically builds flexibility into your design. Do you remember the Communication Medium abstraction structure we discussed in Chapter 9? Instead of having separate data elements representing Phone Number and Email Address, we stored them as rows in an abstracted Communication Medium data element. This allowed us to have the flexibility to handle new communication media that become requirements, such as pager numbers, fax numbers, Web sites, and so on.

Accuracy means correctly representing the data requirements on the models. Every data element or business rule present within the scope of an application should be captured and correctly represented on the model. This includes all of the meta data around the data elements, entities, and relationships. Everything that characterizes the components of the models should be captured and validated as being correct: definition, format information, nullability, and cardinality. Tools such as the Data Element Family Tree from Chapter 7, "Logical Data Analysis," and the Normalization Hike in Chapter 8, "The Normalization Hike and Denormalization Survival Guide," are necessities for capturing this type of information.

Context means correctly representing the scope of the application. We want to make sure that we have the right functionality included within the scope of our application, and that our application is consistent and properly fits into the larger enterprise model or data dictionary. Context also includes consistency in the way data elements and entities are named and used. Subject area tools (such as those mentioned in Chapters 5 and 6, "Subject Area Analysis" and "Subject Area Modeling," respectively) are very useful for determining and agreeing on scope and context.

If someone were to ask me to describe what makes a great data model in three words, the answer would be: flexibility, accuracy, and context. If you apply the tools in this book and follow my advice, you will improve the design in your logical and physical data models.

The best example from my experience that shows the benefit of all three of these concepts is the Reality Check Subject Area Model I created for a group of managers, which showed how a potentially new data mart fit with the existing data warehouse architecture. It was flexible, meaning that abstract concepts, such as Business Party and Transaction, allowed us to represent a wide range of future data requirements within the data mart or data warehouse. It was accurate, because several experts from both the data mart and data warehouse side validated the content and structure and agreed that it was correct. It had the appropriate context, because by using different colors I was able to show what was in the data warehouse, in the data mart, in both, and in neither. Green entities existed in both the data warehouse and data mart, red entities existed only in the data mart and not in the data warehouse, and so on.

2. Modeling is Only a Small Piece of Your Job

Data modeling is a very small part of your job as a data modeler. Think about the topics included in this book. Even though this is a book for data modelers, only a few chapters are solely dedicated to data modeling. There is a lot of content dedicated to meta data, education, and analysis. Once we actually have captured, understood, and validated the data, we are almost done with our data modeling. Even though we may not have even created a single entity in our modeling tool, we have already done most of the work. That is because most of the effort is around analyzing data requirements and capturing the appropriate meta data for the design. The more complete the analysis and capture is, the easier and quicker the data modeling will be.

Sometimes a great model can be a total failure because of the lack of analysis and meta data capture done before the modeling. A large subject area within a data warehouse that I reviewed recently was never properly analyzed. Even though the data model and resulting design appeared to function correctly, there was a lack of definitions and understanding as to the data elements within this structure. This made walking through the structure almost impossible, and when we needed to modify the structure, it required much more time and effort than anyone ever anticipated. With a little more work up front, the data modeling is just an easy and quick transition from the analysis. Applying the Definition Checklist from Chapter 3 ("Ensuring High-Quality Definitions"), completing the Data Element Family Tree and Subject Area Grain Matrix from Chapter 5 ("Subject Area Analysis"), playing an exciting game of Meta Data Bingo from Chapter 2 ("Meta Data Bingo"), and so on, all contribute to a complete and full analysis before any modeling is actually done. Asking the right questions and knowing the outstanding issues and areas of confusion are extremely important before beginning any data modeling.

3. Try On Other Hats

Seek opportunities to play other roles in the software life cycle. I have been data modeling a very long time. Recently, I had the opportunity to move from being a modeler to being a developer. As a developer, I would be creating several new data marts within an existing data warehouse architecture. I jumped at this opportunity. The developer is one of the customers and recipients of the data model. If I could better understand the needs and requirements of the developer, I could design a better model. Sometimes the best way to understand the needs of someone is to put yourself in that person's shoes. That is exactly what I did. After several months, not only did I learn an incredible amount about development but I also became a better data modeler! It is ironic but true: By not doing data modeling for awhile, I actually became a better data modeler.

I remember being asked which of two data model designs I would prefer. I briefly examined both designs and then replied that going with the first one would mean that the balancing procedures that the developer would need to write would be extremely complicated if not impossible to code. I would not have made this observation without the development experience. I am amazed how much can be learned by temporarily performing a different function in the software life cycle.

Over the years, I have noticed that some of the most impressive data modelers that I have worked with played many different roles in the software life cycle. They have been database administrators, project managers, report designers, and the list goes on. What I encourage you to do is to look for opportunities where you can temporarily try on someone else's shoes and learn more about what they do. Make sure training will be provided!

TIP

A good source for looking for a new hat or role in the software life cycle is the In-the-Know Template from Chapter 5, "Subject Area Analysis." You can use this template to identify roles you might want to try on and identify people with whom you can discuss your interests in taking on a temporary assignment in a different area.

The worst-case scenario from this experience is that you will not like this new function and return to data modeling a little bit wiser. Most of the time, however, you will find that you learn an incredible amount. You not only learn how to do this other role in the life cycle but also new design approaches and techniques for data modeling.

WARNING

While you are trying on a new role in the life cycle, it is better not to do data modeling. This is because sometimes there are conflicting interests between the data modeler and other roles in the life cycle. One time in particular I was working as a developer and was looking for the quick solution, yet the modeler in me wanted the three most important words: flexibility, accuracy, and context. This caused a real dilemma for me. I eventually forced myself to make the right decision and chose flexibility, accuracy, and context.

4. Be Aware of the 95/5 Rule

The 95/5 rule means that 95% of your time will be spent on 5% of your data elements. Have you ever noticed how often this statement is true? If you are working on a data model with over a hundred data elements that require modeling, most of your time will be spent on five or fewer of them. There might be some difficult questions or issues that arise regarding these data elements. There might be some integration concerns. There might be differences in the meanings or values of these data elements. Regardless of the types of issues, fixing this handful of data elements will take most of your time.

Try to identify as early as possible those data elements that will require the most effort. Review the Data Element Family Tree document in sufficient detail to know where the problem data elements are hiding. What I have done in the past that appears to work well is to get access to actual databases or files containing the problem data elements and do whatever I can to examine the data and resolve the problems quickly. In the list below are examples of some problems or issues that I have found take a relatively large amount of time to resolve. I use very specific examples, but after reading these you will easily see that they can appear in a number of different situations. As you read these, think of how many times you have encountered similar problems and how long it took you to solve them:

■ The Customer Number on the Order entity does not match the meta data or data from the Customer Number within the Customer entity.

■ The data in Product Description Text does not match its definition.

■ Both Francis and Maxwell, two business experts from the employee area, strongly disagree on the future use of the Employee Code.

■ The primary key, Order Number, repeats every 90 days.

■ The data elements that we thought composed the alternate key for Customer are not unique.

Use the Data Quality Capture Template and the Data Quality Validation Template from Chapter 7, "Logical Data Analysis," to help identify and resolve the issues for the handful of data elements that will require additional effort.

5. Data Modeling Is Never Boring

It is amazing how many years someone can keep data modeling and still be learning and enjoying the work. Almost every day I learn new business or design tidbits that will help me in future design efforts. I never find the field of data modeling boring. When I find that the learning curve is leveling off, I move on to another assignment or position. And then this new company, industry, or assignment renews the data modeling field once again, and I continue to learn and enjoy what I do.

In data modeling, there are always new industries, assignments, companies, and technologies to keep the work fresh and exciting.

WARNING

■■■■■ **If you have been data modeling and find yourself being bored often, it is definitely time for a change. It may not be that the field of data modeling is boring but that your particular assignment, company, or industry is not exciting anymore. Take a risk and try data modeling a different project or industry!**

6. Stay Sharp

Stay on top of the most current technologies in the data modeling industry. The data modeling industry changes much less frequently than other areas of technology. It is amazing that there are decade-old data modeling texts that are still in circulation and actively being read. Not much has changed. Normalization today is the same as normalization was in the mid-1980s. Data modeling does not exist in a vacuum, however, and technologies and trends have been impacting our industry. Here are some examples of changes and trends that have impacted and will impact the data modeling industry:

CWM. The Object Management Group is an organization that defines and maintains a standard for capturing and transporting meta data called the Common Warehouse Metamodel (CMW). The industry has agreed on this set of meta data standards, and many tool vendors have started designing import and export facilities to match this standard so that meta data can be shared across tools. Our data modeling tools, meta data repositories, and many other tools will be able to cleanly exchange meta data.

Data Martsmarts. Our data models need to be even more streamlined for retrieval in our data marts. Denormalized reference entities become known as dimensions; normalized transaction entities become know as fact tables. Reference data history becomes very important. Applying the Denormalization Survival Guide from Chapter 8, "The Normalization Hike and Denormalization Survival Guide," will help guarantee that you make the right decisions here.

Downsizing. Companies are always looking for ways to do more with fewer resources. For some reason, the data modeling area seems to be always plagued with this attitude. I hope that by using some of the analogies within this text, you might be able to convince the powers that be within your company how valuable and important our roles are, especially with so many large global and integration efforts within our organizations.

ERP. Enterprise Resource Planning (ERP) applications are broad-scoped third third-party packaged software programs that are designed to use a single robust application to replace many home-grown legacy applications. ERP packages are usually brought in with little data analysis and lots of hype. A data model mapping exercise must be completed before the ERP package is used. This mapping exercise translates existing requirements into the ERP structures. Essentially, you will need to map your existing data models to the ERP's data model of the ERP. If you are evaluating an ERP package to see if it will meet the needs of your company's needs, this mapping exercise can be a good test to see if your existing structures fit cleanly into the ERP data model. The Early Reality Check subject area model from Chapter 6, "Subject Area Modeling" can be a very powerful tool for capturing the evaluation results at a subject area level.

Faster computers. This trend towards faster machines and less-expensive memory and storage will slowly lead to physical designs that are more normalized in nature. Joining several tables to get reporting results will eventually only take a blink longer than having all of the information denormalized into a single table. When answering the questions in the Denormalization Survival Guide, remember to adjust your point values accordingly as computer speeds becomes faster and faster.

Globalization. There is a trend towards very large scale projects, including many global efforts within and between companies. This means there is even more of a need for consistent data modeling and standards. This also means more data integration and subject area analysis will be required and performed. More time will need to be allocated for analysis and meta data validation. Remember to use the Subject Area Family Tree from Chapter 5, "Subject Area Analysis," and the Data Element Family Tree from Chapter 7, "Logical Data Analysis," to assist with these large mapping efforts.

UML. Unified Modeling Language (UML) is a standard language for documenting and representing everything about an application. Although it is mainly designed for object-oriented applications, it can also be used for applications built upon a relational database. Because of the rigor and flexibility of UML, I think that over the near term it will become more and more widespread for use in relational database applications.

XML. Extensible Markup Language (XML) has been a very successful and widely used method of capturing and exchanging data. It is possible to transform a data model into an XML structure, with even more integrity and business rule checking than we can capture on the data model. It is also very easy to understand and parse. XML will be the structure for meta data to be passed between development tools, such as data modeling tools and meta data repositories.

Which trends or technologies are impacting the data modeling in your organization or industry?

7. Try Not to Get Emotionally Attached to Your Model

I was once in a data model review where the data modeler was almost in tears toward the end of the meeting. This data modeler was taking everyone's comments very personally. The modeler needs to understand that people's comments during the review are not directed at the creator of the model but, rather, at the content of the model. The goal of a data model review is to try to find structural problems and issues so you can leave the meeting with a better design. If I walk out of a data model review without any changes, I know that the reviewers were not paying attention or did not understand something. I expect my data models to change during a walk-through, especially when there are several other data modelers in the room that voice their opinions and ideas freely. Keep in mind that corrections to your model during your review are beneficial to the resulting design. You want to avoid making corrections to the model after the database and substantial code have already been written.

8. Let Your Imagination Soar

Be as creative as possible in thinking of new ways to capture your data requirements and improve your design. Being creative might involve modifying some of the tools in this text. It also might involve coming up with your own spreadsheet or other tools to get the job down. Remember, as mentioned previously, most of the work of the data modeler happens before any data modeling is actually done. If you can creatively apply the techniques in this text or customize them to your own needs, you could potentially save lots of time and have a better data model in the end.

9. Theory Alone Is Too Expensive

I once worked for a company where it was rare to have tight time deliverables and where ideas and theory alone were encouraged. One project in particular that I worked on was almost in its 10th year and had delivered very little! Today it is very rare to find such an environment, one that promotes research and theory. Most companies want practicality. They want to see the completed analysis and data modeling deliverables on time and within budget. During your design activities, make sure that you keep this perspective in mind. The departments or organizations paying the bills for this application expect to see tangible and practical results.

10. Become a Great Storyteller

Storytelling is a very important part of being a data modeler. We need to tell stories or anecdotes to help educate and influence project managers and others who lack understanding of our industry. Anecdotes and analogies have been discussed in detail in Chapter 1, "Using Anecdotes, Analogies, and Presentations to Illustrate Data Modeling Concepts." We need to be able to make a data model come to life. That is, we need to describe it to users or functional analysts as if it is telling the story of the business or application: "The Customer Bob can buy many Widgets." In fact, a common trait of the data modelers I have admired most over the years is that they are great storytellers. I encourage you to practice telling brief stories with the purpose of education or influence. It is a great skill for a modeler to have.

Summary

This chapter discussed those rules and beliefs that I follow as a data modeler. I have learned these lessons over the years from my own experiences and from the successes and failures of those around me. I believe that by practicing and customizing the tools in this book and by applying the advice in this chapter, you will produce higher-quality analysis and modeling deliverables. In the data modeling industry today, and in the future as data modeling plays an increasingly important part in software development and integration, the tools in this text will continue to play a critical role in improving the efficiencies and effectiveness of our data modeling tasks.

Suggested Reading

Books and Articles

Date C.J. 1990. *An Introduction to Database Systems.* Reading, Mass.: Addison-Wesley Publishing Company, Inc.

This is one of the classic texts in our field. In a very straightforward fashion, Date discusses many relational database characteristics, including normalization. If you are looking for a formal walk-through of all levels of normalization, this is your text.

Fleming C., and von Halle B. 1989. *Handbook of Relational Database Design.* Reading, Mass.: Addison-Wesley Publishing Company, Inc.

This was the first book I read on data modeling. The authors use lots of examples to highlight database design techniques, and they have a fairly extensive methodology for completing a database design.

Kimball R. 1996. *The Data Warehouse Toolkit.* New York: John Wiley & Sons, Inc.

This is a classic text on data warehousing. If you have ever designed a data warehouse or will design one, this is an excellent reference.

Kent W. February 1983. "A Simple Guide to Five Normal Forms in Relational Database Theory." *CACM.*

This short article contains one of the clearest explanations of normalization I have seen.

Reingruber M., and Gregory W. 1994. *The Data Modeling Handbook.* New York: John Wiley & Sons, Inc.

This is a great introductory text on data modeling. Although many texts in our field focus on database design (that is, physical data modeling), this text dedicates much of its content to logical data modeling and best practices.

Silverston L., Inmon W., and Graziano K. 1997. *The Data Model Resource Book.* New York: John Wiley & Sons, Inc.

This book provides a valuable set of reusable abstract designs that make great starting points for your data models.

Simsion G. 1994. *Data Modeling Essentials.* International Thomson Computer Press.

Once you have an introductory understanding of data modeling, this is an excellent book to read. Simsion has a conversational and easily understandable writing style and, therefore, clearly describes some difficult and challenging modeling scenarios.

Web Sites

Here are some of my favorite Web sites on data modeling:

www.dmreview.com—Excellent article archive and portal site.

www.infogoal.com/dmc/dmcdmd.htm—Excellent data modeling portal site.

www.tdan.com—Periodic newsletter on data administration topics, including modeling and meta data.

www.wiley.com/compbooks/hoberman—Last but not least! Here you will find additional tools and templates and updates to existing templates in this book.